VERLAINE

ALSO BY JOANNA RICHARDSON

Théophile Gautier: His Life and Times
Princess Mathilde

VERLAINE

Joanna Richardson

WEIDENFELD AND NICOLSON
5 Winsley Street London W1

SBN 0 297 00354 2

Printed by C. Tinling & Co. Ltd,
London and Prescot

L'art, mes enfants, c'est d'être absolument soi-même

Paul Verlaine, Bonheur, XVIII

CONTENTS

A*

ILLUSTRATIONS

INTRODUCTION

VERLAINE did not lack publicity in the last years of his life. Critics, diarists, journalists were constantly discussing him. Monographs were written about him and about contemporary poetry; foreign visitors hunted him down, like eager entomologists, in the Boul' Mich', and hastened away to publish their impressions. Artists and photographers were busy recording his Socratic features. He himself was still writing poetry, though his best days were long since over, and publishing his reminiscences. When he died, on 8 January 1896, there was a flood of appreciation (and sometimes vilification), and during the seventy years that have passed since then, it has never ceased. Verlaine's complete works and much of his correspondence have been published, the memoirs of his former wife have appeared in print. His religion, his relationship with Rimbaud, his lifelong, fruitful relationship with England, his influence on music, his debt to earlier writers, his relation to the Parnassians, the Decadents, the Symbolists, and to the English literature of the nineties: all have been repeatedly discussed. Again and again, new letters have appeared in periodicals, illuminating friendships and uncharted periods in his life. The biographies of his friends and acquaintances have filled in his *ambiance* in remarkable detail. This is the first attempt at a synthesis. This is the first full-scale critical biography.

To say so is not to disparage the work by Edmond Lepelletier, which appeared in 1907; but Lepelletier wrote too soon after Verlaine's death. Besides, he was the poet's friend, anxious to present a respectable image to posterity. His biography suffered from special pleading, from naïveté (or was it *suppressio veri?*), from a lack of literary judgment and from ignorance of the countless facts and documents which have appeared in the last sixty years. The most recent study of Verlaine, by Professor Carter, says much that is new about the poet's son, but it does not present Verlaine himself, or his background, in satisfactory detail. The most original study of Verlaine by an English writer has been Dr V. P. Underwood's *Verlaine et l'Angleterre*, but, as its title shows, it has its limits.

It therefore seems more than time to attempt a full-scale life of Verlaine, and I have been bold enough to do so. I have been led on by an instinctive love of his poetry; it seemed to me the moment to examine its significance, and to assess its place in French literature. I have also been led on by the fascination of the man: perhaps the most remarkable 'double nature' in literary history. It is curious that a man as weak and vicious as Verlaine, a man who, by all accounts, was physically repulsive, could create such warm affection; but one has only to read his letters, to catch the tone of his conversations, to understand his hold on his contemporaries. He is endearing, and, behind this disarming manner, one is suddenly aware of the presence of genius.

I am glad to thank Dr Robert Baldick, who kindly put his collection of Verlaine books at my disposal, and Dr W. G. Moore, who facilitated my research at Oxford. I must also express my gratitude to Sir Henry d'Avigdor Goldsmid, Canon P. B. G. Binnall, Miss Lillian Browse, Miss J. M. Bunker, Mr R. E. Coley (Town Clerk of Boston), M. Serge Grandjean, the Rev. L. C. Hodge (Rector of Stickney), Dr J. F. A. Mason (Librarian of Christ Church, Oxford), Mr F. Mulhern, Mr Vivian Ogilvie, Mr Michael Pakenham, Mr Alan Parkes and Mr Robert Speaight. I am grateful to the staff of the Bodleian Library and the Taylor Institution, Oxford, the British Museum Reading Room and Newspaper Library, the Bibliothèque Nationale and the Bibliothèque littéraire Jacques Doucet.

I owe my most lasting debt to the late Dr Enid Starkie, not only for her study of Rimbaud and for her generous interest in this book, but for years of encouragement, criticism and help, and for a constant example of scholarship. To her, with love and gratitude, this *Verlaine* belongs.

J.R.

London – Paris
May 1970

PART ONE

Le Petit

(1844–69)

I

METZ is nearly two hundred miles north-east of Paris; it is
on the eastern edge of France, almost on the borders of
Luxembourg and Germany. Critics who see a poet's
birthplace as an explanation of his nature and his poetry might
infer that Verlaine, the supreme poet of mood, owed some of his
temperament to this geographical fact. His gloom, his gentle
melancholy, his sentiment, his ferocity, his preference for northern
landscapes, his coarseness and pugnacity, his profound awareness
of music: all, no doubt, might be ascribed to the fact that he was
born much nearer to Germany than to the heart of France.

Such reasoning would be mistaken. If Verlaine was born at 2,
rue Haute-Pierre, at Metz, that was because his father, Nicolas-
Auguste Verlaine, a captain in the engineers, happened to be
stationed there. 'Paul Verlaine,' wrote the poet himself at the end
of his life, 'was born in Metz as if by an ominous Fate. Fate has
always tossed him about, and in a sense it has deprived him of a
native land.'[1]

Yet, through both his parents, the future poet could have claimed
northern ancestry. His mother, Élisa-Julie-Josèphe-Stéphanie
Dehée, came from an Artois family. The Dehées, oil merchants
from Arras, had settled in Fampoux, a nearby village, in the mid-
eighteenth century; and there Élisa had been born in 1809, the

3

daughter of Julien-Joseph Dehée, a farmer, and an ex-mayor of the commune. The Dehées were solid bourgeois, with an affection for the soil. From them Verlaine inherited his deep-rooted bourgeois instincts and his attachment to a country life.

Captain Verlaine was forty-six at the time of his son's birth. He had been born in 1798 in Bertrix, which later became part of Belgian Luxembourg. It was then part of the French Département des Forêts.

'Au pays de mon père on voit des bois sans nombre . . .'[2] the poet was to write; and, as if to recall his Walloon origins, Verlaine's name is that of a village near Longlier. It is also that of a hamlet between Hamoir and Tohogne.

'I am of Walloon origin,' Verlaine would remind an Antwerp audience. 'My father came from an old family in the Belgian Ardennes.'[3] M. Le Febve de Vivy traced the family back to a certain Gilles de Verlaine, who was living in 1577; he had claimed to be the natural son of Gilles d'Ochain, seigneur de Verlaine. The d'Ochains are among the oldest noble families in Belgium.[4] And yet one must remain a little cautious about the claim. If there had been any such romantic legend about his family, Verlaine would have been the first to disinter it.

Besides, his near relations do much more to explain his nature; and if Captain Verlaine, that irreproachable army officer, seems to have little in common with his son, one must remember that heredity sometimes shows itself in irregular ways. Characteristics are not always passed down, simply, from one generation to another. They may disappear for years before they recur. The father of Nicolas-Auguste had died when the boy was seven; his young widow had left Bertrix and settled with her parents, the Grandjeans, at Jehonville. She had soon remarried and gone away, leaving the Grandjeans to bring up her three children in an atmosphere of rigid piety. The children knew nothing about their father, except that he had been a lawyer. Posterity knows that Henry-Joseph Verlaine had spent his youth between the chapel and the tavern, with occasional bursts of wild behaviour. If, for a moment, he had thought of entering the Church, his religious feeling was short-lived. When the French armies invaded

Belgium, he had become an ardent revolutionary. One Sunday in 1804, after mass, he stood drunk at a tavern door, and shouted such abuse of Napoleon that he was summoned to explain his behaviour to the procurator in Luxembourg. In Luxembourg he suddenly died. It is worth noting that this hot-tempered drunkard had had his literary pretentions; but Henry-Joseph did not only bequeath his wit and aggressiveness to his grandson, he also seems to have given him his alcoholic tendencies. Perhaps Henry-Joseph suffered from syphilis. This might explain why the wife of Nicolas-Auguste suffered three miscarriages before, at last, she gave birth to a child.

If we look back beyond the exemplary Captain Verlaine, we discover other disturbing figures: among them the Captain's grandfather, Jean Verlaine, a hard-drinking waggoner who was fined six gold florins for blasphemy; and there are others, nearly all of them violent and unstable, but no doubt well-intentioned in their youth, since they married into solid families. These families included a good many priests.[5]

Such was Verlaine's inheritance from his father's side: violence, originality, a tendency to vagabondage and to alcoholism, and a strong element of piety. It was, perhaps, also from his father that he inherited his ardent – if platonic - love of France.

After the Hundred Days, when Bertrix became part of Belgian Luxembourg, Nicolas-Auguste, then a soldier of seventeen, chose to keep French nationality. Verlaine was to remember him in his captain's uniform which seemed a constant symbol of patriotism.

I was so proud of my father's fine uniform: the French-style tunic with velvet facings and his two decorations from Spain and France, Algiers and Trocadero, the two-cornered hat with tricolor plums of a captain-adjutant-major . . . And I was very proud, too, of his splendid bearing. It was that of a very tall man, 'a kind they don't make any more,' with a martial yet gentle face. All the same, the habit of command had left the mark of authority upon it, and this was just as well, for I was as wicked as a devil when I was allowed to get up to mischief . . .[6]

And this, one suspects, was all too often. Verlaine's mother was thirty-five when he was born. She had been married for more than twelve years before, at last, she gave birth to this son. She had longed for children with such morbid intensity that she kept the results of her earlier pregnancies in alcohol, in a cupboard, even when, at last, she became a mother. As for her son, Paul-Marie, who was born on 30 March 1844, she loved him with the doting love that only such a mother could give. At an early age, Verlaine understood that she would let him have all he wanted, and that she would forgive him all his failures. Her tolerance was almost saintly; and yet, perhaps, it led to his undoing. It allowed him to indulge his weakness, it deprived him of the discipline essential to the child and to the man. It also created the intense relationship between mother and son which is a breeding-ground of homo-sexuality.

2

Soon after Verlaine's birth, the Captain's regiment was trans-ferred to Montpellier, and the family moved from north to south of France, from one cathedral city to another. Verlaine would long remember the religious processions in Montpellier. He would also recall how, when his parents went out in the evening, his nurse took the chance to go out, too, and entrusted him to two old women living in the house. They were toysellers, and he found himself in a paradise of puppets, drums and trumpets, buckets and spades. The Verlaines were still at Montpellier in 1848, at the time of the February Revolution. Louis-Philippe abdicated, and the Republic was proclaimed. Wearing an em-broidered jacket, knee-length pantaloons, and a peaked cap with a long tassel, Verlaine stood with his mother in the place d'Armes and, for the first time, heard *La Marseillaise*.

Then the family returned to Metz; and he was old enough, now, to appreciate his native city. 'I lived there only a few years,' he would write, 'but it was there that my mind and senses opened to life.'[1]

Le petit, as he was called at home, began to be aware of the world. 'My visual sense,' he remembered, 'was especially precocious. I took in everything . . . I was constantly pursuing shapes, colours and shadows. I was fascinated by daylight, and, though I was a coward in the dark, I was also attracted by the night. I was drawn to it out of curiosity, I sought in it I know not what: white, grey, tints, perhaps.'[2]

> Car nous voulons la Nuance encor,
> Pas la couleur, rien que la nuance!
> Oh! la nuance seule fiance
> Le rêve au rêve et la flûte au cor!

The author of 'Art poétique' was already there, in embryo.

Yet, as Verlaine said in his *Confessions*, he did not, at that moment, have the slightest vocation for poetry. He was a practical little boy, an extrovert (in the modern phrase), 'a perfect little bourgeois, a *balanced* child if ever there was. How people change!'[3] He dreamed, very naturally, of being an army officer like his father.

But, looking back on his early childhood, Verlaine also wondered if a psychologist might already have discovered a tendency to amativeness. The Esplanade at Metz was a magnificent terrace, overlooking the valley of the Moselle, and the vineyards stretching down to the river. Behind the Esplanade rose the elaborate silhouette of the cathedral. In the middle of the Esplanade was a bandstand where, on Thursday afternoons, and on Sundays, after vespers, a military band used to play, and *le tout Metz* used to take the air. It was there that Captain Verlaine's son, nearing his seventh birthday, met a little girl of eight or so, some functionary's daughter. She had red-gold hair, and freckles, and she was called Mathilde. The friendship grew so demonstrative that the children became known as Paul and Virginie.[4]

This happy, carefree early childhood ended in 1851, when Captain Verlaine resigned his commission. He was fifty-three, and still only a captain; there was clearly no future for him in the army. Besides, there was no financial need for him to remain there. His wife was comfortably off, and they were not dependent on his pay. (At the moment of their greatest wealth, calculates a critic, they had no less than 400,000 francs.)[5] Despite a flattering letter from his colonel, Captain Verlaine refused to withdraw his resignation.

Perhaps he had come to tire of his garrison life, and wanted to find a permanent home. Perhaps he was tired of a provincial existence. Certainly, if he and his wife had ambitions for their son – and Mme Verlaine wanted him to be a lawyer or an engineer – it was obvious that they should move to Paris, and that the boy should begin his education.

This was probably the main reason why, in 1851, when Paul was seven, they arrived in Paris. Verlaine had imagined it would be a city of gold and pearls, a city from the *Arabian Nights*. As they rattled in an evil-smelling cab from the Gare de l'Est to their temporary home, he looked out of the dirty window at the tall, drab buildings, and wept bitterly.

3

A week later, when the furniture had arrived from Metz, the family settled at 2, rue Saint-Louis, in what Verlaine called 'Batignolles, près Paris'. Les Batignolles, which lay outside the city barriers, was a suburb favoured by retired army officers, and the Verlaines were likely to make many friends. Paul was sent as a day-boy to a local school in the rue Hélène. He made enough progress for his parents to think of entering him at a lycée. Two events intervened. The first was the *coup d'état* of 2 December 1851. Louis-Napoleon, the Prince-President, dissolved the National Assembly and assumed full powers. It was now just a matter of time till the Empire was restored. But the event mattered little, in practical terms, to the Verlaines; a more significant event, to the small boy, was his mild attack of typhoid fever. The illnesses of childhood do not often leave their mark; but his mother's devoted nursing intensified an already deep relationship, and – one suspects – it made him more than ever dependent on her. When, on a winter day, he was taken to the

Institution Landry, in the rue Chaptal, as a boarder, he was horrified by the roughness of school life. At the end of the afternoon he escaped, and fled back to the rue Saint-Louis.

Within a few minutes he was home; and, as he wrote, years later: 'In the eyes which expressed no real surprise, in the outstretched arms . . . in the long, gentle kisses of my mother and my cousin Élisa, the quick, bristly kisses of my father and my cousin Victor, I soon perceived every indulgence – if not some ill-concealed approbation.'[1] He wept 'delightfully', he was regaled with a sip or two of wine, and – well aware that he had done wrong – he promised to return to school next day.

Victor – a sergeant in the *chasseurs* – escorted him back to the Institution Landry. As they made their way to the rue Chaptal, he exhorted Verlaine to be a man. He spoke to such effect that Verlaine returned to school almost joyfully. He entered the elementary class in which he was to spend a year before he prepared for the Lycée Bonaparte; and, in this class of children who came from bourgeois backgrounds like his own, he settled down very happily. He could hardly feel abandoned by his family. Every day in term time, without fail, for the next nine years, his father would come and see him; and every day he would bring him some little delicacy.

Verlaine received religious instruction and took his first communion. In October 1855, two years after he had entered the Institution Landry, he entered the *septième* at the Lycée Bonaparte (now the Lycée Condorcet). He continued to board at the rue Chaptal, while he followed the courses at the lycée. In these conditions he finished his education.

In his *Confessions*, written at the end of his life, Verlaine maintained that he had been a dunce. He had, he said, shown mild interest in Latin, but he had been bored by mathematics, history and geography. He had generally come between twenty-fifth and thirtieth in a class of thirty-five.

Verlaine, in his later years, felt a curious need to pose as a *mauvais sujet*. In 1864, as it happens, M. Landry gave him a handsome testimonial.[2] On 16 August 1862, Verlaine took his baccalauréat. He seemed equipped for a solid and conventional career.

Yet, on his own admission, his schooldays had not followed an entirely conventional pattern, His dreams of being a soldier had gone. When he was in his fourteenth year, the poet had been born in him. He had read not only such classics of their kind as the licentious *Œuvres complètes* of Piron, but – far more important – he had discovered *Les Fleurs du mal*. An usher had inadvertently left a copy lying about, and Verlaine read it with passionate interest. It was a remarkable book to find in a school in 1857: in its very year of publication. Perhaps Verlaine did not know that it was the subject of a *cause célèbre*, and that its author had been accused of *outrages aux mœurs*. In any case, the so-called perversity of the book escaped him. But Baudelaire had a profound and immediate influence on him: an influence which could only grow with time. Baudelaire's Romanticism and his saturnine temperament were strangely akin to those of Verlaine; and perhaps, even now, Verlaine recognised the power of the poetry.

He was not only impressionable, he was eager to read and discover. One day, on leave from school, he discovered *Les Cariatides* in a bookshop, and he fell instantly under the spell of Banville. By the age of sixteen he had read widely in almost every field, 'poetry, novels from Paul de Kock to Paul Féval and from Alexandre Dumas to Balzac; travels, translations (all of them under cover of my desk) and *Les Misérables*, which had just appeared.' He himself was writing, too. On 12 December 1858 he sent Victor Hugo his earliest known poem: 'La Mort'. 'I have some taste for poetry,' he explained, with youthful frankness, 'and I feel the need to open my heart to a skilled master. To whom, Monsieur, could I better venture to show these first steps in the stormy career of poetry – the first steps of a pupil in the *quatrième* a little over fourteen years of age?'[3]

Hugo does not seem to have answered. But the taste for poetry remained. While Verlaine was still at the lycée, he sketched out a drama about Charles VI, and he planned a *Charles le Sage*, and a *Louis XV* in six acts. If we are to believe him, he also wrote most of the *Poèmes saturniens* as they would appear in 1866.

Verlaine's poetic development was remarkably precocious. His personal development was far from satisfactory. In 1860, at the lycée, he met his lifelong friend, Edmond Lepelletier. Lepelletier was then fourteen, and Verlaine was over sixteen, but 'he was still rather young for his age'.[4] Verlaine had suffered from the loneliness of an only child, from the excessive indulgence which was shown him by his family. The Captain was alternately authoritative and doting; Mme Verlaine could not bring herself to contradict or criticise her son. She had pampered him too much and too long. She refused to recognise that he was no longer a child. She still called him *le petit*, years after he had outgrown the name. She allowed him – perhaps she wanted him – to remain weak and dependent.

But Verlaine's character cannot be blamed entirely on her possessiveness and inordinate love. From an early age he was aware of his remarkable ugliness. Schoolboys are not renowned for tact, masters have their obvious dislikes, and girls can make it clear that they find an admirer unattractive. Verlaine, closely bound to his mother, soon understood that he was unlikely to be loved or indulged by other women. It was the classic situation in which a boy would turn homosexual.

As a boy, perhaps, Verlaine was homosexual by force of circumstance. As he wrote in later life: 'I felt for several friends who were younger than myself, either in succession, or all at once, I can't remember, the pretty little romantic love of the Esplanade at Metz. But now, as puberty was coming, it was not so pure.'[5]

4

On 18 August 1862, immediately after he had taken his baccalauréat, Verlaine went to Lécluse, near Douai, to stay with his cousin Élisa Dujardin. She was the daughter of one of Mme Verlaine's sisters. A photograph shows a demure young woman in her twenties: her hair is tightly drawn back, and held in a snood; her dress is provincial, her expression gentle, pious and unpretentious. She had known Verlaine since his childhood, and she loved him as a sister might have done. Since she was eight years his senior, she also showed him the kind of maternal affection which he most needed. She knew him too well to be conscious of his ugliness or shyness; she understood him, she could give him reassurance and sympathy, and she could encourage the literary dreams which, perhaps, he could confide in her alone.

Had Élisa not been a married cousin, she might, in time, have been an excellent wife for Verlaine; but the previous year she had made a *mariage de convenance* with a rich beetroot grower, M. Dujardin. Since Dujardin was immersed in his business affairs, she had much time to give Verlaine, and he stayed on, now, at Lécluse, reading, wandering in the woods, hunting, and dancing at the village fêtes.

Though he was to write few poems about the countryside, Verlaine always loved a rural life. 'He often stayed in Artois, his mother's country,' wrote Lepelletier. 'He found a charm in this sombre part of the world . . . He had a strong affection for country life. He liked to stroll through the fields of beetroot and colza, breathing the morning air, damp in the dew . . .'[1]

In October, after two months' holiday, Verlaine returned to Paris, entered himself at the École de Droit and took a course in arithmetic. He intended to sit for the examination of the Ministry of Finance. Throughout his career, he would always keep the deep, inherited instinct to lead a regular existence; and he could never entirely disown the middle-class values. Throughout his career, he would also be drawn, with equal fervour, towards a bohemian life: towards the life essential to his poetry. From the moment that Verlaine divined his vocation, he was a dual character; and the contradiction, the constant struggle between the two men within him, the conventional and the bohemian, the pious and the sensual, the gentle and the violent, would determine the course of his life and his poetry.

In August 1863 he made his first appearance in print: he published his sonnet 'Monsieur Prudhomme' in *La Revue du progrès moral, littéraire, scientifique et artistique*. This ambitious review was edited by Louis-Xavier de Ricard. Louis-Xavier's father, General de Ricard, had been an aide-de-camp to King Jerome, and he and his wife entertained their son's friends in their salon in Les Batignolles. Verlaine was a frequent visitor; and in the Ricards' salon he met the young poets soon to be known as the Parnassians.

The salon was to end with the death of General de Ricard, and the war of 1870. But Mme Alphonse Daudet, in her memoirs, remembered that, when she was a girl of eighteen, it had seemed to her the very temple of poetry.

Léon Dierx, grave and handsome, exactly like Leconte de Lisle (and, like him, a creole), let us enjoy the wonderful lines of his *Filaos* ... José Maria de Heredia, with his black eyes full of sun ... hammered out every line of *Les Trophées* ... Edmond Lepelletier used to come with Paul Verlaine ... Verlaine was rebarbatively ugly, and when he recited those lines from one of his poems:

> 'Et nous n'aurons jamais de Béatrice!'

the young girls who were present could not help smiling.[2]

Verlaine was increasingly drawn to a literary life. Predictably, he abandoned his legal studies. In January 1864, his father found him a position with an insurance company. Two months afterwards, he became a copying-clerk at the *Mairie* of the ninth *arrondissement*, attached to the Bureau des mariages. He later moved to the central administration, in the Bureau des Budgets et Comptes at the Hôtel de Ville – again as a copying-clerk. He did not deign to rise any higher, although he had had an excellent education.

His friendship with Lepelletier was deepened by the friendship between their parents. Mme Lepelletier was a soldier's daughter, and she found much in common with Mme Verlaine, who was an officer's wife. M. Lepelletier (whose brother was an officer in the Zouaves) was soon on excellent terms with the Captain. Invitations were exchanged, and nearly every Wednesday evening, when Mme Lepelletier was 'at home', *les Verlaine* would come for tea and music and whist. On another evening, *les Lepelletier* went to the rue Saint-Louis where – piano apart – the programme was repeated. The two young men took advantage of these receptions to shut themselves in their rooms, and talk literature. Lepelletier lent Verlaine the works of Hugo, Rousseau and Balzac. Verlaine lent Lepelletier *Les Fleurs du mal*, and the poems of Leconte de Lisle, Gautier, Banville and Glatigny. They read the Greek classics, historians like Michelet and Louis Blanc, philosophers like Descartes, the *Lundis* of Sainte-Beuve, and Taine's *Histoire de la littérature anglaise*. They read the Vedic poems which had just been translated into French. They read Shakespeare and Calderon (Verlaine wanted to translate one of his plays), Lope de Vega and Gœthe. They read Dickens and Thackeray; they read secondary but picturesque French writers like Petrus Borel and Aloysius Bertrand. Verlaine's choice of reading 'was almost entirely romantic, as a reaction against academic teaching'. Years later, in his life of Verlaine, Lepelletier would add: 'His vast brain was open to every manifestation of art. We made frequent visits to the Louvre, and to the Musée du Luxembourg. He did not miss the exhibitions of painting which were then held at the Palais de l'Industrie.' Verlaine was one of the first assiduous visitors to the popular concerts founded by Pasdeloup. He was one of Wagner's early admirers.[3]

The year 1865 was to be eventful. On 30 March he was twenty-one. On 30 December, as if to remind him that he had come to manhood, Captain Verlaine died. He had lost much of his money in financial speculations. As the result of a heavy fall, he had also contracted a disease of the spinal marrow. This had manifested itself in increasingly frequent fits, and, eventually, in intermittent senility. It must have been almost a relief for his wife and son when he died at last. On 1 January 1866 he was buried in the cemetery at Les Batignolles. Verlaine ensured that he was given the military honours to which his rank and decorations entitled him.

The year which had brought Verlaine the official beginning of manhood also brought him his entrance into poetry. In 1865 he was one of the habitués of Lemerre's bookshop, in the passage Choiseul.

5

Just as the Romantics of the 1830s had found their publisher in Eugène Renduel, so the Parnassians, thirty years later, found theirs in Alphonse Lemerre. 'He was thickset, massive, squat,' remembered the poet Laurent Tailhade. 'His broad face, framed by a fair beard ... was both peasant-like and sculptural; it reminded one of a Roman proconsul and of a cattle-driver. So appeared Alphonse Lemerre, from 1865 to 1910, in his bookshop in the passage Choiseul. This little shop, dim and airless though it was, remained a place of singular renown.'[1]

Lemerre had begun his career by selling religious books; but he had a love of poetry, and he readily agreed to publish *Le Parnasse contemporain, recueil des vers nouveaux*. The first issue appeared on 3 March 1866. The eighteenth and last appeared on 14 July. The poets who contributed to the first series – and Verlaine was among them – became known as the Parnassians; and in November they received their critical accolade when the tempestuous critic Barbey d'Aurevilly attacked them in an article in *Le Nain jaune*. It took the Franco-Prussian War of 1870 to disperse the Parnassians who had gathered in the passage Choiseul. But the second series of *Le Parnasse contemporain* was published in 1871, after the war, and a third series appeared five years later.

One of those who gathered in Lemerre's back room was a small, squat, round-faced man with protuberant eyes, a composer of music called Emmanuel Chabrier. Three years older than Verlaine, he had been born at Ambert, in the Puy-de-Dôme, in 1841. His family had settled in Paris, for his father – a lawyer –

hoped that the boy would qualify for a Government post. Chabrier had duly taken a degree in law, and in 1863 he had become a copying-clerk; but, just as Verlaine continued the pursuit of poetry, so Chabrier had continued his study of music, and by 1869, when he entered the Ministry of the Interior, he knew many people in the musical world.

Verlaine was one of his earliest friends. 'For two or three years,' wrote Chabrier, 'from 1860 to 1863, I used to dine nearly every Saturday at Mme Verlaine's, in the rue Lécluse.'[2] The Verlaines did not move to 26, rue Lécluse until 1866, after the Captain's death; no doubt Chabrier had gone to the rue Saint-Louis, or to their later apartment in the rue Lemercier. However, Verlaine himself would happily recall these evenings in his sonnet to Chabrier; and there would be another memorial to their friendship, for he wrote the libretti for Chabrier's operettas *Fisch-Ton-Kan* and *Vaucochard et fils Ier*. Desaymard, in his book on the composer, dated these libretti between 1864 and 1869. Poulenc, in his study of Chabrier, placed them between 1863 and 1864. Only once, wrote Poulenc, in 1961, had the fragments of these operettas been performed in public: this had been in 1941; he himself had played the piano in *Fisch-Ton-Kan*.[3]

Chabrier was a remarkable man: he remained not only a life-long friend of Verlaine, but a close friend of Manet, and his collection of pictures included Manet's *Un bar aux Folies-bergère*, and *Les Moissonneurs* by Cézanne. Long before he died in 1894, he had become a legend in the musical world, with his broad-brimmed hat, his white scarf and his mustard-coloured ulster. In the days of the passage Choiseul, he was already bubbling over with fantasies, musical and otherwise; and with Charles de Sivry and Cabaner, the Bohemian composer, he was one of the few musicians admitted into the intimacy of the Parnassian poets.[4]

Another versatile friend of Verlaine's was Émile Blémont. When he left the Lycée Louis-le-Grand, Blémont had begun to study law; but early in 1866 he published a book of poems, and he hopefully sent a copy to Banville. Banville opened the world of literature to him, and in Banville's salon he met Verlaine. In about 1867 Verlaine introduced him to François Coppée.[5]

The Parnassians could be gay as well as intense; and they were certainly gay in the Bohemian salon of Nina de Callias. Nina was the daughter of a Lyons barrister; she had inherited a fortune, and married a journalist, Hector de Callias. Unfortunately Callias was addicted to absinthe, and she was obliged to separate from him. She consoled herself by entertaining talented young men. 'There's no need for evening dress with me,' she used to say. 'A sonnet is enough.'

As her biographer emphasised, she demanded originality.

At one of her gatherings, Verlaine first recited, and brought into fashion, one of those slang poems which Aristide Bruant later made his own ... The regulars at Nina's salon applauded it warmly for its novelty ...

But Verlaine did not only write songs. He sang himself – and heartily; he sang couplets from Offenbach and refrains from Paulus, changing the words as the spirit moved him, to the intense delight of Nina's guests. What was still better, they saw him act comedy, and one evening he earned a well-deserved triumph in *Les Deux Aveugles* . . .[6]

One may linger for a moment at this *salon*, which played its part in the history of *le Parnasse*. Nina did not merely keep open house. She was eager to learn from her guests. She had a remarkable knowledge of literature, she wrote presentable poetry, and her literary judgment could be acute. But her first love was music; and she often played the piano at public concerts, where she was acclaimed for her interpretations of Chopin, and for her own compositions.

She was not strong enough for a life of such intensity and, in 1884, she died insane. She was thirty-eight. According to her last wishes, she was buried in a kimono, pink silk stockings and silk slippers. This carnival costume symbolised her life.

She was to earn some unexpected immortality, for in 1906 she appeared, as the Comtesse Ninon de Calvador, in George Moore's *Memoirs of my dead life*.[7]

It was in 1867 that Charles Cros met Verlaine in the *salon* of his brother Antoine. Even in an age of remarkable men, the Cros family were outstanding. Simon Cros was a former professor of philosophy; Antoine, his eldest son, was a doctor and writer. Henri was a sculptor and ceramist, and he eventually held a post in the Sèvres factory. Charles, born in 1842, was an intellectual phenomenon. 'When only four years of age he began to "commit" poetry ... At eleven, he was already a philologist ... Michel Bréal, later of the Institut de France, and professor at the Collège de France, was his pupil in Hebrew, and M. Paul Mayer, another professor at the Collège de France, his pupil in Sanskrit.' In 1867, at the age of twenty-five, he showed his automatic telegraph in the International Exhibition in Paris. He also gave the Académie des Sciences an outline of the procedure for colour photography. In 1869 he published his essay on communication with the planets. He also made his poetic début in *L'Artiste*. In 1868 he had been introduced to Nina de Callias, and soon afterwards he became her lover. In 1870 he became friends with Charles de Sivry, 'an exquisite and far too modest musician', and, during the siege of Paris, when his father's house was destroyed, he and his brothers were taken in by Sivry's mother, in the boulevard Saint-Germain. There it was that he wrote his monologue, *l'Hareng saur* (set to music by Cabaner), and many of the poems which appeared in his *Coffret de Santal*. In 1878 came his break with Nina, and his marriage. Ten years later he died, an alcoholic.[8]

There were a number of salons in which the Parnassians assembled; but the Parnassus to which they went in pilgrimage was a fourth-floor apartment in the boulevard des Invalides. There lived the author of *Poèmes antiques* and *Poèmes barbares*. Leconte de Lisle had been forced by poverty to accept an Imperial pension, but he still dominated his disciples by his poetic achievement, his lofty nature, and - for he was nearing fifty - by the prestige of years. Like his poetry, he was exotic and stern, glamorous and un-bending. He had been born on Reunion Island, in the Indian Ocean, in 1818, the son of a former surgeon in Napoleon's armies; his mother, who belonged to the island, was a cousin of the poet Parny. Leconte de Lisle had come to France as a youth of nineteen, and studied law; and since 1846 he had lived in

Paris. The Revolution of 1848 had ruined his family and ended his private allowance, and for some years he had struggled to subsist on journalism, translations and private tuition. In the intervals of such work, he had devoted himself to poetry. His legal training, his financial straits, and his literary creed combined to make him rigidly self-disciplined; and his character – like his poetic principles – remained inflexible. He was a dedicated poet and a natural master.

In 1884, in *La Légende du Parnasse contemporain*, Catulle Mendès would recall his salon. 'None of those who were admitted will ever forget those sweet and noble evenings which, for so many years ... gave us our finest hours ... To this little drawing-room ... we came to discuss our plans, bring our new poems, and ask for the judgment of our comrades and our great friend ... He was, and still remains, our poetic conscience in person ... He condemns or absolves, and we submit.'[9] Mendès was not the only poet to pay tribute to this awesome master. Nearly thirty years after *Le Parnasse contemporain* first appeared, François Coppée remembered: 'My friends and I used to go to Leconte de Lisle every Saturday evening – Victor Hugo was too far away, in Guernsey – as the faithful make their pilgrimage to Mecca.'[10]

Verlaine did not go to Guernsey, but he worshipped at both shrines. Among Hugo's papers is a letter in Verlaine's most careful hand, written with a schoolboy's admiration.

14 September 1867.

Dear, illustrious and venerated Master,

For all my efforts, I have found it impossible to carry out the two commissions with which you kindly honoured me. The first was to send you the article by Leconte de Lisle on *La Légende des Siècles*, and the other was to pass on to Albert Glatigny your kindly words about his poems and his request to perform in *Ruy-Blas*.

As for the first of these commissions, I have communicated your wish to Leconte de Lisle, who has lost the article and completely forgotten the date – even the approximate date – of its publication ...

As for Glatigny, he has disappeared so utterly from Paris since the beginning of August that his closest friends do not know where he is living now ...

It remains for me, *cher Maître*, to beg you to excuse this chatter and to accept the expression of my immense respect, and the unchangeable affection of my profound gratitude [*sic*] . . .

Dear, illustrious and venerated Master,

Your most humble and devoted servant and admirer,

PAUL VERLAINE.[11]

If Verlaine paid effusive tribute to the exiled god, he found a less rarefied atmosphere in the boulevard des Invalides. But, according to Leconte de Lisle's biographer, he was unwelcome there. When, in the early years of the twentieth century, Fernand Calmettes published *Leconte de Lisle et ses amis*, he dismissed Verlaine with scorn. Perhaps he saw him through the eyes of Leconte de Lisle, who had come to detest him. Perhaps he judged the Verlaine of the late 1860s by the Verlaine of the 1890s. 'Verlaine,' he wrote, 'did not yet get drunk when he began to frequent the salon of Leconte de Lisle; but, when he was sober, he took little part in the conversation . . . As soon as he took to drink, just before the war, his bad manners made it unpleasant to associate with him. He disappeared after the Commune. Despite his "musical soul", he was not in tune with the salon.'[12]

6

The truth was that Verlaine was not an unquestioning disciple of the master; and while he wrote his poetic essays in Parnassian style, as a form of literary discipline, he was already drawn, instinctively, to poetry of quite another order.

This was clear from his first book of poems. In 1866 – on the same day as he published *Le Réliquaire*, by Coppée – Lemerre published Verlaine's *Poèmes saturniens*. Most of the poems, Verlaine said, were written while he was still at the Lycée. 'Three-quarters of them were written in the *rhétorique* [the top class but one], and in the second class, and some, I'm afraid, were even written in the third.'[1] The book, added Lepelletier, had been finished in the first months of Verlaine's undemanding career at the Hôtel de Ville.

It is evident that *Poèmes saturniens* is an early book. 'Nocturne parisien' is little more than a scholastic tour de force. 'Monsieur Prudhomme', which had been Verlaine's first published poem, is a sharp but trivial caricature, and it bears no relation to the rest of the collection. Verlaine is still under the influence of older contemporary poets. From Hugo, the author of *La Légende des Siècles*, he borrows the grandiose rhetoric of his 'Prologue', the idea of the poet as a visionary (but Hugo's influence was relatively slight: Verlaine was one of the very few poets of the time who escaped his domination). From Leconte de Lisle, Verlaine takes the heroes of classical mythology, the interest in Indian epic, and the ideal of impassibility.

> Ainsi que Çavitri faisons-nous impassibles,
> Mais, comme elle, dans l'âme ayons un haut dessein.[2]

This was the Parnassian doctrine; and, in his 'Épilogue', Verlaine casts aside the Romantic belief in inspiration, dismisses the sentimentality of Lamartine, and insists, with all the force of a convinced Parnassian, with all the conviction that Gautier had expressed in 'L'Art', on the supreme importance of unremitting work and technical perfection.

> À nous qui ciselons les mots comme des coupes
> Et qui faisons des vers émus très froidement,
> À nous qu'on ne voit point les soirs aller par groupes
> Harmonieux au bord des *lacs* et nous pâmant ...
>
> Ce qu'il faut à nous, c'est l'étude sans trêve,
> C'est l'effort inouï, le combat nonpareil,
> C'est la nuit, l'âpre nuit du travail, d'où se lève
> Lentement, lentement, l'Œuvre, ainsi qu'un soleil!
>
> Libre à nos Inspirés, cœurs qu'une œillade enflamme,
> D'abandonner leur être aux vents comme un bouleau;
> Pauvres gens! l'Art n'est pas d'éparpiller son âme!
> Est-elle en marbre ou non, la Vénus de Milo?[3]

'For some time afterwards,' Verlaine said at the end of his life, 'I considered this epilogue as the cream of aesthetics. These verses and theories have since come to seem puerile.'[4]

The 'Épilogue' is not the only poem in this collection to suggest the influence of Gautier; and elsewhere there are reminiscences of Glatigny. But these influences are largely intellectual: they are not in accord with Verlaine's instincts, with the personal feelings which he is at pains to conceal. It is, however, neither Hugo nor Leconte de Lisle who leaves the clearest imprint on this book: it is Baudelaire. 'It is to Baudelaire,' Verlaine would write, 'that I owe the awakening of poetic feeling, and what is deep in me.'[5]

The influence of Baudelaire may be seen in Verlaine's interest in modern Paris, occasionally in his use of a title or a phrase, but, above all, in mood. The very title 'Crépuscule du soir mystique' recalls Baudelaire's 'Le Crépuscule du soir' and 'Le Coucher du soleil romantique', and the whole poem is redolent of *Les Fleurs du mal*. Verlaine's 'Sérénade' is directly inspired by Baudelaire's 'Le Beau Navire': it has the same schema, and it, too, is a catalogue of the beauties of the poet's mistress – though one suspects that Verlaine's mistress is an ideal. 'Lassitude' is distinctly Baudelairean in mood. In 'La Dahlia' the poet gazes at the impeccable body of a cold and indifferent courtesan. The poem recalls the Baudelairean sonnet 'La Beauté': 'Je suis belle, ô mortels! comme un rêve de pierre.'

The influence of Baudelaire was instinctive and profound; and Verlaine had acknowledged it before his *Poèmes saturniens* appeared. Late in 1865, in the periodical *L'Art*, he had published a critical study of the poet. It was remarkable, since Baudelaire received little recognition in his lifetime; it was also remarkable as the work of a youth of twenty-one. Verlaine was writing from his heart; he was using a critical judgment which would be sadly impaired in later years. *Charles Baudelaire* was perhaps the most searching and considered appreciation that he would write; and in it he sensed the poet's true distinction.

The profound originality of Charles Baudelaire is, to my mind, his powerful presentation of the essential modern man: . . . the physical man of today, as he has been made by the refinements of an excessive civilisation: modern man, with his sharpened, vibrant senses, his painfully subtle mind, his intellect steeped in tobacco, his blood burned up by alcohol . . . It is Charles Baudelaire, I repeat, who presents the sensitive man, and he presents him as a type, or, if you like, as a *hero* . . . The future historian of our age should study *Les Fleurs du mal* with pious attention. It is the quintessence, the extreme concentration, of a whole element of this century.[6]

Some of the *Poèmes saturniens* suggest a more or less strong literary influence; some suggest mere literary exercises. One or two reflect, perhaps, Verlaine's love for Élisa Dujardin; but none is written with the undoubted passion, the physical need, the spiritual longing, which was to mark certain poems in later years. The Verlaine of *Poèmes saturniens* is still ostensibly Parnassian, still trying to impose impassibility on a supremely personal art, and on a nature which – like that of Baudelaire - is Romantic and intensely subjective. The Parnassian principles offered a useful discipline to a young poet, a sound professional training, but they were the last principles which Verlaine was created to profess. Already, in his first book, his literary debts revealed his own saturnine and Romantic nature. The most memorable *Poèmes saturniens* were, already, poems of mood: the poems in the series 'Mélancolia' and some of the 'Paysages Tristes'. 'The more people read me,' Verlaine would write, a quarter-century later, 'the more they will be convinced that there is a sort of unity between my early works and those of my maturity. "Paysages tristes", for example: are they not, in a sense, the egg which hatched a whole flight of singing lines of poetry . . . birds of which I was perhaps the first fancier?'[7]

Among the 'Paysages tristes' was 'Le Souvenir du crépuscule'. Years later, Jules Lemaître analysed it as an example of Symbolist poetry. It was, as he perceived, 'the poetry of twilight expressed still in dream, before reflection, before the images and feelings which the half-light awakens had been set in order . . . This poetry almost comes before words: it is the poetry of limbo, it is re-corded dream.'[8] Among the 'Paysages tristes' is also the 'Chanson d'automne,' which is pure, unadulterated Verlaine. Critics would later cite it as a reflection of *fin de siècle* decadence, but it was written at the zenith of the Second Empire. Even now, the poet has dropped the mask of impassibility; he has brought poetry close to music, not merely in sound, but in emotional power.

He has somehow defined an indefinable mood, and given permanence to a transient, dream-like and infinitely suggestive state of mind.

> Les sanglots longs
> Des violons
>   De l'automne
> Blessent mon cœur
> D'une langueur
>   Monotone.
>
> Tout suffocant
> Et blême, quand
>   Sonne l'heure,
> Je me souviens
> Des jours anciens
>   Et je pleure.
>
> Et je m'en vais
> Au vent mauvais
>   Qui m'emporte
> Deçà, delà,
> Pareil à la
>   Feuille morte.[9]

On 22 November 1866, Verlaine wrote his first known letter to Mallarmé, and sent him a copy of *Poèmes saturniens*.

Monsieur, would you allow a friend of your friends, who is also a sympathetic admirer of your poetry, to send you this first book? Its whole merit – if it has merit – consists, perhaps, in the respect of the Masters and of the Tradition which it proclaims in its little way. I venture to hope that these attempts will interest you and that you will recognise . . . at least an effort towards Expression, towards the record of Sensation . . .[10]

Mallarmé replied with his gentle, customary charm:

Monsieur et cher Poëte,

Allow me to see your exquisite attention . . . not only as a gesture of literary sympathy, but as a wonderful presentiment of an unknown friendship. You have forestalled a wish I felt when I read your poems in

Le Parnasse – a wish to shake you by the hand ... Poets inherit old forms from each other; you have decided to begin by forging a new and virgin metal ...[11]

Poèmes saturniens brought Verlaine the lifelong friendship of Mallarmé. They brought a condescending letter from Leconte de Lisle: 'Your *Poèmes* are those of a true poet, an artist who is already very skilful and will soon be a master of expression.'[12] *Poèmes saturniens* also brought an appreciation from one of the foremost critics of the day. Verlaine had sent a copy of his book to Sainte-Beuve, and in December Sainte-Beuve acknowledged it.

The talent is there, and, before I do anything else, I recognize that. Your aspiration is lofty, you do not content yourself with fugitive inspiration ...

As a landscape artist, you have some very piquant sketches and night scenes. Like everyone who deserves to attain the laurel, you attempt to do what has not been done. You do well ...

You need not be afraid, at times, to be more harmonious and a little more pleasant, and a little less sombre and hard where emotions are concerned. Don't take that poor fine Baudelaire as your point of departure.[13]

It was strangely mistaken criticism. Sainte-Beuve had failed to recognise the fruitful influence of Baudelaire. He had praised some of the poorest poems in the collection. Verlaine was flattered by the letter, but he did not follow Sainte-Beuve's advice to continue writing descriptive poems like 'César Borgia' and 'Philippe II'. He wisely pursued his own way.

7

Élisa Dujardin, affectionate and encouraging as ever, had paid for the publication of *Poèmes saturniens*. Three months after the book appeared, on 16 February 1867, Élisa died in childbirth at Lécluse. Verlaine had been summoned by telegram. He arrived as the coffin was being carried out of the house.

Throughout his life, especially in moments of crisis, he would seek escape from reality: sometimes in travel or poetry, sometimes in religion, but all too often in sexual orgy or drink. In 1861, at the age of seventeen, he had already lingered in the Paris brasseries. The following summer, after the strain of his baccalauréat, he had been drawn to the taverns at Lécluse, where gin cost only a sou a glass, and the local inhabitants drank a savage mixture of coffee and alcohol known as *bistouille*. He was all too dependent on drink: Alphonse Lemerre was to remember that Verlaine never left the bookshop in the passage Choiseul 'without pausing for a break in a little café at the end of the passage. There he sometimes drank more than one absinthe, and very often Coppée had great trouble in dragging him away.'[1] Now, in 1867, the death of Élisa sent him back to the taverns at Lécluse; and for three days, to his mother's despair, to the horror of the village, Verlaine drank solidly to drown his grief. He was weak by nature, and the blood of Henry-Joseph, the dissolute lawyer, was, alas, too strong.

Verlaine was not yet twenty-three, and his alcoholism was already plain. So, too, was another trait which would help to make and destroy his life. Verlaine had not only been devoted to Élisa Dujardin: he had shown excessive interest in a young Dujardin boy, and he felt passionate friendship for Lucien Viotti, a pretty youth whom he had known at the lycée. He had not outgrown the *garçonneries* of his schooldays; he would always have a homosexual element in his nature. Probably – as I have already suggested – it owed something to his intense relationship with his mother; certainly it owed something to his ugliness. Lepelletier's mother thought that he looked like an orang-outang. Lepelletier agreed that his ugliness was astonishing. A master at the lycée said that 'his hideous head made one think of a brutalised criminal'. Verlaine himself was acutely aware of his *gueusard de physique*: in his early years it made him understandably timid with women. The accident of his appearance, as well as the circumstances of his life, confirmed what was no doubt an inborn tendency.

Yet though the supreme relationhip in his life was to be a liaison with a man, though he would have many homosexual

experiences, Verlaine was bisexual. At the age of seventeen he
had paid his first visit to a brothel. It had been an ignoble initiation
– miraculously transformed into poetry.

> Ah! les oaristys! les premières maîtresses!
> L'or des cheveux, l'azur des yeux, la fleur des chairs,
> Et puis, parmi l'odeur des corps jeunes et chers,
> La spontanéité craintive des caresses . . .[2]

Verlaine was not only enamoured of men. He would marry,
he would spend the last years of his life torn between two
middle-aged women, he would have countless casual heterosexual affairs. In 1868, a slim book of sonnets, *Les Amies*, was
published in Brussels by Poulet-Malassis (who, eleven years
earlier, had published *Les Fleurs du mal*). It was a delicate celebration of Lesbian love by a poet who disguised himself under the
transparent pseudonym Pablo de Herlagnez. The subject owed
some of its glamour to the fact that it was illicit love; but the
poems (which Verlaine would reprint in *Parallèlement*) showed
a sensuous appreciation of women. Two later collections of
poems, *Femmes* and *Hombres*, emphasise the point. Indeed,
Femmes reflects much more lust than its counterpart. The poems
which, in later years, Verlaine addressed to his mistresses, show a
sexual appetite which recalls that of Hugo in old age.

Verlaine, in his early twenties, was already bisexual. He was
already a potential alcoholic. And – another inherited trait – he
could be violent. Violence lay all too close to the surface of his
nature. Neurotic young men with a family taint of insanity (one
recalls the wild Henry-Joseph) are often affected by alcoholic
mania. They may need only a little wine to reach a state of excitement and fury which leads to attempted murder or suicide, and
this state may last for hours or even days. In Verlaine himself,
drink would remove any trace of inhibition, and the slightest
contradiction would fire him. His family and his dearest friends
were not safe from him. Lepelletier recorded how, after a night
of drinking, he and Verlaine were coming home through the
Bois de Boulogne. Verlaine had wanted to go back to the Pré-
Catalan for another drink; Lepelletier had tried to restrain him.

Verlaine had torn himself away, drawn his swordstick, and plunged at him. Lepelletier had fled.[3]

If Verlaine's weak and vicious nature was already clear, so, too, was his devotion to poetry. In August 1867 he paid a visit to Belgium to offer his respects to Victor Hugo. Every summer, Hugo left his voluntary exile in Guernsey to stay in Brussels with his son Charles. Now Verlaine called at the place des Barricades, and Hugo asked him to dinner, praised his *Poèmes saturniens*, and criticised the affectations of Leconte de Lisle, and Parnassian impassibility. 'You will get over it,' he assured Verlaine.[4] Verlaine had already passed beyond it. He owed much less to Leconte de Lisle than to Baudelaire, whose funeral he attended in September.[5]

On 2 January 1868, *Le Hanneton* published *Qui veut des merveilles?* It was a light-hearted review of 1867 which Verlaine had written with Coppée. Almost exactly a year later, on 14 January 1869, with all the Parnassians of the passage Choiseul, all the habitués of the Marquise de Ricard and Nina de Callias, Verlaine attended the first performance of Coppée's *Le Passant*. The evening was to leave a lasting impression on him. He would not forget the young Sarah Bernhardt playing the minstrel boy, Zanetto; and at the end of his life, when he was writing a three-act *Louis* xvii he imagined her in the part of the Dauphin.[6]

The triumph of *Le Passant* did not immediately change the friendship between Coppée and Verlaine, but it marked the parting of their ways. Coppée became the protégé of the Emperor's cousin, Princess Mathilde, and embarked on the conventional career which led him to the Académie-Française. Honours are not always a final measure of distinction. Posterity might set the author of *Le Passant* lower than the author of *Fêtes galantes*.[7]

8

Only three years lay between the publication of *Poèmes saturniens* in 1866 and that of *Fêtes galantes* in 1869; but between the two books lay a chasm. *Poèmes saturniens* had been marked by literary exercises and experiments, and strongly coloured by literary influences. Verlaine had revealed his instinctive sympathy with Baudelaire, and he had begun to establish himself as a poet of mood. In *Fêtes galantes*, with remarkable suddenness, he showed himself to be a poet of extraordinary technical accomplishment, a poet of exquisite sensibility. He re-created a distinctive world.

Fourteen poems out of the twenty-two in *Fêtes galantes* had appeared in *L'Artiste* before they were published in the book; and it has been asked if Verlaine owed a debt to Arsène Houssaye, the editor of *L'Artiste*, who was himself a lover of the eighteenth century. Houssaye had not only published articles and poems on eighteenth-century subjects in his periodical, he had published a substantial work of his own, *Galerie des Portraits du XVIIIe siècle*, and he had invited Verlaine to his *hôtel* in the avenue Friedland, where Verlaine could admire his pictures. It must, however, be said that the Goncourts dismissed Houssaye's gallery as a wonderful collection of fakes; and Jacques Robichez has written that 'Verlaine came unscathed through the traps which were set for him'.[1]

In his edition of Verlaine's poems, Robichez also says that the only historical and critical work which almost certainly influenced him is that of the Goncourts. It was, he writes, from the Goncourts' work that Verlaine took certain details for *Fêtes galantes*. 'Their study of Watteau ... already figured in the first volume of the *Portraits intimes du XVIIIe siècle* in 1857. Verlaine certainly read the brilliant chapter on La Camargo in the same volume.'[2] However, Robichez fails to mention a more distinguished writer who should certainly be considered as an influence on *Fêtes galantes*. This was Théophile Gautier, a fellow-contributor to *L'Artiste*, a friend of Houssaye and the Goncourts, and the pre-eminent art critic of the day.[3]

As early as 1838, Gautier had affirmed the importance of that eighteenth-century quality, *l'esprit*, and declared it to be unjustly disdained by his fellow-countrymen; he had expressed his sympathy for the eighteenth-century theatre. His affection for the period extended, naturally, to its visual arts. This affection is reflected in his early poetry; and there is a clear touch of Watteau and Lancret, of the *déjeuner sur l'herbe*, about the ideal theatre in Gautier's novel, *Mademoiselle de Maupin*.

This affection for the eighteenth century is distinctly seen in Gautier's criticism; and in 1860, when the Louvre exhibited only one Watteau, one Fragonard and three Chardins, and refused to buy others, Gautier attacked his compatriots for scorning their national art. He also wrote a series of enthusiastic, beautifully visual appreciations of eighteenth-century masters. On 5 September that year, in *Le Moniteur universel*, he published the second of seven articles on the current exhibition of old French masters in the boulevard des Italiens. It was a warm appreciation of Watteau.

He can, with good reason, be called a genius [Gautier declared], for he has completely created his world, a wonderful world, full of harmony and illusion, where the landscape is just artificial enough to make the characters seem real, where there is not a note out of tune with its charming unreality, where nature blends, with perfect tact, into the operatic décor. Watteau reigns over this legendary land which Breughel had half seen; his gilded galleons with silken sails have landed the pilgrims of Cythera on the azure shores of the happy islands; he has raised there, as a standard, and in sign of possession, a maypole crowned with roses ... It is a strange thing, but these fairytale woods, peopled by the masks of Italian comedy, this perpetual festival of youth, beauty and gallantry, all these visual delights were drawn by a failing hand. These dreams of happiness came from a sombre spirit, and life was sad for the man who, in his painting, made it so beautiful ... Only his palette glowed, and, in that century of licence, the painter of the *fêtes galantes* led a life that was almost austere ...

In his commentary on *Fêtes galantes*, Bornecque writes: 'It has long been thought, because of Lepelletier's statement, that Verlaine had been able to admire the Watteau paintings in the Lacaze collection at the Louvre. Ernest Dupuy has pointed out a mistake in the dates. The only Watteau canvas which was accessible to the public before the *Fêtes galantes* was *L'Embarquement pour Cythère*.'[4] Verlaine, adds Robichez, must therefore have been inspired by the legend of Watteau, which had been popularised for some years in Paris; he could not have been inspired by the paintings themselves.

It seems that Robichez and Dupuy have both been mistaken. The Lacaze collection of Watteau's paintings had been shown in the boulevard des Italiens long before it was presented to the Louvre; and, in his appreciation of Watteau in September 1860, Gautier made this clear: 'It is rare,' he wrote, 'for artists who are used to small canvases to enlarge their paintings with impunity . . . This is not so with Watteau; the *Gilles* of the Lacaze collection shows that the author of so many charming little pictures had nothing to fear from this decisive test . . .'

The *Gilles* in the Lacaze does not seem directly to have inspired any poem in *Fêtes galantes*; but round him, in the picture, were 'those happy masks of the *commedia dell'arte*, Mezzetin, Scapin, Colombine . . .' who are present in spirit in the poetry. The *Rendez-vous de chasse*, which was also in the exhibition, bears a slight relation to Verlaine's 'Sur l'herbe'.

The *Rendez-vous de chasse* is a rare piece in the master's work [wrote Gautier], although it is not worth the *Gilles* of M. Lacaze or *L'Embarquement pour Cythère*, which belongs to the Museum . . .

A band of young noblemen and fine ladies have paused in a forest clearing during the hunt . . . The gallantry has already begun, and one nobleman is paying court to a pretty woman who is listening to him over her shoulder with that feigned distraction, that affected non-chalance which spur on the madrigal and change it into a declaration of love; this occupation does not prevent the suitor from playing with his dog with his other hand.

The scene anticipates Verlaine's 'Sur l'herbe', in which a marquis and an abbé, drinking wine on the grass, pay court to two women, and the marquis declares: 'Je voudrais être petit chien !' In *L'Heureuse Chute*, another Watteau picture, a certain ardour seemed to disturb the elegant libertinage. 'A young woman is wearing one of those fine coquettish *déshabillés*, where the folds fall from the shoulder and add such grace. She has fallen on the grass. No doubt the high heel of her slipper has twisted under her pretty foot . . . The cavalier has his arms round the young woman, but certainly not in order to pick her up . . .' Here, perhaps, in

Watteau's picture, described by Gautier, is a foretaste of Verlaine's 'Les Ingénus':

> Les hauts talons luttaient avec les longues jupes,
> En sorte que, selon le terrain et le vent,
> Parfois luisaient des bas de jambe, trop souvent
> Interceptés! – et nous aimions ce jeu de dupes ...[5]

It is also worth looking at Gautier's description of *L'Indiscret*:

Sitting on a grassy bank, writhing with the suppleness of a viper, is a Harlequin, diamond-patterned in every colour, paying court to a nearby Columbine ... The Columbine is defending herself as best she can, and holding her slender hand to her white breast, in disdainful protest.

While Harlequin is delivering his little speech, the other comedians, indifferent to amorettas, are leaning against a tree, and going over their parts, and the music which they must sing this evening.

It is possible that Verlaine had this picture in mind when he wrote 'Pantomime':

> Pierrot, qui n'a rien d'un Clitandre,
> Vide un flacon sans plus attendre,
> Et, pratique, entame un pâté.
>
> Cassandre, au fond de l'avenue,
> Verse une larme méconnue,
> Sur son neveu déshérité.
>
> Ce faquin d'Arlequin combine
> L'enlèvement de Colombine
> Et pirouette quatre fois.
>
> Colombine rêve, surprise
> De sentir un cœur dans la brise
> Et d'entendre en son cœur des voix.[6]

'The work of Watteau,' wrote Gautier, 'is like an Elysium where the spirit is consoled for the brutalities of realism ... His *Fêtes galantes* are never orgies or bacchanals; Watteau paints the pleasures of gentlefolk, the delights of the refined ... The greatest intimacies of his lovers do not go beyond those comedy kisses, indicated rather than emphasised, which respect the powder and the rouge.' The atmosphere would characterise the *Fêtes galantes* of Verlaine as well as those of Watteau; and Gautier suggested the world of the *Fêtes galantes* still more clearly when, on 1 April 1862, again in *Le Moniteur universel*, he discussed the first four issues of the Goncourts' *L'Art du XVIIIe siècle*. They included an illustrated appreciation of Watteau.

'In this operatic Arcadia,' wrote Gautier, 'in this Tempe of Italian comedy with velvet lawns, with bluish trees, with fountains blowing out their vaporised waters, a whole carefree population strolls, talks and plays the guitar, forgetful of the real world, and apparently not sharing its passions.' It is a strange anticipation of Verlaine's 'Claire de Lune', where the lute-players with their songs move the very fountains: 'Les grands jets d'eau sveltes parmi les marbres.'

Love [wrote Gautier] occupies these couples on the flower-enamelled grass, but it does not disturb them; no lasciviousness, no sensual ardour. The women display a calm coquetry, and, sure of being respected, they smile vaguely as they acknowledge the madrigals. These madrigals are sung by suitors whose restraint astonishes the marble Fauns in the groves. The greatest liberties are discouraged by a little tap of the fan, and even when they leave for Cythera on that ship with silken sails, and cupids for its crew, the pilgrims have a rhythmic walk as if they were in a ballet.

And yet, through this perpetual festival, one divines a hidden languor, a melancholy which will not be confessed . . .

If Verlaine, like Watteau, caught the elegance and comedy, the restrained sensuality of the world of the *commedia dell'arte*, he also shrouded it in his own melancholy. There is a touch of cynicism about the stylised love; there is also a constant sense of the transience and futility of passion. Verlaine, like Watteau, stands in the corner of his exquisite pictures, a quiet and sombre observer of the scene.

> Un vieux faune de terre cuite
> Rit au centre des boulingrins,
> Présageant sans doute une suite
> Mauvaise à ces instants sereins

Qui m'ont conduit et t'ont conduite,
– Mélancoliques pèlerins, –
Jusqu'à cette heure dont la fuite
Tournoie au son des tambourins.[7]

Yet the fundamental melancholy cannot obscure the brilliance of these tiny verbal pictures, these miniature conversation-pieces and declarations of love. Perhaps Verlaine was inspired by the exhibition in the boulevard des Italiens, perhaps he was inspired by Gautier's writing. The source of his inspiration remains an academic point. In the twenty-eight poems of *Fêtes galantes*, as in some kind of amber, he catches and enshrines the world of Watteau. He preserves, in its theatrical light, the world of the *commedia dell'arte*. *Fêtes galantes*, explained George Moore, 'is lit with dresses, white, blue, yellow, green, mauve, and un-decided purple; the voices? strange contraltos; the forms? not those of men or women, but mystic, hybrid creatures, with hands nervous and pale, and eyes charged with eager and fitful light.'[8]

Fêtes galantes was, in many ways, an impersonal book; it re-vealed little about Verlaine, except, possibly, his own cynicism and his own melancholy about love. But its technical mastery, its musical quality, its intense and subtle evocation, showed that the poet had come into possession of his powers.

Dans le vieux parc solitaire et glacé,
Deux formes ont tout à l'heure passé.

Leurs yeux sont morts et leurs lèvres sont molles,
Et l'on entend à peine leurs paroles.

Dans le vieux parc solitaire et glacé,
Deux spectres ont évoqué le passé.

– Te souvient-il de notre extase ancienne?
– Pourquoi voulez-vous donc qu'il m'en souvienne?

– Ton cœur bat-il toujours à mon seul nom?
Toujours vois-tu mon âme en rêve? – Non.

Le Petit

– Ah! les beaux jours de bonheur indicible
Où nous joignions nos bouches! – C'est possible.

– Qu'il était bleu, le ciel, et grand, l'espoir!
– L'espoir a fui, vaincu, vers le ciel noir.

Tels ils marchaient dans les avoines folles,
Et la nuit seule entendit leurs paroles.[9]

PART TWO

Mathilde

(1869–71)

9

FÊTES GALANTES was published by Lemerre on 10 July 1869. By the time it appeared, Verlaine's life had changed dramatically.

For some time, now, it had become increasingly clear that he needed the discipline of marriage. His drinking habits were as grave as ever. In the rue Lécluse the concierge was all too often woken by his drunken homecoming in the small hours. When Mme Grandjean, tante Louise, died in March 1869, Verlaine had attended the funeral at Paliseul, and behaved as disgracefully as he had done, two years earlier, at Lécluse. A local tavern-keeper sent in a bill: 'Five francs for gin for Monsieur Paul.' Since gin – or *gnief*, as the locals called it – cost a sou a glass, Verlaine must have bought a hundred glasses in two and a half days. Such drinking-bouts – though no doubt he had companions – produced intellectual atony as well as physical violence.

Verlaine was just twenty-five. He was not indifferent to his disgrace; at moments he felt profound disgust at his behaviour, and (for he had pious ancestors) he would enter a church, and make his confession. He would avoid the temptations of cafés, show himself to be a model *employé* at the Hôtel de Ville. Then, once again, heredity and weakness would prevail, and he would succumb to temptation.[1]

His family were anxious about him. His mother was forgiving –

37

all too forgiving – and she maintained that *le petit* was not fundamentally bad. Verlaine asked only to be saved from himself, from an endless prospect of timid reform and perpetual relapse. In March 1869, his mother and her sister Rose suggested that he should marry one of his cousins: a girl of strong and energetic character.

The project came to nothing. Three months later, Verlaine met his future wife.

Mathilde-Sophie-Marie Mauté was just sixteen. She had been born at Nogent-le-Rotrou, Eure-et-Loir, on 17 April 1853. She was the daughter of Théodore-Jean Mauté (and if he or one of his ancestors took a fancy to the name Mauté de Fleurville, it does not appear on any official records).[2]

Théodore Mauté was forty-six at the time of his daughter's birth; on her birth certificate he was described as a man of independent means. When, years later, Lepelletier came to write his book on Verlaine, he described M. Mauté as a retired solicitor. The description offended Mathilde. 'There's certainly no harm in being a solicitor,' she explained in her memoirs. 'But Lepelletier is wrong: my father never did anything but live as he pleased.' According to Mathilde – who became a ludicrous social snob – her father was sent to Paris at the age of twelve, to attend the Lycée Henri IV. One of his fellow-pupils there was the Duc d'Orléans, the son of Louis-Philippe. Among his other contemporaries at the Lycée, said Mathilde, were Alfred de Musset and Paul Foucher, the future brother-in-law of Victor Hugo. Foucher and Mauté were to remain lifelong friends. Mauté (so his daughter continued) had an excellent academic record; but instead of entering the Conseil d'État, as his father wanted, he showed a preference for a naval career. At this moment, his destiny was decided for him. One of his brothers died, accidentally, at the age of twenty; and Mme Mauté could not bear the thought of losing her second son to the navy. Théodore dutifully renounced the career he had chosen, but he refused to follow any other, and he insisted on travelling for pleasure. He went to England, Scotland, Italy, Switzerland and Algeria, and he was

about to leave for Turkey and Greece when, instead, he became a
married man.

Every year he had loyally spent the summer with his parents,
and gone shooting on what Mathilde called his father's estate. He
used to spend his winters in Paris, where he was socially in demand,
for he was an eligible bachelor. When his father died in 1851,
explained Mathilde, Théodore had come into a fortune which
assured his independence. He had inherited some land, 'some
houses in the provinces and about 60,000 francs in banknotes
hidden in books in the library.'[3] He had spent his time of mourning
with his mother; then he had resumed his life in Paris until the
day he met a young widow, Mme de Sivry.

Mathilde herself was to create such a legend about her mother's
family that it is difficult, even now, to ascertain the truth. François
Porché, introducing the memoirs of Mathilde, remarks that she
never stops talking about her maternal grandmother, *née* Leroy
d'Honnecourt; and perhaps this 'd'Honnecourt' is non-existent
like 'de Fleurville'. And yet, as Porché says, Mathilde was devoid
of imagination; she would have been incapable of inventing
everything. As for her account of her parents' life 'in the world
of the faubourg Saint-Germain', of their long annual visits to the
Château de Reynel, Porché observes, very plausibly, that
domestics used to include tutors, governesses and companions,
and that perhaps the link which bound the 'Fleurvilles' to the
aristocracy was a link of this kind. Mme Mauté was an excellent
musician.[4]

When Antoinette-Flore Chariat, the future Mme Mauté, was
a child of five, her parents had left Douai and settled in Paris. By
the age of fifteen, she had become an accomplished pianist (there
is an unsubstantiated legend that she was a pupil of Chopin). She
was soon sought after in society – as Mathilde herself explained,
it was because of her musical talents. She was a pretty brunette
with blue eyes and a fine complexion; she was also gay and good-
natured. If we are to believe Mathilde, she did not only know the
nobility; in the salons of the Russian and Polish colonies she met
such celebrities as Balzac, George Sand and Musset. She was

(said Mathilde) a friend of Wagner, and it was in Wagner's box that she listened to the tempestuous first performance of *Tann-hauser*. At a soirée at the Comtesse d'Hautefeuille's, she had met M. de Sivry, her first husband.

The Marquis de Sivry, Mathilde would write,

was thirty years old; he was good-looking and extremely learned. He knew eighteen languages: apart from the European languages, he knew nearly all the Asiatic dialects [*sic*], and he did translations, chiefly for the clergy. His family is one of the oldest in France. The eldest son of Jean, Duc de Brienne, Emperor of Constantinople, had received the title of Marquis de Sivry from King Charles VI. The Marquis de Sivry fell in love with my mother and married her. Unfortunately he died soon after the birth of my brother [Charles].

Unfortunately, it has also been proved that the 'Marquis' was a hatmaker's son.[5]

However, Mme de Sivry remained a widow for five years; and then (continued Mathilde), in the salon of the Comtesse de Borck, she met Théodore Mauté.

After their marriage in 1852, M. Mauté moved into his wife's apartment at 45, rue du Miromesnil; and Mathilde would no doubt have been born there had it not been for old Mme Mauté, who insisted that the birth took place in her house. It was there-fore in the rue Charronnerie, at Nogent-le-Rotrou, that Mathilde came into the world, and thenceforward the Mautés spent the six months of spring and summer 'in Normandy'.

When Mathilde came to write her memoirs, she forgot to record that her grandfather Mauté had been a grocer. She seems to have found Nogent-le-Rotrou too common to mention. She was also vague about her grandmother's house. Perhaps this vagueness was due to the fact that she did not see the place after she was seven; but perhaps her recollections of the house in the rue Charronnerie owed something to her social pretentiousness, for she implied that it had been a château, standing in considerable estates.

These summers 'in Normandy' came to an end when old Mme Mauté died in 1860. Théodore Mauté sold the house and bought a house in Montmartre. Much of the furniture from the rue Charronnerie was installed in 14, rue Nicolet, and some of it was later given to Mathilde on her marriage.

The house in the rue Nicolet had a courtyard in front, a garden behind, and its own stables and coach-house. On the ground floor were two salons and a large dining-room; on the first floor were the bedrooms of Mathilde and her parents; and on the second floor were the rooms of Mme Mauté's mother and Charles de Sivry, the library, and the laundry. The Mautés (so Mathilde recalled) became friends of the Mayor of Montmartre, and she and the Mayor's daughters were educated together. 'We followed the courses of M. Lévy-Alvarès. He transformed the education of young girls, which until then had been rather neglected. He tried to develop his pupils' intelligence rather than their memory, and one learned a good deal of literature and history at his courses; several of his pupils have become remarkable women . . .' Alas, she herself was not among them, and – judging by her memoirs – she had very little intelligence, natural or developed. Very often, as M. Porché writes, 'the *Mémoires* which she wrote at the age of fifty-four seem the work of a girl of fourteen: a girl with a certain good sense, honesty, and a stubborn attachment to all the bourgeois precepts or prejudices of her family . . .'[6]

One of the precepts instilled into her was respect for religion. She did not only take her first communion, she remained a believer all her life. It was, however, characteristic of Mathilde that she remembered taking her first communion in the same year as her friend Osine de Beurges, grand-daughter of the Duc de Rohan.

If the Mautés could no longer go to Nogent-le-Rotrou for the summer, they had, it seems, a more distinguished address for the shooting season. 'Every year,' remembered Mathilde, 'my parents were invited to spend the shooting season at the Château de Reynel. We generally set off in the first days of October, at the same time as the owners of the château, and we used to come back with them about 5 or 6 January. This continued for fifteen years.' It was this statement which seemed to Porché 'to indicate a special familiarity which is not exactly that of friends or guests. Friends or guests "in the world of the faubourg Saint-Germain" would have had their own châteaux and shoots. To say the least one cannot imagine them digging themselves in at Reynel for three months a year, and this for fifteen years in succession.' But whatever the Mautés' social status at the Château de Reynel, and whether or not Mme Mauté justified their presence by her accomplishments as a pianist and as a teacher of music, it is clear that the châtelaine's daughter, Osine de Beurges, was a friend of Mathilde.

Mathilde kept an enchanted memory of Reynel, and something of the same aura suffused her memories of Bouëlle, the château in Normandy where she and her family stayed with Mme de Bouëlle, a cousin of the de Beurges. The year 1867 stood out in her mind because her half-brother, Charles, had spent his holidays at Bouëlle.

Charles de Sivry had just finished his education.[7] He had clearly inherited his mother's musical talents; he had learned the piano when he was five, and, by the age of eighteen, he had begun to compose. He was vivacious, witty and engaging. It was this admired elder brother who, in 1868, on her return from the Château de Reynel, took Mathilde to meet Nina de Callias. That evening, so Mathilde remembered, she saw Verlaine for the first time. 'He did not appear to notice me; personally I found him ugly and badly dressed, with a poor appearance.'[8]

She was to see him a second time at a party in Montmartre. It was given by the sculptor Mme Léon Bertaux. Mme Bertaux was a friend and neighbour of her mother's; she had also taken Charles de Sivry as her model for her statue *Un jeune Gaulois prisonnier des Romains*. She was now giving a farewell party before she left for a holiday in Normandy, and there were to be a concert, recitations and a dance. Sivry's friend, Edmond Lepelletier, decided that there should be an operetta. Sivry was to write the music; Lepelletier and another friend were to act *Le Banquiste. Parade à deux personnages*. 'You know my voice,' explained Lepelletier. 'Don't write anything too hard for me. About my friend: he's a poet with a very nice tenor voice. You can give him the lyrical parts.'[9]

And so it was in Montmartre, at the performance of *Le Banquiste*, that Mathilde saw Verlaine for the second time. He was wearing the sort of clothes with which he would always be associated:

. . . an Inverness cape, a checked muffler and a felt hat. The inelegance of his dress hardly improved his appearance. I think [Mathilde remembered] that he was intimidated by the audience; he looked gentle and a little alarmed. He didn't notice me that evening, any more than he had done at Mme de Callias'; and yet I looked nice with my white muslin dress, and pink sash. I wore my hair in ringlets, with a plain ribbon. But I was fourteen [*sic*] and I looked as if I was twelve.

When we got home, my brother talked to me about his new friend: 'He's a very gentle young man,' he said, 'and very good. He adores his mother. She's a widow and he's living with her. He's very intelligent, he's gifted, and he'll certainly be famous one of these days.'

And he gave me *Poèmes saturniens* and *Fêtes galantes* to read.

I found some very beautiful things in the first book; the second seemed to me exquisite, and it completely charmed me. Charles set some of these poems to music, including *Le Parc* [*sic*] and *Colloque sentimental*. I learned to sing them. My brother soon became more friendly with their author, whom he often met at Mme de Callias'. As for me, after Mme Bertaux's soirée, I didn't see Verlaine again for some months. It was by the purest chance that I actually met him in our house, when he came, one day, to see my brother.

One day, when Charles had spent the night at a party at Mme de Callias', and I hadn't seen him at *déjeuner*, I went up to his room and found myself face to face with Verlaine. He certainly saw me for the first time, and if it had been the same with me, I should probably have been surprised by the strangeness of his face; but . . . I was already used to his face and – to be honest – to his ugliness. And so I smiled as I said good-morning to him.[10]

10

Verlaine was overwhelmed by the grace and innocence of Mathilde, and, above all, by the fact that she seemed to be unaware of his *gueusard de physique*. He felt the attraction which he would always feel towards the young. He felt grateful because she admired his poetry. He felt secure at the thought of her moral rectitude. Here was the guardian angel who would save him from himself. Perhaps, deep in his consciousness, he felt safe in her surroundings; here, in the rue Nicolet – so different from the rue Lécluse – he sensed the material security which he needed.

After a few minutes' conversation [Mathilde herself remembered], I disappeared, leaving my brother with his friend. I had no idea of the effect I had produced.
And yet I had noticed a complete change in his face while he was talking to me: his face seemed as if it was illumined by some inner joy; his glance, which was usually dark and shining, had become gentle and tender as he looked at me. He was smiling. He seemed both moved and happy. At that moment, he ceased to be ugly, and I thought of that pretty fairy tale, Beauty and the Beast, where love transforms the Beast into Prince Charming.[1]

In his *Confessions*, written at the end of his life, Verlaine himself would still recall the sudden inspiration he had felt, 'the tranquil joy . . . Was it not chance (I hadn't believed in God for ages, now): was it not a happy, unhoped-for chance which had put this sweet girl on my path – on the path which I knew to be the path of perdition?' That evening he drank no absinthe.[2]
Absinthe was to take its revenge; and nothing shows more clearly the eternal double nature of Verlaine than his behaviour this momentous summer. At the end of June, he had met Mathilde, and he had been transformed by their meeting. On 4 July, drink took possession of him. Victoire Bertrand, a young girl from the Ardennes, a friend of the Grandjeans, was staying in the rue Lécluse. In a letter of 18 July, addressed to M. Pérot, the mayor of Jehonville, she described the events.

Three or four days after I arrived, Verlaine came back at five o'clock in the morning. I heard his mother get up; then I heard a commotion in her room; then Mme Verlaine came in and cried: 'Get up, quick, he wants to kill me!' I rushed in at once and saw the wretch: he was holding a dagger, a sabre and a big knife, and saying he wanted to kill his mother and then kill himself . . . He was in a terrible state, his mother said to me: 'He's ill, and he sometimes gets very excited.' But he was excited by drink.[3]

Mme Verlaine was too loyal, too loving, to refuse to live with her son; still less did she think of sending for an *agent de police*. If she had done so, Verlaine might well have faced a prison sentence. Instead she sent for her elder sister, Rose, who was nearly seventy. Verlaine respected Tante Rose, and Mme Verlaine thought that perhaps her presence would restrain him. Out of her misguided love, she continued to treat her son of twenty-five as if he was still a difficult child. Tante Rose arrived in Paris on 6 July, and Verlaine behaved better during her visit; but she left again two days later. On 10 July, Victoire Bertrand

. . . suddenly heard a noise during the night. It was him coming in. It was one o'clock. He called out to his mother, and said he was coming in with a friend. He began to make such a row that a poor woman [on the floor below] had to get up, she thought the ceiling was going to fall down. I didn't dare get up for fear of annoying him; but suddenly there was a cry. I rushed into his room, and there I saw him with his sabre. He wanted to throw himself on his mother; but the young man who was with him seized hold of him, and Mme Verlaine and I snatched the sabre from him. He wanted his mother to give him 200 francs.[4]

It was at this moment, said François Porché, that Verlaine wrenched open the cupboard where Mme Verlaine still kept the foetus of her three unborn children. He hurled the jars to the floor. (She buried the foetuses that night in the courtyard.)[5]

Verlaine – went on Victoire Bertrand – continued to demand money from his mother.

Then he said to her: 'You've got four thousand francs of mine, you must give them back this moment.' At last the young friend went off to bed. We stayed alone with Verlaine; once he knocked his mother over and grasped her by the throat and said he was going to kill her and then himself . . . In short, M. Pérot, we were struggling with the wretched man from one to eight . . . After this affair, I advised his mother to go away with him for a while. She left that evening for Fampoux.[6]

She and Verlaine went to stay with her brother, Julien Dehée.

She had intended to stay at Fampoux for at least a month, but after four days she returned to Paris.

I thought at once that something else had happened [continued Victoire]. She said it hadn't, but I'm sure it had ... Mme Verlaine insisted that it was the first time her son had given her trouble, but I know, when she wrote to you that she was at Fampoux at the beginning of June, that it was because of a quarrel he had had in a café. That time, they only stayed for four days. He wanted to come back. I think that if he goes on like this, he'll commit a crime sooner or later ...[7]

Mme Verlaine had perhaps come back to Paris out of fear and despair. Verlaine himself, left in Fampoux, indulged in several orgies. It was after an evening spent in the bars and brothels of Arras that he wrote to Charles de Sivry, asking him for the hand of Mathilde.[8]

Mathilde herself was only aware that she had turned the Beast into a prince; she did not know that, for most of his life, the Beast and the prince would struggle for possession of Verlaine. Sivry was surprised by the letter, but he was not displeased, for he was very fond of Verlaine. He showed the letter to Mathilde, and then, together, they went to Mme Mauté. She was astonished by this *coup de foudre*.

My brother then told us [Mathilde continued] that Verlaine was a good young man, very affectionate, but sensitive, extremely nervous and a little susceptible. He said that his unpromising physique had made him very timid with women, and that I must certainly be his first love. He also said he had talent and a future.

We all three went into my father's room to show him the astonishing missive. He said flatly that it was madness to talk of marriage at my age, that I was just fifteen [she was sixteen] and that he wouldn't have me married before I was nineteen or twenty, either to Verlaine or to anyone else. He said he had no antipathy at all towards the young man, but he hardly knew him and wouldn't make any promises for the moment.[9]

Considering that M. Mauté had not met Verlaine, it was a sensible reply. Even if Verlaine had been a brilliantly eligible suitor, even if Mathilde had been in love with him, she was much too young to commit herself. At the age of sixteen, coming, as she did, from a comfortable bourgeois family, she should still have waited to make her choice. It seems strange that Sivry did not, at this point, warn his family of Verlaine's drinking habits; but perhaps he considered Verlaine's drinking to be a normal custom, and perhaps he was not aware of his violence and his homosexuality. Mathilde herself wrote, convincingly: 'He did much to ensure my marriage with Verlaine, and he always regretted that he caused my misfortune. But my brother, like my mother, was so benevolent that he found it hard to believe in evil . . . He lived his whole life full of illusions about everything and everyone.'[10]

Sivry was not sure how he should answer Verlaine; and as Verlaine ended his letter by asking him to Fampoux, he decided to go, and he wrote a few lines to announce his arrival. He added, simply, that there was cause for hope. Before he left, he and Mathilde had a long conversation; they agreed, Mathilde remembered, 'that the poor poet mustn't be hurt. On the contrary, he must be told that I felt great sympathy for him, though I was not committing myself. Since my father wouldn't hear any talk of marriage for three or four years, we should have time enough to know one another better.'[11]

One of the first to hear the news of Verlaine's proposal was Lucien Viotti, whom he had known since the days of the Lycée, and for whom he felt passionate friendship, and intense physical attraction. In an undated letter, presumably addressed to Charles de Sivry, Viotti expressed his surprise at Verlaine's behaviour. Clearly he did not consider that Verlaine was meant for marriage. 'You didn't mention the overture which you made on behalf of our friend,' went Viotti's letter. 'What has happened about it, and how has the family taken the proposal, and, finally, have they agreed to it? I have answered [Verlaine's letter] without alluding to it at all, but I shall be curious none the less to know the result . . .'[12]

Sivry arrived at Fampoux on about 25 July; and Verlaine, who had probably feared a refusal, was more than content with the vague hope which was given him. Almost at once, he wrote the first poem of *La Bonne Chanson*.[13]

II

On about 2 August, Sivry left Fampoux. He took the poem to give to his sister. Then the Mautés went to spend August and September at Bouëlle, near Neufchâtel-en-Bray. Mathilde recalled that summer in her memoirs much as Emma Bovary might have done.

A mass of pleasures were awaiting me [at the château]. Charles and his friend, the Marquis de Forget, began by organising a theatrical performance, followed by a ball ...

I cannot list everyone who was received at the château; but I particularly remember M. de Jouvenel, a former Prefect, his daughter Marquerite, an exquisite young girl ... and the Vicomte and Vicomtesse des Roy ...

In the midst of all these distractions, what was happening to my poor poet? Lord, I must admit that I was a little forgetful of him. However, he was still thinking of me, because he wrote to my brother, and asked him to give me one of the prettiest poems of *La Bonne Chanson*.[1]

It was the poem which recalled Mathilde at their June meeting:

> En robe grise et verte avec des ruches,
> Un jour de juin que j'étais soucieux,
> Elle apparut souriante à mes yeux
> Qui l'admiraient sans redouter d'embûches;
>
> Elle alla, vint, revint, s'assit, parla,
> Légère et grave, ironique, attendrie:
> Et je sentais en mon âme assombrie
> Comme un joyeux reflet de tout cela;
>
> Sa voix, étant de la musique fine,
> Accompagnait délicieusement
> L'esprit sans fiel de son babil charmant
> Où la gaîté d'un cœur bon se devine.

Aussi soudain fus-je, après le semblant
D'une révolte aussitôt étouffée,
Au plein pouvoir de la petite Fée
Que depuis lors je supplie en tremblant.[2]

Mathilde was naturally touched by a poem about herself. She was 'so charmed' that she asked her mother's permission to write to the author and thank him. Mme Mauté agreed, but she did so without consulting her husband. As Mathilde was not yet engaged, he would have considered the letter incorrect. Besides, though he had no open antipathy for Verlaine, the idea that Verlaine should marry his daughter never pleased him, and 'to bring him round to what we wanted', Mathilde herself remembered, 'my mother, brother and I had to use a great deal of diplomacy.' Monsieur Mauté had more knowledge of the world than they did. It is remarkable that a woman of Mme Mauté's age and social standing let her daughter encourage Verlaine. At best, he was an unknown quantity.

However, with her mother's permission, Mathilde began an anodine correspondence with her suitor. Verlaine, exalted by his love and imagination, read much into the letters which was not there. The first innocent note filled him with such joy that he wrote 'Puisque l'aube grandit . . .', the poem in which he proclaimed his confidence in his future Paradise. It is curious that, in this poem, which he sent to Mathilde, he clearly specified his weaknesses: his moods of violence and his indulgence in drink.

. . . Arrière aussi les poings crispés et la colère
À propos des méchants et des sots rencontrés;
Arrière la rancune abominable! arrière
L'oubli qu'on cherche en des breuvages exécrés! . . .[3]

Perhaps Verlaine felt a need to make his confession; perhaps, for some perverted reason, he was defying destiny. But presumably the poem was not shown to Théodore Mauté. 'Not for a moment,' wrote Mathilde, 'did he suppose that his future son-in-law drank. Otherwise he would inexorably have refused his consent to the marriage.'[4]

Verlaine hoped, for a moment, to join the Mautés at Bouëlle;

considering how far he was from an actual engagement, such a project seems extraordinary. No doubt, if he had erupted into the Emma Bovary world where comtes and vicomtes danced cotillions, and former Prefects chaperoned their daughters, Verlaine would have lost his glamour for Mathilde, and any hopes of pleasing her family. But he abandoned his thoughts of Bouëlle; he stayed at Fampoux until 7 or 8 August, and then went to stay with a cousin at Lécluse. There, where he recalled Élisa, a touch of melancholy crossed his mind, but it was lost in his new mood of euphoria. At Lécluse, in about mid-August, in another poem, he expressed his infinite happiness and *tendresse*. It is said that he took the structure of his poem – the two interlacing themes – from a poem by Villiers de l'Isle-Adam. But, whatever his technical debt, the delicacy of touch was his own.

> Avant que tu ne t'en ailles,
> Pâle étoile du matin,
>   – Mille cailles
> Chantent, chantent dans le thym.–
>
> Tourne devers le poète,
> Dont les yeux sont pleins d'amour;
>   – L'alouette
> Monte au ciel avec le jour.–
>
> Tourne ton regard que noie
> L'aurore dans son azur;
>   – Quelle joie
> Parmi les champs de blé mûr!.–
>
> Puis fais luire ma pensée
> Là-bas, – bien loin, oh, bien loin!
>   – La rosée
> Gaîment brille sur le foin.–
>
> Dans le doux rêve où s'agite
> Ma mie endormie encor . . .
>   – Vite, vite,
> Car voici le soleil d'or.–[5]

One other poem in *La Bonne Chanson* – written at about the same time – created the same mood of love and peace, of a tranquillity shared by the whole of nature. And here the influence of Baudelaire fused with the inspiration of Mathilde. It was a poem which explains why Fauré and Debussy were to set Verlaine to music; and yet it comes so close itself to the emotive power of music that a setting seems superfluous. Verlaine never wrote a more perfect poem than this.

> La lune blanche
> Luit dans les bois;
> De chaque branche
> Part une voix
> Sous la ramée . . .
>
> Ô bien-aimée.
>
> L'étang reflète,
> Profond miroir,
> La silhouette
> Du saule noir
> Où le vent pleure . . .
>
> Rêvons, c'est l'heure.
>
> Un vaste et tendre
> Apaisement
> Semble descendre
> Du firmament
> Que l'astre irise . . .
>
> C'est l'heure exquise.[6]

Mathilde had at first felt pity for the young man who was so ugly and unhappy, and she had therefore welcomed him more kindly than she did her brother's other friends. She had also admired his poetry; and now she was flattered that she had inspired such real and immediate love. From the moment that Verlaine asked for her hand, she had begun to fall in love with him, and, so she said herself, she grew more attached to him every day.

Verlaine had sent her five '*bonnes chansons*' before he returned to Paris on 23 August. In the train between Arras and Paris he composed another, and in it he contrasted the noise and restlessness of the journey with the pure and luminous vision within him. Late in August, from Paris, he sent yet another poem to Bouëlle:

> Une Sainte en son auréole,
> Une châtelaine en sa tour,
> Tout ce que contient la parole
> Humaine de grâce et d'amour . . .[7]

Mathilde now wanted to reply with more than a letter. One day, a local photographer took a picture of the Mautés with their host and hostess at the château; he also took a photograph of Mathilde with her younger sister, Marguerite. She asked her mother's permission to send a copy to Verlaine, and he thanked her with another poem.

Looking back on this idyllic summer of 1869, Mathilde took care to emphasise that she had not then been engaged to Verlaine, and, indeed, that she had had three other suitors. One (she said) was a vicomte who asked Mme Mauté's permission to call on them in Paris. But, as Mathilde herself explained, 'one does not escape one's destiny.' On the eve of her departure she received another poem ('La dure épreuve va finir . . .'); and, as she was getting into the train, she received yet another.

> Va, chanson, à tire-d'aile
> Au-devant d'elle, et dis-lui
> Bien que dans mon cœur fidèle
> Un joyeux rayon a lui,
>
> Dissipant, lumière sainte,
> Ces ténèbres de l'amour:
> Méfiance, doute, crainte,
> Et que voici le grand jour!
>
> Longtemps craintive et muette,
> Entendez-vous? la gaîté
> Comme une vive alouette
> Dans le ciel clair a chanté.

top left The poet's father: Nicolas-Auguste Verlaine (1798–1865). A sketch, presumably after the family portrait.

top right The poet's mother: Élisa-Julie-Josèphe-Stéphanie Verlaine (1809–86).

Verlaine *collégien* – a photograph taken in 1856, when he was twelve, and a pupil at the Lycée Bonaparte.

'Cocodette un peu mûre':
ex-Mme Paul Verlaine, from a
photograph taken in later life.

Arthur Rimbaud, aged
seventeen. From a photograph
by Étienne Carjat, taken soon
after the meeting with Verlaine.

Va donc, chanson ingénue,
Et que, sans nul regret vain,
Elle soit la bien venue
Celle qui revient enfin.[8]

On the evening of the Mautés' return to the rue Nicolet, Verlaine arrived.

He was so moved when I came into the salon [Mathilde remembered], that his emotion affected me, and I was a little intimidated. I remained silent for a moment when I had grasped his hand. My dear mother, who had come down with me, began to talk of one thing and another to put us at our ease, and, when my father came in, nothing betrayed our feelings any more – except our glances, because he was quietly watching me, and I found the same gentle expression in the eyes, the same happy, confident smile I had seen before.
For the first time, he had taken trouble with his appearance; Verlaine, incidentally, had a very good figure. He was tall and slim, and only his face was ugly – but, as I've said, love had transfigured it.[9]

Next day he returned to the rue Nicolet with another of the '*bonnes chansons*'; and this time he brought his mother with him.
Mme Verlaine no doubt approved of the solid comfort of the house. The albums on the salon table, the flowers brought back from Bouëlle, the furniture from Nogent-le-Rotrou: all bespoke the bourgeois luxury which remained her ideal. She dismissed her memories of Verlaine's drunkenness and violence. He was *le petit*, her only son, and she wanted to see him married.
Mathilde considered Mme Verlaine with predictable snobbery.

She looked astonishingly like her son, with this difference that she must have been pretty when she was young, and that she was still nice-looking, but she had the same slanting eyes, the same thick, rather bristly eyebrows. That day, she was wearing a black silk dress, but usually she wore a faded woollen dress which made her look like a beggar-woman. My first impression was sympathetic: wasn't she Paul's mother?
I must have pleased her, too, because she looked at me kindly; then she smiled, came up to me, and kissed me on the forehead.
Now that the ice was broken, we talked about trivialities; when she

left, she asked my father to come and see her next day to talk business. It was premature and inopportune.[10]

It was, indeed. Perhaps Verlaine had led her to believe that he was virtually engaged; but, whatever Mathilde's emotions, M. Mauté had decreed that she was too young to marry. He was no doubt still unaware that she had been writing to Verlaine; presumably he was unaware that Verlaine had been sending her poems. Now, out of civility, he promised to call on Mme Verlaine; but, when she and her son had left, he said angrily that things were moving too fast, and that people were trying to force his hand. He had, he repeated, asked for time; he would not have his daughter married for three or four years, and he was not having Verlaine to the house as her fiancé.

Mathilde was miserable, and Mme Mauté intervened. She said that Verlaine seemed a good young man, and genuinely in love. He did, admittedly, have a modest position at the Hôtel de Ville, but he was gifted, and he would make his name. 'As for my future mother-in-law,' recorded Mathilde, 'we were all agreed: she was obviously well brought up and correct, very provincial and of mediocre intelligence. But what did that matter? She adored her son and would love me because of him.'[11]

It was apparently at this point that M. Mauté saw himself outmanoeuvred. His daughter was clearly in love, his wife and stepson supported her, and they sang the virtues of Verlaine. He could not, for all his authoritarian manner, for all his social ambitions, for all his personal forebodings, oppose his daughter's happiness. 'My father,' so Mathilde continued, 'seemed a little shaken. He said that, if this marriage really pleased me, he would not oppose it; I was sensible enough to choose a husband myself. He really only wanted my happiness.'[12]

Next day he called on Mme Verlaine. The visit left a lamentable impression. Number 26, rue Lécluse was a humble house; she had a little apartment on the third floor. She had Louis-Philippe furniture: faded furniture, the kind which soldiers dragged from garrison to garrison. Everthing was clean and neat; it seemed 'proud and decent poverty, but poverty all the same'.[13]

The impression was so bad that M. Mauté wondered if the marriage was just a financial speculation of the Verlaines, and he told Mme Verlaine that he would not give his daughter a dowry. He secretly hoped that this statement would end the romance. Mme Verlaine was disappointed by this extraordinary behaviour, but she said that her son loved Mathilde and that money was unimportant to him. Apart from his salary of 3,000 francs at the Hôtel de Ville, he had a small capital of 20,000 francs from an aunt; besides, she would give him 40,000 francs on his marriage. She offered to give Mathilde and Verlaine her apartment, and to go and live with her sister in Arras.

For all the taunts of provincialism and low intelligence which were made by the Mautés, she showed a noble selflessness which was far beyond them. Perhaps even Théodore Mauté recognised this quality. When he returned from the rue Lécluse, he said that, considering the modest situation of the Verlaines, he would not give his daughter any capital, but he would give her an income equal to that of her fiancé. This, said Mathilde, was duly done.[14]

12

During the autumn and winter of 1869-70, Verlaine called at the rue Nicolet every evening. He was now accepted as Mathilde's fiancé; and the poems which he wrote for her reflect his confidence and tranquillity. The twenty-one poems which were published in *La Bonne Chanson* represented (he said, later) one-tenth of those which he had addressed to her. The statement is almost certainly a wild exaggeration, but he did withhold a number of poems. He felt they were too bold for such an innocent, sheltered girl; he could not risk endangering the idealised love which, by a miracle, had begun to grow in her own mind. Nor could he risk damaging his own sudden prospects of happiness.

The published poems of *La Bonne Chanson* were, then, written for Mathilde, and, after their engagement, they were possibly written with the knowledge that her family might see them. They show Verlaine as he tried to appear to this eminently bourgeois family which he hoped to make his own; and, implicitly, they reveal Mathilde herself. They portray her as a conventional lover would portray her; they describe her as a captivating fairy, a source of inspiration and – ridiculous hyperbole – as a source of wisdom. But they suggest an *ingénue*, a colourless young girl; and, despite the dream-like beauty of one or two of the poems, *La Bonne Chanson* gives the impression of a poet writing a correct epithalamium. Verlaine simplifies his metre and his vocabulary; he simplifies his thoughts to make them both intelligible and socially acceptable. He imposes restraint on himself, as he would in the rue Nicolet. *La Bonne Chanson* already reveals the impossibility of his happiness.

It also discloses and emphasises, with discretion, what Verlaine hopes to find in marriage; and this is not only tranquil domesticity, the comfort of a lamplit fireside, of constant and admiring companionship. It is also an upright, unfailing guide, a strong moral character which will safely dominate his own. Now, in Mathilde, this girl of sixteen, Verlaine - who was twenty-five when he met her – sought a maternal guide. From this genteel, naïve, unimaginative girl he sought an almost masculine discipline. He wanted Mathilde to be the dominant partner in the marriage. She was not only to inspire him, she was to cleanse him of his past and relieve him of his moral responsibilities.

This was not the only impossible demand that Verlaine made of her. He also demanded (though he took care not to emphasise the fact) his permanent physical happiness. He was intensely passionate, and he needed a response. But sexual compatibility demands more than physical attraction; it demands emotional intimacy, and imagination. From all we know of Mathilde, and all that can be deduced, she was cold and unemotional. Reading her memoirs, her accounts of provincial dances, one is ineluctably reminded of Emma Bovary. Mathilde, too, saw herself as the heroine of some romantic novel, she was flattered to find an accepted poet at her feet, writing poems to her (the ones she most appreciated were the ones most concerned with herself). But she had no instinctive warmth, no imagination, and – one infers –

she was not a sensual creature. Here again *La Bonne Chanson* is a sad indication of the disillusionment to come.

But it is also an honest indication of Verlaine's aspirations; it records – and this must be remembered – his genuine longing for domesticity. It illuminates a stage in his spiritual progress. And, in the poems where his love for Mathilde is generalised, Verlaine reveals himself as a poet of rarefied and exquisite happiness.

Poèmes saturniens had been poems of autumn and of twilight, of dank and melancholy landscapes; *Fêtes galantes* had been stage revelries, lit by the artificial light of the theatre. *La Bonne Chanson* is suffused by daylight, lit by the hopeful dawn, warmed by the morning sun and by Verlaine's vision of 'la lueur étroite de la lampe'. It was perhaps this vision that Fernand Gregh had in mind when he said that Verlaine 'felt and translated the particular poetry of urban and suburban life . . . He even recreated the bourgeois dream.'[1]

In the autumn of 1869, when Verlaine became engaged to Mathilde, it was agreed that the marriage would take place in two years' time; and though one can see the wisdom of a long engagement for a girl as young as Mathilde and a fiancé who was so little known, the delay was unduly long, and it imposed an evident strain on Mathilde and, even more, on a man who confessed himself 'impatient des mois, furieux des semaines'. But M. Mauté had pleased his daughter and soothed his family; now he satisfied himself. He hoped that within two years some event would occur to break the engagement.

It almost did, for in November the vicomte from Bouëlle paid two visits to the rue Nicolet, and – according to Mathilde – he begged Mme de Bouëlle to ask the Mautés for their daughter's hand. 'Had it not been for Verlaine,' said Mathilde, 'I should probably have accepted the brilliant marriage, but I had already given my heart away.' The vicomte was followed, in December, by a young army subaltern on leave; his mother (a friend of Mme Mauté's) praised him to Mathilde with such effusion that Mathilde guessed her intention. 'Oh, I shan't marry early,' said Mathilde. 'My father isn't giving me a dowry.' She heard no more of this prospective suitor. There was a third whom she had often met at Reynel and Bouëlle, and he was a rich only son. Mathilde was terrified that he would speak to her parents, 'for my father already found it hard to accept Verlaine, and he would have been still more difficult if he had seen that I was sought after.' She played a prank on this final suitor and he disappeared from her life.[2] It seemed to her as if Verlaine sensed the dangers that beset their betrothal, for it was now that he wrote the poem:

> J'ai presque peur en vérité,
> Tant je sens ma vie enlacée
> À la radieuse pensée
> Qui m'a pris l'âme l'autre été . . .[3]

Mme Verlaine now invited Mathilde to the rue Lécluse; and at her little soirées Mathilde saw her fiancé loved and appreciated. In the rue Lécluse, Verlaine recited his poetry, and Chabrier and Sivry improvised on the piano. Villiers de l'Isle-Adam read *Ellen* and *Morgane*; and Mathilde met some of the poets she had glimpsed at Mme de Callias': Valade, Mérat and Louis-Xavier de Ricard. Mme Verlaine hardly ever invited her own friends to these soirées: they were nearly all the wives of retired army officers and they found themselves out of their element among poets. She thought, however, that Mathilde would like to meet a girl of her own age, and she invited Mme Lepelletier and her daughter Laure. Mme Lepelletier's son, Edmond, was Verlaine's closest friend. Some forty years later he would publish the first biography of Verlaine, and the book would rouse Mathilde to write her memoirs.[4]

The winter of 1869 passed quickly, and 1870 began. In about April – when Mathilde was seventeen – Verlaine urged, understandably, that the date of the marriage should be advanced. Mathilde and her mother pleaded with M. Mauté and pursuaded him that it should be in June. 'What was the use of waiting, since we now knew each other well? Indeed,' wrote Mathilde, 'throughout the engagement, Verlaine was perfect; we had never once seen him drunk, and it was precisely because we knew him well, or believed that we knew him, that my parents did not seek for information.'[5]

Verlaine now came to the house more than ever. He spent all his evenings there; he spent every Sunday with Mathilde, and then stayed on to dine in the rue Nicolet. He took Mathilde to the Pasdeloup concerts, where he introduced some of his friends to her, among them Catulle Mendès and his wife. The *ménage* Mendès were a handsome couple: Catulle, the Parnassian poet, had a fair, Christ-like head, and Judith – who was the elder daughter of Théophile Gautier – was renowned for her classical beauty; it would dazzle Wagner as it had delighted Baudelaire.

As the date of the marriage approached, Mathilde and Verlaine spent their Sundays looking at apartments. Mathilde found a romantic apartment on the corner of the quai de la Tournelle. It had a large balcony, with a panoramic view of the Seine below, of Notre-Dame, the Hôtel de Ville, and, in the distance, Montmartre. Mathilde rejected Mme Verlaine's offer of furniture (she could hardly have accepted the chairs upholstered with imitation leopard-skin). She chose everything herself. Her own room was hung with pink chintz, and furnished with antiques from her grandmother's house in Normandy; Verlaine's room, next door – which served as a guest room – was dignified with a marquetry desk. In the salon was a Pleyel grand piano. It was an elegant décor – '*convenable*', thought Mathilde – but Verlaine was given no part in choosing it; he was content with the promise of comfort, and with the lack of responsibility.

On 23 and 24 June, the marriage contract was drawn up. It did not entirely agree with the statements which – said Mathilde – Mme Verlaine had made to M. Mauté; but it emphasised the fact that Verlaine was much richer than his wife. Verlaine's contribution was 20,000 francs, and a further 6,960 francs which he had inherited from his aunt, Mme Grandjean. His mother also gave him a dowry of 20,000 francs. Mathilde contributed 4,206 francs, and a quantity of furniture. This included a sofa and two arm-chairs quilted in silk damask, an oak dresser and four oak chairs, and four lacquered chairs upholstered in red silk. There were an inkwell in gilded bronze, a hand-mirror, and a green-and-white dinner service; there were a bronze cartel clock, a rosewood desk, a sofa, four chairs, and an easy chair in the Louis xv style, upholstered in chintz. There were also four red silk damask curtains, a white woollen bedspread, and two dozen pairs of sheets.[6]

The wedding was now arranged for 29 June; but it was finally delayed until 11 August, because Mathilde was stricken with smallpox. For three days she was critically ill. Verlaine, she recorded, 'was so afraid of catching smallpox that he only just dared to come to ask for news at the garden gate. He left to spend a fortnight in the country, which gave me time to get well again.'

On 15 July, as the marriage approached, the Franco-Prussian war was declared. It was the result of reckless political stupidity, and it proved to be a political and military disaster. On the eve of Verlaine's wedding, a decree was issued calling up all single men of the 1844 and 1845 classes. Verlaine arrived in anguish at the rue Nicolet, and insisted that the decree would prevent the wedding from taking place. His fear was quite illogical. Mathilde suspected – probably with justice – that he was afraid of fighting, married or not.

On Thursday, 11 August 1870, a few days after the Siege of Paris began, Verlaine and Mathilde were married at the *Mairie* of the xviiith *arrondissement*, and then at Notre-Dame de Clignancourt. The bride's witnesses were Paul Foucher, brother-in-law of Hugo, and a M. Sédillot, an orientalist friend of her father's; the bridegroom's witnesses were Léon Valade and a M. Istace, a friend of old Mme Verlaine's. 'There were very few people at our wedding,' remembered Mathilde. 'All our friends used to leave Paris after the Grand Prix.'[7]

Elsewhere, in her *Mémoires*, written at the end of her life, she added: 'I can say in all sincerity that, when I married Verlaine, I loved him as much as he loved me.'[8]

13

For the first week of their honeymoon, until their own apartment was ready, the Verlaines lived in the rue Nicolet. It was a lamentable arrangement, and it almost symbolised Verlaine's dependence on his wife, his social and financial disadvantage. However – so Mathilde remembered – they were both content. Verlaine was gentle, kind and affectionate. 'I *alone* knew a Verlaine who was quite different from what he was with other people: Verlaine in love, that is to say morally and physically trans-figured. I have already explained that, when he looked at me, his physiognomy changed and he ceased to be ugly. Morally, the change was almost as complete.'[1]

He and Mathilde used to set out after *déjeuner* and wander round the environs of Paris. It was to be their last chance of seeing Saint-Cloud before the palace was burnt by the Prussian invaders; it was to be their final opportunity of going as far afield as Versailles, for Paris was now almost cut off from the world, and in September it would be isolated.

Mathilde records nothing of this in her memoirs. 'A week after our marriage,' she wrote, 'we were able to move into our own apartment; and for me – I was still such a child – it was a delight to play the mistress of the house. As for Paul, he was enchanted by our pretty apartment, gay and bright, with its exceptional view of Paris'.[2]

Verlaine's wedding-present to his wife had been – it might be said – *La Bonne Chanson*. Lemerre had published the twenty-one poems as a book; the printing had been finished on 12 June. On 5 July, Verlaine had written a dedicatory poem in the copy destined for Mathilde. Ten days later, war had been declared. There could hardly have been a less propitious moment for poetry.

However, Leconte de Lisle had acknowledged his copy of the book with remarkable warmth. The great impassible had been touched.

Saint-Ideuc-Paramé,
9 August 1870.

My dear friend,

I have received *La Bonne Chanson*, and I thank you most cordially for your kind remembrance of me. Your poems are delightful, they breathe forth peace of mind and tranquil fullness of heart. Please accept my warmest congratulations ... We live in terrible anxiety, here, about events. If we lose the battle which must be fought at the beginning of the Vosges, the Prussians will be in Paris in a week. Everyone in this part of the country is in consternation ...

I will see you soon, *mon ami*, if you are not sent to the front ...[3]

Verlaine was not sent to the front; he remained at the quai de la Tournelle. 'Oh, those sweet little *déjeuners*!' wrote Mathilde. 'How happy they used to be! They were like little dinners, with the new china, the shining silver, and the white linen embroidered with our monogram. After *déjeuner*, we used to have coffee on the balcony, with that fine panorama in front of us; then we used to send the maid out for tobacco or something, so that we could kiss as much as we liked.' The idyll continued. On 2 September, Lepelletier expressed his regret that military duties had kept him from their wedding. He sent a lengthy poem which he had written in their honour.[4]

On 3 September the news reached Paris. Napoleon III had surrendered with his army at Sedan. Next day the fall of the Bonaparte dynasty was decreed; Verlaine came home, delighted, to announce the proclamation of the Republic. He was fiercely republican at the time, and he had converted his conventional young wife to his way of thinking. That day, the two of them went out into the streets, where Parisians were celebrating the new régime, and lustily singing *La Marseillaise*.

But though the Emperor had surrendered, hostilities continued, and the Prussian troops continued their march on Paris. M. Mauté installed an ambulance unit in the rue Nicolet, and continued to live there, alone. Mme Mauté left Montmartre, which was dangerously exposed, and settled in the boulevard Saint-Germain; it was near the quai de la Tournelle, and Verlaine often took Mathilde to spend the evening with her mother. Mme Mauté had wisely provided her daughter with jars of butter, and Mathilde used them when she cooked steak for Verlaine. But the steak was no doubt horseflesh, and when the family met for their New Year's dinner, Mme Mauté was obliged to give them jugged cat and leg of dog.

Verlaine had not entirely abandoned his former friends. On 29 November, one of the peaceful evenings of the Siege, Félix Régamey, the artist, had sketched him at the Café du Gaz. After the fall of the Empire, Hugo had returned to Paris, and settled in the hôtel du Pavillon de Rohan. Mathilde was welcomed there as the heroine of *La Bonne Chanson*. Victor Hugo, she remembered, 'congratulated Verlaine on these pretty poems, which he called "a bouquet in a shell [*obus*]" '. She was 'absolutely enchanted', and so was Verlaine, who still kept an unqualified admiration for the Master. Verlaine also took Mathilde one evening to call on the Leconte de Lisles, who were back in Paris, and sharing their apartment with the Mendès. A few days later, he took her to see Philippe Burty, the art critic, and his wife; Mathilde claimed, afterwards, that she had met the Goncourts at their apartment. (Jules de Goncourt had in fact died before her marriage to Verlaine; Edmond left no record of this meeting.) On Friday evenings, the Verlaines entertained in their apartment; old Mme Verlaine used to come to dinner and stay at least a night. 'The poor woman's only fault,' wrote Mathilde, with her usual condescension, 'was her maternal weakness. If Paul had become a drunkard long before our marriage, that was because she had never dared to give him a stern rebuke. On the contrary, she affected to laugh at his drunkenness, and to believe that it didn't really matter . . . When I think that, for . . . more than two years, Verlaine did not once get drunk, I think he must have made a very commendable effort for love of me. It's true that he could sometimes have had a drink without actually getting drunk.'

It was indeed true. One day she found Verlaine in the salon, with his hat on; he did not take it off when she came in. He was irascible; he criticised the food, and said that in future he would have his *déjeuner* at the Café du Gaz. Mathilde was in tears; but he had his *déjeuner* at the Café du Gaz for a fortnight. He later gave an embroidered account of the incident in his *Confessions*; but Mathilde insisted, in her memoirs, that at this time she was still perfectly happy.

However, she did dispel the legend that Verlaine was a patriot. He had no wish to be killed in a war which he believed unnecessary; and old Mme Verlaine – an officer's widow – encouraged him in his cowardice. Verlaine, as a married man, was a *garde national*, not a serving soldier; but during the winter of the Siege his mother was afraid that *le petit* might develop bronchitis on the ramparts. She told him to find a way of avoiding service. Verlaine sent a note to the captain of his battalion, saying that he had urgent work at the office; he also sent a note to the head of his department saying that he was needed on the ramparts. This trick allowed him to enjoy some unofficial leave, but it was discovered. He was sentenced to two days' imprisonment.

As soon as he was freed, he decided that he and Mathilde must live with his mother in the rue Lécluse. He wrote to his captain that he had changed his address, and that he now belonged to another battalion. As the captain did not verify the fact, Verlaine avoided all national service. It is not surprising that when, in time, Mathilde read his ode to Metz, she found his patriotism 'somewhat platonic'.

Up to the third week in January, nobody in Paris doubted that salvation would come if only they could wait; but the provincial armies never came to their rescue, and the great, decisive sortie, the magnificent French victory never occurred. On 28 January 1871, the 132nd day of the Siege, and the 25th of the bombardment, the city capitulated – to famine, rather than the Prussians. On 26 February, Thiers signed the shameful peace with Bismarck. On 1 March the victorious Prussians entered the city. On 18 Marc h,incensed by Thiers's capitulation, the Commune seized power in Paris, and French troops were obliged to begin a second siege of the capital.

The Commune would be marked by a bitterness and brutality which are, perhaps, found only in civil wars; and among the Communards were a good many malcontents and anarchists who seized the chance of 'licensed' violence. But – at least at the beginning – the Commune seemed an act of patriotism: a positive gesture at a time of official weakness, a heroic rejection of defeat. There seemed, in these early days, more nobility about the Commune than about the Thiers government at Versailles.

'At that legendary time,' Verlaine wrote, later, 'I found myself an *Hébertiste* [an extreme and violent revolutionary], full of historical facts, and more innocent about what was happening than an unborn child. I liked a revolution which had cartridges in its cartridge-box. I liked a revolution that looked so proud.'[5] Mathilde remembered that, at the beginning, nearly everyone in Paris had felt the same. Several of Verlaine's friends were in the new government. Old Mme Verlaine was afraid that her son would lose his post at the Hôtel de Ville, and she advised him to continue his work at Versailles. But Mathilde would not persuade him to go. She had money of her own, she considered Verlaine's salary insignificant, and she thought that if he lost his job (which he clearly found distasteful), he could write, and live as he pleased. Verlaine was now in charge of the Press Department at the Hôtel de Ville. It was an inoffensive task, which consisted of reading the Versailles papers and publishing corrections of their errors. He used his influence to find a post at a *mairie* for Charles de Sivry.

The Verlaines had returned to their apartment on the quai de la Tournelle. It was during the Commune, in mid-April, that Sivry's wife had to go away for a few days, and she asked Mathilde to look after him while she was away. Verlaine seemed delighted; but Sivry had hardly arrived before Verlaine displayed such bad humour that Sivry felt responsible and offered to go. Verlaine insisted that he stayed, grew angry with Mathilde, and with the maid, whom he wanted to dismiss.

Verlaine must certainly have been drinking; but how could I have guessed it [asked Mathilde]. He spoke clearly and coldly, he didn't stagger, although his gestures were a little staccato ... But it made such a painful impression on me that during the night I had a high temperature and became delirious. Apparently I saw big black flies running over the bed. I had then begun my pregnancy, and Verlaine was very worried ...

Next morning, when I woke, he was kneeling by my bed, weeping bitterly, and begging my forgiveness ...

Before my brother left, I begged him not to speak to my parents about what had happened, because it was something exceptional. He promised to be silent, but he went away sadly.[6]

It would have been impossible, even now, to have cured
Verlaine of his love of drink. For many months he had been so
sober and conventional that no-one would have guessed his
besetting weakness. But the strains of the war and the Commune,
and the strain of bourgeois life were finally beginning to appear.
Since his marriage, he had been a remarkably good husband; but
now Mathilde was three months pregnant, and he had small
chance of physical pleasure. He was frustrated, and he was possibly
jealous of affections soon to be divided. He had enjoyed his
mother's whole and intense devotion; until now he had enjoyed
the single-minded love of Mathilde. Perhaps he resented the
thought of this child who would share the love of both women.
And perhaps, even now, there was another cause of frustration:
Verlaine might have been tempted, again, by homosexual love.
Lucien Viotti, for whom he had conceived intense affection, had
been captured by the Prussians during the war, and he had died
in a German hospital. Years later, in a prose poem, Verlaine was to
recall him:

Your eyes shine vaguely at me as they used to do, your voice comes
to me, grave and veiled like the voice of former times, and the whole
delicate, elegant creature which you were at twenty. That charming
head . . . the exquisite proportions of your youthful body under your
conventional clothes: I see it all through my tears, which are slow to
fall . . .[7]

Those lines appeared in *Mémoires d'un veuf*, in 1886, fifteen
years after Lucien had died. There is no poem to Mathilde written
with such feeling.

On 10 May 1871, the Treaty of Frankfurt was signed, and the
Franco-Prussian War was officially over. It became increasingly
clear that the Commune would be overthrown, and that Thiers's
armies, the Versaillais, would soon capture Paris. Verlaine
remained in constant terror.

Late in May a friend arrived at the quai de la Tournelle to
announce that the Versaillais had entered Paris and that they were
shelling Les Batignolles. Verlaine was too afraid to go in search
of his mother, but he spent the night weeping and moaning. At

five the next morning, Mathilde suggested that they should both
go and fetch her. Verlaine's answer was astounding. He said that,
if he went out, he might be forced to fight at the barricades.
Mathilde then offered to go alone, and he readily agreed. 'I must
add,' Mathilde continued, 'that neither of us thought that I should
be exposing myself to danger. My only merit was that I set off
at six in the morning, and I have always hated getting up and
going out early.' Mathilde was just eighteen, and she was four
months pregnant; her conduct was little less than heroic.

While Verlaine stayed at home, and tried to relieve his frustra-
tions by seducing the maid, Mathilde made her way through the
Communard barricades. She heard the rebels firing at unseen
Versaillais, and she heard the Versaillais replying. A spent bullet
fell at her feet; she picked it up, still hot, and put it in her pocket
as a memento. Suddenly she realised that she was in the midst of
the battle. She changed her plans and ran to the rue Nicolet. The
firing lasted till five that evening, but she thought only of
Verlaine's anxiety. She and her father finally set out together,
and picked their way between the corpses in the chaussée Clignancourt. A stray bullet came so near that M. Mauté insisted on
taking her back to the rue Nicolet. Next morning, at six o'clock,
he escorted her to the boulevard Montmartre, and then, as everything seemed calm, he let her go on alone. His behaviour, too,
seems indefensible. Mathilde soon met a cordon of soldiers. The
Hôtel de Ville, the Tuileries and the Cour des Comptes were on
fire. She was forced to turn back again, and she returned to
Montmartre, this time to her brother's. It was on the third day
that, at last, her mission unfulfilled, she came home to the quai
de la Tournelle.

Old Mme Verlaine had arrived an hour before her. The
Commune was over, and, after *déjeuner*, they sat on the balcony and
watched Paris burning.[8]

Everyone who had stayed in Paris now felt apprehensive about
their future. There was a wave of accusation, recrimination and
punishment. Lepelletier, who had been a leading Communard,
went into temporary hiding. On 28 May, the day that the

Commune was overthrown, Edmond de Goncourt had been talking to Philippe Burty. Burty 'was suddenly accosted by Mme Verlaine, and they discussed means of hiding her husband.'[9]

Verlaine's war record had been despicable. At that moment of national crisis, he had been afraid of active service; he had avoided his duties as a *garde national*, he had even escaped his work at the Hôtel de Ville. But what alarmed him, now, was not his record of cowardice and evasion, it was the fact that he had not gone to Versailles, the fact that he had chosen to stay – nominally, at least – and work for the Communard administration. 'Verlaine had kept his job at the Hôtel de Ville in April and May,' explained Clerget in his life of Blémont, 'and now they were looking for the civilians who had been employed by the Commune. Blémont was worried about him.'[10] As Lepelletier wrote, later: 'After the events of the Commune, he felt he should abandon his work and, so to speak, go into hiding.'[11] This was one of the reasons which led him, in June, to leave Paris with Mathilde.

His mother came to stay with them for a week before they left; Mme Mauté helped Mathilde to pack, and both of them could see that she and Verlaine were happy. On 13 July Verlaine wrote to Blémont, who was about to get married: 'Try to draw a lucky number. I've no reason to complain of my own.'[12]

Mathilde was received with open arms by Julien Dehée and his wife and daughters at Fampoux. She assessed them with polite condescension, but she remained good friends with the daughters, Victorine and Zulma, for many years. Verlaine played cards and drank beer with Zulma's husband, but he never drank too much. Mathilde went out very little, because of her condition, but she felt quite content.

This serenity was broken by the news that Charles de Sivry had been arrested as a Communard. Mathilde felt sure that he had done nothing blameworthy, and that he would soon be released – as indeed he was. But Verlaine thought that Charles had been arrested because of the modest post which he himself had procured him during the Commune. He was very worried about his own future, and said that, when they returned to Paris, he would not go back to the Hôtel de Ville. The situation was resolved on 11 July, when he and his colleagues were dismissed by the Prefect of the Seine.

Since Verlaine would in future have no regular employment, Mathilde wrote to her father, pointing out that their income would be depleted. M. Mauté could not have had a high opinion of Verlaine, but he did not want his daughter to suffer; he offered them the second floor of the house in the rue Nicolet. Verlaine was not humiliated. 'My husband,' wrote Mathilde, 'seemed delighted with this arrangement, which left him free and made us richer than we had been before.' In August, after a visit of some weeks to Auguste Dujardin, at Lécluse, the Verlaines returned to Paris. M. Mauté – 'with his usual egotism,' said Mathilde – had left to go shooting in the country. There seems no reason why he should have stayed in Paris to help her move.

The apartment on the quai de la Tournelle was abandoned, and the Verlaines moved to the second floor of the rue Nicolet. They also shared the Mautés' drawing-room and dining-room.[13] Verlaine had virtually resigned his independence when a letter arrived from Arthur Rimbaud.[14]

PART THREE

Rimbaud

(1871-3)

14

ARTHUR RIMBAUD had been born in Charleville, in the Ardennes, on 20 October 1854. He was the son of an army officer. Captain Rimbaud had not only earned some military distinction in Algeria; he had translated the Koran into French, and he left the plans for several literary works. He had intellectual powers of no mean order. Mme Rimbaud came of a solid Ardennais family, of good yeoman stock; but one of her brothers had earned the nickname of 'the African' on account of his Algerian adventures, and her other brother ended as a vagrant, whom she sometimes paid to keep away. She was determined that her own children should become respectable. Her husband was tolerant and generous; she was all the more rigid and parsimonious. They finally separated, and, from the age of six, Arthur was brought up by this high-principled, undemonstrative and unbending woman.

Mme Rimbaud – 'la Bouche d'ombre', Arthur called her – intended her two sons to rise in the social scale. Until Frédérick was sixteen, and Arthur was fifteen, she escorted them home from school every day, to ensure that they did not meet undesirable acquaintances. She supervised their homework, and took them to mass each Sunday. When Arthur began to show promise at school, she overcame her innate thrift in order to pay for private lessons for him. He was soon the most distinguished pupil that the local school had known; but he became a solitary boy, for his mother showed him no affection, and his contemporaries at school were mentally so behind him that he needed friends much older than himself. His first adult friend was Georges Izambard, who came to the Collège de Charleville as a master in 1870. Izambard was the first important influence in his life.

Izambard encouraged Rimbaud's love of literature, lent him books of his own, and urged him to read more widely. During Rimbaud's last year at school, when he was fifteen, he began to write poetry. In the summer of 1870 he did brilliantly in his examinations; but his personal triumphs were soon forgotten. The Franco-Prussian War broke out, and Izambard left Charleville. Late in August, determined to escape from his provincial prison, Rimbaud secretly boarded a train for Paris.

He arrived without papers and without the money to pay his fare, and since he refused to give his name and address, he was imprisoned at Mazas. After a week he wrote to Izambard, asking him to come and rescue him. Izambard came, and took him back to his own home at Douai; since war conditions made it hard to get in touch with his mother, Rimbaud remained at Douai for three weeks. Eventually Izambard escorted the prodigal back to Charleville. In the first week of October he had a letter from Mme Rimbaud, begging him to help her. Rimbaud had vanished once again, and she had no idea where he might be.

Rimbaud was in fact tramping happily through France and Belgium. About a fortnight later, Izambard found him back in Douai; he was busy copying out his poems. But he was still under age, and Izambard had no right to keep him; once again he had to return to Charleville. In February 1871 he sold his watch, to pay his railway fare. On the 25th he left again for Paris. He was there when the Prussians arrived, and he stayed there for a fortnight. He was penniless, he ate the food he could scavenge from dustbins; he slept under bridges, and possibly he spent a few nights in barracks with the soldiers or the National Guard. During this fortnight he seems to have had some brutal initiation into sex –

possibly into homosexuality. He returned to Charleville a changed being.

His poem 'Cœur supplicié' was the outcome of this experience. He sent a copy to Izambard and, for the first time, Izambard failed completely to understand him. Rimbaud was so disillusioned that their friendship ended.[1]

He now sought escape for his feelings in obscene and blasphemous poetry; but inwardly he sought for an ideal in which to lose himself, for some sudden illumination. He turned to occult philosophy, magic and the cabala, and he turned to Baudelaire, particularly to the dreams and visions which Baudelaire had described in *Les Paradis artificiels*. But while Baudelaire accepted the conditions of life, Rimbaud determined to alter them. Baudelaire, as a Christian, was not prepared to sacrifice his soul; Rimbaud wished, whatever the cost, to penetrate into eternity. Rimbaud believed that the poet must experience all forms of love and madness so that he might keep their quintessence; he believed that the poet must degrade himself to break down his discipline and training. 'Le poète se fait *voyant* par un long, immense et raisonné *dérèglement* de tous les sens.' For Rimbaud, however, debauchery was not vice; he felt he was above the reach of sin. Suffering was an essential part of his doctrine; it was, he wrote, 'the most exquisite torture, and the poet will need all his faith, all his superhuman strength, for he becomes *le grand malade, le grand criminel, le grand maudit et le suprême savant*.' Rimbaud's aim, all through his artistic life, was to become *le suprême savant*. Verlaine, years later, would write *Les Poètes maudits*: appreciations of certain poets, Rimbaud among them. For Verlaine, *les poètes maudits* meant *les poètes absolus*.

Rimbaud was an 'absolute', a dedicated poet. He meant to dedicate himself to experience, to cultivate his powers to the full, and to reach infinity. He believed that the poet must reveal the visions of the new world which he found, that he must find a new language to express the hitherto unknown. He believed that, by his intense refinement of language, he had restored their full meaning to words, he had invented a new poetic language and recorded the inexpressible. Between April and June 1871 he composed his obscene and blasphemous poems; between April and September he was making bold experiments in vocabulary. Before September he also wrote his longest, and perhaps his greatest, poem: 'Le Bateau Ivre'.

Rimbaud's point of departure is Baudelaire's 'Le Voyage'. But, in his poem, Baudelaire had kept to this world; only at the end had he conceived a journey beyond it. Rimbaud began where Baudelaire ended. In his boat, *le bateau ivre*, he drifted alone, seeing sights that none had seen before him; and then, at last, as he was about to burst into eternity, just as he seemed to be rising up, away from the world, the water suddenly dropped, and he was hurled down again to reality.

Rimbaud longed to escape in his life, as he had tried to do in his poetry. Once again he determined to go to Paris, but this time he wanted to earn his living and to give himself leisure for writing. A friend from Charleville, Charles Bretagne, a tax official and a frequenter of cafés, suggested that he wrote to Verlaine. Bretagne – whose morals were dubious – had met Verlaine at Fampoux, and he gave Rimbaud a letter of introduction.[2] Rimbaud considered Verlaine to be Baudelaire's successor as a *voyant*. He wrote to him immediately, and sent copies of some of his poems. Verlaine was away from Paris when the letter arrived, but on his return he answered at once, giving Rimbaud praise and criticism. He hinted that he might ask him to Paris, but said that he must first consult some friends. He showed the poems to Burty, Cros and Valade. They were all astounded by Rimbaud's originality. Verlaine summoned Rimbaud to Paris. 'Venez, chère grande âme, on vous appelle, on vous attend.' He sent him the money for his fare, and invited him to stay.

Rimbaud arrived early in September 1871. He was not quite seventeen. He was drawn to Paris by his admiration for Verlaine's poetry, and by the generous invitation which Verlaine had sent him. Here was a recognised poet who would understand and help him, and introduce him to Parisian life. Here was a poet akin to himself: one who was also in debt to Baudelaire, one who was already breaking the bounds of prosody, freeing poetry from convention, exploring new worlds of emotion. This was a man with whom he could share his voyage of discovery. They could become *voyants*, demi-gods, together.

Verlaine had entered the life of Rimbaud at a crucial moment; Rimbaud entered that of Verlaine with devastating precision. Verlaine was living with the genteel and oppressive Mautés, and (though perhaps he did not know it) he had reached the end of his marriage. The vision of Mathilde, the dream of domesticity, had proved to be more enthralling than married life. The marriage had been strained by the war, the Siege and the Commune; it was also strained by Verlaine's disillusionment. He had not only failed to find tranquil domesticity. Mathilde – one suspects – had proved to be physically unimaginative. Now – with all the moods which her condition may have involved – she was eight months pregnant.

Verlaine was frustrated and disappointed, he longed for a relationship which would sweep him out of his bourgeois surroundings, satisfy all his physical and emotional needs. He wanted someone younger than himself, someone whom he could dominate, yet he wanted someone who would direct him, someone with a stronger character than his own, someone who would satisfy his mind and his body. Since his marriage, fourteen months earlier, he had tried to accept convention, to live an irreproachable married life, but at moments it had seemed that he was acting a part. Since his marriage he had not satisfied a fundamental need of his nature. He had written no poetry. If he was to write again, this new, irresistible influence was essential.

Now, in the words of Rodenbach, there arrived 'a handsome youth with cruel blue eyes, a pimento mouth, and . . . enormous hands, hands that could grasp the clouds'.[3]

15

If M. Mauté had been at home, he might have been less ready to accept a stranger in his house. But he was away, and Mme Mauté was always good-natured. She and Mathilde, as it happened, were the first to set eyes on Rimbaud, for Verlaine had gone to meet him at the station when Rimbaud arrived at the rue Nicolet.

As they waited for Verlaine in the salon of *La Bonne Chanson*, none of them felt comfortable. Mathilde and her mother were disconcerted by this sturdy peasant boy with his wild hair and his outgrown clothes. His trousers were too short for him, and they could see the crude blue socks which his parsimonious mother had knitted for him. Mathilde remembered, later, that he had fine blue eyes, with a sly expression which, at first, they mistook for timidity. He had no belongings except the clothes he was wearing. Rimbaud must have assessed Mathilde and her mother with equal distaste. They symbolised the bourgeoisie whom he despised.

More than twenty years later, on the eve of his own death, Verlaine would recall his first impression of Rimbaud. He had, he remembered, 'a real child's face, chubby and fresh-cheeked, and a tall, thin, rather awkward body – the body of an adolescent who was still growing. He spoke with a strong Ardennais accent, almost a patois, and his voice had ups and downs because it was breaking.'[1] Perhaps at that first meeting, as Porché has suggested, Verlaine already felt disturbed, aware that he had met his destiny.[2]

Rimbaud made no attempt to be sociable; he was taciturn throughout dinner, and then he went to bed, saying that he was tired from his journey. Mathilde saw little of him in the days that followed, for Verlaine used to take him out immediately after *déjeuner*, and often neither of them returned for dinner.

Verlaine introduced him to Banville, Burty, Mérat, Valade and the Cros. Rimbaud was well received everywhere, and treated as a coming poet of genius – except, perhaps, by Lepelletier. In 1900, Lepelletier recalled his first impressions of Rimbaud. They may have been coloured by the knowledge of later events, but no doubt they contain a certain truth.

Arthur Rimbaud [he remembered] was a tall, gawky young man, very thin, with the look of a rather fierce street Arab. He was taciturn, with a sneering solemnity, very impressed by his own importance, affecting a universal scorn of men and of things. He struck Baudelairean attitudes ... He conscientiously played the part of sublime child and infant prodigy. Verlaine imposed him on all his circle ... Although Verlaine was more than ten years older than Rimbaud, he allowed his despotic companion to lead him like a child. Verlaine was weak in everything except in poetic talent ...[3]

Mme Mauté, understandably, did not admire Rimbaud. She could hardly have felt happy to see Verlaine ignore Mathilde, who was so soon to give birth to her child. Rimbaud also stole an ivory crucifix which had been in the family for years, and Verlaine had some difficulty in making him return it. He then, wrote Mathilde, 'deliberately broke some things that I was fond of, and he behaved several times with indelicacy.'[4] At last Mme Mauté asked Verlaine to lodge his friend elsewhere. She explained that M. Mauté was coming home.

There are various accounts of what happened during the next few weeks. Rimbaud's biographer, Dr Enid Starkie, says that Rimbaud did not wait to be turned out. 'He fled, of his own accord, without telling anyone where he was going ... It was only some weeks later that Verlaine met him by chance in the street.'[5] Rimbaud, writes Dr Starkie, had been living in destitution; Verlaine was moved to tears by the change in him, and took him to Charles Cros and André Gill, who were to look after him until some permanent arrangement could be made. Cros, we learn elsewhere, put him up for some time in his studio; but Rimbaud tore up an issue of *L'Artiste* which contained five of Cros's poems, and relations between the two men grew stormy. Verlaine then approached Banville, and Mme Banville gave Rimbaud a bed. The neighbours complained of his behaviour – it is said that he stood naked at the window – and he was forced to leave. He then camped with the composer Cabaner, and slept on his sofa; afterwards he spent some weeks 'in the studios of those willing to grant him the charity of a night's shelter'.[6]

Wherever Rimbaud was living, Verlaine was less and less at the rue Nicolet. One evening, however, when he and Mathilde had been dining in the rue Lécluse, Verlaine told her how Rimbaud had stolen books from a shop at Charleville, and had then sold them for fear of being caught. Mathilde expressed her disapproval.

The effect was electric. Verlaine pulled her out of bed, and threw her on the floor.

A week later, on 30 October 1871, Georges Verlaine was born.

That day, Verlaine left in the morning, and did not come home till midnight. 'He seemed pleased to have a son,' remembered Mathilde. 'He kissed me and the baby and went to bed in his room, which was next to mine.' A nurse was hired to look after mother and child, and for three days all was well. Verlaine dined with the Mautés and spent the evenings with Mathilde. On the fourth day, he came home at two in the morning, 'horribly drunk. He had an evil expression, and he threatened me. The nurse was terrified,' wrote Mathilde, 'and wanted to call my parents. I forbade her to do so. In vain she begged my husband to go and sleep in his room. He lay down, fully dressed, on my bed, wearing his felt hat, with his filthy shoes on the pillow by my face. He was soon sleeping like an animal, and my mother found him like this when she came into my room in the morning.'[7] Verlaine did not wait to be admonished; he leapt off the bed and ran down into the street.

He had once dressed with punctilious care. Since Rimbaud's arrival, he had 'returned to the awful mufflers and felt hats. Sometimes he spent a whole week without changing his linen or having his shoes cleaned; but that day,' recalled Mathilde, 'since he had spent the night fully dressed, he was especially dirty and ill-kempt. Yet it was in these clothes that he went, that evening, to the Théâtre-Français, to the première of *L'Abandonnée*, a play by François Coppée. There ... accompanied by Rimbaud, he strolled in the foyer.' Rimbaud was equally dirty and dishevelled. Next morning one of the papers announced: 'Among the men of letters who attended the performance of Coppée's play, we noticed Paul Verlaine, the poet, giving his arm to a charming young lady, Mlle Rimbaud.'[8]

This audacious comment, said Mathilde, had been made by Lepelletier. It was not the only occasion on which he showed his strong disapproval. Years later, his son recorded that Verlaine had shocked Lepelletier's young wife by his appearance and his outrageous remarks; and, when Rimbaud was asked to *déjeuner*, he had sat down at the table like a waggoner, 'and retreated into a sullen silence, from which he had only emerged to throw an occasional filthy word into the conversation. At last my father . . . had taken the youth by the shoulders and thrown him out.'[9]

Lepelletier had been the first to create a scandal. At about the same time another paper published a note about an anonymous Parnassian poet; he had, it was said, come home very drunk, and he had nearly killed his wife and new-born child.[10]

Mathilde herself said that when Verlaine left the theatre, after Coppée's play, he and Rimbaud went off and got drunk. He had come back at three in the morning, more violent than ever, and threatened to set light to a cupboard in which M. Mauté kept his cartridges. He said that he wanted to blow up the house, and Mathilde as well. It seemed as if his love had changed into inexplicable hatred. Next day Mme Mauté remonstrated with him. He wept, and protested his love for his wife.

In mid-December, he announced that he was going to Belgium to collect a small sum of money from a lawyer; it had been left to him by an aunt. On the eve of his departure he came home drunk, once again, this time with Rimbaud and the young artist, J.-L. Forain. He settled them both in his own room, and slept with Mathilde. At five in the morning, he got up and asked her, before he left, to see that his friends were given soup when they woke. When the Mautés' cook took the soup to their room, they had already gone.

Verlaine was away for three days. During his absence, his mother came to the rue Nicolet. She seemed surprised and annoyed that he should have gone to Belgium to collect a legacy. She was even more concerned and vexed when Mathilde told her that, in the last six weeks, Verlaine had spent two thousand francs on pleasures. They were never able to explain where this money had gone. It was true that Verlaine now kept Rimbaud, for all his other friends had abandoned him; but Rimbaud lived in a little room, and dressed like a beggar, and drunkenness was then the least expensive of vices.

Mme Verlaine was practical. She made enquiries, and discovered that her son had been dismissed from the Hôtel de Ville only for prolonged absence. If he returned to work, she said, he would drink less, spend less, and earn some money. She also discovered that an aunt of Lepelletier's knew a head of department at the Hôtel de Ville; she went to see her, and contrived to meet the official himself. Devoted mother that she was, she invited him to dinner at the end of December. He was to meet her son, and Verlaine's future would be assured.

Mme Verlaine was always thrifty, but she could spend her money in a good cause. There were twelve at dinner, and even Mathilde considered that the food was excellent. Verlaine arrived nearly an hour late, despicably drunk.

Fantin-Latour was now beginning his picture *Coin de Table* for the first post-war Salon. It was intended as a sequel to his painting *L'Atelier de Manet*, and he decided to portray the young poets and writers who frequented the passage Choiseul. On 18 March 1872 Edmond de Goncourt was dragged off to see Fantin-Latour, 'distributor of glory to the *gens de brasserie* . . . And on the easel there was a huge canvas which represented a Parnassian apotheosis of Verlaine, d'Hervilly, etc., an apotheosis in which there was a large gap, because, he innocently told us, so-and-so and such-and-such had refused to be portrayed in the company of colleagues whom they considered to be pimps and thieves.' This was a reference to Albert Mérat. He had found Rimbaud so repugnant that he had refused to pose with him; he was replaced by a pot of geraniums.[11]

Verlaine, so Mathilde remembered, made this picture an excuse for staying away from the rue Nicolet, sometimes for days. M. Mauté was astonished that Verlaine deserted Mathilde like this, but he remained remarkably innocent. Mathilde somehow contrived to hide Verlaine's drunkenness from her father, and he did not know her real unhappiness. Besides, she wrote, 'my father was an extremely correct man of the world, and he was too discreet to interfere in our marriage without good reason.' There would have been excellent reason, now, for his intervention; but Verlaine was already lost to them.

Early in the new year, 1872, he attempted to set fire to Mathilde's hair. The match went out, but she had made no attempt to stop him. She seems to have been past caring.

Mathilde wrote later that from October 1871 to January 1872 her life had been threatened every day. 'As for the child, Verlaine was absolutely indifferent to him. He never kissed him or looked at him; he simply ignored him.' One day, in mid-January, he came in when dinner was nearly over. Mathilde was unwell, and staying in her room. Verlaine went upstairs to find her sitting by the fire, holding the baby. He demanded money so that he could go out and have some coffee. Mathilde replied that he did not need to find an excuse to go out: he left her more alone every day. Verlaine was exasperated. He seized his son (then three months old) and flung him against the wall.

Providentially, Georges was not hurt; but he might have been killed, and Mathilde screamed with terror. Her parents rushed upstairs to find Verlaine with his hands round her throat. M. Mauté tore him away. Verlaine fled from the house. Then the Mautés questioned Mathilde, and Mathilde 'confessed everything'.

Next day the Mautés called in a doctor. He could still see the bruises on her neck. At M. Mauté's request, he wrote out a certificate recording the violence that she had suffered; he then said that she needed absolute rest.

Mathilde set off with her father, her baby and the nurse; they spent the next six weeks in Périgueux.

Verlaine vanished for two days; then he sent a letter to the rue Nicolet. Since he received no answer, he came himself. Mme Mauté said that Mathilde had gone away with her father until the spring; she would not give Verlaine the address, but she said that she would forward letters.

Verlaine – according to Mathilde – went back to live with his mother. That was his official address, but he had rented an attic for Rimbaud in the rue Campagne-Première; and there, no doubt, he spent nearly all his nights – his 'nuits d'Hercules'. However, he wrote often, and affectionately, to Mathilde and he begged her to come back. Even now, despite his drinking and his violence, she still loved him. She made one condition for her return: that he sent Rimbaud away.

In his *Confessions* [wrote Mathilde, at the end of her life], Verlaine accuses me of having been *jealous* of Rimbaud. Let me say here, frankly, that I never did such honour to that misguided youth. I was also far from accusing him of a vice which was then quite unknown to me. Verlaine – one must do him this justice – had respected the innocence of the young girl he had married . . . , and he had kept me in ignorance of many unpleasant things which I knew only later. To my great surprise, he resisted my very legitimate wish that Rimbaud should be sent away; he answered, at first, that it did not rest with him to stop Rimbaud from living in Paris. I pointed out that he needed only to stop giving Rimbaud money to make him go.[12]

Verlaine refused to send Rimbaud away. At this point, M. Mauté took charge of the situation. He wrote to his solicitor, Maître Guyot-Sionnest, and asked him to file a demand for separation; he enclosed the doctor's certificate. Rimbaud was not mentioned; but the threat had its effect. Verlaine wrote at once that Rimbaud was leaving. As soon as Rimbaud had left, Mathilde returned to Paris. M. Mauté stayed in the country for another two months. He intended to avoid any further scenes.

Verlaine seemed delighted by Mathilde's return, and, for a while, all went well. Mme Verlaine, still determined to make her son lead a regular life, had found him a job with an insurance company. Once again, Verlaine went to the office every morning; he came back to the rue Nicolet for dinner, and generally he and Mathilde went out in the evening. He even refrained from getting drunk, though every day he had a drink with Forain. 'Forain was a nice young man, not at all intemperate; hence the relative sobriety of Verlaine. I am grateful to him,' wrote Mathilde, 'for this brief lull in my life.'

Her tranquillity was not to last. One day, Verlaine came home with two slashes on his wrists, and three wounds on his thigh; they seemed to have been inflicted with a knife. He said that he had hurt himself fencing. The explanation was improbable, but

M. Mauté, who had come back that morning, helped Mathilde to dress her husband's wounds, and both of them pretended to believe it.

Soon afterwards, Verlaine and Mathilde went to dinner with Mme Verlaine. The moment the old lady left the room, Verlaine took a knife from his pocket and threatened his wife. She pretended not to take any notice. After dinner, they left early. It was a Thursday, the day when Philippe Burty was at home. On the way to the Burtys, Verlaine continued to threaten her. He was so drunk and malevolent that the Burtys called a cab, and they sent Mathilde home, alone, while they kept him occupied in the salon. In the half-hour's grace which was given her, she reached the rue Nicolet and told her parents about her husband's threats. The baby's cradle was brought downstairs, and Mathilde was settled in the room next to her mother's. Verlaine came back in a savage mood, and he drew his swordstick, but M. Mauté ordered him to bed.

Next day, when Mathilde went to thank Mme Burty, she was told that Rimbaud had been back in Paris for some time. Everything was suddenly clear. 'Where have they gone,' wrote Forain to Verlaine, years later, 'where have they gone, the days when we used to wait for you, Rimbaud and I, in a little café in the rue Drouot, smoking clay pipes and refreshing ourselves with numerous curaçao-bitters?'[13]

And then the bad days began again. The Mautés hardly slept at night, when they heard Verlaine's heavy, uncertain steps. Sometimes, in the morning, he would repent his drunkenness and weep, and swear that he would never drink again; and, that evening, he would drink once more. 'He was always the man of periodic repentances,' wrote Mathilde. 'He spent one half of his life doing wrong and the other half repenting it. He had a double nature.'

He had the most remarkable double nature in literature. It was now, in May 1872, when Rimbaud was back in Paris, and Verlaine was murderously violent to Mathilde, that *La Renaissance littéraire et artistique* published the opening poem of *Romances sans paroles*:

C'est l'extase langoureuse,
C'est la fatigue amoureuse,
C'est tous les frissons des bois
Parmi l'étreinte des brises,
C'est, vers les ramures grises,
Le chœur des petites voix . . .[14]

One night Verlaine did not come home. Mathilde was afraid that he might have had an accident, and early next morning she went to the rue Lécluse. Her mother-in-law said that Verlaine and Rimbaud had come to dine and sleep there, and that Verlaine had just left for his office.

About a fortnight later, Mathilde had acute neuralgia, and a high temperature. Verlaine seemed sorry to see her ill; he said that he would call on Dr Cros on the way to his office, and ask him to come. There had been no quarrel the previous evening. He kissed Mathilde good-bye. Then he left the rue Nicolet, as her husband, for the last time.

16

When Rimbaud arrived in Paris, he had been 'in a state of feverish mental exaltation, with his sexual curiosity aroused and his senses stimulated but not yet satisfied'. He was, writes his biographer, ready to be initiated, and it was chance which made him meet Verlaine at this crisis in his development. Rimbaud does not seem to have been a natural homosexual, 'and he could never overcome his sense of guilt or inferiority in this relationship. Nevertheless, there is no doubt that, with Verlaine, Rimbaud, for a time, experienced complete physical and spiritual ecstasy and complete freedom from all inhibitions.'[1]

According to sober-minded witnesses, wrote Charles Maurras, Rimbaud had 'a rather ugly face: a flat nose, a full mouth, and pale, vague eyes. But he was big and vigorous, and a passionate sensuality emanated from all his features.' Verlaine, who had been living with a dull and pregnant wife, was stirred to the depths of his being by this sensuality, which matched his own.

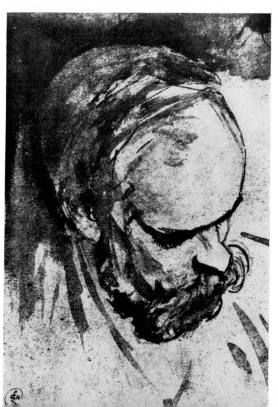

'Coin de table', by Fantin-Latour (1872). From left to right, seated: Verlaine, Rimbaud, Léon Valade, Ernest d'Hervilly, Camille Pelletan. Standing: Elzéar Bonnier, Émile Blémont, Jean Aicard.

Verlaine in London, October 1872. This sketch by Félix Régamey shows Verlaine during his odyssey with Rimbaud, and at the height of his poetical powers.

Verlaine with some of his pupils from St Aloysius' School at Bournemouth, where he taught from 1876–7. An impression by Max Beerbohm.

Years later he still talked about 'that perfect oval face, the face of an exiled angel'.[2] His relationship with Rimbaud was, without question, the paramount experience of his life. If Rimbaud was an exiled angel, Verlaine was prepared to sacrifice his family and sell his soul to go into exile with him.

Possibly Rimbaud knew something of homosexuality. Verlaine was ten years older than Rimbaud; he now initiated him into a life of depravity. Rimbaud soon 'plunged his teacher into depths of vice he would not have explored alone.' Verlaine had found a friend to persuade him that all his appetites were legitimate; it seemed to him that the prison gates were open. He himself satisfied his appetites as a hedonist; Rimbaud did so as an explorer. But in the early months of their relationship they found perfect fulfilment in one another.

Verlaine had always had a streak of violence in his nature, and it had always been intensified by drink. Rimbaud, too, was violent; at a literary dinner, le Dîner des Vilains Bonshommes, he had seized Verlaine's swordstick, and rushed at Étienne Carjat, the photographer. He would have done him bodily harm if some of the other guests had not restrained him. Valade told Blémont that Rimbaud's imagination, 'full of unheard-of power and corruption, fascinated or terrified all our friends'.[3] Lepelletier thought him 'strange, fantastic and disturbing'.[4] Maurice Rollinat, the poet, told Goncourt that Rimbaud was the very genius of perversity. 'Yes, the genius of perversity . . . He had a malevolent imagination . . . and he spent his life inventing acts of ruthless malice.'[5]

Verlaine was not exempt from them. The two of them fought with knives. On one occasion Rimbaud asked him to put his hands, palm upwards, on the table; then he stabbed them. It was not merely to prove to himself his unbreakable hold on Verlaine; it was not simple indulgence in wrongdoing. It was part of his creed, 'le long, immense et raisonné *dérèglement* de tous les sens'.

The quickest way to achieve degradation was to get drunk on absinthe; and early in 1872, when he and Verlaine began to be shunned even by Bohemian friends, they spent much of the day in the cafés of the Boul' Mich', spending Verlaine's inheritance on absinthe, and living in a more or less continual state of intoxication. When the cafés finally closed, they used to go to the rue Campagne-Première.

It cannot be proved that they practised sodomy. In the medical report on Verlaine in 1873, it was said that his body showed signs of recent active and passive sodomy; but some doctors now consider that the facts revealed by such an examination are not reliable evidence. However, it is impossible to believe that Verlaine and Rimbaud contented themselves with a romantic friendship; there is no doubt that both men felt physical rapture, and, repeatedly, in his poems, Verlaine proclaims his passion. In 'Le Poète et la Muse', he recalls the attic in the rue Campagne-Première:

> Seule, ô chambre, qui fuis en cônes affligeants,
> Seule, tu sais! mais sans doute combien de nuits
> De noce auront dévirginé leurs nuits, depuis.[6]

'Le Bon Disciple', a poem later found in Rimbaud's pocket-book, leaves little doubt of their relationship. There can be no question of the meaning of 'Ces Passions': 'Ces passions qu'eux seuls nomment encore amours . . .' And in 'Læti et Errabundi', written when Verlaine no longer knew if Rimbaud was alive or dead, he hails him as 'mon grand péché radieux'. When this poem appeared, it was thirteen years since Verlaine had seen Rimbaud, but the poem blazed, and blazes still. It shows the passion of this supreme relationship: one which had been spiritually and physically complete.[7]

The day after Verlaine's departure from the rue Nicolet, Mathilde asked her father to go in search of her husband. M. Mauté went to the rue Lécluse, but Verlaine had not been there. He went to Verlaine's office, but they had not seen him for a week. He went to the Morgue, to police headquarters, and to the cafés in the Latin Quarter where Verlaine and Rimbaud used to meet. There he heard 'the most scandalous suppositions' about their relationship. He came home in sombre mood. Some days later, Mathilde received a letter from Verlaine, in Brussels. 'My poor Mathilde, don't worry and don't be sad. I'm having a bad dream, I'll come back one day.' He did not say why he had gone or when he would return.

His letter was both affectionate and incoherent [Mathilde remembered]. But, after the anxiety I had been through, it was a relief to know that he was alive . . .

A few days later, I received a second letter. Verlaine told me that he had got into touch with some Communard refugees in Brussels, and that he wanted to write a book on the Commune and the atrocities which had been committed by the Versailles army. He added that, as he would be staying in Belgium for some time, he would be glad if I would send him his belongings, and various papers which were in the *unlocked* drawers of his desk.[8]

When she wrote her memoirs, Mathilde emphasised that the drawers had been unlocked, and – whatever Lepelletier's accusations – that she had not forced them. In Verlaine's desk she found, ironically, the manuscript of *La Bonne Chanson*; she found letters from Leconte de Lisle, Banville and Victor Hugo, congratulating Verlaine on the book. She also found 'a few poems of Rimbaud's which have all been published . . . I emphasise this, too,' she wrote, 'because, for many years, Verlaine *let his friends believe* that I had stolen and then destroyed a "sublime" work by Arthur Rimbaud.' What she did find, however, in the unlocked drawers of her husband's desk, was a whole correspondence from Rimbaud.

These letters were so strange [she recalled] that I thought they had been written by a madman, and I was terrified to think that Verlaine had gone away with such a companion.

At the same time I was angry at the way he had cheated me, because these letters had been exchanged while I was staying in the South [of France]. As I've said, I had demanded that Rimbaud should be sent away before I returned. Verlaine had been forced to give in for fear of a separation, and he had written to me that his friend had left Paris for good. At the same time, however, he had written to Rimbaud to tell him to be patient for a few days, that he had sent him away regretfully; as soon as his wife came home, he would ask him back.[9]

Rimbaud had not hidden his displeasure at being sacrificed to

'a whim'. Verlaine had asked advice from his mother, who said
that the young man should look for work. Rimbaud had answered,
in obscene terms, that he had no intention of working. He had
not gone back to his mother's: he had gone to Arras, where he
had lived at Verlaine's expense until he was invited to return.
'There were many other things in these letters which I don't want
to repeat here,' Mathilde continued. 'I was very upset by this long
correspondence. Then my father came into the room, and he
took the letters out of my hands.'

Next day, she told Dr Cros and his brother, Charles, about her
discovery. Dr Cros thought that Verlaine and Rimbaud were both
unbalanced by their abuse of absinthe, and Charles then explained
the slashes which Verlaine had received a few weeks earlier.
'We were all three at the café du Rat-Mort, Verlaine, Rimbaud
and I, when Rimbaud said to us: "Put your hands on the table,
I want to show you an experiment." We thought it was a joke,
and put out our hands; he pulled an open clasp-knife from his
pocket and cut Verlaine's wrists quite deeply. I had time to take
my hands away and I wasn't hurt. Verlaine left with his sinister
companion, and received two other stab-wounds in the thigh.'
Cros added: 'Another day I was sitting in the café next to Rimbaud. I left the table for a moment, and when I came back I saw
that my beer-glass contained some bubbling liquid. Rimbaud
had just poured sulphuric acid into it.'[10]

Cros's account of Rimbaud's vicious behaviour made Mathilde
more anxious than ever. It is astonishing that she kept any vestige
even of loyalty to Verlaine, but she determined to try to rescue
him from this relationship. It seemed to her certain to drive him
insane. Mathilde had never lacked physical courage. She decided
to go to Brussels and make a last attempt to bring Verlaine home.

Her father, strangely enough, agreed with her decision, and
Mme Mauté offered to go with her. She wrote to Verlaine that
she would arrive the following day, and that she would wait for
him at the Hôtel Liégeois.

I can now say [wrote Mathilde in 1907], that this journey was an act
of pure devotion on my part. For the past year I had suffered continu-
ally, I had been the victim of violence, insults and ill-treatment of every

kind, I had trembled for the life of my child, which was threatened quite as much as mine. I had also just had the proof that the letters which my husband had sent me during my stay in the South were only traps and lies to make me come back. All this had very largely detached me from him, and, if I attempted the journey to Brussels, I did so out of duty much more than affection. I felt that he was going to ruin not only my life but his own, for ever, and I made an effort to save him.

On the way to Brussels, I was thinking what means I could use to decide my husband to come with me. There could be no question of returning to the rue Nicolet; nothing in the world would have made me oblige my poor parents to go on suffering the life which they had led for the past ten months. Verlaine did not seem anxious to live in Paris any more. Since his friends had cold-shouldered Rimbaud, he bore a grudge against them. A journey would certainly be the best thing, but it had to be a long journey to some far-distant place, so that Rimbaud could not find us again.[11]

It was then that Mathilde thought of New Caledonia. Henri Rochefort, the political journalist, was living there; so was Alphonse Humbert, the fiancé of Lepelletier's sister. He had been deported for his Communard activities; he was to stay in New Caledonia for ten years, until an amnesty allowed him to come home and marry the patient Laure. Louise Michel, 'the Red Virgin', the ferocious Communard, a friend of Charles de Sivry and the Verlaines, was also there. Verlaine would find stimulating company on this Pacific island; he would find all the inspiration he needed to write his book on the Commune. He and Mathilde (so she decided) would stay there for about two years, and then return to Paris. The baby could not be exposed to such an exhausting voyage, and it could remain with the Mautés.

It was with these arrangements in mind that Mathilde reached Brussels at five a.m. on 22 July 1872. At the Hôtel Liégeois she was told that Verlaine and his friend were no longer staying there, but that Verlaine would come at eight o'clock. There were two hours and more to wait, and she and her mother went to their rooms to rest.

Verlaine arrived punctually. Whatever Mathilde professed about her overriding sense of duty, she threw herself, laughing and crying, into his arms.

Then I told him how utterly miserable he made me by his absence, and I begged him to come back with me. I won't repeat his answer here; it wasn't very clear, especially to me. I only really understood the meaning of his words very much later. What is certain, however, is that he began by refusing, because he didn't want to leave Rimbaud. Then I explained my plan to go to New Caledonia. To my great delight, the idea seemed to please him and to alter his intentions. He promised, with conviction, that he would come back with me.[12]

He arranged to meet her at four that afternoon in a public garden in Brussels. They were to catch the five o'clock train for Paris.

At four o'clock, as he had promised, Verlaine was waiting; but in the interval he had seen Rimbaud again, and he was drunk. As usual in his drunken moods, he seemed sullen and irascible, but he got into the train and began to eat a cooked chicken, which he had just bought. He ate it like a glutton, tearing it apart with his hands. Then he fell asleep, and slept until they had almost reached the frontier.

At Quiévrain, the frontier station, there were customs formalities. Everyone had to get out of the train. When the formalities were over, Verlaine disappeared, and Mathilde and Mme Mauté could not find him. The train was about to leave for France. As the doors were being shut, they finally caught sight of him on the platform. Mme Mauté cried out: 'Hurry up!' Verlaine rammed his hat down over his eyes, in a gesture of defiance, and shouted back at her: 'No, I'm staying!'[13]

17

Vous n'avez pas eu toute patience:
Cela se comprend par malheur, de reste
Vous êtes si jeune! Et l'insouciance,
C'est le lot amer de l'âge céleste!

Vous n'avez pas eu toute la douceur.
Cela par malheur d'ailleurs se comprend;
Vous êtes si jeune, ô ma froide sœur,
Que votre cœur doit être indifférent! . . .[1]

In 'Birds in the Night', the poem which he wrote two months later, Verlaine accused Mathilde of showing too little patience and gentleness. Almost incredibly, he had come to believe in his own innocence. Incredibly, too, he persuaded himself that Mathilde had not loved him, while he had loved her, 'ma Belle, ma Chérie'. And, recalling his final vision of her – an ironic companion-piece to his first vision in *La Bonne Chanson* – he was moved by a feeling of charity, singularly misplaced, and he accorded her his forgiveness.

> Je vous vois encore! En robe d'été
> Blanche et jaune avec des fleurs de rideaux.
> Mais vous n'aviez plus l'humide gaîté
> Du plus délirant de tous nos tantôts.
>
> La petite épouse et la fille aînée
> Était reparue avec la toilette
> Et c'était déjà notre destinée
> Qui me regardait sous votre voilette.
>
> Soyez pardonnée! . . .[2]

Yet, though the forgiveness was misplaced, it was true that Verlaine's destiny had been fulfilled. He had been more fortunate than he could have dared to hope, far more fortunate than he deserved, in his marriage. His vision had materialised, his poetic dream had, by a miracle, turned into reality. He had had a wife and child. He had known the bourgeois way of life which part of him always wanted, a regularity which henceforward he would often crave.

But Verlaine, as Mathilde herself and many others knew, was a double man. In her own words, he was Prince Charming and the Beast. He was anxious to conform and anxious to be free. He was not made for marriage, for he could not have been bound. No woman could have tolerated his drinking and his homicidal violence for life. Nor could they have borne the fact that he was passionately drawn to men.

All the troubles of his life, Verlaine once said, came from the fact that he was feminine. He needed to be dominated where he should have led. He needed to be admired where he should have felt admiration. He had fallen in love with Mathilde as if he had grown enamoured of a dream; but, if he needed a woman at all, he had needed a maternal figure: endlessly forgiving, unfailingly strong. He needed to be tolerated, cherished and directed. In making love he preferred, himself, to be the passive partner – or, rather, he preferred a man to love him. Verlaine was bisexual, but the attraction of Rimbaud was, for him, overwhelming. Beside this savage, passionate love, this love without constraint, his love for Mathilde seemed a pale and artificial *fête galante*. Nothing else in his life – which was a life of many passions – ever approached it.

It was strengthened by poetic kinship, by poetic inspiration. In May and June, when Rimbaud had returned from Arras to Paris, Verlaine had broken his poetic silence. He had written what would be the opening poems of his next collection, *Romances sans paroles*. These were his *Ariettes oubliées*. When Verlaine came to write about Rimbaud in *Les Poètes maudits*, he observed that people should not take Rimbaud's lessons in naïveté too seriously: they were belied by Rimbaud's life and character. But Verlaine himself had taken Rimbaud's lessons to heart. He wrote his *Ariettes oubliées* in the style of the Rimbaud of 1872. He had never been more sincere. He had found a style which was made for him.[3]

18

Three days after Mathilde's return to the rue Nicolet, she received a note from Verlaine. He had written it on leaving her at the Belgian frontier; he had clearly been drunk at the time, and demented by anxiety about Rimbaud. 'Misérable fée carotte, princesse souris, punaise qu'attendent les deux doigts et le pot, vous m'avez fait faire tout, vous avez peut-être tué le cœur de mon ami; je rejoins Rimbaud, s'il veut encore de moi après cette trahison que vous m'avez fait faire.'[1]

This time Mathilde gave the note to her father, and told him that she wanted a separation. She asked him to arrange it but not to speak of it again. The very mention of Verlaine was now painful to her. Rimbaud's letters were sent to Maître Guyot-Sionnest. Verlaine himself continued to write to Mathilde, but she put his letters unopened into a drawer. It was five years later that she brought herself to read them, and saw how he had set himself up as a martyr, as a misunderstood man who asked only to forgive her. Sometimes he also asked Mathilde to forgive him, sometimes he explained that he could not come back because he would be arrested as a Communard (which, remarked Mathilde, was untrue). Once, at least, he invited her to live with him and Rimbaud.

Divorce was not legally possible at the time, and the future would be difficult for a girl of nineteen with a broken marriage; but Mathilde remained determined on separation.[2]

Meanwhile, in the summer of 1872, Mme Rimbaud asked the Belgian police to discover the whereabouts of her son, who had left France with Verlaine. It was disclosed, in August, that Verlaine was living at an hotel in the rue de Brabant in Saint-Josse-ten-Noode, but that nothing was known of Rimbaud – who, presumably, was living with him.[3] The series of 'Paysages Belges' in *Romances sans paroles* was to pinpoint some of the stages in their odyssey. 'Walcourt', written in July, suggests not only the town itself, but the wholehearted happiness of Verlaine's life with Rimbaud, his life of wandering, drinking and making love. 'Charleroi' shows a touch of the melancholy which, at moments, clouded his happiness. In the first of the Brussels poems, the 'Simples Fresques', written in August, he senses the first breath of autumn, the kind of gentle sadness which had suffused the 'Chanson d'Automne' in *Poèmes saturniens*. The second of the 'Simples Fresques' suggests a more aggressive mood. Verlaine and Rimbaud, on their wanderings, admire a noble château: they also dream of desecrating the place and making it the setting for their passion. The poem is more than a graceful vignette: it is an anti-social comment, no doubt inspired by Rimbaud, and by the refreshments at the Estaminet du Jeune Renard, from which it is dated. Brussels also inspired Verlaine with 'Chevaux de Bois'. Wandering in the fairground in the suburb of Saint-Gilles, he revelled in the popular amusements, the vulgar vertigo of those who rode on the merry-go-round; the poem ended in a tone of gentle parody. August also brought 'Malines', in which he admired the lush Flanders countryside.

'Birds in the Night', which followed 'Malines', was Verlaine's comment on his marriage, and on Mathilde's visit to Brussels. It was written in September and October, in Brussels and in London.

On 7 September, Verlaine and Rimbaud embarked at Ostend for Dover. On 10 September, remembered the artist Félix Régamey, there was a knock on the door of his London studio:

> It was Verlaine ... He was fine-looking in his way, and though he was very ill-equipped with linen, he did not seem in the least overcome by fate.
> We spent some delightful hours together.
> But he was not alone. A silent companion was with him – a companion who was not remarkable, either, for his elegance.
> It was Rimbaud.
> Naturally we talked about absent friends.
> As Verlaine watched me draw and paint, inspiration seized him, and he enriched my album with two pearls: Napoleon III after Sedan, and the Prince Imperial.[4]

Verlaine's anti-Imperial feelings were no less strong now that he found himself among the Communard exiles. Régamey helped his two compatriots to find lodgings, and they settled in the room which had recently been occupied by the journalist Eugène Vermersch, at 35, Howland Street, off Tottenham Court Road. Fifty years later, Paul Valéry unveiled a plaque on this eighteenth-century house where Verlaine had written some of *Romances sans paroles* and Rimbaud had probably begun *Les Illuminations*.[5]

Within a few days of his arrival in London, Verlaine was sending Lepelletier his first impressions of the Victorian capital: of the little, soot-blackened houses, of the grandiose neo-Gothic and pseudo-Venetian mansions, of restaurants where people did not drink, and coffee-houses not licensed to sell spirits. ' "We don't

have spirits," replied a maid to whom I put this insidious question:
"One absinthe, if you please, mademoiselle".'[6] It was a far cry
from the Latin Quarter.

Verlaine was fascinated by the boot-blacks, in their scarlet
coats, who polished boots from morn till night, at a penny a time.
Even the beggars, clad in rags, seemed to have shining boots.
'Dans les cafés-concerts, Alhambra, Grecian Theatre, etc. ...
on danse la gigue, entre deux *God save* ...'[7]

Dansons la gigue!

J'aimais surtout ses jolis yeux,
Plus clairs que l'étoile des cieux,
J'aimais ses yeux malicieux.

Dansons la gigue!

Elle avait des façons vraiment
De désoler un pauvre amant,
Que c'en était vraiment charmant!

Dansons la gigue!

Mais je trouve encore meilleur
Le baiser de sa bouche en fleur,
Depuis qu'elle est morte à mon cœur.

Dansons la gigue!

Je me souviens, je me souviens
Des heures et des entretiens,
Et c'est le meilleur de mes biens.

Dansons la gigue![8]

This poem, dated from Soho, was perhaps suggested by a
barrel-organ as much as by any theatrical performance. It was also
inspired by Mathilde, whose image appeared to Verlaine super-
imposed, as it were, on the street scene. The frivolous refrain

showed, at least, a determination to be indifferent, but it is hard to believe that she still left him unmoved.

By the Treaty of Frankfurt, which had ended the Franco-Prussian War, Alsace and Lorraine had been ceded to the new German Empire, and all natives of Alsace and Lorraine were now obliged to choose either French or German nationality. On 18 September, in the presence of the French consul-general in London, Verlaine made his inevitable choice. He was later to proclaim the fact in his *Confessions* in terms which hardly matched his behaviour during the war and the Siege.[9]

On 24 September, he wrote again to Lepelletier. 'Here are two little poems to follow the one I sent you; I mean to have them printed, with others (congeneric, and completely different in style) under the title of *Romances sans paroles*. They will be printed here, in a month. I count on you for advertisements.'[10]

According to Van Bever, the poems sent in this letter were the first stanzas of 'Birds in the Night'. The three first stanzas were also sent to Blémont on 5 October. Presumably it was later that month that Verlaine wrote the four final stanzas. *Romances sans paroles* was not to find an English publisher; it was to be published in France in 1874.[11]

19

Poèmes saturniens are coloured by Baudelaire; *Fêtes galantes* show the influence of Watteau and his century. *La Bonne Chanson* was inspired by Mathilde. *Romances sans paroles*, which some consider Verlaine's finest book, bears the ineffaceable mark of Rimbaud. For Rimbaud broke with conventional poetry which, to him, was merely a rhythmical record of action. Poetry, he believed, should be in advance of action. He rejected subjective poetry, the psychological analysis, the Parnassian picturesqueness organised by man around man. He demanded objective poetry which, through a new, creative language, reached realities so far unknown. '*Je* est un autre,' wrote Rimbaud. 'J'assiste à l'éclosion de mes pensées.'[1] It was Rimbaud whom Verlaine followed in the poems of *Romances sans paroles*, in which he created an original, unacademic language. Verlaine showed his technical whims, disdained the conventional alternation of masculine and feminine rhymes, systematically wrote false rhymes, and dislocated lines. Determined not to be academic, he went to the opposite extreme: sometimes his poetry touched surrealism.

> Je devine, à travers un murmure,
> Le contour subtil des voix anciennes
> Et dans les lueurs musiciennes,
> Amour pâle, une aurore future!
>
> Et mon âme et mon cœur en délires
> Ne sont plus qu'une espèce d'œil double
> Où tremblote à travers un jour trouble
> L'ariette, hélas! de toutes lyres!
>
> Ô mourir de cette mort seulette
> Que s'en vont, cher amour qui t'épeures,
> Balançant jeunes et vieilles heures!
> Ô mourir de cette escarpolette![2]

Rimbaud advocated pictorial simplicity, a return to popular sources, to simple refrains and simple rhythms. Verlaine gladly and instinctively followed Rimbaud's guidance, bringing some of his poems close to popular songs, seeking a new simplicity and a new complexity. Here, perhaps, he practised the theories which he was later to preach in 'Art poétique'. Now he was already showing his technical emancipation; and he was exploring the *correspondances*, the relations between the senses, which Baudelaire and Gautier had revealed, and Rimbaud believed in. He was attempting to spiritualise his poetry. Just as Rimbaud freed Verlaine from bourgeois domesticity, swept him out of mediocrity, so he shook him free from certain literary conventions, and swept him into a splendid adventure: the search for a new poetry, for the powers of the seer, and for the forgotten god-like status of man. Some of the poems of *Romances sans paroles* – those which were written in the spring and summer of 1872 – clearly show the influence of Rimbaud. Verlaine became more temperate in his language in the later poems of the collection.

It was natural that Verlaine should be influenced by the poet to whom he was ineluctably drawn. In some ways, Rimbaud was only appealing to instincts and beliefs which were already present: to Verlaine's sympathy for the simple and popular, to his love of technical experiment, his lifelong pleasure in exploring and exploiting language and syntax, his interest in *correspondances* and in expressing moods. Verlaine was already a supreme poet of mood; under Rimbaud's influence he attempted to eliminate himself from his poetry, to record mood and atmosphere without the intervention of self. This was the ultimate refinement of poetry.

Yet if Rimbaud's theories marked the logical continuation of Verlaine's progress, they were not theories which Verlaine could permanently accept. Rimbaud, despite his comparative youth, was already masculine in his attitude to life and to literature. He believed in objective poetry, in the philosophical meaning of poetry, he believed in poetry as a means to a more glorious end: as a means of rediscovering man's forgotten dignity. Rimbaud was an extrovert, a man of action, to whom – as history would show – poetry would prove a useless tool, an abandoned creed, a disillusioning stage in a life of action. Verlaine was always feminine in his attitude to life and to poetry. He could not, at any moment, have abandoned literature, let alone turned to a life of adventure. His life was poetry, and subjective poetry. The poetry which came to him most naturally was the poetry he spun from his own entrails, the poetry which faithfully mirrored his own infinite, changing moods.

> Il pleure dans mon cœur
> Comme il pleut sur la ville;
> Quelle est cette langueur
> Qui pénètre mon cœur?

> Ô bruit doux de la pluie
> Par terre et sur les toits!
> Pour un cœur qui s'ennuie
> Ô le chant de la pluie!

Il pleure sans raison
Dans ce cœur qui s'écœure.
Quoi! nulle trahison?...
Ce deuil est sans raison.

C'est bien la pire peine
De ne savoir pourquoi,
Sans amour et sans haine,
Mon cœur a tant de peine![3]

If the intense but impermanent influence of Rimbaud is seen
in Verlaine's technical experiments, his simplified vocabulary,
his brilliant grammatical unorthodoxy, it is not always easy to
define Rimbaud's more personal presence in *Romances sans paroles*.
Sometimes there is an apology for their liaison, a moment of
apprehension, a defiant proclamation of their relationship, a more
precise charting of their odyssey. Yet there is no poem here which
suggests the intensity of Verlaine's passion for Rimbaud; and
there are several poems which recall – without hatred, and still
with a certain love – the figure of Mathilde.

Le piano que baise une main frêle
Luit dans le soir rose et gris vaguement,
Tandis qu'avec un très léger bruit d'aile
Un air bien vieux, bien faible et bien charmant
Rôde discret, épeure quasiment,
Par le boudoir longtemps parfumé d'Elle ...[4]

The fifth of the *Ariettes oubliées* gently recalls the tone of *La
Bonne Chanson*; and 'Child Wife' (the title is taken from *David
Copperfield*) gives a disingenuous portrait of Verlaine, but a
plausible likeness of a young wife. 'Birds in the Night' recalls,
very vividly, the attempted reconciliation in Brussels, the final
vision of Mathilde in her white-and-yellow dress.

One can hardly accept the self-portrait which Verlaine draws
in this poem: the portrait of a loving husband who needed only
patience and understanding; and yet, in 'Birds in the Night', he
suggests, with complete conviction, one of the fatal flaws in the
marriage:

... Vous êtes si jeune, ô ma froide sœur,
Que votre cœur doit être indifférent![5]

Mathilde had now returned to her bourgeois milieu, and, perhaps, she had come to hate her husband. But she could never have given him the love which he had demanded. She was young and sexually inexperienced. She had been, perhaps, in love with love. Her feeling for Verlaine had been a young girl's day-dream, a cerebral romance; and Verlaine, too, had been enamoured of an ideal created by his own imagination. Perhaps he was not made for marriage. But his marriage with Mathilde had been a predictable disaster.

Twenty years after his meeting with Rimbaud, he was asked by a journalist how the prestige of love could be restored. He spoke of the Greek philosophers' love for young athletes. 'All this,' he said, 'is certainly in the lofty realm of the ideal. But some noble spirits of our own day ... have felt that ordinary passion could never reach the height of disinterestedness which is so easily attained in friendship between men. Passionate friendship – that is the remedy you are looking for.'[6]

It may also have been an attempted explanation of his own disillusionment in marriage, of his overwhelming love of Rimbaud. Rimbaud had shown Verlaine – perhaps for the only time in his life – the power of physical passion. He had combined it with the attraction of poetic genius.

20

Throughout October and November 1872, Verlaine wrote copious letters to Lepelletier: letters which recorded the continual fascination of London, his intellectual life, and his persistent worries about Mathilde.

The fog is beginning to show the tip of its filthy nose [this in October]. Everyone is coughing here, except me. It's true – you know me – that I'm full of flannel, mufflers, cotton-wool in the ears, and other precautions which are as *honourable* here as they are silly in Paris ...

and so I'm as well as my poor head will let me be, all fraught as it is with out-manoeuvring these wicked plans [for a separation] . . .

In a few days' time, I expect to go into a big establishment here, where you earn quite a lot. In the meanwhile, I am working for some American papers, which pay pretty well. In fact I'm not vegetating as much as the good folk in the rue Nicolet expected, though I am still very sad about this revolt of my wife's. As you know, my mother had done everything, and I had suffered everything, for her.[1]

Madame Verlaine had indeed been generous; but, even to Lepelletier, Verlaine's past 'suffering' must have been unconvincing.

The next letter was probably written in the same month. In the interval, Lepelletier had sent Verlaine some advice on retrieving his property from the rue Nicolet.

Thank you for your helpful practical details [came the answer]. I shall make use of them. I've written to my wife about returning my belongings. If she's recalcitrant, I'll do something else.

I'm very sad all the same about this indelicacy, this churlishness and vulgar treachery, this criminal breaking open of drawers. It's even sadder that my wife should abandon me in favour of a father-in-law like that. I say abandon, because I have never ceased to ask her to come to me, and she doesn't even write to me any more, after she'd been and ranted like a lunatic about me, and insulted my mother, *to whom she doesn't even send my son*! Tell all that to our *wondering* friends.[2]

Mathilde's one concern was now her child; she was too aware of her mother-in-law's reckless devotion to Verlaine to entrust her with his year-old son. And if the Mautés asked old Mme Verlaine to the house, Mme Verlaine refused the invitation. Mathilde would not have been sorry; she only wanted oblivion.

If Verlaine's list of his possessions was correct, there were still too many reminders of him in the rue Nicolet. There were his summer and winter clothes (never again could he afford to dress according to season); there was a bayonet-belt, a memento of his 'service' as a *garde national*. There were a lithograph portrait of his mother, a watercolour by his father of the Château de Carlsbourg in the Belgian Ardennes. There was a quantity of books, including *Les Épaves* by Baudelaire, signed copies of works by

Hugo, and issues of *Le Parnasse contemporain*. There were a photo-graph of Élisa Dujardin, two photographs and four self-caricatures of Rimbaud. There were about ten letters from Rimbaud, con-taining poems and prose poems. There was, above all, a manu-script of Rimbaud's in a sealed envelope: the manuscript of *La Chasse spirituelle*.[3]

Old Mme Verlaine gave this list to Lepelletier, and it was he who asked that the Mautés should return Verlaine's belongings. 'I think,' he wrote, 'that most of the items in this list were given back to Mme Verlaine *mère*.' The letters from Rimbaud to Verlaine were part of Mathilde's grounds for demanding a separation. They were now with Maître Guyot-Sionnest. After Verlaine's death she destroyed them, for fear that her son might read them; and Rimbaud's sister, Isabelle, informed of the destruction, wrote to her: 'I am glad that you burnt those papers, whatever they contained, rather than leave them in the hands of strangers.' Mathilde herself emphasised 'that the destruction of the letters addressed to Verlaine by Rimbaud can in no way have lessened Rimbaud's glory. If his family and friends had read them, as I and my father did, they would be grateful to me for destroying them.'

The destruction must be bitterly regretted, but at least the fate of the letters is known. The manuscript of *La Chasse spirituelle*, in its sealed envelope, has not yet been found. In 1907, Mathilde determined 'to finish once and for all with the repeated accusation that I maliciously destroyed some of Rimbaud's manuscripts out of revenge. I say categorically,' she wrote, 'that all I found among Verlaine's papers was the correspondence between the two friends.'[4] If Mathilde herself did not destroy the manuscript, it is possible that Monsieur Mauté committed it to the flames. Or perhaps it still survives, waiting to be found, this work full of 'étranges mysticités, et les plus étranges aperçus psychologiques', which Verlaine considered to be Rimbaud's supreme achievement.

On 8 November 1872, from Howland Street, Verlaine wrote again to Lepelletier. 'Thank you for your good advice. I'll take it, though it would have been nice to scotch the abominable calumnies at once ...'[5] The 'calumnies' were, no doubt, the accusation of a homosexual relationship between himself and Rimbaud. When Lepelletier came to write his life of Verlaine, he recalled how indignant Verlaine had been at this accusation, how he had wanted to publish letters in the papers, enlist support from friends, demand a medical examination for himself and Rimbaud. Lepelletier suggested that this demand was itself enough to absolve him. But Lepelletier was excessively loyal. He was trying to establish an image which he knew to be untrue. Lepelletier had seen Verlaine and Rimbaud together, he had publicly criticised the behaviour of his friend and 'Mlle Rimbaud'. Besides, in this same letter to him, on 8 November 1872, Verlaine, with his usual duality, both rejected the accusation of homosexuality and let him understand that it was justified. Having mentioned the 'calumnies' of the Mautés, he told Lepelletier that he had written a memorandum on the subject, and that he intended to use it.

In this memorandum I set down, clearly, and, I think, with effective feeling, all that the wretched woman made me suffer ... As for the filthy accusation, I completely and utterly pulverise it and cast all the disgusting opprobrium of it on to these wretched people. In my memorandum, I record the unheard-of betrayals which I have recently suffered, and I show, as clear as day, that this unnatural affair, with which they have the infamy to reproach me, is simply intimidation (if not blackmail) in order to get a larger sum of money ... And in a psychological analysis, without fine words or paradoxes, I set down the highly honourable and sympathetic motives of my very real, very deep, and *very enduring* friendship for Rimbaud – I won't add *very pure* – for shame![5]

Verlaine added his comments on the Victorian Sunday. His sketches of London, in his letters to Lepelletier, were a verbal counterpart to the drawings of Gustave Doré. They had, it is true, an element of obscenity which was lacking in Doré, an anal-erotic tone which suggested the childishness in Verlaine's nature; but they still present a critical, admiring and lively picture of the Victorian capital. It is, of course, raining, and the rain has driven people into the theatres, to see *Macbeth* (with Métra quadrilles played in the intervals), or the English version of Hervé's *L'Œil crevé*. In the wine rooms and 'alsoops bars', with their frosted glass, their zinc-topped mahogany counters, their dark green painted woodwork, the décor looks, through half-closed eyes, like a background by Delacroix; and blowsy barmaids half encourage broad compliments from the customers. Coffee, observes Verlaine, angrily, 'coûte six pences, sans cognac'; and all the fish in the restaurants is cooked till it looks like octopus. 'Je profite de cette lettre,' he adds on 10 November, 'pour maudire comme il faut l'abominable *ox-tail soup*.'

In Leicester Square, which had long been a centre for the French colony, Verlaine discovered the Café de la Sablonnière et de Provence: no doubt the Hôtel Sablonnière where Théophile Gautier had stayed, some twenty years earlier. He listened to the German bands, visited Mme Tussaud's, the music-halls, and the National Gallery, where he admired the Italian primitives. He saw the guys ('les mannequins de Guy Fowks') made to celebrate 5 November, and he watched the procession on Lord Mayor's Day. He admired the Grenadier Guards '(splendides hommes en rouge, frisés et pommadés'), felt nervous at the thought of the Tower subway, noted the photographs of Stanley and Livingstone, Napoleon III and Eugénie, in the shop windows ('ô que d'Ugénies!'). He determined to go to Speakers' Corner one Sunday afternoon; he heard the organ-grinders grinding out a familiar tune: the serenade from Coppée's *Le Passant*. He was fascinated by the City, and he went down the Thames by boat as far as Woolwich. 'The docks are unheard-of: Carthage, Tyre and everything in one!' 'It is probable,' he wrote, 'that English life has a poetry which I cannot yet see. I'm waiting, and, while I'm waiting ... I'm "collecting impressions"!'[6]

The vitality and variety of London life could not entirely distract him from the question of a judicial separation. Lepelletier had once advised him to resist the demand for separation; he had urged him to contest the statements which had been made. He knew that it was impossible for husband and wife to live together, but he had felt that if Verlaine was silent he would seem to accept the imputation of immorality. Now, however, that Verlaine was staying in London with Rimbaud, the Mautés' case was strengthened, and Lepelletier felt it prudent to restrain him. He advised him, above all, not to publicise this allegation. He advised him to entrust his battle to his solicitor, Maître Pérard. He took it upon himself to reclaim Verlaine's possessions from the rue Nicolet.

On 14 November Verlaine wrote dejectedly:

My dear Edmond,

I'm writing to you a lot because I'm very worried, and it's good to talk to an old stick like you, especially an old branch I can cling to – in such a horrible situation. And then I think it's a good idea to tell you about my latest actions. Rimbaud has recently written to his mother to warn her about everything that was being said and done against us, and I am at present in regular correspondence with her. I've given her your address, and my mother's, and the Mautés', and those of M. Istace and the two lawyers. You know that mine is Me Pérart [*sic*], rue du 4 Septembre; you have also received my powers of attorney ...

Who were those people who went to my mother's about Rimbaud, so they said ... ? Mme Rimbaud herself (so she's written to me) has received anonymous letters against her son on several occasions. I'm waiting for another letter from her which will tell me where they come from, and other details. All these circumstances are clearly part of a network, and the meshes can and must be broken ...

On 23 November, he returned to the subject: 'Give me as many details as possible about the 'dear child' and her august family. Do you still see the Sivrys? Mme Rimbaud is passionately concerned about the affair. She thinks that, if I part from her son, I should *bend* them. What do you think? I believe, myself, that it would be giving them their *one weapon* ...' He again insisted that he and Rimbaud were ready to undergo a medical examination.[7]

In December, it seemed as if Mme Rimbaud's advice had prevailed. Some time before Christmas, Verlaine announced, soberly:

Rimbaud is leaving this week for Charleville, and my mother is going to come here. Her presence won't only give me the greatest pleasure, it will be very useful from the point of view of *respectability*.

We shall probably rent a little house in one of the cheaper neighbourhoods; there are many of them here, and life is a hundred times cheaper than it is in Paris, the climate a hundred times healthier, and work is infinitely easier to find. And then my life will be happy again, and I shall completely forget those wicked people. I shall find serenity again, and – who knows? – perhaps a *ménage*: Lord, I am entitled to any revenge.[8]

Rimbaud had left London by Christmas. Verlaine consoled himself with roast goose. 'But I am very sad,' he added. 'All alone. Rimbaud (you don't know him, I'm the only one who knows him) isn't here any more. The emptiness is dreadful! I don't care about anything else.'[9]

His mother had not yet arrived. In January he caught influenza; and, dramatic as ever, he saw himself dying, alone, on foreign soil. In desperation – or was it simply adolescent self-pity? – he posted off his letters of farewell.

Mon ami [this to Blémont],
   I am *dying* of grief, of illness, weariness, and desertion. Rimbaud will send you this. Forgive this brevity from someone who is *gravely ill*.
   Goodbye, or perhaps farewell for ever.

P. VERLAINE.[10]

In the same theatrical mood, he summoned his wife and mother. The telegram to Mathilde was ignored. Mme Verlaine arrived with all speed, and, two days later, after an absence of a month, Rimbaud returned (Mme Verlaine had sent him fifty francs). Together they saved Verlaine, 'not from imminent death', as he now confessed, 'but from a crisis which, in my solitude, would indeed have been mortal.'[11]

In February, Mme Verlaine returned to France, and urged him to come home. She assured him that there was no danger of anti-Communard reprisals; she implied that there might be a reconciliation with the Mautés. For a moment, he thought of going to Paris, 'to put an end to all these affairs *myself*. I count on your kind help in my task,' he told Lepelletier. 'And tell me, too, if there's a way of hastening things; it's become ridiculous, especially as my defence is so simple. It is the pure and simple denial of everything, the challenge to produce a proof or a witness. And, above

all, it is the impossibility of my staying with the Mautés, and my
wife preferred to destroy her marriage rather than give in to me
on that point.'[12]

Verlaine could not, finally, persuade himself that it was safe for
him to return to Paris. Perhaps he still hoped that in Belgium,
away from the influence of her parents, Mathilde would agree to
a meeting, and their differences might be resolved.

On 4 April, he and Rimbaud crossed from Dover to Ostend.
On board the *Comtesse de Flandres*, Verlaine wrote the last poem of
Romances sans paroles.[13]

21

It is possible that he and Rimbaud spent some days together in
Brussels. On 11 April, Good Friday, Rimbaud returned, un-
announced, to his mother's farm at Roche, in the Ardennes.
There, soon after his arrival, he began *Une Saison en Enfer*. It was
'the explanation of his poetry of the magician period, an indictment and repudiation of it . . . He had thought himself a *mage*
and a *voyant*, an angel, the messenger from God . . . But he had
been mistaken. What he had thought were *Illuminations* were
only *Hallucinations* after all.'[1]

While Rimbaud was making his rigorous *examen de conscience*,
Verlaine took refuge with his aunt, Mme Évrard, at Jehonville,
in the Belgian Ardennes. He was far from happy. At Namur, on
his way to Jehonville – so near Rimbaud's Charleville – he had
received a note from Mathilde, telling him to stop writing to her.
He professed not to understand Mathilde's change of mood. With
his infinite capacity for self-delusion, he had convinced himself
that she was unjust, and that he would win any lawsuit, if it
occurred. The previous summer, she had begged him to return to
her. Now 'this strange *deserted* woman' had rejected him. Despite
his relationship with Rimbaud, he was even indignant at the
thought that she might be unfaithful. 'I ask you, confidentially,
what you know, infer and advise,' he wrote to Lepelletier on
15 April. 'This is just *because I must* take everything into account,

and I want to retrieve everything (I could even bring myself to forgive).'² Lepelletier answered that he had not heard anything untoward about Mathilde. But if her own life was beyond reproach, she seemed to be happy with the prospect of release from Verlaine.³

Verlaine remained undecided how he should behave towards her. Lepelletier said that he still hoped, secretly, for a reconciliation; Rimbaud's absence made him feel more sure of it.⁴ But Verlaine's letter to Émile Blémont, written on 22 April, a week after his letter to Lepelletier, does not suggest any wish to be reconciled. It does record his despondency, and his wish for Rimbaud's company.

My dear friend,

On my return from a *prudent* little excursion in the direction of Sedan, I've found a very nice letter from you. It has been a welcome diversion from the mortal weariness which has preyed upon me since I left London. I left for imperative reasons, but I left *provisionally*, and I'm burning to go back. I'm staying here with an old aunt, who shows me every possible kindness, and I'm waiting for my mother and hope very much to persuade her to cross the Channel. But I have no books (they're keeping all mine at the rue Nicolet, not to mention manuscripts, linen, etc. . . .). I have no-one to talk to, and no distractions except for enormous walks. And it's only at far distant intervals that I see the friend to whom I've given all my affection – an affection which he wholeheartedly returns. So here I am, very sad and disheartened. I'm working hard, however. Apart from the little book [*Romances sans paroles*] which I hope to get printed in Paris, I'm preparing a collection of all my unpublished poems (sonnets, old *poèmes saturniens*, political poems and a few obscenities), and I'm going to have them printed in Brussels, with an enormous preface in which I hit out at a good many things and people. And then I'm occupied with the lawsuit which they're determined to bring against me, and with my will, and with a memorandum for my son, in case of my death. – For on two occasions I've thought I was dying. The first time, in London, I was saved only by my mother's care, and the admirable devotion of Rimbaud, who had come back specially from Charleville. Quite recently, here in Belgium, at Namur, I had a sort of cerebral attack, which I survived alone only through taking quantities of sedative. All this makes me do a lot of thinking, and that is largely why I'm here, in a little village in the

Belgian Ardennes, where I'm busy putting my poor affairs in order. I still don't know when the lawsuit will take place. My wife has had the incredible malice and cynicism to bring it against me, after a thousand protestations and a thousand promises to the contrary, but I hope it takes place as soon as possible, so that the fools and cowards will have their mouths shut once and for all. After all that, I shall no doubt lead a wandering life abroad. I don't want any more to do with Paris, and, if I'm ever seen there again, I'll just be passing through . . .

Mon ami, I am atrociously weary. Your letters do me good; make them longer and more frequent . . . I am so grateful to the people who show me affection.[5]

On 16 May, Verlaine wrote again to Lepelletier about the impending lawsuit.

After more than six months of actual separation (though there was not the least wish for it on my part, quite the contrary), after a judgment which *temporarily* but *indefinitely* deprives me of all powers over my wife and son; after all the rumours which have been spread around and legally recorded, I think that an *amicable* separation is impossible. It would not prevent my adversaries from returning, if they chose, to judicial proceedings (which might then be called *blackmail*). It also seems to me a half-measure which would look like a tacit confession on my part – and therefore it is impossible. What I want is not a re-conciliation – I myself have never been 'at variance' – it's my wife's *immediate* return to me; I have just written to her in these terms, warning her that this would be the last time. I am waiting for her reply, and it's clear that if she doesn't give me satisfaction very soon, I shall have to act . . . I have said everything, done everything, I've come here (and left London and my hopes of living there in comfort) for her sake; I've prayed and reasoned, appealed to her good sense, her heart, and even her maternal love! The answer was that *I was afraid of the lawsuit, that that was why I said these affectionate things, that she wasn't afraid of the lawsuit*, BECAUSE SHE KNEW SHE COULDN'T LOSE IT . . .

So if you see Mme Bertaux [the sculptor, a friend of the Mautés] – even go and see her if you can – tell her that if she sees my wife and if she sees fit, she should show this misguided woman all her madness and all her shamelessness, and all her indifference to her son's future and all the unhappiness for her, for me, and for the child that would be implied and determined by the pursuance of such a revolting act as this filthy and grotesque lawsuit . . .

My health is unsettled. Oh, if I only had a little happiness in my emotional life, how well my intellectual life would go![6]

For all his worries about Mathilde, his loneliness without Rimbaud, Verlaine was working intensively. Emotional stress never restrained his creative powers. The quality of his writing might vary, but, throughout his life, with one notable exception, Verlaine was always formulating or writing something new. He had the incessant creative urge of the natural writer. It is ironic that his least creative period was precisely that of his married life. He was not inspired by domesticity.

Now, in Jehonville, where he remained in a state of tension, he lost himself in writing. He was (so he told Lepelletier, on 16 May) working on a prose drama, *Madame Aubin*. It dealt, not surprisingly, with the theme of infidelity. He was finishing a comic opera which he had begun, two or three years earlier, with Sivry. He was relieving his feelings in 'a ferocious novel, as sadistic as possible and very drily written'. He was writing a series of sonnets, to go with *Les Amies*, the sonnets on Lesbian love, which he had already sent Lepelletier; now he sent him a prologue for the whole series. He was working on the preface to a new collection of poems, *Les Vaincus*. This was, apparently, the book which he had mentioned to Blémont. It was later advertised, but it never appeared. Verlaine also told Lepelletier that he was toying with the idea of a book of didactic poems

... from which *man* will be completely banished. Landscapes, things, the malice of things. – Here are a few titles: 'La Vie du Grenier'. – 'Sous l'eau' – L'Île. Every poem will have 300 or 400 lines. – The lines will be according to a system which I'm evolving. It will be very musical, without puerilities à la Poe ... (I'll talk to you about him, some day, because I've *read him all* in English), and it will be as picturesque as possible. The life of Rembrandt's 'Grenier'; 'Sous l'eau', a real water-sprite's song; 'L'Île', a great picture of flowers, etc., etc. Don't laugh until you know my system: I may have got a capital idea ...

This last book of poems did not appear; but *L'Île* was advertised the following year as being in preparation. In 1888, thanking Francis Poictevin for his *Paysages*, Verlaine wrote: 'I once had an idea, too, of the pure and simple landscapes of a *Robinson* ïCrusoeï without Robinson or Friday. It would have been in verse, and it's called *L'Isle* . . . I abandoned the idea, but your book has brought it back to me.'[8] It was, as Verlaine came to imply, an almost Baudelairean poem on the beauty and goodness of unspoilt creation.

The poems 'from which *man* will be completely banished' recall Rimbaud's search for objectivity. '*Je* est un autre.' As for the poetic system which Verlaine was evolving, in the early summer of 1873, it was, one suspects, a system which owed much to Rimbaud's purifying doctrine: to the refinement of poetry to a point where it expressed the hitherto unknown. Perhaps Verlaine was already coming to the creed which he would formulate in 'Art Poétique':

> De la musique encore et toujours!
> Que ton vers soit la chose envolée
> Qu'on sent qui fuit d'une âme en allée
> Vers d'autres cieux à d'autres amours . . .[9]

All the arts, Baudelaire had said, constantly aspired towards the condition of music. There was the essence of Verlaine's work. But Verlaine was not so much concerned with the music of verse as with the nature of music. The finest and most typical of his poems were closer to music than they were to literature.

In his letter to Lepelletier, on 16 May, he had not spoken only of his writing. He had also spoken of his unsatisfied sexual appetite. 'Hélas! je suis *chaste* . . .' He relieved his feelings in the 'beaux versses' which he sent him: a sonnet here called 'Invocation'.

> Chair! O seul fruit mordu des vergers d'ici-bas,
> Fruit âcrement sucré qui jutes aux dents seules
> Des affamés du seul Amour, – bouches ou gueules,
> Que fait? – O Chair! dessert des forts et leur repas!
>
> Amour! L'unique émoi de ceux que n'émeut pas
> L'horreur de vivre, Amour qui blutes, sous tes meules,
> Les scrupules des libertins et des bégueules
> Pour le pain des Damnés qu'élisent les Sabbats!

Chair! Amour! Ô *tous les appétits* vers l'Absence,
Toute la délirance et toute l'innocence,
Toi qui nous es si bonne et toi qui m'es si cher,

Je vous supplie, et je vous défie, et je pleure
Et je ris de connaître, en ignorant qu'épeure
Le doute, votre énigme effroyable, Amour, Chair.[10]

When this sonnet appeared, eleven years later, in *Lutèce*, it had been significantly changed. The final tercets were re-written, and simplified into an allegory of the conciliation of physical and spiritual love. In 1873, when Verlaine wrote the poem, it was an unmistakable tribute to his love for the absent Rimbaud. 'Ô *tous les appétits* vers l'Absence...'

This absence was made all the more oppressive by the thought that Rimbaud was at Roche, so near him. They had written to one another. They had already met several times during the last few weeks: once, no doubt, on Verlaine's '*prudent* little excursion towards Sedan' (he had carefully not mentioned this to Lepelletier), sometimes on the 'enormous walks' which he had also failed to mention to him. To Blémont, who was not concerned with the impending lawsuit, he could reveal that he still saw Rimbaud – and to Blémont he could hint at the importance of the relationship. In none of the published letters to Lepelletier does he disclose so much.

However, on 19 May he wrote again to Lepelletier, announcing that he had sent him the manuscript of *Romances sans paroles*. He suggested that though the accusations of immorality were unfounded, Rimbaud remained significant in his life. 'I am very anxious,' he wrote, 'to have the dedication to Rimbaud. In the first place *as a protest*, and then because these poems were written when he was there and repeatedly urging me to write them. Above all, I want to have it as a token of gratitude for the devotion and affection which he has always shown me, and especially when I nearly died. This lawsuit mustn't make me ungrateful. You understand? However, write to me if you see any objection....'[11]

Romances sans paroles appeared without a dedication; but on

23 May Verlaine announced: 'I'm leaving tomorrow for Bouillon, where I have arranged to meet friends from Mézières-Charleville.' Lepelletier must have known the identity of one of the friends from Mézières-Charleville – as Charleville was sometimes called. Certainly, when he came to write his life of Verlaine, he was in no doubt of the situation.

The projects of reconciliation had vanished. The writs were flying to and fro. A judgment was expected from the civil tribunal, decreeing a judicial separation, for divorce did not then exist. Arthur Rimbaud, recalled by Verlaine, had come to join him at Bouillon. The return was celebrated by an orgy of drinking. Verlaine and his companion wandered round the Ardennes for a little while, and then, once more together, embarked for England.

Verlaine arrived in London with Rimbaud on 27 May.

22

It is hard to understand his behaviour. He asked Lepelletier to keep him informed about the Mautés' 'lack of principles', and he announced his conviction that 'my wife is a proper villain, and her mother is a wretch (I'm not even speaking about the old louse of a father)'. He intended, he continued, 'to act very soon and very severely'.[1] And yet, presumably, he had abandoned hope of a reconciliation. On 30 May he wrote to Blémont: 'Here I am, back in London again, – after the final, and, I venture to say, *the most delicate* efforts. I am now sure of my wife's terrible stupidity, – or her profound malice. But we'll forget that, if you don't mind. I won't bore anyone else with my affairs. It will be Justice which settles them.'[2] He must have known that – if the lawsuit was to be brought against him – his new journey with Rimbaud would weigh heavily against him. But perhaps he had come to be indifferent or defiant.

When he and Rimbaud arrived in London, they rented a room at 8, Great College Street – now Royal College Street – in Camden Town. It was clearly very different from what it is today.

It's a very gay neighbourhood [Verlaine told Blémont, in the same letter]: you'd think you were in Brussels. I firmly intend to work here – as I don't expect to come back to Paris till *all* these affairs are settled. Lepelletier must have told you that he has my book. I hope it will appear soon. I'm also working hard at some poems. You'll have some extracts from them one of these days, and I think they're really original; and I'm working at a play and a novel.[3]

On 21 June, when Blémont had not answered, Verlaine wrote again, and asked for news.

London is delightful, now [he reported]. As I think I told you, this neighbourhood is very gay ... In the north-west, the countryside is lovely. I often go there, when I don't go to the Reading Room at the British Museum, where they give you *every* possible book. In the evening, I exchange language lessons with *des Angliches*. I'm going to give PAID French lessons – which is no misfortune ...

I don't read French papers any more. But what harm in that?[4]

Four days later, the long-expected letter arrived from Blémont, and Verlaine sat down to answer it.

Here I am, a *tutor* [this on 25 June]. After some fifteen advertisements in the *Daily News, Echo, Daily Telegraph*, etc. . . . a 'pupil' has come to me. A two-hour lesson every day, three shillings [*sic*] the lesson. It's no Potosi [silvermine], but it's enough to pay for my lodging and my tobacco ... I'm still waiting for an answer to certain propositions, including one from the principal of a 'college' ... It would be a question of being an *usher*, fed, etc. . . . , quite well paid and a good deal of free time: four hours of lessons and 'supervision' a day – *et des Hégards*. I want to accept, *for I should soon learn English perhaps*. That would be for six months ...

I have a mass of plans in my head, but let me say that my main care at present is [*daily*] *bread* and learning English, especially pronunciation. Every evening – or nearly every evening – I have "tea-parties' at which I struggle to catch the subtlety of spoken English. I'm making slow progress. What efforts, and how slow! ...

My drama is written – in my head. So is my novel. So is my next book of poems, 'L'île' – 'la Vie au Grenier', 'Sous l'eau', 'le Sable', etc. . . . As soon as I've earned some daily bread and I know English *well* (practical English, because I read Swinburne almost fluently), I'll settle down to them. I have regained my courage and my health.[5]

Judging by these letters to Blémont, Verlaine was active, happy and confident. Lepelletier later published a letter which Verlaine wrote that June, and said that nothing in it suggested the events which were to follow. And yet, in his letter to Lepelletier, who – Rimbaud apart – was his closest friend, Verlaine confessed that giving French lessons 'killed the *ennui*, and that's a great point'.[6]

Verlaine was living on his earnings from his French lessons, 'about 100 or 150 francs a month', and on the money which his patient mother was sending him. It was not much, and perhaps financial straits created difficulties between him and Rimbaud. Lepelletier said later that there were frequent quarrels, 'caused by Rimbaud's despotic character and by Verlaine's nervous and capricious temperament. With the help of drink, these disputes soon grew bitter.'[7]

During his weeks at Roche, Rimbaud had made a deep and painful *examen de conscience*; and, in *Une Saison en Enfer*, he had begun to write his repudiation of his creed. 'There can be little doubt,' says his biographer, 'that in the portion of *Une Saison en Enfer* on which he was now engaged, he was liquidating all his previous dreams and ambitions, but he had not yet begun to formulate his positive beliefs for the future, nor his plans for his work.'[8] Rimbaud was profoundly unsettled. He had allowed himself, perhaps from love, or simply from compassion, to return to England with Verlaine. Now he resented his decision. He had wanted to escape from the relationship; now he felt that he was being dragged back into vice, drained of his vitality and will-power. He was repelled by Verlaine's weakness; and, to assert himself, he was driven into sadism. He would be cruel to Verlaine, he would humiliate him, and then, in a moment of remorse, he would try to make amends for his behaviour. In *L'Époux Infernal et la Vierge Folle*, Rimbaud describes how he tried to prepare Verlaine for their separation. They were both desperately unhappy.

At last – it was on 2 July – Verlaine could not bear the emotional strain any longer. Rimbaud later said that he had accused Verlaine of being lazy and of behaving badly to some friends. Verlaine said that Rimbaud had mocked him. Whatever the reason, Verlaine said nothing, but left the house at once.

When Rimbaud finally realised that Verlaine had gone, he was overcome by remorse. Verlaine must often have threatened to go back to Belgium, for Rimbaud knew instinctively, now, where to find him. He rushed to the docks, and arrived on the quayside just as the Antwerp boat was about to leave. Verlaine was on deck. But when Rimbaud made signs that he should disembark, he turned away.

On board the ship, Verlaine wrote once again to Mathilde. He told her that he had left Rimbaud for ever, and that he would blow his brains out if she did not come to him in Brussels. 'As I said,' wrote Mathilde in her memoirs, 'I did not open his letters, but, if I'd read them, I shouldn't have gone. You don't fall into the same trap a second time.'⁹

On 2 July, on board the ship, Verlaine had also written to Rimbaud. He said he could no longer bear their quarrels, and he was going to seek a reconciliation with his wife. If they were not reconciled within three days, he would shoot himself. He still, he said, loved Rimbaud greatly, and if he were obliged to kill himself his last thought would be for him. He asked Rimbaud to write to him, *poste restante*, in Brussels.

On 4 July, before this letter reached him, Rimbaud wrote to him in intense emotion. He protested his devotion, begged Verlaine's forgiveness, and implored him to return to London, or to send for him. Possibly, in the correspondence which Mathilde destroyed, there were letters comparable to this; but nothing else, in Rimbaud's published work, testifies so clearly to the intensity of his relationship.¹⁰ Then came Verlaine's letter about a reconciliation, and his threat to kill himself. Rimbaud wrote again, and this time in much more sober mood. He brushed aside the threat of suicide, and the possibility of Mathilde's return. But he still wanted to continue his life with Verlaine. 'Do you imagine,' he asked, 'that your life with others will be happier than it is with me? *Think it over.* Of course it won't be happier. You're only free with me, and as I promise I'll be very nice in future, that I'm sorry for all the wrong I've done, that I'm now clear in my mind, that I do love you: if you won't come back or let me join you, you're committing a crime, and *you will repent it* . . . Remember what you were before you knew me.' Rimbaud added that he was going to Paris as soon as he could, and that he would have to sell Verlaine's clothes, in order to raise money. If Mathilde returned, he would not compromise him by writing again; but if Verlaine followed his true instincts, he would come back to him. 'The only real thing is: come back again,' added Rimbaud. 'I want to be with you. I love you.'[11]

Verlaine himself had reached Brussels in a highly emotional state; and, seeking, perhaps, to touch his wife, he had gone to the Hôtel Liégeois, where, almost a year ago, they had been reconciled. He had written to his mother, giving her his address, and warning her that he would shoot himself if Mathilde did not return to him. A few months earlier Mme Verlaine had rushed to London to rescue him from death; now she hurried to Brussels to prevent his suicide. Verlaine was behaving once again like a maladjusted adolescent. He sent a characteristic announcement to Lepelletier: 'I'm going to kill myself! But no-one must know until the thing is done.' He also wrote to Mme Rimbaud, telling her of his intended suicide. Mme Rimbaud showed excellent sense and unexpected feeling. She told him that his suicide would not only be cowardice, it would be infamy.[12]

In the meantime – as Rimbaud had predicted – Verlaine had abandoned the thought of suicide. The time limit he had set Mathilde had now expired, and she had not come. He had presumably received both Rimbaud's letters. He sent him a telegram, and summoned him to Brussels. Lepelletier says that he begged Rimbaud's forgiveness and begged him to come and live with him again. Rimbaud came to Brussels on 8 July.

He found Verlaine with his mother. Verlaine – as Rimbaud later said – had no definite plans, but he did not want to stay in Belgium, because he felt he would have no future there. Rimbaud did not want to return to London, as Verlaine suggested, because their abrupt departure had made such a bad impression on their friends. He still wanted to go to Paris – as he had mentioned in his letter.

Lepelletier declared that Rimbaud had no intention of resuming the relationship, and that he simply came to Brussels to demand the money to stay in Paris.[13] This interpretation seems demonstrably untrue. Rimbaud would have not come from London to Brussels merely to extort money. If he had really wanted to end his relationship with Verlaine, he would not have answered his summons. The truth is much more likely to be found in his own statement (which Lepelletier discounted).

I determined to return to Paris. At one moment, Verlaine declared his intention of coming back with me, to take his revenge on his wife and his parents-in-law; the next moment, he was refusing to come back with me, because Paris had too many unhappy memories for him. He was in a state of great exaltation; but he insisted vehemently that I should stay with him. Sometimes he was desperate, sometimes he was furious; there was no coherence in his ideas. On Wednesday evening, he drank excessively ... On Thursday morning, he went out at six, and he did not come back until about noon. He was drunk again; he showed me a revolver he had bought, and when I asked what he thought he'd do with it, he replied, jokingly: 'It's for you and me and everyone!' He was very over-excited.

While we were together in our room, he went downstairs again, several times, to drink; he still wanted to stop me from going back to Paris. I remained resolute, I even asked his mother to give me my fare ...[14]

It is thought that Rimbaud meant to catch the mail train which left Brussels at 3.40. It was the last Paris train of the day.[15]

I can see us again in Brussels [Verlaine himself told Adolphe Retté, in 1892]. We were in that squalid hotel in the rue Pachecho ... I was sitting on the end of the bed. He was standing near the door, with folded arms, his whole attitude one of defiance ... Oh, the wickedness, the cruel flame in his eyes! They were the eyes of a fallen archangel! I had said everything I could to make him stay with me. But he wanted to go, and I felt that nothing would make him alter his decision ...[16]

When, said Rimbaud, he finally showed his determination to go, Verlaine locked the door, and sat down on a chair against it, to bar his way.

I was standing with my back to the opposite wall [Rimbaud continued]. Then he said to me something like: 'That's for you, as you're going!' He aimed at me, and fired a shot which struck my left wrist; the first shot was almost immediately followed by a second, but, this time, the weapon was pointing towards the floor.

Verlaine at once expressed the most acute despair at what he had done; he rushed into the adjoining room, which was occupied by his mother, and threw himself on to the bed. He was like a madman, he put his revolver into my hands and he told me to shoot him through the head.[17]

The last train to Paris had long since gone. At about five o'clock, Verlaine and his mother accompanied Rimbaud to the hospital, to have his wound dressed.

When we came back to the hotel [Rimbaud went on], Verlaine and his mother suggested that I should stay with them, so that they could look after me, or that I should go back to the hospital till I was completely cured. Since the injury did not seem at all serious to me, I said that I would go back to France that evening, to my mother's, at Charleville. This news cast Verlaine into despair once again. His mother gave me 20 francs for the journey, and they went out with me to take me to the Gare du Midi.

Verlaine was like a madman: he did all he could to keep me; he also had his hand constantly in his pocket, where he kept his revolver. When we got to the place Rouppe, he went on a few steps ahead, and then he turned round and came towards me. His attitude made me afraid that he was going to abandon himself to some new excess. I turned round and fled. It was then that I asked an *agent de police* to arrest him.[18]

Verlaine was arrested on the afternoon of 10 July 1873. Mme Verlaine later said in her evidence that he had not threatened Rimbaud; but Rimbaud might have been forgiven for thinking that his life was in danger. That evening, at the police station at the Hôtel de Ville, he made his first statement, and, as a result, Verlaine was taken to L'Amigo prison, and then to the Prison des Petits-Carmes. The charge – substantiated by the revolver which Verlaine was carrying – was, at first, a charge of attempted murder.

When Rimbaud had made his statement, he returned to hospital. The bullet could not be removed from his wrist, because he was still too feverish, and the doctor considered that he was unfit to give evidence in court. On 12 July, he therefore made his statement in hospital. Perhaps the Mautés' lawyer had already been in touch with the authorities, for, at the end of his statement, Rimbaud was asked if Mathilde had objected to his intimacy with Verlaine. 'Yes,' he replied, 'she even accuses us of an unnatural relationship, but I can't be bothered to deny such calumnies.'[19]

On 17 July, the bullet was extracted from Rimbaud's wrist, and, two days later, he left hospital. When he came out, he went to the law courts and said that he did not wish to bring a charge against Verlaine, he was convinced that the shooting had been an accident; Verlaine had been in no condition to know what he was doing. The charge was reduced to one of criminal assault, but it could not now be entirely dismissed, because the machinery of the law had been set in motion.

On 8 August, when the case was heard, Verlaine's medical report was read in court. It was irrelevant to the charge, and modern doctors do not consider that the evidence produced was reliable. However, the prison doctors said that Verlaine showed signs of recent active and passive sodomy. It was this report, not the actual shooting, or Rimbaud's wound (which was far from serious) which led the judge to impose the maximum penalty. Verlaine was sentenced to a fine of two hundred francs, and to two years' hard labour.

PART FOUR

Mes Prisons

(1873–5)

23

RIMBAUD had left hospital on 19 July; but he had now spent the twenty francs which Mme Verlaine had given him, and he was obliged to walk home to Roche. His arm was in a sling, his face was worn, and at the first expression of sympathy he burst into tears. Since he found his mother unexpectedly gentle, he told her of his unhappiness, and of his plans for finishing his book. It was his last hope in literature.

Mme Rimbaud had moments of nobility. She promised to help him, financially, to publish his work, and she promised to leave him in peace until it was finished. The following month, Rimbaud finished *Une Saison en Enfer*.[1]

On 21 August the Prefect of Police in Paris sent a report to Brussels about Verlaine's Communard sympathies, and about his 'shameful passion for the aforementioned Rimbaud'. On 27 August, Verlaine's appeal was naturally rejected, and his sentence was confirmed by the Cour de Brabant.[2]

Some days before the shooting he had written to Victor Hugo, asking him to see Mathilde, and to intercede in his favour. 'It was a clever idea,' Mathilde said, acidly. One day, when she called on Hugo, he told her that he had just received a letter from Verlaine, 'asking him to intercede for him so that I would resume our life together'. Mathilde's reply was to tell Victor Hugo of her

sufferings; and – so she maintained – she showed him the note
which Verlaine had sent her after their last meeting. 'Misérable
fée carotte, princesse souris . . .' Hugo replied, pontifically, that
Mathilde had done her duty, that he would always be glad to see
her, and that she would never meet Verlaine at his house.[3]

However, he had already answered Verlaine's letter.

My poor poet,
    I shall see your charming wife and speak to her in your favour in the
name of your little boy. *Courage et revenez au vrai.*

VICTOR HUGO.[4]

It has been suggested that, in the last phrase, Hugo urged Verlaine
to return to heterosexual love.[5]

Even before the shooting in Brussels, there had been no question
of a reconciliation; but Hugo's interest brought Verlaine an
unexpected benefit. He was summoned by the governor of les
Petits-Carmes, who handed him the letter with the comment:
'I've just read this note and I'm astonished to see you here, if you
have such correspondents.' Mme Verlaine had already asked permission for her son to be *à la pistole* – to have a separate room in
the prison. 'On the strength of this letter,' the governor continued,
'I shall authorise this at once.'[6]

Verlaine had been sleeping in a hammock, living on barley
mash and water. Now he was given a bed and – thanks to a
financial arrangement – his food and a little drink were brought
to him from outside. The imprisonment itself remained as
rigorous as ever. His cell was opened for an hour a day so that he
could take his solitary exercise in the yard. At the bottom of the
yard, on the other side of the wall, he used to see 'the voluptuous,
trembling leaves on the top of some tall poplar in a neighbouring
square or boulevard. At the same time,' he recalled, 'I used to
hear the distant, muffled sounds of gaiety.' These symbols of
nature, of everyday life across the prison wall, seemed to be the
symbols of his whole misguided youth. They stirred the mood
of melancholy which, since the days of 'Chanson d'automne,' he
had always known how to express.

Le ciel est, par-dessus le toit,
    Si bleu, si calme!
Un arbre, par-dessus le toit
    Berce sa palme.

La cloche dans le ciel qu'on voit
    Doucement tinte.
Un oiseau sur l'arbre qu'on voit
    Chante sa plainte.

Mon Dieu, mon Dieu, la vie est là,
    Simple et tranquille.
Cette paisible rumeur-là
    Vient de la ville.

– Qu'as-tu fait, ô toi que voilà
    Pleurant sans cesse,
Dis, qu'as-tu fait, toi que voilà,
    De ta jeunesse?[7]

In *Mes Prisons*, published twenty years later, Verlaine was to recall his Belgian imprisonment almost with affection; indeed, he told Byvanck, the Dutch writer, that it was 'a real haven, after all the sufferings of the past.'[8] He felt the claustrophobia of the prisoner, he was oppressed by the unremitting monotony of existence. But in *Mes Prisons*, in his poems, in his correspondence, there were no acute regrets for Rimbaud; nor did he constantly lament Mathilde. He seems to have been intensely relieved to find his escape from the violent emotional problems, the ever-present temptations, of the world. He had always needed to be ruled; and now an inevitable discipline was imposed on him. He was sheltered, given adequate food and strictly limited drink; he was forced to accept an austere routine. In the calm and austerity of his prison life, he was also free to turn in upon himself, to examine his emotions, to question his beliefs, and to express and lose himself in poetry.

On 11 July, the day after the Brussels drama, he had written 'Impression Fausse', which would later appear in *Parallèlement*. It was a strangely lyrical impression of his first night in prison, and it attests his astonishing duality. Here, within a few hours of his shooting Rimbaud, when the prison gates had closed on him, he could lose himself in a poem touched by gaiety and humour. In July, in les Petits-Carmes, he had also written the lines 'Au lecteur', which would one day appear in *Parallèlement* as 'Prologue d'un livre ...'

> J'ai perdu ma vie et je sais bien
> Que tout blâme sur moi s'en va fondre:
> À cela je ne puis que répondre:
> Que je suis né Saturnien ...[9]

The same month, in 'Autre,' Verlaine described his fellow-prisoners at their exercise in the torrid heat. In July he also wrote 'Sur les eaux' (later to appear in *Sagesse*); and in August he set down the poem which, in later life, he would choose to recite to his admirers.

Gaspard Hauser was a youth of fifteen or sixteen when, in 1828, he had been discovered wandering in the streets of Nuremberg. He had known nothing of his origins; doctors said that he seemed to have been imprisoned throughout his childhood, and to have been kept in a state which bordered on imbecility. He was adopted and cared for, but it soon became evident that he had some mysterious enemy. After two attempts at suicide, he was murdered in 1833. Verlaine, *le poète saturnien*, was naturally drawn to this hero of misfortune. Like Gaspard, he sometimes felt that he had been born too late or too soon; he, too, questioned his purpose in the world.

> Je suis venu, calme orphelin,
> Riche de mes seuls yeux tranquilles,
> Vers les hommes des grandes villes:
> Ils ne m'ont pas trouvé malin.
>
> À vingt ans un trouble nouveau
> Sous le nom d'amoureuses flammes
> M'a fait trouver belles les femmes:
> Elles ne m'ont pas trouvé beau.

> Bien que sans patrie et sans roi
> Et très brave ne l'étant guère,
> J'ai voulu mourir à la guerre:
> La mort n'a pas voulu de moi.
>
> Suis-je né trop tôt ou trop tard?
> Qu'est-ce que je fais en ce monde?
> Ô vous tous, ma peine est profonde:
> Priez pour le pauvre Gaspard![10]

Verlaine, like Gaspard, beat his head against the bars of his life; and yet it was his irregular life, marked by catastrophes and miseries, which gradually distinguished him as a poet. Now, in August, in les Petits-Carmes, he made a remarkable experiment in prosody. 'Crimen Amoris' was written in lines of eleven syllables, and (as Gide was to note in his *Journal*), it was curiously perfect.[11] Forty years after it was written, it would inspire Debussy. But the poem also had its personal meaning. Mankind had rebuked Verlaine for his acts of love; in 'Crimen Amoris', the wicked angel of sixteen – the transfigured Rimbaud – is rebuked, for his god-like ambition, by God Himself.

> ... Or le plus beau d'entre tous ces mauvais anges
> Avait seize ans sous sa couronne de fleurs.
> Les bras croisés sur les colliers et les franges,
> Il rêve, l'œil plein de flammes et de pleurs ...
>
> Qu'est-ce qu'il dit de sa voix profonde et tendre
> Qui se marie au claquement du feu
> Et que la lune est extatique d'entendre?
> 'Oh! je serai celui-là qui créera Dieu!' ...
>
> Il dit tout bas une espèce de prière,
> Les yeux au ciel où le feu monte en léchant ...
> Quand retentit un affreux coup de tonnerre
> Et c'est la fin de l'allégresse et du chant.[12]

The search for god-like status had ended in retribution and failure. The superb, audacious quest on which Rimbaud and Verlaine had embarked, some two years earlier, had ended in disaster;

and they acknowledged their failure at the same moment. Verlaine wrote 'Crimen Amoris' in the month when Rimbaud finished *Une Saison en Enfer*, and recognised the futility of his ambition to be a seer or a demi-god. 'Moi! moi qui me suis dit mage ou ange,' wrote Rimbaud, 'dispensé de toute morale, je suis rendu au sol, avec un devoir à chercher, et la réalité rugueuse à étreindre! Paysan!'[13]

'Crimen Amoris' was followed, in August, by 'L'Impénitence finale' (later to appear in *Jadis et Naguère*). For the first time since 'La Mort de Philippe II', in *Poèmes saturniens*, Verlaine wrote a dramatic verse narrative. But while the earlier poem had been a simple essay in the Hugolian style, which might have found a place in *La Légende des siècles*, 'L'Impénitence finale', a mediocre poem, continued the theme of 'Crimen Amoris', and it had its relevance to Verlaine's life. The Marquise Osine, unfaithful to her husband, had a vision of the sorrowing Christ; and then, on her death-bed, she dreamed that Christ had rejected her prayers. 'La Grâce', composed at about the same time, is again an indifferent poem, with an uncomfortable air of Romantic melodrama. The errant Comtesse is addressed by a death's-head which assumes the voice of her late husband, and, indeed, the voice of conscience. She begs divine pardon for her sins, and asks God to kill her in sign of forgiveness. Her prayer is immediately answered. In 'Don Juan pipé', also written in August, Don Juan blasphemes and is turned to a figure of ice.

September brought 'Un Pouacre', a poem in a more conventional Verlainian style, in which Verlaine looked back, regretfully, on his past:

> Avec les yeux d'une tête de mort
> Que la lune encore décharne
> Tout mon passé, disons tout mon remord
> Ricane à travers ma lucarne.
>
> Avec la voix d'un vieillard très cassé,
> Comme l'on n'en voit qu'au théâtre,
> Tout mon remords, disons tout mon passé
> Fredonne un tralala folâtre . . .[14]

According to the Barthou manuscripts, it was also in Brussels, in September, that Verlaine wrote his 'Almanach pour l'année passée'; however, when he sent Lepelletier these poems, at the end of the year, he was writing from Mons, and he described them as 'a few poems recently written here'. He had changed the title to 'Mon Almanach pour 1874'. Perhaps the actual dating is an academic point; perhaps it is enough to say that three of the four poems reflect the poet's growing melancholy. As 'Chanson d'Automne' had suggested, in his first book, autumn had always been the season most in accord with Verlaine's temperament. At the time of his *Poèmes saturniens* his melancholy had perhaps been a general mood, with no one obvious cause. Now, in 'Automne' (which would appear, as 'Vendanges', in *Jadis et Naguère*), his melancholy could be explained all too clearly.

> Les choses qui chantent dans la tête
> Alors que la mémoire est absente,
> Écoutez! c'est notre sang qui chante . . .
> Ô musique lointaine et discrète!
>
> Écoutez! c'est notre sang qui pleure
> Alors que notre âme s'est enfuie
> D'une voix jusqu'alors inouïe
> Et qui va se taire tout à l'heure . . .[15]

On 28 September, Verlaine wrote to Lepelletier. It was now more than eleven weeks since he had first been committed to prison, and his imprisonment had begun to weigh upon him. Early in September his mother, who had stayed on in Brussels, returned to France, and he felt oppressively alone.

My dear friend [he wrote to Lepelletier],

As soon as you get this letter, would you answer by return of post? You'll understand how much it means to me. I haven't had any visits for three weeks, as my mother's gone, and I've only had one letter from her since . . . Tell me a little about Paris, and about our friends, and, if you have news of it, about the rue Nicolet. Have the Paris papers talked about this wretched affair, by any chance? Is Victor Hugo in Paris? Would you send me his address?

My mother must have told you how much importance I attach to the rapid printing and publication of my little book [*Romances sans paroles*]. So, if you can't look after it, give the manuscript back to my mother with the notes I sent you, so that she can busy herself with it at once.

I have hundreds of literary plans: especially in the theatre, because, as soon as I get out, I mean to bestir myself until I really earn money with *my pen* . . .

I don't know when I'm leaving here. It may be at any moment. That is why you must write to me very quickly . . . I am dreadfully unhappy – I've been so, especially, for the last fortnight. And my health isn't marvellous; I sometimes have terrible headaches and I'm more nervous than ever. Don't say anything about this to my mother, please, and if you see her before I've written to her, tell her that you've heard from me and that I'm well.[16]

One more poem belongs to Verlaine's imprisonment at les Petits-Carmes. This is 'Kaléidoscope', which was later to appear in *Jadis et Naguère*. As the title suggests, it is a collection of impressions, with no logical connection. Here, before Proust, Verlaine experiences those rare, mysterious, transient moments which have more savour than the actual events which they revive. The setting of the poem cannot be identified; there are elements of London, elements of Paris. In the last verse, Verlaine destroys any lingering vestige of reality, and leaves the whole poem, suspended, in a dream. Like certain poems by Rimbaud, 'Kaléidoscope' catches a world beyond the world. It is in this sort of poem that Verlaine shows the extent of his powers.

> Dans une rue, au cœur d'une ville de rêve,
> Ce sera comme quand on a déjà vécu:
> Un instant à la fois très vague et très aigu . . .
> Ô ce soleil parmi la brume qui se lève!
>
> Ô ce cri sur la mer, cette voix dans les bois!
> Ce sera comme quand on ignore des causes:
> Un lent réveil après bien de métempsychoses:
> Les choses seront plus les mêmes qu'autrefois
>
> Dans cette rue, au cœur de la ville magique
> Où des orgues moudront des gigues dans les soirs,

Où les cafés auront des chats sur les dressoirs,
Et que traverseront des bandes de musique.

Ce sera si fatal qu'on en croira mourir:
Des larmes ruisselant douces le long des joues,
Des rires sanglotés dans le fracas des roues,
Des invocations à la mort de venir,

Des mots anciens comme un bouquet de fleurs fanées!
Les bruits aigres des bals publics arriveront,
Et des veuves avec du cuivre après leur front,
Paysannes, fendront la foule des traînées

Qui flânent là, causant avec d'affreux moutards
Et des vieux sans sourcils que la dartre enfarine,
Cependant qu'à deux pas, dans des senteurs d'urine,
Quelque fête publique enverra des pétards.

Ce sera comme quand on rêve et qu'on s'éveille!
Et que l'on se rendort et que l'on rêve encor
De la même féerie et du même décor,
L'été, dans l'herbe, au bruit moiré d'un vol d'abeille.[17]

'Kaléidoscope' was written in prison in Brussels in October 1873. That month, Verlaine was transferred to Mons, where he was to serve the rest of his sentence. If we are to believe *Mes Prisons*, his first impression of his new jail was far from unhappy. It was, he wrote, 'the prettiest possible thing. Outside, it is pale red brick – almost pink; inside . . . it is whitewashed and tarred, with sober architecture of iron and steel.' In 1875, as a free man, in the serenity of Lincolnshire, he would write a poem in gratitude for his incarceration. 'J'ai naguère habité le meilleur des châteaux . . .' He would look back, almost with regret, on the long months of silence, 'la paix réelle et respectable', on the very austerity of his cell, on the days which he had devoted to study and to prayer.

C'était la liberté (la seule!) sans ses charges,
C'était la dignité dans la sécurité!
Ô lieu presque aussitôt regretté que quitté,
Château, château magique où mon âme s'est faite.[18]

When Verlaine entered the prison at Mons, his prison clothes were brought to him: a leather cap, a rough greenish suit, and a pair of clogs. He was taken to an ordinary cell, until he had been permitted, again, to serve his sentence *à la pistole*. Then the prison barber shaved him according to regulations.

Some ten days later, he became a prisoner *à la pistole*. He was moved to another part of the jail, where he had the luxury of a bed. He asked for books, and he was allowed a whole library of his own. 'I had dictionaries, classics, a Shakespeare in English, which I read from beginning to end (just think how much time I had!). I read the valuable notes of Johnson, and all the English, German and other commentators: they helped me to understand the great poet properly – though Shakespeare never made me forget Racine, any more than Fénelon or La Fontaine.'[19]

Verlaine was not only reading poetry, he was writing it. In the month of his arrival he wrote 'Le Bon Alchimiste' (later known as 'Images d'un Sou'). At the end of October, he wrote 'Réversibilités'. This was the poignant poem in which he contrasted freedom and imprisonment, and meditated on the monotony of prison life. In this life, the repetition of daily tasks seemed to have an accelerated rhythm, while the hours themselves passed more slowly.

Dear friend [he told Lepelletier on 22 November],

This is a prayer, an urgent prayer: *write to me* from time to time. Would you do so every fortnight or three weeks? I hope it isn't too much . . . I go out for an hour a day, during which I can smoke. All the rest of the time it's solitary confinement, in the strictest sense of the word . . . My health is still poor, and the courage which always sustained me at the end of my time in Brussels looks like deserting me now, when I need it more than ever. They are very good to me and I am as well as possible. But my poor head is so empty, so echoing, still – so to speak – with all my recent griefs and misfortunes, that I haven't yet been able to acquire that kind of somnolence which seems to be the *ultimum solatium* of the prisoner. And so I need people to remember me a little, *on the other side of the wall*, and to show me that they do.

When will the little book appear?[20]

The 'little book' was *Romances sans paroles*, the book which

Rimbaud had so largely inspired. It was to appear in unexpected fashion. Lepelletier had been working for a republican paper, which had been suppressed by the military governor of Paris for a so-called tendentious article. The editor of the paper had determined to continue publication outside the governor's jurisdiction, and Lepelletier was sent to take charge of the paper at Sens. There he printed *Romances sans paroles* on the presses of *Le Suffrage universel*.[21]

He sent a sample page to Verlaine. On 24 November, Verlaine approved it, gratefully; but he could not give it all his attention. He was now obsessed by the behaviour of his wife and son and the Mautés, and, as Lepelletier said, 'he was the captive of memory and of his old love, even more than the captive of his jailers.' It was extraordinary that he could still harbour illusions about his wife's feelings; but the hope of regaining his lost happiness had not, even now, disappeared.

Would you believe that one of my griefs is *still* my wife [he asked]? It's extraordinary how . . . I pity her, with all my heart, for everything that happens: for knowing her to be there, in those unworthy surroundings, deprived of the only person who understood her at all, I mean *myself*. They have done so much, they have made her do so much, that she is now, as it were, 'on her honour' to persist in her plans, and to rot. Deep down, I'm sure, she is fretting herself away with grief and perhaps remorse . . . She would like to come back, and she can't – even though her father's house is now a hell to her![22]

Verlaine was all too far from the truth. Mathilde herself, in her memoirs, denied Lepelletier's suggestion that her family had contributed to Verlaine's conviction.

We were all trying to forget him; we talked about him as little as possible, indeed so little that my demand for a separation stayed in the files for a year, and no-one tried to bring it out.

When Me Guyot-Sionnest heard of Verlaine's conviction, he took advantage of the occasion to bring the affair to a quick conclusion. He asked Brussels for the whole dossier; he was sent not only Rimbaud's statement, the charge and the verdict, but something which [Lepelletier] doesn't mention, probably because he has never known of its existence.

As for me, I only knew of it after my father's death, and I have hidden it from everyone.[23]

This document was undoubtedly the medical report on Verlaine.

We all wanted to avoid a scandal [continued Mathilde]. Since divorce did not exist, I had to go on bearing the name of the man from whom I was separated; and then, I had a son. Verlaine's name was already known, and my father was afraid that it would attract the Press to the hearing; and so my lawyer merely said that his client had been the victim of her husband's violence and desertion. There was no question at all of the scabrous comments which some of his friends had made about him. My lawyer asked only to show the judges the horrible document in question. It was not read aloud at the hearing, but it did determine the harsh conditions of the separation.

After Verlaine's conviction, the silence about him was even more complete. As for me, oblivion gradually came to me . . .[24]

On 24 April 1874, with no official mention of Rimbaud, Mathilde obtained her judicial separation, and she was given custody of her child. The prison governor took a copy of the decree to Verlaine in his cell at Mons. Verlaine recorded that he wept; an hour or two later, he asked that the prison chaplain should come to him.

24

There is no doubt that Verlaine turned, in all honesty, to religion. He was not, in the strict sense, an intellectual, and – though he now asked for religious books, and discussed theological points with the chaplain – his return to Catholicism was not primarily made from intellectual conviction. It was made, above all, from emotional need. In his isolation and fear, he felt a need to return to the comfort and security of his beginnings.

I have nothing to say to anyone about my conversion [he would tell Jules Claretie, years later]. It's my personal affair, my private happiness, the belated flower of my soul. I alone must watch over it, and cultivate it with love and care if I want to see it grow into autumn fruit.

But, speaking generally, what is surprising if a man returns to the faith of his childhood, to the religion of his ancestors, of his country, to the God of Whom his mother taught him, the God in Whose arms his father died? . . .[1]

Verlaine – like many prisoners – sought comfort in religion. He needed the sense of a constant spiritual presence, of a perpetual guide, of a God Who would raise him from his state of misery.

If Jesus had been a man [he explained, towards the end of his life], He could not do anything for me. How can people represent Him like that? Like a bigger and better [General] Boulanger? What would that mean to me? If I am to be saved from my misery, I need a God, not a person who once lived on earth, a person whose life can be reconstructed with the help of documents . . . Oh, the fools who think that Jesus is contained within a few wretched little books! Do they believe, then, that Christianity has derived from the Gospels? . . . No, no, it's the poor little working-class women who have faithfully kept the memories of the Passion and the Cross; it is Nero, maker of martyrs, who saved belief in Christ and made it into a thing of grief and blood. For me, Jesus is The Crucified. He is my God because He suffered, because He suffers still. I see Him before my eyes, covered with dreadful wounds, sweating in His final agony, as the peasant women of Judea actually saw Him.[2]

Verlaine's need of God was that of the simple, humble folk. His religion was primitive. He was to speak of himself – with some truth – as a medieval Catholic; and George Moore would declare that 'he abandoned himself to the Church as a child to a fairy-tale'.[3] Verlaine could not have become a Jansenist or a Protestant; he needed the richness, the spiritual and emotional release of Catholic belief and ritual. 'How I hate everything Jansenist or Protestant – everything mean! To want to belittle human nature, to take away from me the supreme delight of communion! The communion by which I partake of the body of God! Whoever thinks that my faith is not sincere does not know the ecstasy of receiving the very flesh of the Lord into one's body. For me, it's a dizzying happiness: a physical emotion.'[4] Verlaine felt cleansed by religion. 'I really had faith,' he said, 'during the years I spent away from Paris, after my misfortune. I felt I was pure, I was chaste, I was happy and well. No evil thoughts crossed my mind. I was calm in spirit, and the feeling was almost physical. I felt as if I was always wearing clean new linen.'[5] He felt at peace within himself. He felt he could shed his past: and, now that his marriage was destroyed and Rimbaud had gone, he could give his love to God, Who would not fail him.

Not for a long time [wrote Edmond Pilon] have I known a man who loved as much as Verlaine. This love, in him, rose gradually, like an initiation; after he had shown his kindness and passion for human beings, his soul ascended, slowly, cleansed and purified, towards God. I do not say that his prayers go beyond the prayers of Lamartine – which were most sincere – but I think that they have all the more merit, because Verlaine had a deeper love of humankind before he reached the state of superior grace.[6]

Such conviction was not always shared. Lepelletier remained cynical about Verlaine's conversion. In his biography of Verlaine, he was prepared, in the face of all the evidence, to proclaim the innocence of his relations with Rimbaud. But, even in the interest of public approval, he could not bring himself to believe in his return to religion.

Was this conversion deep and real? I don't believe it was . . . He was not converted by force of examination, by persuasion, by the appearance of evidence, but only by the violence of a stormy life, by the moral and material tempest in the heart of which he found himself borne away. During the hurricane, he invoked the saint. When the danger passed, he felt the proverb had to be verified.[7]

Lepelletier recalled that Verlaine, like everyone else, had made his first communion at the lycée, but that his religion had been superficial. As a young man he had found religious practice tedious, and he had disdained and denied the faith. He and Lepelletier had read the same materialistic books; they had come to believe that the supernatural did not exist, and that there was no tutelary providence. Verlaine, at the age of twenty, had been a rational atheist. But heredity and early education had left religiosity in his soul; and it was 'this old sediment' which, said Lepelletier, had suddenly caught fire. Over Verlaine's bed, in the prison cell, were the regulation copper crucifix, and a lithograph of the Sacré-Cœur, the heart that bled and shone. These, too, said Lepelletier, had influenced his conversion. And he made a much more cynical suggestion. 'Verlaine did not see his conversion only as a renewal of his soul . . . He thought that, in Catholic feeling, he might find a sort of renewal of poetry.'[8]

Verlaine was aware of Lepelletier's lack of sympathy. He wrote to him late in August, about the state of his soul, but he did not send the letter. Instead, on 8 September, he wrote, assuring him that 'one has to have gone through all that I have suffered for the past three years . . . to know what wonderful consolation, reason and logic there are in this religion.'[9] In the same letter (Lepelletier did not quote them in his book) were ten sonnets which would later appear in *Sagesse*. They were Verlaine's dialogue with Christ. Christ tells Verlaine that he must love Him, and Him alone, for He had loved men even unto death. Verlaine pleads that he had sought Him and could not find Him, and that he is unworthy to worship Him. Christ insists that the poet should love Him – but love Him of his own free will. Verlaine hesitates; Christ assures him that there is a place for him in Heaven, if he only wishes to deserve it.

> Et pour récompenser ton zèle en ces devoirs
> Si doux qu'ils sont encor d'ineffables délices,
> Je te ferai goûter sur terre mes prémices,
> La paix du cœur, l'amour d'être pauvre, et mes soirs
>
> Mystiques, quand l'esprit s'ouvre aux calmes espoirs
> Et croit boire, suivant ma promesse, au Calice
> Éternel, et qu'au ciel pieux la lune glisse,
> Et que sonnent les Angélus roses et noirs,
>
> En attendant l'assomption dans ma lumière,
> L'éveil sans fin dans ma charité coutumière,
> La musique de mes louanges à jamais,
>
> Et l'extase perpétuelle et la science,
> Et d'être en moi parmi l'aimable irradiance
> De tes souffrances, enfin miennes, – que j'aimais![10]

Verlaine felt the terror and the joy of being chosen by Christ, and he finally accepted in ecstasy.

Lepelletier maintained that, at this moment in his life, Verlaine abandoned objective poetry, and became a subjective, intimate poet. This statement is clearly untrue; Verlaine had expressed certain personal moods in *Poèmes saturniens*, he had recorded his love of Mathilde in *La Bonne Chanson*, and his odyssey with Rimbaud in *Romances sans paroles*. He would still write poems which bore no relation to himself. What is interesting is the diversity of his inspiration at Mons. The Barthou manuscripts show that in April he wrote his famous 'Art poétique': 'De la musique avant toute chose. . . .' In June and July he wrote 'Via dolorosa' (which would appear, untitled, in *Sagesse*); in August he wrote the banal and vulgar 'Amoureuse du Diable' (to be published in *Jadis et Naguère*). In October followed the twenty-two verses of his hymn to the Virgin: 'Bouquet à Marie'.

As Lepelletier emphasises, Verlaine's conversion was not his only emotional experience. He also felt a sensual exacerbation, which was the result of continence. It was intensified by cerebral passions. 'It disturbed his poetry, which until then had been somewhat chaste, objective and impersonal. He had fits of lyric eroticism of which his later books retain the trace.'[11] It was true that, in his solitude, Verlaine at times indulged in erotic dreams; but they were not necessarily dreams of conjugal passion. The sonnet later published as 'Le Poète et la Muse' is dated from Mons in 1874; but its title is 'A propos d'une chambre, rue Campagne-Première, à Paris, en janvier 1872'. This was the room which Verlaine had rented that month for Rimbaud, the attic where he and Rimbaud had lived together. The 'Muse' of the published title was no doubt the attic itself, personified as an inspiration.

> La chambre, as-tu gardé leurs spectres ridicules,
> Ô pleine de jour sale et de bruits d'araignées?
> La chambre, as-tu gardé leurs formes désignées
> Par ces crasses au mur et par quelles virgules?
>
> Ah fi! Pourtant, chambre en garni qui te recules
> En ce sec jeu d'optique aux mines renfrognées

Du souvenir de trop de choses destinées,
Comme ils ont donc regret aux nuits, aux nuits d'Hercules!

Qu'on l'entende comme on voudra, ce n'est pas ça:
Vous ne comprenez rien aux choses, bonnes gens.
Je vous dis que ce n'est pas ce que l'on pensa.

Seule, ô chambre qui fuis en cônes affligeants,
Seule, tu sais! mais sans doute combien de nuits
De noce auront dévirginé leurs nuits, depuis![12]

Verlaine was fiercely sensual; his need to express his sensuality can only have been intensified by his months of solitary confinement. It was natural that he should recall his passionate past and ease his present longings in poetry. His physical lust, for men or for women, did not invalidate his spiritual needs, or his religious conversion. The truth, which Lepelletier failed to understand, was that Verlaine was two men simultaneously – or, to use his own word, *parallèlement*. Rémy de Gourmont said, perceptively: 'He always sings the same love-song, whether his love is a love of a woman or of angels, and it is almost the same sensuality.'[13]

If Verlaine's physical lust was real, so also was his yearning for religion; and if Verlaine's religion was primitive and childlike, that did not make it less honest, or less satisfying. 'Some people have considered his conversion as hypocrisy,' wrote his former wife. 'I am convinced that it was quite sincere.'[14] If Verlaine's unsophisticated religion made him feel purified, if it had a profound and long-lasting effect on his life, if it changed him from an intellectual atheist to a practising Catholic, even a lapsed Catholic, then his conversion was genuine. Verlaine was incapable of theological argument, but perhaps this is the least important part of religion. What mattered was the effect of religion on himself.

Yet though his conversion was honest, every creative artist has a double view of experience. He has his human awareness of life; he also has his artistic sense of it. He can be genuinely sad, but he can see his sadness as a fitting subject for a sonnet. He can instinctively admire a view, but he can also see it as a composition for a canvas. Lepelletier failed to recognise the artist's duality.

Verlaine did not embrace Catholicism as a promising new source of poetry. He was converted, and he found it natural to write about his religious experience. Just as he had charted the progress of his love for Mathilde, so he was now recording his spiritual odyssey. It was an honest personal record, but, since he was a poet, he strove for literary perfection. His emotions were spontaneous, but he kept his judgment.

In prison at Mons, he made a full confession, and received benediction. On 15 August, the Feast of the Assumption, he was allowed to take communion. It gave him a feeling of complete renewal. Imprisonment had sobered him, made him more tranquil and perhaps more tolerant; now he was filled with goodwill to all mankind. Suddenly, he felt innocent; and this vast sense of relief, this elating sense of innocence, remained with him until he was freed.

There had been various appeals to mitigate his sentence. Lepelletier maintained that these had all been ignored. Verlaine should have had a maximum sentence of a few days' imprisonment. If he was released after serving eighteen months, instead of staying in prison for two years, that was only because the law allowed this remission for prisoners in solitary confinement.

On 15 January 1875 he was given back his watch, his wallet (which contained a few banknotes) and his clothes. Next morning, he found his mother waiting at the prison gates. 'It was recently proposed,' wrote Rémy de Gourmont in 1912, 'to set a commemorative plaque on the jail. I think that silence would be better, if silence was possible. And yet one cannot forget that it was there that he wrote *Sagesse*: the book which made him one of the greatest Catholic poets of France.'[15]

PART FIVE

Moi Professeur

(1875–7)

25

VERLAINE and his mother were escorted to the frontier by two gendarmes; and there the French police received them 'with no great cordiality'. 'And, whatever happens,' said the sergeant to Verlaine, 'don't do it again.' The exhortation was recorded in *Mes Prisons*; it was echoed in the opening poem of *Sagesse*:

> Mais le bon chevalier, remonté sur sa bête,
> En s'éloignant me fit un signe de la tête
>
> Et me cria (j'entends *encore* cette voix):
> 'Au moins, prudence! Car c'est bon pour une fois.'[1]

Verlaine needed rest, and his mother took him to stay with her brother at Fampoux. 'I have been here, *en famille*, since the 16th,' Verlaine told Lepelletier on 25 January. 'They are so nice to me, here, it's so good to breathe the country air, even if it's northerly, that the great city barely tempts me. All the same, I don't think it will be much longer before we see one another.'[2]

They met, briefly, in February; possibly the meeting was in Paris. It is said that Verlaine went to Paris that month, and tried to see his former wife and child, but he was not permitted to do so. He also hoped for an interview with the Mautés' solicitor; but Me Guyot-Sionnest did not receive him. Verlaine was still under the influence of his conversations with the prison chaplain, and he wondered, now, if he had a vocation. He went for a probationary period to the Trappist monastery at Chimay; but he soon left, disillusioned. He had no other plans for his future, and he thought again – indeed he had never ceased to think – of Rimbaud. Rimbaud was in Stuttgart. Verlaine extracted his address from their mutual friend, Rimbaud's old school-friend, Ernest Delahaye; he wrote to him, begging him to return to Catholicism. He ended his letter: 'Let us love one another in Jesus Christ.'[3]

It is hard to know Verlaine's intentions. There is no doubt that, at this time, he felt strong religious convictions. And yet – *parallèlement* – the old faun remained within him. He felt more than spiritual brotherhood with Rimbaud. He still felt, and would always feel, an overwhelming physical attraction.

Rimbaud blasphemed when he received the letter; but he agreed that Verlaine might visit him. Late in February or early in March, after an interval of some nineteen months, they met again in Stuttgart. Any attempt at conversion failed. They trekked from bar to bar. Finally they went for a walk on the banks of the Neckar, and quarrelled violently. Verlaine was excited by unwonted alcohol, and he attacked Rimbaud; Rimbaud struck back, and left him unconscious by the river. He was found next morning by some peasants, who took him back to Stuttgart in their cart. Two days later, he returned to France. 'The other day,' Rimbaud told Delahaye, on 5 March, 'Verlaine arrived in Stuttgart with a rosary in his paws, but three hours later he had denied his God, and made the ninety-eight wounds of our Blessed Lord bleed again.'

This is said to have been the last time that Verlaine and Rimbaud met.[4]

Verlaine now considered his situation. He wanted, above all, to avoid the temptations and the unhappy memories of Paris. He thought of leading a farmer's life, but he had had no farming experience, and, for the moment, he set the idea aside. He needed to escape from France until his past was forgotten. He needed to find himself again: to lead a sober, steadfast life, a life of regular work among upright people. During his imprisonment he had read a good deal of English literature and persuaded himself that he understood it; he had even thought of founding a publishing house to undertake translations from English. Rimbaud himself, in Stuttgart, had advised him 'to go and finish his studies *là-bas, dans l'île*'.[5] Verlaine decided to teach French in England.

On about 20 March, he arrived in London. He saw it, now, with the eyes of a bohemian who was grateful to find stability, of a convert who was thankful for the discipline of English life. One day, he hoped, Catholicism would bring the ultimate happiness to this moral and deserving nation. He expressed his new feelings in a somewhat Wordsworthian poem, which would later appear in *Sagesse*:

> L'immensité de l'humanité,
> Le Temps passé, vivace et bon père,
> Une entreprise à jamais prospère:
> Quelle puissante et calme cité!
>
> Il semble ici qu'on vit dans l'histoire.
> Tout est plus fort que l'homme d'un jour.
> De lourds rideaux d'atmosphère noire
> Font richement la nuit alentour.
>
> Ô civilisés que civilise
> L'Ordre obéi, le Respect sacré!
> Ô dans ce champ si bien préparé,
> Cette moisson de la seule Église![6]

Verlaine settled at 10, London Street, Fitzroy Square, only a few yards from his old lodgings in Howland Street. He immediately went to an agency for teachers and tutors. 'I wanted,' he wrote in his *Notes on England*, 'to be employed upon terms of mutual exchange: that is to say, I would teach French, drawing, and the dead languages, in return for my board, lodging and laundry. I waited for about a week, . . . and at the end of that time I received a notice from the agency in question, informing

me that a schoolmaster in Lincolnshire had agreed to engage me
as French and drawing master in a village called Stickney.'[7]

The grammar school at Stickney had been founded in 1678,
but it might have been invented by a benevolent Dickens. It was
a model of an unpretentious Victorian country school. It was
graphically summed up, a few years later, in an educational
directory.

Endowment £126. Pupils receive an English middle-class education,
with French, Latin, and Music. Scholars in attendance, 60. Stickney
children free, from other parishes £1 per annum. Pupils admitted any
age if child knows the rudiments of reading. Vacations: 2 weeks at
Christmas, 4 in the summer. Head Master, W. Andrews, London
University, certificated, with assistant Masters.[8]

The day after Verlaine heard from the agency, he set out from
King's Cross for Sibsey, the nearest station to Stickney. There, he
remembered,

. . . the schoolmaster's pony-chaise and groom were to meet me . . .
At Sibsey, I was met by a chubby-faced urchin about twelve years old,
a pony and the chaise mentioned above, in which a porter and the
groom stowed my luggage. Then a touch of the whip, and we were
off . . .
  The last rays of daylight were shedding lustre upon a landscape which
was exquisite in its rich sweetness of pasture and trees – those English
trees with their branches capriciously twisted and 'intricated', if I may
be allowed the barbarism, which the Bible somewhere says are those
that bear the best fruit; both sides of the road, which was flourished
[sic] with fine quickset hedges, were studded, so to speak, with big
sheep and nimble colts roaming free. I made a sketch of the scene in
these few verses, which are taken from my book, *Sagesse*:

> L'échelonnement des haies
> Moutonne à l'infini, mer
> Claire dans le brouillard clair
> Qui sent bon les jeunes baies . . .[9]

Verlaine felt at home in this Lincolnshire landscape, which
recalled his beloved northern France. It would be ungenerous to
observe that he arrived in the early spring, and that, in his *Notes*

on England, which he bravely wrote in English, some years later, he described an autumnal countryside; it would be ungenerous, too, to observe that the 'jeunes baies' of *Sagesse* belonged to some distinctly autumnal hedgerow. But Verlaine's moods and land-scapes had often recalled the moods and the landscapes of a con-temporary English poet; now, without reading Tennyson, he found himself in sympathy with Tennyson's native county.

He found himself immediately in sympathy with his employer, Mr Andrews, 'a man in the thirties, with a large moustache and enormous whiskers, whom I could just distinguish in the dusk.' Verlaine spoke doubtful English and the schoolmaster possessed 'not less questionable French', but Verlaine was presented to Mrs Andrews, and they all communicated with gestures.

Next morning Verlaine woke early, as usual, and went down to explore the garden. There he met another early riser, the rector of the parish. Canon Coltman spoke tolerable French and was, added Verlaine, 'a good, a very good man'. As the nominal director of the grammar school, he had doubtless hoped to meet the new teacher. Foreigners were rarely seen in this remote corner of East Anglia, and Verlaine's appointment was considered audacious. That morning, before breakfast, the Protestant clergy-man and the Catholic convert engaged in a conversation on 'all kinds of subjects, literature, art, and even theology'.

Before the working day began, Verlaine was shown over the school – which he later described in his unconventional English.

I was delighted with the building, properly so called. In construction it was of a Gothic, should I say, nature . . . Then, for it was past eight o'clock, we went into the school-room. After commanding silence, . . . Mr Andrews read prayers.

Then I was introduced.

'Monsieur Verlaine, who is a Bachelor of Arts of the University of Paris, is willing to assist me in teaching the French language and the art of drawing. He knows English as well as an Englishman, and most certainly far better than all of you put together, but, of course, he cannot pronounce it . . . quite well. I am convinced that you will respect and like this gentleman. But should any of you take advantage

of his foreign accent to show him the least want of respect, I shall lose
no time in ... correcting the error.'[10]

Verlaine was to look back on his life at Stickney with affection.
Once – as his correspondence shows – he had come to England
full of prejudice and cynicism. Now he was grateful for the
serenity of English country life. After his first drawing-lesson he
was summoned by 'the dinnerbel' to lunch.

Grace was said by one of the day boarders ... Next appeared the
roast beef. Not one of those crimson lumps that are set before us even
in our best restaurants, but a wellcut joint, daintily streaked with fat and
lean, emitting rich and appetising odour, full of promise of nourish-
ment. No sauce, no gravy! The vegetables were potatoes boiled in
their jackets, and bursting through their skins. They were served upon
a plate to the left, and were the substitute for bread ... It is true that the
latter article of food, which here is only eaten when cut in slices with
bread or jami [*sic*], appeared in a pudding with lemon peel (lemon
pudding), a delicious sweet. It displayed its white roundness in the
place of dessert, which was represented by it alone, but it was quite
enough.[11]

After this succulent lunch, Verlaine and his employer agreed to
further each other's education. Mr Andrews undertook to perfect
Verlaine's English, and Verlaine to help him with Greek and
Latin. They began work next day.

Here I am, an *au pair* professor in an English village [wrote Verlaine
to Lepelletier early in April]. No-one round me speaks a word of
French, a single word! I'm teaching French, Latin ... and drawing!
I get through my three tasks quite well ... and – strangest of all – I
teach in *English*. What English! But, in the week I've been here,
I improve ...

How long shall I stay here? Three or six months, according to how I
can speak and *understand*. Then I shall see about earning *my living* in
earnest – probably in this country, where I hope mother will more or
less settle in the end.

I have no distractions and I don't look for any. I read enormously, I
go for walks with pupils (not in *ranks*, you know – there's nothing
usher-like here) through magnificent *meadows* full of sheep, etc. It's

astonishing how well I've been, morally and physically, for the last week . . .

You must send me masses of gossip. No doubt there have been new rumours about my 'mysterious' departure around Montmartre . . . If they [the Mautés] could see me in my new incarnation, I venture to say that they would be 'astonish'd'.[12]

By the end of April, Verlaine was already enlarging his circle of acquaintances. Mr Andrews found private pupils for him. Verlaine taught French to the daughters of a local doctor, and – twice a week – to the children of Colonel Grantham, of Keal Hall. He made such a gentlemanly impression that the Colonel and his wife asked him to dinner. The Colonel recalled his campaigns, and Verlaine, not to be outdone, gave an account of his valorous deeds during the Siege of Paris. He had, he said, been condemned to death, and he had only been saved by the personal intervention of Thiers.[13]

Verlaine did his best to take part in English village life. He was often asked to dinner by Canon Coltman, he went to the annual Sunday school party, and he attended the Wesleyan chapel in the village to find the points of divergence between church and chapel. 'Mister Mossou', as he came to be called, even ventured to learn football from a pupil, and he learned to drive Mr Andrews' gig. Some of his older pupils used to go with him on his long walks through the fens, and it was perhaps a Lincolnshire sunset which Verlaine recalled in a sonnet in *Sagesse*:

> Les faux beaux jours ont lui tout le jour, ma pauvre âme,
> Et les voici vibrer aux cuivres du couchant . . .[14]

Everything at Stickney combined to strengthen the convert in his good resolutions. He was living in a family which led a Christian life, and he belonged to a Christian institution. He felt increasing admiration for Canon Coltman, who set an example of charity, goodness and zeal. Perhaps the Canon even had his influence on *Sagesse* and *Amour*. In this atmosphere of tolerance and piety, Verlaine was tolerant and pious, too. The English Sundays, which he had once considered oppressive, were to become 'the good Sundays of rest and fraternal joy in a country where everyone is a believer, when, at morning service, he has savoured the fresh and tender poetry of the English hymns'. The services at Stickney were Low Church, and Verlaine missed the Catholic ritual; nor could he understand biblical English. But 'my life is madly calm,' he assured Delahaye, 'and I am so happy about it ... I have an appalling need of calm. I still don't feel I have recovered properly from my past idiocies, and I am struggling with a kind of ferocity to confound the old Self of Brussels and London, 72–73 ... and also, and above all, of Brussels, *July* 73.'[15]

One wonders how hard he was struggling. Even in the fens of East Anglia, he was thinking repeatedly of Rimbaud. 'If you have news from Stuttgarce, or other places,' he added, to Delahaye, 'let me know, and if you write there, send a (really) very cordial greeting from me.' In June, Delahaye reported: 'Rimbe is at Marseilles, having, so it seems, done a tour of Liguria on foot.' It was about now, between Rimbaud's peregrinations, that Delahaye asked him discreetly if he had any literary plans. Rimbaud answered, simply, that he did not write any more. 'There was no suggestion of regret or pride.' Delahaye mentioned Verlaine, and found that Rimbaud avoided 'the memory of behaviour which he now considered excessive'. 'What news, anyway, of *L'Œstre*?' Verlaine asked again, on 3 September. 'And what about L'Œstre?' he repeated, on 26 October. Delahaye said that L'Œstre was drinking excessively and would probably end in a lunatic asylum. Verlaine wrote to Rimbaud, exhorting him to repent his sins. Rimbaud replied, yet again, with blasphemies.[16]

Rimbaud remained in Verlaine's life; but Verlaine had no sins of the flesh to confess when he went to St Mary's Catholic chapel at Boston. At most he needed to confess persistent homosexual desires. But he needed spiritual relief, he needed to shed the burden of his thoughts, and he made his regular confession because it made him more self-critical, and because it maintained his Christian humility. The ardour of the convert remained. He counteracted the influence of Protestant services by attending mass; and he made his confession every Saturday. Sometimes he rose at dawn to walk the nine miles to the church, sometimes he went into Boston in the carrier's spring cart, squashed among half-a-dozen farmers' wives on the way to market. It was said to be on his return from a visit to Boston that he wrote 'Ô vous, comme un qui boite au loin . . .'': the sonnet in *Sagesse* which records the euphoria of communion.

He was not only an ardent Catholic; he was now an ardent patriot. For all his 'vaguely socialist' youth, his republican fervour, his evasion of military service, his passive part in the Commune, he now proclaimed legitimist views, and emphasised his belief in authority. Modern France needed to be reformed, and Verlaine maintained that only the monarchy, in alliance with the Church, could save it. In April 1875, he told Delahaye: 'My patriotic book will be short and simple. I hope I shall soon be able to send you part of it. I venture to believe that it will be new, very gentle, very touching, and, as far as possible, very French.'[17] Verlaine's patriotism was no passing emotion, born of his self-imposed exile abroad. But, as for the patriotic book, it was probably the pamphlet which materialised, some years later, as *Voyage en France par un Français*. It was far from gentle. Verlaine did not only express his legitimist politics, he wrote a savage indictment of modern France, and he contrasted his country with Victorian England: moral, dignified, and prosperous. *Voyage en France par un Français* did not find a publisher until after Verlaine's death.[18]

26

It must be admitted that Verlaine gained more than pious satisfaction from his weekly visits to Boston. In Stickney he did not dare to be seen in a public-house; it would have ruined his reputation. In Boston he could briefly enjoy a less restricted life. He came to know the German priest, Father Hermann Sabela, who invited him to his house; and he made friends with an Italian photographer who attended the church and, to Verlaine's intense relief, spoke French. Sometimes Mrs Andrews observed that

Verlaine was gayer than usual when he returned to Stickney on Saturday evenings.

But the clearest memory which she kept of her husband's colleague was that of a man who, every day, after school hours, paced up and down in the playground or the garden, writing constantly in a little book. Verlaine was planning poems (among them a long religious poem, 'Le Rosaire', which was never written). In his black trunk he had brought not only his books, but manuscript poems he had written in prison.

During his first term at the school, he wrote:

> Ô mon Dieu, vous m'avez blessé d'amour . . .

The poem – which would appear in *Sagesse* – bears witness to continued piety. It is above all interesting as a sign of a powerful new influence in Verlaine's poetry. Verlaine, who believed intensely in the music of poetry, and was now especially susceptible to religious literature, had discovered *Hymns Ancient and Modern*.[1]

A new edition of the hymnal was in fact published this year, 1875, and there is evidence that he had a copy of his own. In 1872, when he was in London with Rimbaud, he had laughed at the hymn-singing of Victorian England. Now he was in sympathy with the religious fervour of the time. He was moved by the inescapable feeling, the robust assurance of the music which he heard on Sundays at Stickney. In the enlarged hymn book, which included nearly five hundred hymns, he found a rich mine of poetry after his own heart. There were hymns by Cowper and Herbert, Wesley, Keble and Newman and in this edition, for the first time, there appeared the hymn by Bishop Ken:

> Arise, my soul, and with the sun
> Thy daily stage of duty run . . .

Verlaine translated this hymn, and many others. England and English literature were to mean more to him than to any other French poet of his time; and some of these hymns were, he wrote, 'real poems of tender and melancholy mysticism, with a depth of thought, an emotion, a power of expression, a richness of imagery, a delicacy of feeling – not to mention a search for the fantastic which is reminiscent of Shakespeare – which the authors of our French hymns have never dreamed of.' Verlaine became impregnated with the English hymnal, and some of the poems later to appear in *Sagesse* and *Amour* reflect not only the general inspiration, but actual turns of phrase. Hymn 180, for example, speaks of the 'wound of love' in the heart of Christ: Hymn 191 declares:

> To Thee my heart and soul belong;
> All that I have or am is Thine . . .

These phrases may be found, almost textually, in the poem in *Sagesse*:

> Ô mon Dieu, vous m'avez blessé d'amour . . . ,

the poem which ends:

> Mais ce que j'ai, mon Dieu, je vous le donne.

In the English hymnal there was a series of hymns in praise of God, the giver of the harvest:

> He sends the snow in winter,
> The warmth to swell the grain . . .

It would not be surprising if such hymns, and the harvest festival at Stickney, had their effect on the last poem of *Sagesse*:

> C'est la fête du blé, c'est la fête du pain . . .

Some said that *Sagesse* was due to Verlaine's imprisonment in Belgium. Cazals declared, long afterwards, that 'it was in fact in England that Verlaine produced that transcendent work. It had been inspired by those English hymns which he never tired of hearing, and which he never heard again without an indescribable emotion.'[2]

It has been suggested that Verlaine, inspired by English hymns, turned to some of the English mystic poets of the seventeenth century: to Herbert, Donne and Crashaw. Soon after his arrival at Stickney, he himself recorded that he was reading Milton's *Comus*; possibly the influence of *Comus* may be seen in the first two allegorical poems of *Sagesse*.

F

It is almost certain that, during the early days at Stickney, Verlaine was also reading Tennyson. It would have been difficult for him to live near Canon Coltman, the Poet Laureate's friend and admirer, without being advised to read his work. Tennyson was also, beyond question, the most popular poet of the time; any self-respecting schoolmaster would have owned some, at least, of his books. On 20 November, Verlaine told Blémont that he was reading Tennyson; on 8 February he mentioned Tennyson's drama *Queen Mary*, which had recently been published, and on 23 May he asked Delahaye how to get a cheap edition of Tennyson's works. It seems a strange request to send from England to France, but it shows a serious literary interest. No doubt Verlaine was drawn to the *Idylls of the King*; they appealed to his love of the Middle Ages, and they also professed a stern morality which was in keeping with his current mood. Yet one suspects that, in Tennyson, Verlaine discovered a much deeper and more permanent affinity. He found a man whose moods, whose dream-like, symbolic landscapes bore a remarkable likeness to his own.

Even in his juvenilia, Tennyson had written of his need to believe in God; and *In Memoriam*, which was written over a period of seventeen years, and eventually published in 1850, records his painful search for faith: his desperate need, after the death of his friend Arthur Hallam, to believe in immortality. *In Memoriam* was probably the most widely read of Tennyson's poems; its theme of the search for faith would have suited Verlaine's religious mood, and it seems certain that he later turned to it at a time of bereavement. But now, at Stickney, he must already have been impressed by the Lincolnshire landscapes it contained, and he must have found much in Tennyson after his own heart. One of the tapestries in *The Palace of Art* showed a strangely familiar dream-picture:

> One seem'd all dark and red – a tract of sand,
> And some one pacing there alone,
> Who paced for ever in a glimmering land,
> Lit with a low large moon.[3]

There is a curious affinity between such lines and the mood of 'Soleils couchants' in *Poèmes saturniens*:

> . . . Et d'étranges rêves,
> Comme des soleils
> Couchants sur les grèves,
> Fantômes vermeils,
> Défilent sans trêves,
> Défilent, pareils
> À des grands soleils
> Couchants sur les grèves . . .[4]

Among Tennyson's early poems was the oppressive, autumnal 'Song':

> The air is damp, and hush'd, and close,
> As a sick man's room when he taketh repose
>   An hour before death;
> My very heart faints and my whole soul grieves
> At the moist rich smell of the rotting leaves,
>   And the breath
>   Of the fading edges of box beneath,
> And the year's last rose.
>   Heavily hangs the broad sunflower
>   Over its grave i' the earth so chilly;
>   Heavily hangs the hollyhock,
>   Heavily hangs the tiger-lily.[5]

Such a mood was remarkably in keeping with 'Crépuscule du soir mystique', another of the *Poèmes saturniens*:

> Le Souvenir avec le Crépuscule
> Rougeoie et tremble à l'ardent horizon
> De l'Espérance en flamme qui recule
> Et s'agrandit ainsi qu'une cloison
> Mystérieuse où mainte floraison
> – Dahlia, lys, tulipe et renoncule –
> S'élance autour d'un treillis, et circule
> Parmi la maladive exhalaison
> De parfums lourds et chauds, dont le poison
> – Dahlia, lys, tulipe et renoncule –
> Noyant mes sens, mon âme et ma raison,
> Mêle dans une immense pamoison
> Le Souvenir avec le Crépuscule.[6]

Tennyson was not only a supremely musical poet. Like Verlaine he was a poet of autumnal moods and inexplicable melancholy: a poet of dank and desolate landscapes, of brooding, sometimes sinister nature. Like Verlaine, he was a poet of a lonely, wind-swept countryside, lit by setting suns and by isolated stars.

27

During the summer holidays of 1875, Verlaine returned to France. It was from Arras, on 3 September, that he told Delahaye that he was reading St Theresa and St Thomas Aquinas. Three days later, again from Arras, he sent a reproach to his old friend Émile Blémont: 'It is now more than two months since I posted you a warm letter and some poems for a *Parnasse*, and asked if you would acknowledge them. Since then, silence . . .'¹

Verlaine was alluding to a plan which clearly meant much to him. A third *Parnasse contemporain* was about to be published, and 'it seems to me,' he wrote, 'that . . . if my name did not appear in a 3rd *Parnasse*, it would be a kind of typographical error.'² Verlaine was flippant, but he was serious. If Lemerre chose, now, to publish him with his friends of pre-war days, it would mean his acceptance in literary circles in Paris. It would show that, for all the vicissitudes of the last few years, he had not been forgotten or dismissed. He was to be disappointed. The poems were rejected: clearly on account of his personal conduct. Two of his friends from the passage Choiseul, Banville and Coppée, abstained from voting for him. They accepted the verdict of Anatole France, who decided, briefly: 'No. The author is unworthy, and the poems are some of the worst that we have seen.'³

Verlaine learned of his rejection after he had gone back to Stickney. He had returned there for the autumn term which began on 13 September. No doubt he welcomed his return to a life of 'sobriety, *wisdom*, work – and contentment'. He was reading *The Pilgrim's Progress*, and one may detect the influence of Bunyan on 'Écrit en 1875', which Verlaine wrote in October.

The poem was an affectionate and grateful recollection of the prison at Mons: 'Château, château magique où mon âme s'est faite . . .' The final lines, in which he spoke of his release and his future, strongly recall Bunyan's Christian and his pilgrimage to Mount Sion.

> Ô sois béni, château d'où me voila sorti
> Prêt à la vie, armé de douceur et nanti
> De la Foi, pain et sel et manteau pour la route
> Si déserte, si rude et si longue, sans doute,
> Par laquelle il faut tendre aux innocents sommets.
> Et soit aimé l'AUTEUR de la Grâce, à jamais![4]

It was, apparently, the summer holidays of 1875 which reminded Verlaine of the attraction of 'civilisation'. Late in October, he told Delahaye of his plan to settle in Boston the following month, and to find a more lucrative occupation. Verlaine had first arrived in Stickney early in the spring; now winter would soon be upon him, and his peaceful retreat would become unhappy isolation. 'Il neige ici (*it snows*),' he explained on 27 November. 'Il grésille (*it sleets*), il fait un temps impossible, c'est embêtant comme tout.' Besides, his mother had decided to remain in Arras unless he obtained '*a suitable situation in this country*', in which case she would come and live near him.[5] Verlaine was not only depressed by the wintry landscape at Stickney; he felt he would earn more money in Boston, and enjoy more social opportunities. When he eventually announced his plans to Mr Andrews, he was offered better pay and 'plenty of confortabilities', and he decided to stay until Christmas.

There was a fortnight's Christmas holiday. Verlaine went to Paris, and to see his mother in Arras. In January, he returned to Stickney; and, early in the spring, his mother joined him.

Mme Verlaine lived over the tailor's shop, near the rectory. She soon increased her son's good reputation in the village, and the inhabitants watched benignly as he went to meet her every morning, and brought her back to lunch with the Andrews; they observed, approvingly, as he arranged the hassocks for her in church. She also earned her own success, for she was clearly a model of maternal devotion. Catholic and French though she was, unable to speak a word of English, she readily took part in the religious and social life of Stickney; and Verlaine declared, in 'Moi Professeur', that 'she enjoyed herself immensely, and her only worry was to get bread in proportion to the roast beef, the steak and cutlets and stews.'[6]

Towards the end of March, the Verlaines finally left Stickney. 'The Andrews and I had to part,' wrote Verlaine. 'We were sorry on both sides, and I left, almost in tears.'[7]

Possibly Verlaine had been drawn to Boston by promises from Father Sabela, or from the Italian photographer, who had undertaken to find him pupils. However that may be, an advertisement appeared in the *Boston Guardian* and the *Lincolnshire Herald*:

> Mons. Paul Verlaine, B.L. of University of Paris, will be glad to give lessons in French, Latin and Elementary Drawing. First-class references. Address: 48 Main Ridge, Boston.[8]

The advertisement appeared only once in the *Guardian*, and twice in the *Herald*, but there was another reason why pupils did not flock to Verlaine. No. 48 Main Ridge was in fact The Whale Inn; and no self-respecting pupils were likely to come to a public house. It was small wonder that, in May, Verlaine had a mere three pupils, and thought of leaving Boston for London.

There is some mystery about his movements between 23 May and 26 September. One can only suppose that he left for London about 1 June, as he had predicted to Delahaye, and that he took his mother back to France – if she was still with him. He had presumably stayed in London long enough to get into touch with Mr Frederic A. Remington, the owner of a small but select Catholic school at Bournemouth.

28

Since *A Descriptive Guide to Bournemouth* was published that year, one may recall the town as it appeared to Verlaine. It was an established watering-place and, said the *Guide*,

it has gained for itself a well-merited reputation as a fashionable resort and winter residence. [It presents] highly romantic scenes, offering sites for villas so secluded in character, so healthful, soothing and reviving in their influences . . . as to become of incalculable value to those whom disease, excitement, or fatigue place beyond the reach of satisfactory medical treatment in their homes. And as Bournemouth is the creation of the last quarter of a century or so, the design for its dwellings has been laid out with due care and attention . . . [1]

Bournemouth was a sanctuary for the invalid and a model of Victorian town-planning. It also had abundant charms for a poet. Not only did Shelley's nephew live at Boscombe Manor, two miles from the town, but 'the coast scenery,' added the *Guide*, 'is magnificent and varied.'

Yachts and boats of all kinds flit here and there, careening to the wind, and throwing the white foam from their glittering bows. Every portion of the water has a character of its own. The clear pale green close inshore, where the white sand of the beach shows through, the deep blue further out, the grey where the wind falls heaviest, and the rich purple marking the movements of the flying clouds overhead; while gleams of sunshine strike on the multiform projections of the bounding cliffs, and deepen the shadows in the recesses, or glisten on the windows of the villas above: all makes a very complete contemplative picture. [2]

Verlaine would think so, as he stood on top of the cliffs, gazing at the 'leagues and leagues of sea'.

> . . . Il fait un de ces temps ainsi que je les aime,
> Ni brume ni soleil! le soleil deviné,
> Pressenti, du brouillard mourant dansant à même
> Le ciel très haut qui tourne et fuit, rose de crème;
> L'atmosphère est de perle et la mer d'or fané . . . [3]

It was in September 1876 that he arrived to teach French and Latin at St Aloysius' School, West Cliff, Bournemouth. The establishment prepared pupils 'for the Catholic Schools, Civil Service, and Professions, or finished their education, if desired'. Each pupil was assured of individual tuition,

... special care being taken to ensure progress in those who are backward. The pupils are in every way considered as members of the family, and have the comforts of home combined with a reasonable amount of school discipline.

Bournemouth is especially suited for invalid or delicate boys, for such as suffer from chest affections, and for foreigners, the climate being warm and dry, and considered more equable than that of the South of France.

Mrs. REMINGTON interests herself in the health of the boys, and so arranges household matters as to make them as homelike as possible for the pupils.

Terms: From Sixty Guineas per annum, according to age, health and requirements.

Extras: Modern Languages, Music, Drawing, and Laundress, &c.[4]

Whatever benefits Bournemouth offered for delicate boys, the pupils at St Aloysius' seem to have been far from frail. Some of them were Irish, 'proper devils', said Verlaine, and one of them knocked him unconscious with a snowball in which a stone had been carefully concealed. The malefactor was not identified.

Mr Remington himself was a Cambridge graduate and a Catholic convert. He lived with his wife and sister at 2, Westburn Terrace, in what were then the outskirts of the town. Verlaine lived with them. Mr Remington was bearded and solemn, but he showed his own kind of tolerance. He did not like his pupils to smoke, but he told them that they might do so as long as he did not see them. He was unlikely, one suspects, to be severe on the weaknesses of a colleague.

Verlaine did not only teach at Bournemouth; he was also obliged to escort the pupils on their walks, and to supervise them when they bathed. In *Notes on England* he said he had taken them down to the beach every day, and that he had bathed with them. It seems unlikely that delicate pupils would bathe in autumn or winter, and it is even harder to imagine Verlaine, so addicted to mufflers and overcoats, braving the English Channel. But, what-

ever the truth of the story, Verlaine was popular, and some of the
pupils became his friends.

On Sundays he attended mass at the new Catholic Church of
the Sacred Heart. In his leisure hours he continued to write poetry;
and here, by the sea, he seems to have felt the influence of
Tennyson more than ever. The first verse of the poem 'La mer est
plus belle ...' – originally called 'La Mer de Bournemouth' –
seems to be a memory of a passage in 'Sea Dreams'; and in 'Un
Veuf parle' – said to be written in 1878 – there are probably
reminiscences of Bournemouth, and of Tennyson.

> Tears of the widower, when he sees
> A late-lost form that sleep reveals,
> And moves his doubtful arms, and feels
> Her place is empty, fall like these ...[5]

So Tennyson had written in the thirteenth section of 'In
Memoriam'. The feelings are echoed by Verlaine:

> Je vois un groupe sur la mer.
> Quelle mer? Celle de mes larmes.
> Mes yeux mouillés du vent amer
> Dans cette nuit d'ombres et d'alarmes
> Sont deux étoiles sur la mer.
>
> C'est une toute jeune femme
> Et son enfant déjà tout grand
> Dans une barque où nul ne râme,
> Sans mât ni voile, en plein courant ...
> Un jeune garçon, une femme! ...[6]

In January 1877 Verlaine wrote 'Bournemouth': the impression
of the town which would later appear in *Amour*. He was working
intensely on his poetry: polishing and copying out his earlier
work, and, probably, writing many of the poems which would
appear in *Sagesse*, *Amour*, *Bonheur*, and *Liturgies intimes*.

During his stay at Bournemouth he attempted, once again,
despite the legal separation, to be reconciled with his wife. He
sent her a copy of *Sagesse*, written out in his own hand.[7] During
the Christmas holidays of 1876, when he was in Paris, he also

addressed a poem to Hugo. The incident casts some doubt on Mathilde's veracity. If her account of her interview with Hugo was correct, it is hard to explain why Hugo now acknowledged Verlaine's poem, and told him: 'We shall meet again. Lay me at the feet of your charming wife.'[8]

It has also been suggested that, during his time at Bournemouth, Verlaine saw his son; but Mathilde herself denied this.

In 1877 [she wrote], he was passing through Paris; and, from a café near the house, he sent me a note asking me to return a drawing done by his father, and to entrust his son to the messenger who brought me the letter. The idea of entrusting Georges to this stranger did not appeal to me. I returned the picture and kept the child. I did so all the more firmly as I had had a warning from a cousin of Verlaine's, when I paid her a short visit at Fampoux.

'Beware of Paul,' she had said to me, 'and take good care of your child. He came here when he was released from prison, and we received him because of his poor mother, who is much to be pitied. He told us that he would try to kidnap his son, not because he wants to have him with him, but in revenge for your demand for a separation.'

After this warning [continued Mathilde], I naturally took my precautions to avoid such a misfortune; but it is not true to say that I prevented him from seeing his son.[9]

It is hard to know what was malice and rumour, and what was the simple truth. It seems unlikely that Verlaine, alone as he was, would have wanted to take a child of six back to England. He would also have been well aware of the penalties for taking the child against his mother's wishes; and, if he still aspired to a reconciliation, this behaviour would hardly have ensured it. Even now, Verlaine still hoped, stubbornly, against all hope, that he would be reconciled with Mathilde, and he was seeking for a formula. 'What might decide her,' wrote Delahaye in 1876, 'would be to avoid any contact with papa, and to send the young lady *herself* a few simple, honest words, suggesting that she joined you in England. Who knows if this little coup-d'état wouldn't tear a good many spiders' webs away?'[10]

In 1877, Verlaine decided to return to France. Perhaps he felt that he could no longer play the demanding part he had set himself, perhaps he felt confident that he could withstand the temptations of Paris: 'that Paris which saw my childhood and will probably see my old age, if that is to be.' Most probably he was drawn home by his love of France, and by his intention to launch himself again in literature. *Romances sans paroles* had passed unnoticed; now, with *Sagesse*, he would win the great Catholic public. He left Bournemouth at Easter 1877.[11] 'I approve of your return to our dear Frrrrance,' wrote Delahaye, in his flippant style, '. . . and I'm sure that you'll easily be reconciled with the "modern Babylon" . . . But, if I were you, I'd hesitate to try the Office again, teaching seems to me much less unpleasant.'[12]

Despite his wish to return to France, Verlaine kept great affection for the country which had sheltered him for the last two years. He continued to correspond with the Andrews and the Remingtons, and he presented his friends with his photograph. Equipped, in turn, with two 'splendid testimonials' from his English headmasters, he succeeded Delahaye, in October 1877, as a master at the Collège Notre-Dame at Rethel. It was not far from Charleville, where Rimbaud had been born. It was in the heart of the Ardennes: that bleak north-eastern corner of France to which Verlaine was drawn by his paternal ancestry, his melancholy temperament and, perhaps, by the undimmed recollection of his past.

PART SIX

Lucien Létinois

(1877–83)

29

THE Collège Notre-Dame was an established boarding-school, with about a hundred and fifty pupils. A photograph shows a building of monastic severity, on the outskirts of Rethel, looking out over broad unbroken fields; but the precincts of Notre-Dame were softened by trees, and there were small trees in the courtyard where the pupils played: a courtyard which, with its arcades, had a certain collegiate charm.

How pretty our dormitories were [remembered a pupil]! The good nuns kept them in such precise and elegant order! . . .

Our little green beds were set out, in long rows, with their regular pink eiderdowns. Every bed had its number, and so had the chairs, the bedside tables, and the big wardrobes, lined with cheap red cotton, where we hung up our clothes . . .

Every Saturday evening, we used to find a white bag at the foot of our bed; it contained our change of linen . . .[1]

Life at Notre-Dame continued with comfortable regularity. When the pupils went for their Sunday walk, they wore a uniform which some of them still recalled, with pleasure, in manhood. It was black, and, as one of them said, gilt-edged. 'There was a tunic with gold embroidery, trousers with gold stripes, and gold buttons (oh, the gold, the gold!), all of it enveloped in winter by an ample cloak.' On the Thursday walk –

and presumably for the rest of the week – the boys wore sober grey.[2]

When Verlaine arrived at Notre-Dame, he was thirty-three, and nothing (said Eugène Prévost, who was one of his pupils), nothing then suggested that he was famous.[3] This was not surprising, for Verlaine had disappeared from the literary scene. He was forgotten or ignored in Paris, he was sure to be unknown in this remote part of the provinces. As for his past, he was desperately determined to conceal it; and, anxious to lead an upright life, overawed, it seemed, by the ecclesiastical atmosphere of the college, he played his part with exaggerated care. He was like a miscreant child trying to be good; his anxiety to be correct was comical and touching.

He was earning 800 francs a year [recorded Henri Regnault], and he thought his salary very reasonable. He had found a haven where he could rest from the fatigues and vicissitudes of his past; he seemed to want to forget his vice, and he refused to have any drinks with his colleagues . . . In vain the abbés assured him that 'a little drop' from time to time had never hurt anyone. M. Verlaine would not depart from the rule of conduct he had set himself: sobriety and abstinence.

The new professor had adopted a code of behaviour which he believed to be indispensable. He imagined that he had entered a monastery, and that his ecclesiastical colleagues must be very serious people, and he had composed himself an attitude which to everyone – teachers and pupils alike – soon seemed bizarre . . . He meditated incessantly. He walked like an automaton, and he wore a shabby frock coat. He used to wrap himself up in this, and affect great severity.

When he went to chapel, he stiffened his torso, and folded his big arms across his chest . . . And when he approached the communion table, and again when he served mass, his ostentation caused smiles among the pupils, and the abbé in charge sometimes had great trouble in repressing them. This attitude had earned the new professor the nickname of Jesus Christ . . .

The poet found the way of life at the Collège Notre-Dame was 'excellent'. He was delighted to have a room to himself and never to be obliged 'to supervise, usher-fashion': this allowed him – he told Lepelletier – to devote himself 'in complete calm to literature, which, alas, brings no reward . . . except personal satisfaction . . .'

Verlaine had chosen a father confessor: the Abbé Pierret, the arch-priest from St Nicolas. The church was next to the college, and he took communion every Sunday.[4]

For two years and more, since he had left Mons, Verlaine had fought against his weaknesses. He had chosen a routine which would allow him no chance of relapse. He hoped that a simple life among respectable people would finally cure him.

Nor had he given up hope, even now – how stubbornly the hope lingered! – that one day he might return to his wife and son. In 1878, Georges Verlaine, then a child of seven, was seriously ill. Verlaine heard the news when he came to Paris during the school holidays.

He wrote to my mother [Mathilde recalled] for permission to see his son. My parents replied that he could come ... My little Georges was out of danger, but he was still in bed; my mother greeted Verlaine by the child's bedside, and my father came upstairs to see him. They talked almost all the time about Georges; my name was not mentioned, and there was no allusion to the past. He went away happy; he asked to come back once more before he left, and he was given permission to do so.

A few days later, Verlaine returned, and he had a long talk with my mother; he told her how happy he was at Rethel ... Emboldened by my mother's kind welcome, he told her how he hoped that one day he would come back and live in this hospitable house which he had left on a day of madness ... My mother was touched by Verlaine's repentance and regrets, and by the affection which he said he felt for me. She thought that she should not deprive him of all hope: we were both still so young; we would see later on ...

In her heart of hearts, my mother did not want a reconciliation; we had so often seen Verlaine gentle and repentant, and then succumbing again, so quickly, to his terrible vice. But she did not want to turn him from the path of virtue he had just entered.[5]

> Les chères mains qui furent miennes,
> Toutes petites, toutes belles,
> Après ces méprises mortelles
> Et toutes ces choses païennes,

Après les rades et les grèves,
Et les pays et les provinces,
Royales mieux qu'au temps des princes
Les chères mains m'ouvrent les rêves.

Mains en songe, mains sur mon âme,
Sais-je, moi, ce que vous daignâtes,
Parmi ces rumeurs scélérates,
Dire à cette âme qui se pâme?

Ment-elle, ma vision chaste
D'affinité spirituelle,
De complicité maternelle,
D'affection étroite et vaste?

Remords si cher, peine très bonne,
Rêves bénis, mains consacrées,
Ô ces mains, ces mains vénérées,
Faites le geste qui pardonne![6]

During his stay at Rethel, Verlaine sometimes wrote to Mme Mauté for news of his son, and Mme Mauté always answered him. He sent Georges several presents, including a photograph album and an illustrated English book. 'Unfortunately,' wrote Mathilde, 'these good dispositions did not last. He stopped writing to my mother, he appeared to forget that he had a son, and we did not hear his name again.'[7]

Once more Mathilde distorted the facts. As late as 1879, Verlaine sent Delahaye to the rue Nicolet to plead for a resumption of married life. M. Mauté received him, and told him that 'certain things were irreparable'.[8] It was, one suspects, when these final negotiations failed, and Verlaine's hopes were utterly destroyed, that he succumbed again to his weaknesses.

On the eve of Corpus Christi, 1879, one of the senior pupils at Notre-Dame was sent into Rethel with a number of other *collégiens*. They were to fetch the flowers for the altar of repose which was set up every year in the main courtyard. As they pulled their flower-filled barrow up towards the place de l'Hôtel-de-Ville, they heard a shout from the door of the Café Fleury.

Someone called out to them gaily: it was M. le professeur Verlaine. 'Come and have a drink, children!' he said.

It was hot and they were young. A little awkward at first, then feeling that they were covered by the presence of the professor, the collégiens went into the café; and such was M. Verlaine's munificent hospitality, that, when they left – and the summer sun did the rest – the young boys grew increasingly gay and rowdy, and their flower-filled barrow described strange zigzags across the streets ... They finally collected their wits, some hours later, in the infirmary.

We may now see why, when Verlaine left the college, his 'educative powers' were not greatly missed.[9]

Towards the end of his stay at Rethel, Verlaine's drunkenness became all too apparent. In July 1879 he left the Collège Notre-Dame. According to a note among the papers of Cazals, his course was discontinued. According to another note from the same source, he resigned. Certainly he was not ostracised, for he came back several times to visit his former colleagues. Canon Prévoteaux, who became director of Notre-Dame in October 1880, invited Verlaine to dine with the professors, and seated him at his right hand, in the hope (so legend goes) that Verlaine would be confidential. Verlaine hardly spoke. On another occasion, Canon Lassaux tried to talk philosophy to him, but Verlaine insisted on talking literature.[10] At Rethel, he had written some of his finest poems.

During his last months at Notre-Dame, he had been in correspondence with Mallarmé. In April he had asked him to help find a cheap copy of Poe's poems. 'And, finally, what about that promised Anthology, and those fine and very interesting books on English – which have been announced?'[11]

One of the 'fine books on English' was *Petite Philologie à l'usage des classes et du monde. Les mots anglais.* Mallarmé had published it in 1877, and he inscribed a copy to Verlaine: no doubt to the colleague, as well as the friend. He also sent information about an edition of Poe. Verlaine's letter of thanks revealed Mallarmé's good nature, and Verlaine's constant readiness to exploit it. Verlaine now asked him to suggest a publisher for his *Œuvres poétiques*. 'P.S.,' he added. 'Belated but very sincere thanks for the book on *English Words*. What about other presents?'[12]

Mallarmé sent an encouraging answer. By the time it reached Verlaine, he had left the Collège Notre-Dame, and his literary plans had grown more urgent. On 1 September, he wrote from Arras:

> Have you seen any publishers? Are any of them manageable? Would you let me know as soon as possible?
>
> I shall be in Paris from 1 to 5 October, and I'll see you.
>
> In the meanwhile it would be immensely kind of you to write to me, even if it was only a word . . .[13]

Ten days later, he wrote again. He sympathised with Mallarmé, whose eight-year-old son was critically ill. His letter suggests that his hopes of resuming his own domestic life had now, at last, been destroyed.

> My dear Mallarmé,
>
> . . . It is already some time since I received the letter you sent me here; it made me desolate, for it told me of the great sorrow which still troubles you. Believe me, I can share it, for I am a father, too – and in what conditions! Conditions which are laid down and kept . . .
>
> I don't think I'll go to Paris this year, what's the use? Every happiness, except in God, is denied me . . .

And the English master added, in his deplorable English:

> Kindly write sometimes to your gratefully and so friendly,
>
> VERLAINE,
> 55, rue d'Amiens, Arras, P.-de-C.
>
> In haste, on my travels, I happen to be in a tavern . . . Still sugared, confused. Very worried. Excuse all horrors . . .[14]

In the little tavern, near Arras, Verlaine still had his sugared absinthe in front of him. These last lines were the only ones addressed to Mallarmé in which he alluded to the dissolute impulses of his life.

Verlaine was now considered an outcast, even by some who had been his closest friends; and Lepelletier's son, who was still a child, was carefully kept in ignorance about his father's disturbing acquaintance. Verlaine, he remembered later,

... was two years older than my father, and he was his closest friend. He frightened my mother by his manner ... Nor was his personal past of a kind to make him valued. His adventures with Rimbaud did not yet confer any aura upon him, for in those days the young filibuster from the Ardennes had only the reputation of a terrible rough ...

At this time, then [1878–9], Verlaine was very ill thought of, and he was only received in a few houses. When my mother saw him arriving, she used to send us into the garden or up to our rooms, I didn't understand why.[15]

If Verlaine did not see his son in 1879, it was probably from choice; he was absorbed by a new emotional interest. But after this year Mathilde ensured that Georges was kept from him. There were no meetings, even in the presence of a third person; there were no letters. Mathilde remained inflexible. She was not simply a prudent mother: she showed her lasting rancour and cruelty.

Verlaine needed someone to love. In 1879, when his pupil Lucien Létinois had completed his studies at Rethel, Verlaine left with him. The relationship was a world away from the dazzling relationship with Rimbaud; but Verlaine wanted to be essential, to give his love and to have his love returned, his self-confidence restored. Weak as he was, he could only hope to find this relationship by virtue of his age and his status. It was natural that one of his pupils should fill part, at least, of the void which Mathilde and Georges and Rimbaud had left in him.

30

Lucien Létinois came of peasant stock. His father was a farmer at Coulommes, and there it was that Lucien had been born. Cazals gave his birthday as 2 February 1860; according to Robichez, in was 27 February in the same year. Whichever statement is correct, Lucien was well over nineteen when he left Rethel with Verlaine. He was old for a *collégien*, but he had just failed to obtain his certificate. But Verlaine had not chosen him for his intellectual brilliance. As Cazals explained: 'Verlaine found likenesses to

Rimbaud almost everywhere. Létinois reminded him of Rimbaud by his build, his accent, and, I think, his eyes.'[1]

Lucien was well-built, and had an Ardennais accent; but there the physical resemblance ended. Rimbaud's eyes were blue, and blazing with intelligence; Lucien's were brown and calf-like. Lucien, said Lepelletier, was pale, thin and gawky, 'slightly pretentious and rather sentimental, a shepherd out of a comic opera'.[2] Verlaine did not see him in this light. Exacerbated by years of chastity, he was physically drawn to him. He would speak of him as his adopted son, he would make much ado about his paternal feelings, but the youth of nineteen was not really a substitute for Georges Verlaine, who was seven. Lucien seemed to give Verlaine a chance to relive the past.

It was, perhaps, an urge to relive his odyssey with Rimbaud, as well as his instinct to escape at moments of crisis, which led Verlaine to take Lucien to England. He seems to have heard that his successor at Stickney was leaving. He lauded Lucien to the skies. Mr Andrews was impressed. In the autumn of 1879 – probably in the last half of September – the dull young man assumed the post which Verlaine had once held.[3] Verlaine could still persuade himself that he had shown a paternal interest in Lucien's future; but, when they left France together for England, the first step had been taken towards a more intimate relationship.

When Verlaine had left his protégé at Stickney, he joined the staff of Mr William Murdoch at the Solent School in Lymington. Since Lymington was not far from Bournemouth, perhaps he had already been there. It was a pleasant little town, and the port was much used by visitors to the Isle of Wight. It is possible that Verlaine caught a glimpse of Tennyson on his lordly way to or from his house at Farringford. But there is no record that he himself crossed the Solent.[4]

It is certain, however, that he was enamoured of the Hampshire countryside, and especially of the New Forest.

> Ô Nouvelle-Forêt! nom de féerie et d'armes!
> Le mousquet a souvent rompu philtres et charmes
> Sous tes rameaux où le rossignol s'effarait.
> Ô Shakspeare! ô Cromwell! ô Nouvelle-Forêt![5]

It is not known that Shakespeare ever saw the New Forest; but, to Verlaine, England largely meant Shakespeare, and the New Forest seemed like the Forest of Arden. In his free moments he wandered among the ancient, autumnal trees. It was a tranquil scene.

His emotional life was far from tranquil. On 6 November, the faithful Delahaye announced that he had given M. Mauté – no doubt for Georges – 'the photograph' of Verlaine. M. Mauté had enquired if Verlaine was still at Bournemouth. 'I merely said that you were not,' explained the discreet ambassador. M. Mauté had then asked some embarrassing questions. Why had Verlaine left Rethel? Why had he not come to see Georges during the holidays? Delahaye maintained that conditions at Rethel had so changed that Verlaine had been obliged to look for a post in England or Germany. That, he suggested, was why he had been unable to see his son. 'At this point,' continued Delahaye, in his letter to Verlaine, 'very warm praise of your paternal feelings, and categorical insistence on . . . your no less impeccable behaviour.' Delahaye had spoken so warmly that even M. Mauté had been moved.[6]

The interview illuminates Verlaine's relationship with Georges. Verlaine was often to attack his wife for refusing to let him see his son. But – at least at this moment, in 1879 – he himself had chosen not to see him. At this moment, Georges seemed to be replaced by Lucien.

During this autumn term of 1879, Verlaine's relationship with Lucien was understandably strained. His need to love was frustrated by his lonely, monotonous life; his love of Lucien was intensified by their separation, until it became an obsession. But Lucien remained at Stickney until the Christmas holidays, and they could only write to one another. They wrote, especially, on Sundays, and early in the week Lucien's letter reached Verlaine, who was 'mad with delight'.[7]

By Christmas, the situation had changed. At the end of the term, Verlaine took leave of Mr Murdoch in Lymington. He later said that he had been recalled to France by his mother's ill-health; but there is no other record that she was ill. There was a more valid reason why he and Lucien went home. Lucien knew no English, and he was unable to teach his class, or to keep order. By Christmas, he was obliged to leave Stickney.

He and Verlaine spent Christmas together in London: a London overwhelmed by Victorian fog.

> Ô l'odieuse obscurité
> Du jour le plus gai de l'année
> Dans la monstrueuse cité
> Où se fit notre destinée!
>
> Au lieu du bonheur attendu,
> Quel deuil profond, quelles ténèbres!
> J'en étais comme un mort, et tu
> Flottais en des pensers funèbres.
>
> La nuit croissait avec le jour
> Sur notre vitre et sur notre âme,
> Tel un pur, un sublime amour
> Qu'eût étreint la luxure infâme;
>
> Et l'affreux brouillard refluait
> Jusqu'en la chambre où la bougie
> Semblait un reproche muet
> Pour quelque lendemain d'orgie.
>
> Un remords de péché mortel
> Serrait notre cœur solitaire . . .
> Puis notre désespoir fut tel
> Que nous oubliâmes la terre,
>
> Et que, pensant au seul Jésus
> Né rien que pour nous ce jour même,
> Notre foi prenant le dessus
> Nous éclaira du jour suprême . . .⁸

There has been much argument about the meaning of these lines. Verlaine later made it clear that Lucien confessed he had loved some English girl at Stickney. This was not unnatural for a youth of nineteen; but his confession finally revealed the nature

and the strength of Verlaine's feelings. He did not accept that
Lucien should follow his natural instincts. He told him to repent
his sin; he gave him stern advice, which Lucien accepted with
docility. If Lucien had ostensibly been Verlaine's adopted son,
Verlaine had no time, now, for pretence. All at once, he dropped
his paternal mask. He was overcome by intense, possessive
jealousy.

Some critics maintain that he would not write of religion and
physical love in a single poem. Certainly, in these lines which he
wrote, years later, in memory of Lucien, he was anxious to
emphasize his purity. It is impossible to establish the truth; but
Verlaine's need to love, his *fureur d'aimer*, had long been frustrated,
and it must have been acute and intense. If Verlaine ever became
the lover of Lucien Létinois, he did so on Christmas Day 1879.[9]

31

Early in 1875, on his release from Mons, Verlaine had briefly
thought of turning farmer; but he had put the idea aside. Now,
five years later, once again, he had to change his way of life; he
wanted to lead a simple country existence. The idea was deep-
seated. 'Nature had sculpted him from the heart of some old oak
on the frontier of the Ardennes ... Verlaine was really very
much of the people, very *vieille France*.'[1]

He spent the first months of 1880 between Arras (where his
mother was living), Fampoux, his old refuge, and the Létinois'
farm at Coulommes. At the end of the winter, he demanded
30,000 francs from his mother, and bought a farm at Juniville,
near Rethel. In March 1880 he settled there with Lucien, and
Lucien's parents came to live with them. Since M. Létinois was a
farmer, he served an evident purpose; so did Mme Létinois, who
was a competent cook. To some it may seem as if Verlaine wanted
Lucien's parents to save him from himself; and yet perhaps they
remained as innocent of his behaviour as his mother. Verlaine hid
his address from his friends. He did not want his idyll known in
Paris.

During the summer, he asked his mother to stay at Juniville. She welcomed his idea of turning farmer; she was less happy that the farm was bought in the name of Lucien's father. Verlaine maintained that it would be dangerous if the farm was bought in his own name, since Mathilde might lay claim to it; but it could safely have been acquired in his mother's name. As it was, he was legally bound to the Létinois. It was a proof of his devotion to Lucien.

He settled down to his rustic life; and, lovingly, he recalled Lucien at his daily tasks:

> J'y voyais ton profil fluet sur l'horizon
> Marcher comme à pas vifs derrière la charrue,
> Gourmandant les chevaux ainsi que de raison,
> Sans colère, et criant diah et criant hue;
>
> Je te voyais herser, rouler, faucher parfois,
> Consultant les anciens, inquiet d'un nuage,
> L'hiver à la batteuse ou liant dans nos bois;
> Je t'aidais, vite hors d'haleine et tout en nage . . .[2]

Verlaine himself took little interest in the farm. In the autumn, Lucien left to join the artillery at Rheims. Verlaine had paid the necessary 1,500 francs to reduce his service to a year. He took a teaching post in Rheims, to be near him, and Delahaye said that he followed him when he went to Châlons for manoeuvres.

> Mon fils est brave: il va sur son cheval de guerre,
> Sans reproche et sans peur par la route du bien . . .[3]

Verlaine proclaimed the virtues of Lucien in poetry; he also exhorted Lucien in prose. His open letter 'to my son' was written in 1880. It was part of *Voyage en France par un Français*. In this open letter, Verlaine advised the 'son' who was about to do his military service. Some of the advice came strangely from him. He warned Lucien to drink only in moderation; he urged him to offer daily prayers to the Virgin to help him overcome the temptations of the flesh.[4] There is an air of hypocrisy about such paternalism. Verlaine could not bear the thought that Lucien should love a woman: love anyone, indeed, except himself.

32

In November 1880 *Sagesse* was published by the Société générale de Librairie catholique, formerly the Maison Victor Palmé, with the date 1881. Germain Nouveau and Ernest Delahaye helped with the publicity. They were both friends of Verlaine and Rimbaud. 'I remember,' wrote Delahaye, 'that the two of us took the editor, Dreyfous, the copy intended for Jules Claretie. He was one of the mere four journalists prepared to tell the public about the book which has since become so famous.'[1]

Claretie had known Verlaine in the passage Choiseul; he was cynical about his conversion. 'Effusions of charity after those *Poèmes saturniens*! . . . It is one of the most astonishing literary *cases* I have known . . . This pious book by M. Verlaine might be called an eccentricity.'[2]

My dear Claretie [wrote Verlaine],

By the most remarkable chance I have happened to see the article in *Le Temps* in which you've been good enough to write about me and my book, *Sagesse* . . .

Why treat as an eccentricity the publication of poems which translate my present state of mind with all possible honesty? . . .

Seriously, when you have time, read *Sagesse* again, and I feel sure that, all questions of opinion and doctrine apart, you will find in it at least a new effort, a great literary conscience, and some innovation in rhymes . . .

I have changed totally as an individual, but I pride myself that I have remained at heart with the poets who are still young to-day, and who made their first appearance in *Le Parnasse* in 1866. This group of poets was convinced, tenacious and ardent, and they fought the good fight with great courage and not without glory. It becomes an understanding and generous soul like you to support the veterans of this rear-guard of Romanticism, which is in turn the vanguard of a new but, remember, traditional art – an art which, I believe and trust, is both French and Christian.[3]

Long after Verlaine had died, Claretie published this letter in *Le Temps*. 'It is,' he wrote, 'a fine letter, and to me it proved the good faith of the convert.'[4]

In 1881, when he published his *Documents littéraires*, Émile Zola showed all too clearly how Verlaine had been forgotten. 'M. Verlaine, now vanished, made his brilliant début with *Poèmes saturniens*. He was a victim of Baudelaire, and it is even said that he carried the practical imitation of the master so far that he ruined his life.' Zola revealed himself to be a conservative, if not myopic, critic. Dismissing the work of Baudelaire, and the work of Verlaine, he concluded that 'no really creative poet has appeared since Lamartine, Hugo and Musset ... The great poet of to-morrow will have to begin by making a clean sweep of all the aesthetics current at the moment. I think that he will be pro-foundly modern, that he will introduce the naturalist note in all its intensity.'[5]

It was now, at the height of Naturalism, when Zola's *L'Assom-moir* and *Nana* were in fashion, that Verlaine published *Sagesse*. It was 'like a gentle tinkle of the angelus in the middle of the orgy'.[6] Verlaine, so Maurice Barrès would write, 'is not Pascal. But he has his accent. This pleased us at a time when the life of the spirit needed once again to be honoured.'[7]

Henry Carton de Wiart, the Belgian man of letters, later wrote that Verlaine, in *Sagesse*, was the most Christian poet of the century.[8] In 1888 Jules Lemaître declared, with critical authority: 'M. Paul Verlaine has dialogues with God which may be com-pared (and I say this in all seriousness) with those of the holy author of the *Imitation* [*of Jesus Christ*] ... This is perhaps the first time that French poetry has really expressed *the love of God*.'[9] George Moore explained: 'Verlaine is, in brief, the one literary aspect of Catholicism.' Years later, Verlaine himself ended a discussion on aesthetics by bringing down his fist on a café table, and crying: 'I'm a mystic poet, myself!'[10]

Yet, strangely enough, as Jacques Robichez has emphasised in his edition of the poems, *Sagesse* is not in fact the great Christian collection which it is traditional to admire; or, at least, it is not Christian in the sense which is generally believed. Out of the forty-seven poems in the first edition, fifteen or so have no con-nection with religious feeling, and several date from before

Verlaine's conversion. The remaining thirty poems are religious in inspiration, but one cannot always maintain that they are Christian. Five or six are mediocre, and they contain the elements of a religious attitude, but not the accent of feeling. Claudel told Gide that he had 'never much liked *Sagesse*, in which Verlaine's sleight of hand was always apparent'.[11]

As for the authenticity of the other poems, which are presented in the preface as 'a public act of faith', Verlaine prays once, and only once, to the Virgin; and if he grows weary of the daily round, the common task, the everyday observance of religion, he escapes by repeating prosaic doctrine, or by creating himself a picturesque and heroic religion: a religion which owes more to 'le Moyen Age énorme et délicat' and, perhaps, to Tennyson's *Idylls of the King*, than it does to genuine Christian feeling. In the dialogue with God: 'Mon Dieu m'a dit . . .,' Verlaine is assured that God wants his love, and that if he believes, and repents for his sins, he will find peace of mind on earth and he will finally be received in Heaven. This dialogue is, to certain critics, the summit of *Sagesse*; and yet, while one cannot doubt its orthodox Christianity, or its honesty of feeling, it lacks the conviction of *Hymns Ancient and Modern*, which Verlaine admired and sometimes followed; and it does not reflect the need to believe in immortality which Tennyson had expressed in 'In Memoriam'. Verlaine's Christianity impressed his contemporaries by its novelty, by its appearance in the age of Naturalism and Realism. In a materialistic age, it claimed to speak to them of the spirit. But, in the edition of 1889, the most satisfactory edition to appear in Verlaine's lifetime, the most successful poems were the poems of mood in the *genre* in which he had excelled since the days of *Poèmes saturniens*.

> Le ciel est, par-dessus le toit,
> Si bleu, si calme . . .

No other living poet could catch that mood, and preserve it with such delicacy.

> Je ne sais pourquoi
> Mon esprit amer
> D'une aile inquiète et folle vole sur la mer . . .[12]

This, and the poem 'Le son du cor s'afflige vers les bois', are landscapes of the soul which could be painted by Verlaine alone; but they have no connection with religion. As for the poem which beings 'La tristesse, la langueur du corps humain . . .', it is hard to see it except as a reminiscence of Verlaine's impassioned meeting with Rimbaud at Stuttgart, or as a remembrance of their final 'nuit d'Hercule'. When Verlaine recalls the sins of the past, and dwells upon the temptations which he must now cast aside, when he feels temptation taking hold, he writes with a feeling which is lacking in his more moralising 'Christian' poems.

> Les faux beaux jours ont lui tout le jour, ma pauvre âme,
> Et les voici vibrer aux cuivres du couchant.
> Ferme les yeux, pauvre âme, et rentre sur-le-champ:
> Une tentation des pires. Fuis l'Infâme.
>
> Ils ont lui tout le jour en longs grêlons de flamme,
> Battant toute vendange aux collines, couchant
> Toute moisson de la vallée, et ravageant
> Le ciel tout bleu, le ciel chanteur qui te réclame.
>
> Ô pâlis, et va-t'en, lente et joignant les mains.
> Si ces hiers allaient manger nos beaux demains?
> Si la vieille folie était encore en route?
>
> Ces souvenirs, va-t-il falloir les retuer?
> Un assaut furieux, le suprême, sans doute!
> Ô va prier contre l'orage, va prier.[13]

The profound charm of *Sagesse* lies in its obsession with the past. Verlaine's contrition is frail, but it intensifies the forbidden pleasures of the past, the obsession with Rimbaud, with women ('Femme et l'œillade de tes seins . . .'), with drink, with sin, with the seven deadly sins. 'These sins,' writes Robichez, 'will soon have their complete revenge, and they will have it until the sinner's death. They are still apparently condemned. But it is from them, when their "Voices" are heard in the poet's heart, that there rises in a book which claims to be right-thinking an intoxicating poetry.'[14]

There was no doubt of Verlaine's good faith. When he wrote

Sagesse, he honestly believed that he had entered the path of salvation; he had been tempted, but determined that he would not now turn back. Yet, as Robichez observes, one must distinguish between the man's intentions and the very depth of his soul, which he could not help revealing in his poetry. The essential reality is not edifying. There are a few moments in *Sagesse* when the convert bathes in the purifying love of Christ; and there are many times when he re-lives and regrets a past which is forbidden – and all the more attractive for being forbidden. Verlaine was not a hypocrite, but *Sagesse* presents the two contestants in the unequal fight which God would lose.

33

In the autumn of 1881, Lucien Létinois finished his year of military service. The farm at Juniville was now understandably in financial danger; and, 'alarmed by several writs, and perhaps tired of farming, Verlaine wanted to resume, with Lucien, the wanderings he had once known with Rimbaud. He decided to give up. He persuaded Lucien to follow him.'[1]

Lepelletier maintains that Verlaine and Lucien went to London. It was, as he observes, an almost traditional destination after any crisis in Verlaine's life. Now he and Lucien – said Lepelletier – went there to forget their failure in farming and the malicious gossip of Juniville. 'This peaceful stay in London, where they lived unknown, was cut short by lack of money, and they had to come back to Paris.'[2] This visit to London was perhaps one of the two visits which Verlaine paid to England after he left Lymington. He mentioned it briefly at the end of his *Notes on England*, and said he proposed to write about it later; but he does not seem to have left a record of it. However, in 'Un Tour à Londres', which appeared among his *Souvenirs et Promenades*, he speaks of lunching 'pour la première fois depuis vingt et depuis dix ans à Londres'.[3] This refers to his visit of 1893. If the statement is accurate, he must have been in London in 1883. The date of the visit remains problematical. François Porché dismisses Lepelletier's statement, and suggests that Verlaine and Lucien stayed at Juniville in the autumn of 1881, and that all the Létinois went to Belgium before the farming enterprise was liquidated early in 1882.[4]

Whatever his previous movements, Verlaine returned to Paris in the summer of 1882, and he went to live with his mother in Boulogne-sur-Seine. Lucien took the post of an usher at the Institution Esnault, nearby. On 16 August, Verlaine wrote to Charles Floquet, the Prefect of the Seine, and asked to be re-instated as a municipal *employé*.[5]

One of the most touching features in the complex character of Verlaine is this lifelong need to conform, to lead a purposeful, middle-class existence. Wildly and incurably bohemian though he was, he still longed for the security and the respectability which a common bourgeois life would bring. On 23 August, the loyal Lepelletier recommended his request to Floquet. On 17 September, the former head of Verlaine's department made a statement in his favour. On 21 September Verlaine sent his dossier to the head of the Premier Bureau du Personnel de la Préfecture de la Seine. There was no legal reason why his request should not be granted. On 22 October he wrote to Lepelletier, urging him to take prompt action with the Prefect. Lepelletier did so. 'Verlaine was very impatient,' he remembered. On 7 January 1883, Verlaine wrote again to Lepelletier. 'My dossier is as complete as possible. They can't oblige me to get certificates of a regular life and regular behaviour from a mass of hotel-keepers . . . I have already had enough trouble getting a certificate from the *Mairie* at Arras.'[6]

Such demands were clearly excessive. The fact was that Floquet had asked the Cour d'appel at Brussels for information about Verlaine. On 28 November the Belgian attorney-general replied, and mentioned Verlaine's condemnation and the medical report of 1873. Verlaine, he said, 'was a person of more than dubious morals.' Floquet had now left the Préfecture, but his successor, Louis Oustry, vetoed Verlaine's application.[7]

This rejection determined his future. If he had become an *employé* again, as Lepelletier wrote, 'he would also have re-found his place in literary and social life; he would have been saved.'[8] As it was, he found himself cast into a life of misery. He had moved, now, with his mother, to 17, rue de la Roquette, in Paris; there they lived among furniture worn by years of enforced removals. On the wall hung the Captain's portrait. The background would in time be riddled with holes where Verlaine, in drunken rage, hitting out with his stick, had revenged himself on destiny.

It was now, in 1883, when officialdom had rejected him, that he was overwhelmed by a more personal tragedy. On 7 April, at the age of twenty-three, Lucien Létinois died of typhoid at the Hôpital de la Pitié.

His parents had come to live in Ivry; and there, in the communal cemetery, he was buried. According to barbarous custom, his grave was conceded to him for ten years. The concession was not renewed, and presumably his bones were then thrown away. But, in the years which followed his death, Verlaine would often visit his grave, or – when he was in hospital – send his friends to Ivry.

He had been more loving than loved. Lucien had not been a natural homosexual. In conversation with Delahaye, he had shown his irritation at Verlaine's 'constant emotion'. He had summed up the relationship with crushing moderation. 'If I didn't love him, I shouldn't be worth much; if I accused him, I'd be unfair, because he meant well . . . But it would certainly have been better if we hadn't met him.'[9]

Verlaine saw the years with Lucien in a different light. To him the death of Lucien seemed God's verdict on their relationship, a judgment on the whole of his past.

> Cette adoption de toi pour mon enfant
> Puisque l'on m'avait volé mon fils réel,
> Elle n'était pas dans les conseils du ciel,
> Je me le suis dit, en pleurant, bien souvent;
>
> Je me le suis dit toujours devant ta tombe
> Noire de fusains, blanche de marguerites,
> Elle fut sans doute un de ces démérites
> Cause de ces maux où voici que je tombe . . .

Verlaine

Cette adoption fut le fruit défendu;
J'aurais dû passer dans l'odeur et le frais
De l'arbre et du fruit sans m'arrêter auprès.
Le ciel m'a puni . . . J'aurais dû, j'aurais dû![10]

PART SEVEN

Coulommes

(1883–5)

34

THE death of Lucien would later inspire Verlaine with a series of religious and lyric poems; he would philosophise about his loss, and lovingly recall the more tranquil moments of their relationship. But it would be some time before he could accept his bereavement as divine justice. Its immediate effect was to drive him to despair and to excess.

Whenever Verlaine reached a crisis in his emotional life, he sought escape. Now, faced with the death of Lucien, he wanted to leave Paris. On 30 July, Mme Verlaine bought a little house in the country to encourage him to lead a country life. On 27 August, he told Mallarmé: 'I have decided to go 50 leagues from Paris to make old bones – or what bones God shall please – in a tiny little labourer's house. It belongs to my mother, and it has a big garden all round it.'[1]

Unfortunately Mme Verlaine had chosen to buy a house from the Létinois: Malval, at Coulommes, between Rethel and Vouziers. It was in the very village where Lucien had been born. It was near the Collège Notre-Dame, where Verlaine had met him; it was near Juniville, where they had led their Virgilian life. It was not far from Charleville, which was Rimbaud's birthplace. The house was a constant reminder of past happiness and present regrets. When Verlaine settled there with his mother, early in the autumn, he soon scandalised the district by the degradation of his life.

Ernest Raynaud, the future historian of Symbolism, remembered when he first heard of Verlaine. It was, he would recall, at Sainte-Vaubourg, a village near Coulommes, where he was spending his holidays as a *collégien*.

It was known that Verlaine had come up against the law, which was food for malice and calumny. The gossip spread. His failings were exaggerated until he assumed the proportions of a real criminal. He associated with waggoners and railwaymen, and with the vagrants who had come to be hired during the harvest ... The window of the room where he worked stayed lit up far into the night. That allowed people to suppose that dreadful things were being plotted there, and, behind the red curtains, belated passers-by imagined that they saw a reflection of the flames of hell. As soon as the gendarmes' caps appeared at the turn of the road, there was no doubt that they were coming because of Verlaine, and mothers used his name like that of the Bogeyman, to frighten little children.

One evening, as I was coming back from a walk, along the Attigny road, with my cousins, the young girls suddenly trembled and seized my arm ... They pointed to a man who had passed us and was striding away into the distance, and they whispered: 'It's Verlaine!' in the tone in which they would have said: 'It's the devil!'[2]

One is constantly amazed by Verlaine's duality. He was indeed the vicious and uncontrollable pervert of the legend; and yet, behind the red curtains of the little house at Coulommes, in the intervals of his homosexual orgies, he was working on *Les Poètes maudits*.

Verlaine's appreciations of Tristan Corbière, Mallarmé and Rimbaud first appeared this year in the periodical *Lutèce*. On 16 August, before he left Paris, he had asked Mallarmé for his help.

My dear Verlaine [replied Mallarmé],
   I ought to say no (at the risk of being absurd) to punish you for thinking of me, and for not sometimes coming to tell me so, one Tuesday or several Tuesdays during the winter ... But since you kindly want to recall me as I was in earlier years, ... let us concern ourselves with the photograph; for that is all you ask me for, and you could

not have doubted for a moment the great pleasure it would give me to
be portrayed by you, and in such good company!...[3]

'My dear friend,' Verlaine wrote to Mallarmé on 29 November,
' "Your" chapters will appear in *Lutèce* in a fortnight's time. I
hope you'll be pleased with me, but I should so like to have
something unpublished of yours! Hurry up, hurry up!'[4]

Verlaine was not concerned only with his article on Mallarmé.
His appreciation of Rimbaud showed the intense attraction
which Rimbaud still possessed for him. Perhaps, since Lucien's
death, the memory of Rimbaud was stronger than ever. But if
Verlaine's article was warm with his latent passion, it also showed
his real understanding of Rimbaud's work. Verlaine had been
influenced in his writing by Rimbaud; he was also aware of the
extent of Rimbaud's powers. Now he presented six of his poems,
including 'Le Bateau ivre'. It was a bold and epoch-making
gesture. In these articles, Verlaine opened the gates of renown to
Rimbaud, Corbière and Mallarmé, and he affirmed the sanctity
of poetry. And he was already breaking out into the future. As
Raynaud was to write: 'One can consider Verlaine's little work
as the first manifesto of Symbolism. It became the watchword of
youth ... No innovation was attempted, no reform proposed,
of which *Les Poètes maudits* had not furnished the matter and the
food. It was they who, for the new generation, in the words of
Paul Claudel, illuminated "all the paths of Art, Religion, and
Life".'[5]

Lutèce had launched *Les Poètes maudits*. It soon began to publish
Verlaine's poems, and Verlaine was acclaimed by the younger
generation. Until then he had been unrecognised or misunderstood; now, suddenly, he was discovered. In the offices of *Lutèce*,
in the brasseries, when he went to Paris, he was surrounded by
poets who were eager for something different. There were Jean
Moréas, Henri de Régnier, Rodolphe Darzens, and Laurent
Tailhade. There were Louis Le Cardonnel and Stuart Merrill.
From this sort of circle rose the 'Decadent' movement, from
which Symbolism would in time emerge.

Les Poètes maudits were published in book form by Léon Vanier
in the spring of 1884. Four years later, Vanier would publish a

new, enlarged edition of the work, including studies of Mme Desbordes-Valmore, Villiers de l'Isle-Adam, and a self-portrait by Verlaine. It was *Les Poètes maudits* which established Vanier as Verlaine's publisher.

Léon Vanier had been born in Paris in 1847. After a period selling fishing tackle, and another working in a bookshop, he had opened a shop of his own at 6, rue Hautefeuille, in 1869. He had determined to be, for the Symbolists and Decadents, what Lemerre had been for the Parnassians, and in 1881 he established himself at the address which he would make famous: 19 quai Saint-Michel.

He was a small, brown-skinned, active, intelligent man [remembered Armand Lods, the bibliophile], with an ambition to found a great publishing house . . . When he opened his first shop, Vanier had had very small resources; but, thanks to a good speculation in bookselling, he was able to develop his trade and become a publisher.
The publisher of the Quai Saint-Michel remembered his hard and humble beginnings. He was very economical. He was therefore loath to give Verlaine a sum of any importance. He knew that the poet spent without thinking . . . I have been present at scenes between the publisher and the poet, the latter claiming twelve francs for two poems destined for *Parallèlement*, and Vanier agreeing only to an advance of ten francs. *Sagesse* . . . had been published at Verlaine's expense. It was also at his expense that, in 1884, Vanier published *Jadis et Naguère*.[6]

In his study of Verlaine, Van Bever wrote that the relationship of Verlaine and Vanier was a mere series of hagglings, and that Verlaine always lost in the end. The publisher's contracts, wrote Van Bever, gave the poet meagre provender: 250 francs for a book of medium size, often much less. Vanier usually gave Verlaine five francs a poem.[7]
But Vanier gave Verlaine five francs a sonnet because, he said, 'that obliges him to work.' He could not bear inactivity, nor could he bear improvidence or extravagance. Verlaine used to call on him when he wanted to borrow money, and Vanier was vexed by the habit. What annoyed him most, however, was to see Verlaine arrive by cab. When Verlaine had a little money he would take

a cab in the place Saint-Michel to go to Vanier's, forty yards away. Vanier was all the more enraged by this extravagance, as Verlaine would come in without paying his fare. On each occasion, the irate cabby burst into the shop to claim his due, and only his insults and Vanier's pleading decided Verlaine to acquit his debt. It was probably on one such occasion that Verlaine reminded Vanier of his humble beginnings, and dismissed him as 'a degenerate maggot-merchant'.[8]

On 7 April 1884, Mallarmé acknowledged his copy of *Les Poètes maudits*.

My dear Verlaine,
... It is wonderfully fortunate that you have rescued some of Rimbaud's work ... and taken the poetry of that astonishing Corbière out of the libraries. As far as my own part is concerned, you know what I think of it! Perhaps there exists within me, and perhaps there will emerge, something which is worthy of what you say to-day, and so I accept your dear words with completely new courage. But I have nothing behind me which deserves to be remembered, except by the magnificent highlight of your sympathy, my dear Verlaine, really I have nothing, or almost nothing.
How are you? What are you doing? I have been in very poor health, this winter ... Sometimes I cast my eyes in your direction, and I feel happy to think that you are at peace ... Many young people have a proper cult for you. I'm pleased about that, the evenings when I see them ...[9]

The cult for Verlaine had already spread beyond the rue de Rome, and one of his warmest admirers was Huysmans. 'Would you post me the *Poèmes saturniens* and *Sagesse*, by Verlaine?' Louis Desprez had asked P.-V. Stock on 7 March. 'M. Huysmans .... assures me that, in this last book, Verlaine has given the essence of modern poetry.'[10]

Huysmans did not content himself with such verbal praise. In May 1884 he published his most famous novel, *À Rebours*. The hero, Des Esseintes, was said to be based on the dandy and aesthete, Robert de Montesquiou; and the book is a compendium of fin-de-siècle tastes and interests. Des Esseintes tries to overcome the tedium of life by leading an aesthetic existence; and one of the pleasures he gives himself is to read the *Poèmes saturniens* of Verlaine.

Looking for his antecedents, des Esseintes found a talent already deeply impregnated with Baudelaire ...

He handled metre better than anyone, and he had attempted to give new life to poems with fixed forms ...

But his distinction lay above all in this: that he had been able to express vague and delightful confessions in the half-light. He alone had suggested something disturbing beyond the soul, such faint whisperings of thoughts, such murmured, broken confessions that the ear which heard them remained in doubt . ⸭

It was during the summer of 1884, after the publication of his book, that Huysmans met Verlaine. He found him 'a fascinating character – a combination of a brutal, wheedling pederast and a confirmed drunkard'.[12] Often, in the years that followed (writes Huysmans' biographer), he would admonish the pederast and the drunkard; but he would also help the poet. At the end of Huysmans' life, André Germain used to visit him.

And once he had started on the touching and grievous subject of Verlaine in his last years [remembered Germain], he never stopped. Let me give his own words. There are just a few details too crude for me to be brave enough to print them.

'When Verlaine had his crises of mysticism and remorse, he ... used to come and find me at the Ministry. Or, to be exact, he used to send me some imperious appeal, scribbled on a dirty piece of paper in a nearby café. I couldn't always answer the summons. And then, fifteen minutes later, the messenger would come back: 'Monsieur Verlaine is still waiting for Monsieur; he's crying.' I found myself obliged to leave my office.

And Verlaine mourned his lot. Even the churches weren't a refuge for him. When he asked to make his confession, the sacristan sometimes looked at his ragged clothes, stained with vomit, and turned him out.

On one occasion, it was particularly important: 'It's very serious, I'm in love with ...' (Here came a detail which I think unnecessary.) 'There's only one way to save myself. There's an excellent priest waiting for me in Belgium. I can go off and stay with him, but I need some clothes and my fare.'

I went in search of his publisher, and obtained some money.

I took him to La Belle Jardinière, where he began to alarm me by talking of ordering a corduroy suit. 'You're going to choose a suit for 39 francs 75,' I said to him, and that's what he did.

But when we were in the street again, I soon caught sight of a wretched procession of beggars who were following us, and had somehow sensed that Verlaine had a few sous in his pocket. I realised that it was all no good. He rejoined his companions.'[13]

35

Early in December 1884, Vanier published *Jadis et Naguère*.

The four years which lay between *Sagesse* and *Jadis et Naguère* had been decisive years in Verlaine's life, but they had not influenced the genesis of his latest work. In 1884 he was making a fresh beginning in literature; he was publishing or republishing, in various reviews, many of the poems which appeared in this new collection. But he was not composing them. During these four years, he had composed six or seven at the most; all the rest – five-sixths of the book – were ten or fifteen years old.

The plan of *Jadis et Naguère* seems clear at first sight: it is divided into the distant and the recent past. But in fact the book may be differently divided. Verlaine uses the poems which have not appeared in his five earlier collections, and he goes back, first, to the years before Rimbaud arrived in Paris. He exhumes eighteen poems which reflect the influences and the inspirations of long ago. The sonnet 'Allégorie' is clearly reminiscent of Leconte de Lisle: 'Circonspection' (first published in 1867) might well have found a place in *Fêtes galantes* had it not been too close in inspiration to 'En sourdine'. 'Écrit sur l'album de Mme N. de V.' was a witticism which belonged to the salon of Nina de Villard, Mme de Callias, and it does not bear resurrection. Nor does 'Le Soldat laboureur', the parody which had been recited by the actor Francès in the same salon. 'La Princesse Bérénice' is a sonnet in the style of Banville; and it was to Banville, in 1871, that Verlaine had dedicated his comedy *Les Uns et les Autres*. It appears here, clumsily out of place, an unhappy attempt to exploit the eighteenth-century mood of *Fêtes galantes*. The poems of *Fêtes galantes* had shone with intensity, with power of suggestion. *Les Uns et les Autres* seems like a gross excrescence. By drawing out the dialogue to some four hundred lines, Verlaine has presumed too much of the subject.

A second group of eighteen poems, scattered throughout the book, was written in the years 1873–4. Most of these poems belong to 'Cellulairement', the collection which had been composed in prison. The best poems in *Jadis et Naguère* come from 'Cellulairement', and it is here that the collection echoes *Sagesse*. 'Conseil falot', for example, is closely related to the 'Via dolorosa' of the earlier collection. The other poems from 'Cellulairement' include 'Art poétique', which had appeared in a review in 1882 but only now made its impact on the literary world. They also include 'Kaléidoscope', the brilliant, dream-like, Proustian poem which implies far more about Verlaine's own art. 'Crimen amoris', too, had been written in prison at Brussels; it shows the intense, inescapable influence of Rimbaud. Verlaine also published the sonnet which begins:

Ce soir je m'étais penché sur ton sommeil . . .

The sleeping figure he gazes on with such tenderness, the sleeping lover who arouses his physical passion, is generally thought to be Rimbaud. Nothing proves his identity, or even proves that the figure is that of a man, except the defiant title which Verlaine chose to give the sonnet: 'Vers pour être calomnié'. As if to emphasise his point, he follows the poem with the sonnet once called 'Invocation', and now called 'Luxures'. This is an emended version of the poem which he had sent Lepelletier in May 1873, the poem in which he had expressed his intense need for Rimbaud. In this second version, as in the first, Verlaine extols forbidden love. *Jadis et Naguère* also included 'Le Poète et la Muse': the poem written in Mons 'à propos d'une chambre, rue Campagne-Première'.

In *Sagesse*, the convert who had sought to love God alone had come at last to seek divine sanction for all forms of love; he had persuaded himself that God allowed all human passions and asked only for the offering of the bitterness that followed them. Now he no longer sought to proclaim his religious conviction. With strange disregard for the reputation which *Sagesse* had created, the new reputation he had tried to establish, he reaffirmed the power and delight of his love for Rimbaud. He had since known Létinois, but Rimbaud remained supreme.

There were a few recent poems in this strangely disparate collection, and one of them would be eagerly claimed by the Decadent school of poets. 'Langueur' has the climate of the 'fin de siècle'; it might be illustrated by Gustave Moreau or by Aubrey Beardsley. It suggests solitude, tedium, moral impotence; perhaps it also reveals the secret torments of Verlaine himself.

> Je suis l'Empire à la fin de la décadence,
> Qui regarde passer les grands Barbares blancs
> En composant des acrostiches indolents
> D'un style d'or où la langueur du soleil danse.
>
> L'âme seulette a mal au cœur d'un ennui dense.
> Là-bas on dit qu'il est de longs combats sanglants.
> Ô n'y pouvoir, étant si faible aux vœux si lents,
> Ô n'y vouloir fleurir un peu cette existence!
>
> Ô n'y vouloir, ô n'y pouvoir mourir un peu!
> Ah! tout est bu! Bathylle, as-tu fini de rire?
> Ah! tout est bu, tout est mangé! Plus rien à dire!
>
> Seul, un poème un peu niais qu'on jette au feu,
> Seul, un esclave un peu coureur qui vous néglige,
> Seul, un ennui d'on ne sait quoi qui vous afflige![1]

In the first line of this sonnet, Verlaine had unwittingly suggested the name of a new literary movement. When 'Langueur' had first appeared in *Le Chat noir* in 1883, Félicien Champsaur had promptly discovered and christened the Decadent School. In 1885 the enterprising Vanier had published *Les Déliquescences d'Adoré Floupette*. This accomplished little book of parodies was written by Henri Beauclair and Gabriel Vicaire, and Verlaine appeared in it, thinly disguised as Bleucoton. *Les Déliquescences d'Adoré Floupette* was the fantastic manifesto of these poets of the future – as they considered themselves to be. The following year, Anatole Baju founded a controversial review, *Le Décadent*.[2] Verlaine became a pillar of the periodical.

I like the word decadent [he said], all shimmering with purple and gold . . . It throws out the brilliance of flames and the gleam of precious stones. It is made of carnal spirit and unhappy flesh and of all the violent splendours of the Lower Empire; it conjures up the paint of the courtesans, the sports of the circus, the breath of the tamers of animals, the bounding of wild beasts, the collapse among the flames of races exhausted by the power of feeling, to the invading sound of enemy trumpets. The decadence is Sardanapalus lighting the fire in the midst of his women, it is Seneca declaiming poetry as he opens his veins, it is Petronius masking his agony with flowers . . .[3]

The new Decadent School needed a leader, and it adopted Verlaine. But he himself refused to be called a Decadent, just as he later refused to be called a Symbolist. He had no time for classifications. He thought that the poet must write as it came to him.

36

At Coulommes, disaster was now imminent. Even Lepelletier gave a stern account of the situation.

Verlaine was entirely to blame, and greatly to blame . . . He drank terribly . . . He had also become friendly with a band of young rustic revellers. They used to sit up and tipple well into the night . . .

Money was soon short. Verlaine demanded more from his mother, sometimes he did so imperiously . . . For the sake of peace, Mme Verlaine yielded to his demands. No doubt she also had to face the expenses and the results of several lawsuits, which had arisen from disputes with neighbours, local farmers and tradesmen. She relinquished her ownership of the house at Coulommes.

In a contract drawn up by Me Chartier, a solicitor at Attigny, on

17 April 1884, Mme veuve Verlaine gave her son, Paul-Marie Verlaine, the property at Coulommes; the deed of gift contained a clause of non-distrainability, in order to ensure a home for the donee, who was beset by various creditors.[1]

Throughout 1884 Verlaine continued his degrading life. He drank excessively and mixed with the scum of the neighbourhood, and with ne'er-do-wells, whom he invited, at his expense, from Paris. Mme Verlaine had a neighbour at Coulommes, a Belgian, a M. Dave, and he often remonstrated with him. M. Dave advised her to leave him. One day, early in the new year, after a violent quarrel, she left the house and took shelter with M. Dave.

On 9 February 1885, after his mother had left him, Verlaine went to Paris to see Vanier, and settled at Austin's Hotel, the English tavern in the rue d'Amsterdam. Two days later, violent with drink, he returned to Coulommes, and went to M. Dave's in search of his mother. Mme Verlaine, loyal as ever, later swore that he had not attacked her; M. Dave insisted that he had done so. The court – for the case was taken to court – accepted M. Dave's account. They accepted that Verlaine had seized a knife and threatened to kill her unless she gave him money.

M. Dave must have been influential, and Mme Verlaine could have shown little spirit. It was incredible that she let her son face such a charge. But when Verlaine appeared in court on 24 March, local opinion was heavily against him; and no doubt his past had once again helped to condemn him. Years later, in *Invectives*, there appeared his lines to the magistrate at Vouziers:

> Tu m'as insulté, toi! du haut de ton tréteau,
>   Grossier, trivial, rustre!
> Tu m'as insulté, moi! l'homme épris du seul beau,
>   Moi, qu'on veut croire illustre.
>
> Tu parles de mes mœurs, espèce de bavard,
>   D'ailleurs sans éloquence . . .[2]

Verlaine was sentenced to a month's imprisonment. He entered the jail at Vouziers on 12 April. Among the papers of Cazals is a scrap of paper with the memorandum: 'Maudissons les mères

(m. d'un veuf). Prison de Vouziers. 85.'[3] *Mémoires d'un veuf* contained no chapter with this title, but the idea is still eloquent.

On 13 May, Verlaine came out of prison; but this time no one met him. Mme Verlaine intended to punish him by her absence. He was acutely aware of her gesture, but he celebrated his freedom. He invited the chief warder to the nearest tavern.

He had no wish to seek his mother at Coulommes, especially if she was at M. Dave's. Indeed, she might not even be there, for she had written that she was soon returning to Paris. As for the house at Coulommes, it no longer belonged to him: on 8 March, he had sold it to a local farmer, at a loss.

Nine days after his release from Vouziers, Mathilde's judicial separation was turned into a divorce. Verlaine had irrevocably lost her. It is doubtful when the news reached him. After his release there came a mysterious period when he led a vagabond life in the Ardennes. He is said to have stayed for a while at Corbion, a village near Sedan, where he spent the evenings with the curé. The abbé Dewez had been obliged to renounce a distinguished career, ostensibly for reasons of health; and he found himself, now, in spiritual charge of this obscure Ardennais village. He had been a childhood friend of Verlaine's at Paliseul; and now the presbytery at Corbion echoed into the night with their discussions.[4]

Verlaine himself was to recall his weeks of wandering in 'Poème saturnien' in *Parallèlement*; he had led a drunken, penniless search for homosexual adventure.[5] He would also recall his vagabondage in 'La Goutte', a thumbnail sketch which appeared among his *Œuvres posthumes*.[6] On 31 May he seems to have had some experience at Attigny ('On m'a frôlé. – La nuit sans pareille!').[7] Next day, the day of Hugo's grandiose funeral in Paris, Verlaine tramped the scorching roads of Champagne, wearing a fur-trimmed overcoat and a top-hat. They were, presumably, the only clothes he possessed. He had no money, and a beggar gave him a drink at a tavern. Once he spent the night in a tinker's caravan.[8] In the Ardennes, where he had met Lucien, on the roads which Rimbaud knew so well, he chose to seek his degradation – to make his defiant assertion of independence.

PART EIGHT

6, Cour Saint-François

(1885–7)

37

O N about 13 June, Verlaine settled in Paris: at 6, Cour Saint-François, 5, rue Moreau. The street was in the working-class quarter, at the end of the faubourg Saint-Antoine, and it passed under the sombre arches of the Vincennes railway. The Hôtel du Midi stood mouldering at the back of a damp courtyard, where passing trains disgorged a hurricane of cinders and smoke. The yard was cluttered up with washing, scrap-iron, and a barricade of hand-trucks on which the local children ran wild; night and day, the place was full of clamour.

Mme Verlaine, forgiving as ever, came to join her son. She had a room on the first floor. Verlaine was now suffering from a bad leg; but the 'arthritis' which Lepelletier mentions was probably a symptom of venereal disease. Since he could not climb stairs, he occupied a room on the ground floor. The only light and air came through a window with a grille, which looked on to the yard. The only view was the view of high, blind walls. The bed was hung with black cotton curtains, the wallpaper had faded, and the tiles on the floor were broken. There was a walnut washstand, holding the remains of a basin; there were a rickety stained table and four broken-down chairs. Verlaine was forced to keep to his bed; he had to read borrowed books, because his library had been scattered. All that remained of it were the works of Calderon, a first edition of Corbière's *Les Amours Jaunes*, and Rimbaud's *Une Saison en Enfer*.[1]

Mme Verlaine was seventy-six and still wonderfully good-natured, but age and troubles had somewhat confused her mind. She and Verlaine were now almost ruined. Of the 400,000 gold francs which they had once possessed, only 20,000 remained. Mme Verlaine had managed to save them from the disastrous venture at Coulommes, and she was hiding the bonds from her son. The income was less than 900 francs. This was all they had to live on.

Yet, despite illness and privations, this was not an unhappy period in Verlaine's life. He had determined to write for his living, and he was working fiercely, writing *Amour*, *Parallèlement*, and *Mémoires d'un veuf*. Besides, a number of friends used to come and see him. Raynaud remembered: 'Young writers learned the way to his lodging ... They were all delighted with the genuine welcome Verlaine gave them, with his good-nature and with a zest which, in such circumstances, in such lamentable surroundings, was heroic.'[2]

Late in November, René Ghil, the young poet, went to visit him at the Hôtel du Midi. It was, remembered Ghil, 'a lodging-house of dubious appearance; and, except for the narrow door, the whole of the ground floor was painted a violent red ... The walls in the narrow corridor seemed slimy from wet nights.'[3]

Verlaine himself appeared to be imbued with some of the sinister nature of the place. 'His damp, thick moustache was so long that it mingled with his unkempt beard.' He walked up and down as he was talking (his leg, it seems, was for the moment better). He reviled the Parnassians.

Then he got carried away, the storm suffused the monstrous face, - and he inveighed against Mendès, whose success annoyed him, he compared himself to François Coppée and jeered at him, bitterly. And suddenly, like a mischievous child, he put on his overcoat, picked up his stick and his battered felt hat. 'Now we'll go and have a drink,' he said.[4]

In December, Ghil met him again, this time in the local church.

I found him [he remembered] in a humble, adoring, almost childlike posture before the altar of the Virgin. He was praying sincerely with heart and voice. And certainly, when I touched his shoulder, his pale face ... seemed to me infinitely touching.

'I'm coming,' he said, with the gaze of a blind man. 'Let me finish my prayer.'

The situation underlined his remarkable dual nature; and, as he and Ghil left the church, Verlaine felt called upon to explain the contradictory spirits within him.

'Every man,' he said, 'has two creatures within him, two creatures who hold together and yet remain at variance – very much at variance! – with each other. There are an angel and a beast ... I wrote *La Bonne Chanson* and *Sagesse*: there's the Angel, you see! Now I shall write a book called *Parallèlement*, because I must also give voice to the Beast within me. And so, in time, there will be other books, and it will be like that, *parallèlement* ... There's my plan!'

The conversation continued; then, suddenly, he asked:

'Do you think Mallarmé would come and see me? ... I'd like to see him again: we knew one another in the days of *le Parnasse* ... Can't go and see him, now. They say he lives at Les Batignolles, four floors up. Impossible, with my knee ... And then he's married, Mallarmé, and he's got a daughter ... Leads a regular life. So I couldn't go there. No clothes or manners ... You could arrange that, couldn't you? You'd bring him ... And there's something else ...'

He stopped abruptly, as he often did. Anxiety passed across his face, trembled in his rough voice:

'Mallarmé. He teaches English at Condorcet, doesn't he? Now my boy, you know, my boy, he's a day-boarder at Condorcet. I mustn't see him, that's been settled, because ... there were faults, yes, there were faults, which might have been forgiven. So if Mallarmé wanted? We'd arrange a meeting, and he'd take me into the courtyard and stay there himself – while I was seeing the boy and talking to him. I'd let him know what his father is – and he's a good man, too!'[5]

'My dear Mallarmé,' wrote Verlaine, soon afterwards, 'this morning I had a letter from René Ghil to announce his visit and your own – I look forward to it eagerly ...'[6]

Either that month, or in January 1886, Mallarmé, much moved, came with Ghil to the Cour Saint-François. It was the first meeting, since the days of *le Parnasse*, of the two masters who would soon dominate Symbolism. Verlaine had tidied up his room, and taken trouble with his appearance,

... and his smile was so happy when he put his hands into the out-stretched hands of Mallarmé! Despite all the years which had passed since they had seen one another, both of them naturally resumed the familiar form of address ...

And yet [wrote Ghil] I observed a kind of timidity, even humility, in Verlaine's behaviour. Verlaine was going to be forty-two, and the poet of *L'Après-midi d'un faune* was his senior by a mere two years. But it was with this charming suggestion of homage that Verlaine ... declared their equality in the admiration of the new poetic age.

'Well, Mallarmé, here we are, famous! Leaders of a School!'

'Yes. Who would have thought it?' answered Mallarmé, amused, with a smile which brought delicate creases round his eyes.[7]

At about the time of Mallarmé's visit, another eminent figure appeared in the unspeakable Cour Saint-François.

George Moore had first arrived in Paris in 1873, determined to make his career as an artist. He had stayed there until 1880, and he was probably the first to introduce the English public to the Huysmans of *À Rebours*, to the Goncourts, Rimbaud, Verlaine and Laforgue. He may well have met Verlaine at Nina de Callias' *salon*; but it was now, in the first days of 1886, that Moore (back in Paris as a man of letters) paid his first recorded visit to the poet. He went with his friend Édouard Dujardin: poet, dramatist, novelist, and editor of *La Revue wagnérienne*. They were to collect a sonnet for the magazine. As Moore recalled:

A boy with a face so rosy that he reminded one of a butcher-boy, opened to us, and among some dirty bedclothes we came upon Verlaine. His sinister eyes seemed to reflect the stony silence of the prison cell and yard, and his bald, prominent forehead, his shaggy eyebrows, frightened me; and Dujardin, too, was frightened when Verlaine offered to show us his leg, which he said was better but still gave him so much pain that he might have to return to the hospital [*sic*]. And he would have shown us his leg if he had not remembered as he was about to lift the bed-clothes that his duty as a host was to offer us some wine . . . We were young and enthusiastic and hoped, luck having favoured us so far, that by drinking the wine we should persuade him to recite his sonnet . . . We refrained from expressing our doubts regarding the subject of the sonnet, for when he began to tell the subject, he turned to the butcher-boy and described women as trash . . .

Unable to bear his society and that of the butcher-boy any longer, we departed, saying to ourselves: We shall not be able to publish the sonnet.

Here it is, said Dujardin next day, here is the sonnet which you heard Verlaine speak of as autobiographical. You cannot possibly publish it! I cried. Listen, said Dujardin . . . :[8]

> Parsifal a vaincu les Filles, leur gentil
> Babil et la luxure amusante – et sa pente
> Vers la Chair de garçon vierge que cela tente
> D'aimer les seins légers et ce gentil babil;
>
> Il a vaincu la Femme belle, au cœur subtil,
> Étalant ses bras frais et sa gorge excitante;
> Il a vaincu l'Enfer et rentre sous sa tente
> Avec un lourd trophée à son bras puéril,
>
> Avec la lance qui perça le Flanc suprême!
> Il a guéri le roi, le voici roi lui-même,
> Et prêtre du très saint Trésor essentiel.
>
> En robe d'or il adore, gloire et symbole,
> Le vase pur où resplendit le Sang réel.
> Et, ô ces voix d'enfants chantant dans la coupole![9]

'Parsifal' was published in *La Revue wagnérienne* on 8 January 1886. It was one of eight sonnets written by different poets in homage to Wagner. Paul Dukas, the composer, remembered the publication as an event in literary history.[10]

38

It was now, in the squalor of the slum, in the January cold, that Mme Verlaine fell ill: overcome by age and by years of hardship.

Verlaine was immobilised by his bad leg, and could not climb the stairs to attend to her; at his request a young poet, the pious Louis Le Cardonnel, watched over her in her last moments.

She died on 21 January. Huysmans was to tell Goncourt how Verlaine's drunken friends had kept vigil round her body. 'And then,' added Goncourt, 'there were all the difficulties with the friends and undertakers, all of them equally drunk, to get the coffin down the narrow stairs. While they were bringing it down, the son's door opened for a moment, and someone handed him a holy-water sprinkler so that he could cast holy water from his bed.'[1]

The news of Mme Verlaine's death was given to Mathilde Verlaine by some unknown friend of her former husband's. Even Mathilde was moved.

My poor mother-in-law had just died. Her son was confined to bed with one of his legs in plaster, and he could not attend her funeral; he wanted me to go to it, with Georges.

My son [so Mathilde remembered] was at school at Pons, in the Charente-Inférieure, where I had had him brought up since he was nine. He could not have arrived in time for the ceremony, but I promised to go in his place. After all, the poor woman was very fond of me; if she had stopped coming to Montmartre and seeing her grandson, that was no doubt so as not to seem to lay open blame on my husband's behaviour . . . When she died, she had almost nothing left except her pension as a captain's widow. I arrived at the church with a relation. I was the only representative of the family there. After the mass, I received the condolences of the congregation; there weren't many people and most of them seemed to belong to the lower orders.[2]

Among them was the *patronne* of a little bar-restaurant, Chez Louisou, near the Bastille, which Verlaine frequented. 'Don't cry, Monsieur,' she had told Verlaine. 'You will see your mother again in Heaven . . . . She was so good . . .'[3]

I was asked [Mathilde continued] to get into a carriage which had been reserved for me, and to accompany the coffin to the Cimetière des Batignolles, where the Verlaines had their family vault.

Two other women got into my carriage; they seemed to belong to the working class. One of them was a great gossip, and, since she had no idea who I was, she gave an account of the poor woman's death . . . She seemed to hate Verlaine, and to accuse him of having caused his mother's death by the demands he made of her. He had (she said) sent her in search of a special tobacco in the place de la Bastille, in snowy weather. Mme Verlaine had caught a chill; and, desolate, disheartened, weary of life, she had retired to her bed . . .

My poor mother-in-law contracted inflammation of the lungs, and she refused all food and medicine. She did not speak to anyone, she turned her face to the wall, and she died from inanition, as much as illness, three days later.

This sad story was followed by others which were very painful. The woman, a neighbour from the Cour Saint-François, had often had occasion to see Verlaine . . . I learned from her that, after the sale of the property in the Ardennes, Verlaine received 14,000 francs, put them in his pocket and went out, in spite of his mother's supplications. He was away for three days, and he came back completely drunk, dirty, dishevelled, and stripped of everything. What had happened to him? Had he lost the money or given it away? Had someone stolen it? The mystery remains.

When I returned home [added Mathilde], I told my father what I had heard. He thought that since Verlaine was now completely alone in life, poor and ill, he would do everything to be reconciled with me; and since there was nothing he feared so much as this reconciliation, he urged me strongly to take advantage of the divorce law and to re-marry. He said that he would die in peace if he knew that my son and I were protected.[4]

Mathilde had divorced Verlaine eight months earlier. Her father had kept her for the last fourteen years, he had paid for the education of her son, and he would not have allowed her to suffer any financial stress. Now, in a final moment of rancour, he and Mathilde took revenge on a man whom they knew to be ill, bereaved and destitute. 'On her death,' explained Mathilde, 'my mother-in-law left very little. My allowance had not been paid for fourteen years. There was something to reimburse me with. Me Guyot-Sionnest, my solicitor, took possession of the small inheritance.'[5]

Four days after his mother's funeral, Verlaine received the visit of a tipstaff, sent by Mathilde. He had to give an account of his financial position. He could have answered that he had nothing; but, without hesitation, he drew the packet of bonds – all his resources – from under his mattress. Mathilde declared that she later 'learned' that Verlaine was destitute, and she sent much of the money back to him. He returned a receipt, which she still possessed. Such statements are unconvincing. Mathilde had known of Verlaine's poverty. She had not refrained from taking legal action. Besides, as Porché pointed out, in his introduction to her memoirs, Mathilde did not choose to publish the receipt in her book.[6]

<h2 style="text-align:center">39</h2>

The death of his mother marked a turning-point in Verlaine's emotional life. Like many men with homosexual inclinations, he turned to maternal women. In the past fourteen years, since he had last seen Mathilde in Brussels, he had not approached a woman; now, from February to May, he had an affair with a prostitute, Marie Gambier. She, too, lived in the Cour Saint-François, and she had looked after the dying Mme Verlaine.[1] Marie Gambier was to be followed by several other whores before Verlaine became enamoured of the two plebeian 'muses' of his last years. While the death of Lucien had plunged him into homosexuality, the death of his mother sent him back to heterosexual love – or, rather, to the comfort of the maternal breast.

But Verlaine's immediate instincts were psychological rather than physical; he was not cured of his need for the friendship – and, indeed, the love – of young men. Something of the faith of his conversion remained; but he had had a surfeit of temperance and chastity. Absinthe and his blood, which was 'as fiery as lava', led him to the sins of the flesh. It was now that he met Cazals.

> Mon ami, ma plus belle amitié, ma meilleure,
> – Les morts sont morts, douce leur soit l'éternité ! –
> Laisse-moi te le dire en toute vérité,
> Tu vins au temps marqué, tu parus à ton heure;

Tu parus sur ma vie et tu vins dans mon cœur
Au jour climatérique où, noir vaisseau qui sombre,
J'allais noyer ma chair sous la débauche sombre,
Ma chair dolente, et mon esprit jadis vainqueur,

Et mon âme naguère et jadis toute blanche!
Mais tu vins, tu parus, tu vins comme un voleur,
– Tel Christ viendra – voleur qui m'a pris mon malheur!
Tu parus sur ma mer non pas comme une planche

De salut, mais le Salut même! . . .[2]

Frédéric-Auguste Cazals – like Lucien Létinois – was twenty-one years younger than Verlaine. He had been born in Paris in 1865. His father was a tailor; his mother was the daughter of an orchestra conductor in Strasbourg. Cazals himself had the independence of the Parisian. As a child, in the Siege of Paris, he had chalked caricatures of Prussians on the pavement. He had later worked for a printer, and for a businessman, but he did not take to office work; he soon left his employer, and earned a meagre living by sketching portraits. Gay, irreverent, dandified, 'wearing a frock-coat of the 1830 cut, always sporting lemon-coloured gloves and a monocle', Cazals began, in verse and in drawings, to poke fun at the literary côteries. Ernest Raynaud called him 'that pseudo-Delacroix'; but his gaiety and wit endeared him to everyone else.[3]

It was in about April 1886 that Cazals first met Verlaine. Drawn by his legend, he called at the Cour Saint-François, and, during the next two years, he often went to see him in hospital. Verlaine was despondent about his health, his financial straits, and about the void in his emotional life. From the first moment, he was drawn to Cazals, heartened by his youth and enthusiasm, touched by his *gentillesse ailée*: his readiness to copy out his work, take poems to his publisher, fetch his payment from his editors, find him a room, and help him, when the need arose, to move his belongings. During the first two years of their friendship, when Verlaine spent so many months in hospital, he became dependent on him.

He was also strongly attracted to him; and in 1888 the relationship reached a sudden climax. On 20 August, Verlaine declared that it would be an honour to dedicate *Bonheur* to him; he thought of taking a room near him, and asked him to look for something suitable.[4] Two days later he begged Cazals to forgive him for his 'ardour'.[5] He had clearly attempted to follow his physical inclinations, and he had been rebuffed.

Cazals had no homosexual leanings – and, strangely enough, Verlaine had not recognised the fact. But now Cazals retreated in alarm, and Verlaine was obliged to assure him: '*Je vous reste ami beaucoup, beaucoup,*' and to try to move him to pity: '*Savez comme je souffre de solitude*!!'[6] On 17 November Verlaine went into hospital, and his emotions were intensified by absence. He asked Cazals to visit him as often as possible. 'You know how miserable I am when I don't have news.' As proof of his affection, he began the fifteenth poem in *Bonheur*:

> Mon ami, ma plus belle amitié, ma meilleure ...

But he was careful not to offend Cazals' susceptibilities: '*C'est élevé et affecteux,*' he explained. '*J'espère que ça t'ira.*'[7]

Cazals remained devoted to him, but his devotion had limits. He was still sensitive about Verlaine's physical desires, and he was determined not to satisfy them; he was unable – even if he had wanted – to match Verlaine's emotions. Verlaine was passionate and clinging, Cazals was light-hearted and independent. At times, no doubt, he enjoyed his emotional hold on Verlaine, and he deliberately provoked him. But he was upset by the gossip about their relationship, and this gossip created friction. Again and again Verlaine assured him of the purity of his feelings. 'You are my only real and deep affection in the world. I am in fact jealous, *jealous* like a tiger ... of our fine and noble friendship, this friendship which is and will remain my last *human* passion.'[8]

In June 1888 Verlaine drew up a will, making Cazals his heir; and that month they reached a turning-point in their relationship. 'My dear child,' wrote Verlaine on 20 June, 'People are plaguing me and persecuting me on every side, and reproaching me for my quite pure – at last! – friendship for you. Do I "hanker after" you? Yes, of course, and I've never disguised that from you, and all my jealousies and cruelties (these last, I might add, reciprocated) are an irremediable proof of it. But you can bear witness that I've suppressed all that ... I am capable, you know, of every sacrifice, except the sacrifice of my affection ...'[9] 'I am odiously alone,' he added, a few days afterwards. 'Don't be angry with me if I don't come and see you. I can't *walk* any more!! It's terrible, it would be better to die if I hadn't got you – but I must live a little longer for you.'[10]

The month had begun unhappily, but it ended in serenity; and Providence itself took a hand. On 8 July, Verlaine returned to hospital, and occupied a bed near Cazals. For the next forty days they were neighbours. Verlaine recalled the tranquillity of these days in 'Souvenir de l'hôpital'.[11] Cazals recorded an expedition they made together to Paris to collect what Verlaine called '*des argents*'. They paused so often for a drink that they did not return to Broussais until nightfall. The concierge refused to admit them; and they were let in only after long negotiations.[12]

40

On 11 April 1886 there appeared the first number of *La Vogue*. The review was to be important in the history of Symbolism. When it first appeared – the progeny of the poet and essayist Léo d'Orfer – Gustave Kahn went to see Verlaine in the Cour Saint-François. As Kahn remembered:

I told Verlaine about my plan to publish some works of Rimbaud's in *La Vogue* – not the ones which appeared in *Les Poètes maudits* ... It was a question of finding the manuscript of *Les Illuminations* again. Verlaine had lent it, so that it could be passed round, and it was in circulation. According to Verlaine, if I looked somewhere near Le Cardonnel, I should find myself on the right track ... We had it that evening, read it, assessed it, and published it with alacrity. Verlaine wrote a short preface for the offprint.[1]

'I'm not a critic, far from it,' Verlaine would write, years later,

'I am all enthusiasm and passion.'[2] But we may be grateful for the passion. One cannot overestimate the part that he played in establishing Rimbaud's fame.

Gustave Kahn had also asked Verlaine for a sequel to *Les Poètes maudits*.

At first [he recorded], Verlaine changed the subject, dodged, and talked to me about Mallarmé – knowing me to be one of his disciples. He recited some of Mallarmé's poems, with strange, grandiloquent intonations, and we talked aesthetics – just for the pleasure of doing so ... [Then] Verlaine talked to me about his portrait of Desbordes-Valmore, and went in search, not of his article, but of her poetical works. Then he put on his pince-nez, and, apparently reading over the rims ... he read a few poems with tears in his eyes. When the affair was settled, and he had promised me some poetry, he gave me a letter, authorising me to collect the manuscript of the article from Vanier ...

I often saw him again in the Cour Saint-François. In this picturesque working-class quarter he had created a life for himself. He told me of his early morning pleasures, hobbling along to get his newspapers at the place de la Bastille, and watching the bustle of the omnibuses (which was considerable, even then) ... He was not equable every day, and I refused to publish some very short, sharp pamphlets which he would have liked to let fly at those whom it might concern, in other words at Mme Verlaine.[3]

The only record of Mathilde in the 1880s, except the one she published in her memoirs, was set down by the poet Laurent Tailhade. He used to see her at Charles Cros'. 'People caroused there, and recited poetry; then they chased down a slice or two of cold meat and some crystallised ginger with gin and whisky.' Tailhade found the décor congenial. 'Despite the eccentricity of the place,' he told his mother, in March 1884, 'one finds the most excellent female company ... I've met the separated wife of that infamous Verlaine there. Incidentally, she seems quite consoled for the tragedies of the past.' Two months later, Tailhade met Verlaine, and his prejudices collapsed like a house of cards.[4]

To Laurent Tailhade, just turned thirty, Verlaine was a subject for sorrow rather than scorn; and time was not to change his opinions. When he came to write *Quelques fantômes de jadis* he recalled Mathilde, and showed his unshakeable sympathy for Verlaine. He and the other guests at Cros' had, he said, approached Mathilde somewhat timidly; they knew that this woman who kept in the background and dressed in unrelieved black had inspired Verlaine to write 'Les chères mains qui furent miennes ...'. Since then she had coarsened. Her conversation was bourgeois; she did not seem to remember the past. 'Verlaine had vanished from the rather narrow field of her mind.'[5]

On 26 July 1886, suffering from ulcers on his legs, Verlaine himself entered the Hôpital Tenon. He was to stay there until 2 September, and literary youth went in a kind of pilgrimage to see him. The month after he left hospital, Vanier published *Louise Leclercq. Suivie de Pierre Duchâtelet.*

Louise Leclercq is a meaningless short story about the elopement of a grocer's daughter in Les Batignolles. *Pierre Duchâtelet* is interesting only as autobiography. Duchâtelet – like the young Verlaine – is a government *employé* who serves in the Garde Nationale during the Siege of Paris. He then joins the army, and, while he is away on active service, his wife deserts him. After the Commune, he escapes to London, where he takes to drink, and dies, '*tué par* l'idée *d'une femme.*' The prose is mediocre (as usual with Verlaine); but *Pierre Duchâtelet* has psychological interest. It seems a pathetic revenge for Mathilde's divorce. Verlaine is relieving himself of his indignation, protesting, even now, that he was innocent, presenting himself as a loving husband, a man of principle killed by a little bourgeoise, '*petite brune un peu zézayante, à l'embonpoint naissant*'.

When Mathilde herself, in her memoirs, came to discuss her attitude to Verlaine, she, too, professed her injured innocence. No informed person, so she claimed, 'was surprised that I demanded a separation after Verlaine's departure with Rimbaud; and no-one would have approved if I had taken him back on his release from prison. This excessive, purposeless indulgence would have been considered weak and immoral.'[6]

Since her separation, Mathilde had had no concern for Verlaine.

The divorce law had finally been passed; her parents had long hoped that she would re-marry. Mme Mauté did not live to see her hope fulfilled. She had died in 1884.[7] On 30 October 1886, nine months after she had stripped Verlaine of his small inheritance, Mathilde took a second husband. As if to emphasise her break with the past, she was married at the *Mairie* of the xviiith *arrondissement*, where, in 1870, she had married Verlaine. Mathilde was thirty-three, and her new husband was a year older. Bienvenu-Auguste Delporte was a building contractor from Brussels (Mathilde had long ceased to move in the world of vicomtes and marquis); he, too, was divorced, and he had a daughter by his first marriage. He and Mathilde began their married life (she was careful to note) in '*le quartier de l'Étoile*'.[8]

41

When Verlaine left the Hôpital Tenon in September, he had returned to the Cour Saint-François. A few days after Mathilde's re-marriage, he was evicted, and an anxious Cazals sought help from Rachilde.

Rachilde was the twenty-year-old *femme de lettres* whom Barrès called Mademoiselle Baudelaire. In her long life she would write some sixty novels; but none seemed more daring than her *Monsieur Vénus*, which appeared late in 1886. In this book she imagined the emotional relationship between a virile woman and an effeminate man. *Monsieur Vénus* was published in Belgium, and a Belgian court sentenced its author to two years' imprisonment and a fine of 2,000 francs. But Rachilde, who was accused of inventing a new sin, was in time consoled by the author of *Sagesse*: 'Ah, my dear child, if you had done that, you would be a benefactor to mankind.'

She herself recorded how she had first set eyes on 'a mournful Verlaine, limping like an archangel confounded, and looking like a thief'.

I can still see the young Cazals of yesteryear arriving on my doorstep in the rue des Écoles: 'Monsieur Verlaine is downstairs, in a cab, his landlord has thrown him out and he has a bad leg.'

In the dizzying silence of reading, one had dreamed of some Oriental king . . . , and one saw a man who looked like a poor labourer.

But everything was turned upside down so as to greet him better, the furniture was put in place, the carpets straightened, the embroidered sheets taken out of the cupboard, fragrant scents were sprinkled around . . . There was such commotion, such alarm, . . . and such piety.

Verlaine looked up.

'May I smoke my pipe, Rachilde?'

But his gaze, piercing, terrible, dark, was the gaze of a king.

He was at home everywhere.

'Damn conventions!' I said. 'We're Decadents, here!' . . . [1]

She settled him that evening in her own apartment, and went to sleep at her mother's on the quai de la Tournelle.

On 12 November, from the Hôpital Broussais, Verlaine wrote to thank her for *Monsieur Vénus*. 'I should have liked to know,' he added,

. . . if my things have been moved from Chanzy's (Hôtel du Midi, 6, cour Saint-François) . . . If not, please ask the good Cazals, whom I could never thank enough, and the excellent du Plessys, to move them as soon as possible . . .

A thousand respectful greetings from a man who is very grateful to you. You may have stopped him, the other day, from doing things, not out of despair, oh no! . . . But things which would have been too bizarre. [2]

In November 1886, Verlaine was not only worried about his health, he was naturally anxious about his son. It was eight years since he had seen him; it was seven years since he had been able to communicate with him. Now that Mathilde had re-married, he particularly wanted news of him.

A few months earlier, he had hoped that Mallarmé would arrange and supervise a meeting at the Lycée Condorcet. Now, it appeared, the boy had been moved to the exclusive Collège Rollin; but Verlaine turned again to the understanding Mallarmé for help.

My dear Mallarmé,

I learn that my wife has 're-married'. I am not astounded by the news, and I am sorry for this excommunicated woman; but, unless I am much mistaken, this is the moment when I should concern myself more actively with my son. I have not been able to see him, and I have not been able to communicate with him since '79.

I have heard from Vanier and Ghil – and what pleasure it gave me! – that you were once the child's professor and that you were kind enough to talk to him about me. I ask you now for every possible detail. Is the little brat well, does he seem his age – he's fifteen years old – and does he appear to you to be intelligent? What class is he in, what work is he doing, and what is he probably being prepared for? (*I* should like him to be a soldier – Saint-Cyr or preferably the Polytechnique.)

Finally is he a day-boy or a boarder, and what do you advise me to do, to see him – since the mother refuses to let me see him? Should I write to him? But would letters reach him, if they were addressed to the College? It is impossible for me to go to Rollin myself, because of my illness. And, one more thing: might the child have talked about your conversation with him, hence his withdrawal from your class? Be an angel and answer these questions, won't you?

I am hardly happier every day, as you can see. Sometimes, in the presence of so many offences, so many spiteful actions, I get ideas of suicide, but . . . I believe that literature still wants me . . .[3]

There was little comfort for him. He continued to be disturbed about his poverty, and about the prospect of permanent lameness. 'I confess,' he added, a month later,

. . . that hospital is rather a burden to me, not however that I am so avid for freedom, or indeed for licence, as one might suppose . . . On the contrary, I think that when I am cured and out of hospital I shall just concern myself with living in a humble way, in the wisdom and practice of Christianity. Yes, in the practice of it! I want to be Catholic . . .

While I await this departure – still in the mists of the future – I am working . . . Literature is still captivating and consoling, when you plunge deep into it, your dream and all![4]

On 13 March 1887, Verlaine left Broussais, and returned, once again, to the Cour Saint-François. He was destitute. He had asked his young admirer, Jules Tellier, if he could find him regular office work; he asked Vanier to arrange for him to give English lessons. But these latter-day attempts at respectability failed. Henceforward he would never know material security. He lingered in the wine-shop. He used to work there. He received his friends there. It was an extraordinary milieu in which he was imprisoned by his poverty. The *hôtel* had its little rooms for hire; and, in the evenings, *la patronne*, sitting at her knitting, used to keep an eye on the comings and goings of prostitutes and their clients. Verlaine's friends faced these embarrassing promiscuities for his sake.[5]

Verlaine was then writing *Amour*, in the intervals of apéritifs. 'What can one say?' Mallarmé used to comment. 'It's a way of life . . . It wouldn't suit me.' But he said these words gently, as if to excuse Verlaine.[6]

On 19 April, after a month of freedom, Verlaine returned yet again to hospital: this time to the Hôpital Cochin. On 26 April Maurice du Plessys, the poet, scribbled to Cazals:

Mon cher vieux,

Please be so very kind as to find yourself *to-morrow*, *Wednesday*, *at six o'clock*, without fail, in the waiting-hall at the Gare du Nord. We will arrange to move Verlaine's belongings. The operation must be done before the end of the week. In other words we only just have time.[7]

Verlaine himself, in hospital, continued to worry about Georges.

My dear Mallarmé [this on 28 April],
. . . Here I am back in hospital again, far from cured and more Job-like than ever.
Could you give me the names of my son's professors? . . . Would the boy have talked about you and what you said to him, and would this be yet another *kindness* [from his mother]? I shall try to see him, all the same, as it's my absolute right – and my duty, too.[8]

'My dear friend,' answered Mallarmé, 'I have made a small enquiry among the boys who were his fellow-pupils . . . He is not at the college any more, I assure you . . . What school has he left it for?'[9]

It is clear that Mathilde had done her utmost to keep the child away from Verlaine. When Georges was nine, she had sent him to school in Pons, in the Charente-Inférieure. It was not far from Rochefort, on the Atlantic coast; it could hardly have been further from Paris. Georges's departure from Paris coincided almost exactly with Verlaine's attempts to re-enter the Hôtel de Ville, and with his re-appearance in Parisian literary circles. Verlaine's return to Paris seems the only reason why Mathilde should have sent her son to an undistinguished provincial school. According to her, the boy was still at Pons in January 1886 – when Verlaine believed him to be at the Lycée Condorcet. But Mathilde's account seems suspect, if, by November, Mallarmé had already taught him at the lycée, and the boy had left the lycée for the Collège Rollin. It is unlikely that he would have changed his school twice in a year. After Verlaine's death, Mathilde denied that she had systematically kept Georges from him. 'I shall not discuss this statement,' was Lepelletier's comment. 'The former Mme Verlaine is not a hateful person . . . But we know, from all the correspondence and all the accounts of Verlaine's life, that he always asked for his son's address in vain. This address was always hidden from him, just as the pleasure of embracing the child, when he grew to manhood, was forbidden him to the end.'[10]

Charles Donos, in *Verlaine intime*, said that Verlaine sent envoys to Mathilde, asking to be put in touch with his son. Their eloquence had no effect on 'the rock-like hardness of her heart'.[11] Verlaine wrote to Me. Gouyot-Sionnest, and in the Doucet Collection is his frigid reply, dated 27 June 1887.

I have forwarded to Mme Verlaine, now Mme Delporte, the letter in which you express to me your wish to see your son.

The aforementioned lady has replied that in the interest of her child she does not think she should defer to your wish; at the same time, however, she asks me to inform you that the child is well, that he has a very nice nature and that he is working hard.[12]

Early in August, Verlaine wrote again to Guyot-Sionnest. He had now, it seems, so lost his self-respect that he had tried to get money from Mathilde. 'I have referred your letter of the 4th to

Mme Verlaine, now Mme Delporte,' Guyot-Sionnest replied on
6 August. 'Her answer is that she has no money to send you and
that she does not feel obliged to ask her new husband for money
to support you. In these circumstances I can only refuse your
request.'[13]

On 30 October 1887, M. Mauté died. While Mathilde was still
in mourning, she was told that Verlaine was gravely ill, and that
he was once again asking to see Georges. The request was made
some time before 20 March 1888, when Verlaine left the Hôpital
Broussais. His physical condition was such that he had been in
hospital for six months.

Mathilde was embarrassed by his request. She had recognised
herself as the heroine of *Pierre Duchâtelet*. Verlaine had been 'so
hateful', she said, since her second marriage, that she hardly
felt inclined to let Georges visit him. However, so she wrote in
her memoirs, if Verlaine had been in danger of death, it would
have been cruel not to let him see his son. A young doctor,
married to one of her friends, 'offered to slip in among the house-
surgeons during their round, and to give me an exact account of
the invalid's condition. The news was reassuring. Verlaine
suffered from painful rheumatism, but he was in no danger. I
therefore did not send Georges, but I had a little present sent,
anonymously, to Verlaine ...'[14] In May 1888, Verlaine wrote
again to Guyot-Sionnest, asking about his legal rights in relation
to his son. Guyot-Sionnest replied that Verlaine had been legally
relieved of the care and custody of Georges. 'I think I may add,'
wrote the lawyer, 'that the latter is now with his mother, finishing
his education and preparing for his examinations.'[15] Mathilde
recorded that when he had finished his education, she 'sent him
to a family in England, to perfect his knowledge of English.
He stayed there for eighteen months, and then rejoined us in
Algeria. It is therefore not surprising that Verlaine lost trace of
him.'[16]

Mathilde was to have a son and daughter by her second marriage.
In 1890 she and her family moved to Brussels, to 'a little house
in the avenue Louise'. One wonders what affection she now felt

for Georges. When she wrote her memoirs, she was clearly trying to justify her behaviour.

Lepelletier gave a different account of Georges Verlaine's career:

When he reached adolescence, Verlaine's wife had re-married. She had other children; she wanted to equip her son for manual work at which he could earn his living. The young man was sent as an apprentice to a watchmaker in Orleans. Verlaine knew the occupation his son was destined for, and he approved ...

Georges Verlaine was not to follow the watchmaker's trade. He came back to his mother in Belgium.[17]

He seems to have been a young man of only moderate intellect; he was certainly unsettled by the disturbances of his childhood: by the absence of his father, sometimes left in mystery, sometimes mentioned with pious disapproval. He had, no doubt, suffered from his mother's moods, from his years in a distant boarding-school, and from his mother's second marriage, with all the re-adjustments which it involved. If his past had been disturbed, his present seemed uncertain. He was aware that his father was a famous poet; sometimes he had his own frustrated aspirations. He had little in common with the Delportes. In 1895, after a visit to Algeria, the Delportes returned to Brussels; they left Georges behind, recalled Mathilde, because 'he liked Algeria and wanted to settle there. When we left, I gave him a small sum of money; he had modest tastes, and it was enough to keep him for several months. Within a few weeks, he found himself destitute. He had lost his memory.' He was suffering from amnesia; but one wonders if the unhappy young man had already become an alcoholic.

Whatever the nature of his illness, he was taken to hospital, and cured by hypnosis. 'When he felt he had recovered,' continued his mother, 'the time had come for his military service ... He went to Lille, and joined a service regiment. Unfortunately, he had been discharged from hospital too soon; he had not been completely cured, and he fell again into his lethargic sleep.' He remained in hospital until mid-January 1896. By the time he left, his father had died. As soon as he was demobilised, Georges went

Georges Verlaine (1871–1926).
This is one of the two known
photographs of the poet's son, and
it shows his remarkable likeness to
his father.

'Slightly pretentious and rather
sentimental': Lucien Létinois, for
whom Verlaine wrote much of
Amour.

Verlaine at the Café François Ier, 1892, from a photograph by Harlingue.

Verlaine during his lecture tour of Holland, November 1892.

to see Lepelletier, who was struck by his astonishing likeness to Verlaine. Lepelletier became a virtual father to him. He employed him as a secretary, he represented Verlaine at his wedding, and he found him a post 'in the administration of the Métropolitain'. In 1909, at Catulle Mendès' funeral, Jules Renard noticed 'Verlaine's son, a big, strapping youth, stationmaster at some or other station on the Métro' (it was in fact Avenue de Villiers). Georges supervised the publication of his father's *Œuvres complètes*. He died in 1926, at the age of fifty-four. He left no children.[18]

In 1900 the Delportes had settled in Algiers. It was left to M. Porché to reveal what Mathilde had carefully concealed: that in 1905 her second marriage ended in divorce. At the end of her life she kept a *pension de famille* in the place Masséna, in Nice. She died there, at the age of sixty-one, on 13 November 1914.[19]

PART NINE

'An innocent satyr...'

(1887–90)

42

VERLAINE had entered the Hôpital Cochin on 19 April 1887. He was to spend the next five months in a succession of hospitals. He moved from Cochin to Vincennes, from Vincennes to Tenon, and from Tenon back again to Vincennes, which he left on 9 September. On 20 September he returned to Broussais; he was to remain there for six months.

It was possibly at about this time that he made out a list of errands for some amenable devotee. One was to send him the latest article about him by Jules Tellier.[1]

Tellier was among his most persistent admirers. Born in Le Havre in 1863, he was now a contributor to *Le Parti national*, and he used his journalism and his literary contacts to further Verlaine's fame. 'Time and time again,' wrote Raymond de la Tailhède, 'as if it had been some magic formula, Tellier had mentioned Verlaine's name in his paper. It was only a cry in the night. No echo answered him.'[2]

It had, however, long been clear to Tellier that some more pontifical voice should proclaim Verlaine from the heights. He urged his former teacher, Jules Lemaître, now the critic of *Le Journal des Débats*, to reveal him to the public. On 15 July 1887, from the Hôpital Tenon, Verlaine had gaily announced to Vanier: 'Tellier should be bringing Lemaître to see me one of these days: he's busy writing his article about me. It will give a little fillip to trade.'³ 'Paul Verlaine et les poètes symbolistes et décadents' appeared in *La Revue bleue* on 7 January 1888. It was reprinted the following year, in Lemaître's collected essays, *Les Contemporains*.

Lemaître began with a touch of his habitual irony; and he amused himself a little at the expense of Symbolism.

I do, however, admit [he continued] that the poetry I am trying to define is that of a solitary, a neurotic, almost a madman, who would none the less be a great poet. And the poetry I have in mind would balance on the verge between reason and insanity.

As for the man who writes this poetry, he must, I think, be a strange and exceptional being. Morally and socially speaking, he must be apart from other men. I imagine him almost unlettered . . . He knows nothing of accepted codes and morals. He is as far from us as if he were only an innocent satyr in the great forests. When he is ill, or when he has reached the end of his resources, some friendly doctor sends him into hospital. He lingers there, and writes poetry; strange, sad songs murmur to him in the folds of the white calico curtains. He is not declassed: he has no class. His is a rare and singular case. He lives in a civilised society as if he were living in the heart of nature. To him, men are not individuals with whom he has relations of duty and of interest, but forms which move and pass. He is the dreamer. He has kept a soul as new as that of Adam when he opened his eyes to the light. For him, reality is always incoherent and unexplained, like a dream . . . He may well have been influenced, for a moment, by some contemporary poets; but they merely awakened, merely revealed the extreme and painful sensibility which is his all. He really has no master. He moulds the language at his will, not like great writers, because he understands it, but, like children, because he does not know it . . . But this child has a music in his soul, and, on certain days, he hears voices that none has heard before him.⁴

It was a brilliant impression, if not an academic study. It roused immediate interest in Verlaine. 'All honour to Jules Lemaître,' wrote Raymond de la Tailhède. 'He was the first to dare, with his acknowledged authority, to mark the place of Paul Verlaine in French literature.'⁵

On 13 February 1888, Verlaine wrote from Broussais to Rachilde: '*Amour* will be published soon . . . You remember that one of the poems in it is dedicated to you.'⁶ Early in March, still from hospital, he sent a letter to Huysmans; and on 12 March Huysmans answered:

Thank you very much, my dear friend, for your affectionate letter – and for your promise to come and see us, towards the end of the month, when you have left Broussais.

I await *Amour* with confounded impatience, I assure you, and I am really proud that you've been good enough to dedicate a poem in it to me. So write me a brief word, as soon as you're free – we'll have dinner together, and we'll both of us lick our wounds at table.⁷

On 20 March, Verlaine left Broussais for a furnished room at 14, rue Royer-Collard. Vanier published *Amour* the same day.

43

Amour had originally been conceived in 1875 as a twin book to *Sagesse*; and Verlaine had intended it to present the Christian virtue of charity beside the Christian virtue of faith. But in the thirteen years which had elapsed between the birth of the idea and the publication of the book, Verlaine's life had been troubled, and it had radically changed. In 1875, when he first mentioned *Amour* to Blémont, he had been a schoolmaster at Stickney: a new and ardent Catholic convert who asked only to lead a respectable life. Since then he had moved to Boston and Bournemouth and Rethel, to Lymington, to Juniville and Coulommes; he had abandoned the teaching profession, he had failed in farming, and he had tried in vain to resume his work at the Hôtel de Ville. Society had forced him to live an erratic life. He had been profoundly disturbed by the death of Lucien and the death of his mother. He had now returned, inescapably, to drink and to Bohemia; he was too wretched and too weak, and, now, too unwell to prevent his decline. His plan for a Christian book of verse had long since been abandoned.

Verlaine had not only cast aside his religious hopes, he had apparently lost much of his judgment. The title *Amour* remained, but it was now an empty shell. The book included poems which had no bearing on the theme, and any architectural plan was abandoned. It could only be said that most of the poems were suggested by Verlaine's love for his friends.[1]

The book is dedicated to Georges, and the final poem is addressed to him; but the poem and dedication seem irrelevant. The person who dominates *Amour* is not the poet's son, but the adopted son who had died. The 1888 edition of *Amour* includes forty poems; one of them, 'Lucien Létinois', sub-divided into twenty-four poems, takes up exactly one-third of the work.

The comparison with Tennyson's 'In Memoriam' is inevitable; but Verlaine does not benefit from the comparative study. Tennyson's work matured and grew over a much longer period, seventeen years, but it was more cohesive, and a work of more profound poetry. In the introduction to 'In Memoriam', Tennyson proclaimed his faith in God, and asked Him to forgive him for his lack of comprehension of God's ways, and for mourning the death of his friend. In the opening verses of 'Lucien Létinois' Verlaine, too, proclaims his veneration of divine law. He, too, declares that he had too often forgotten the glory of God in his love of God's gifts; he insists that God had given Lucien to him, and that he returned him to God:

> Vous me l'aviez donné, je vous le rends très pur,
> Tout pétri de vertu, d'amour et de simplesse.
> C'est pourquoi, pardonnez, Terrible, à celui sur
> Le cœur de qui, Dieu fort, sévit cette faiblesse . . .[2]

And here one seems to catch Verlaine striking an attitude before God. Here one finds Tartuffe asserting the purity and virtue of a relationship which was, at best, ambiguous. In the fifth poem, once again, Verlaine proclaims the nobility of the relationship with a fervour which seems excessive and misplaced:

> Ô ses lettres d'alors! les miennes elles-mêmes!
> Je ne crois pas qu'il soit des choses plus suprêmes.
> J'étais, je ne puis dire mieux, vraiment très bien,
> Ou plutôt, je puis dire tout, vraiment chrétien.
> l'éclatais de sagesse et de sollicitude,

Je mettais tout mon souci pieux, toute l'étude
Dont tout mon être était capable, à confirmer
Cette âme dans l'effort de prier et d'aimer.
Oui, j'étais devant Dieu qui m'écoute, si j'ose
Le dire, quel que soit l'orgueil fou que suppose
Un tel serment juré sur sa tête qui dort,
Pur comme un saint . . .[3]

In the sixth poem, Verlaine recalls Lucien on horseback:
a young Christian soldier, without reproach, who scorned the
temptations of the flesh.

Mon fils est bon: un jour que du bout de son aile
Le soupçon d'une faute effleurait mes cheveux,
Mon enfant, pressentant l'angoisse paternelle,
S'en vint me consoler en de nobles aveux.[4]

This was no doubt a reference to Lucien's confession that he
had loved an English girl; and it was this avowal – if not Lucien's
physical surrender to Verlaine – which inspired the poem that
followed:

Ô l'odieuse obscurité
Du jour le plus gai de l'année
Dans la monstrueuse cité
Où se fit notre destinée ! . . .[5]

And here, at last, Verlaine does not pose. He is not pretending
to be teacher, father or saint, he is writing of his intense and
possessive love, of his driving physical desire. He is writing of his
jealousy that Lucien should have loved a woman, or – for the
poem is ambiguous – of the physical passion which abruptly
turned him from an adopted father into a lover.

It is here that we reach the central truth of 'Lucien Létinois'.
When Verlaine recalls the farm at Juniville, and poses as a figure
from *The Georgics*, when he plays the adopted father, imagining a
wife for his son, he writes prosaic verse, for he is not writing from
his heart. When he recalls the eyes, the face, the figure of Lucien:
when, in fact, he touches his deepest feelings, then poetry takes
hold. The finest poems in 'Lucien Létinois' are those which are
illumined by Verlaine's forbidden love.

Il patinait merveilleusement,
S'élançant, qu'impétueusement !
R'arrivant si joliment vraiment.

Fin comme une grande jeune fille,
Brillant, vif et fort, telle une aiguille,
La souplesse, l'élan d'une anguille.

Des jeux d'optique prestigieux,
Un tourment délicieux des yeux,
Un éclair qui serait gracieux.

Parfois il restait comme invisible,
Vitesse en route vers une cible
Si lointaine, elle-même invisible . . .

Invisible de même aujourd'hui.
Que sera-t-il advenu de lui?
Que sera-t-il advenu de lui?[6]

If the poems to Lucien form the most important part of *Amour*, they still make an unsatisfactory whole. They remain a personal lament, a private elegy which is not dignified into a long and honest search for faith. No one could have drawn comfort or wisdom from 'Lucien Létinois', no one could have found in it the loftiness of spirit, the poetic richness of 'In Memoriam'. 'In Memoriam', despite its length, despite its digressions, moves, unimpeded, to its conclusion. The shape of 'Lucien Létinois' is broken by irrelevant poems: by a poem in which Verlaine insults his former wife, by another in which he describes his sufferings, by a third in which – honestly enough – he speaks of his over-mastering need to love.

Amour is in fact two books: an elegy to Lucien, and a heterogeneous collection of poems, of widely differing subjects, moods and merits. 'Écrit en 1875' is an honest, even grateful reminiscence of Verlaine's imprisonment at Mons; 'Bournemouth', written two years later, is an impressionist landscape drawn with Verlainian licence. 'There' is one of his finer London poems. 'Un

Veuf parle' is a touching appeal to Mathilde. But all these poems
date from the 1870s; 'Parsifal' is the only later work to show his
mastery.

44

In November 1888, Vanier shrewdly published the first book to be
written on Verlaine. The monograph, the work of Charles
Morice, had a decisive influence on his fame.

Verlaine's friendship with Morice went back to 1882. On
10 November that year, in *Paris moderne*, Verlaine had published
his 'Art poétique'. It was, it has been suggested, the essentials of a
preface which he did not write, but in which he wanted to set
out his new poetic technique. It is probable that 'Art poétique'
had no influence on the young generation of poets until it was
reprinted in *Jadis et Naguère*; for then, in 1884, Verlaine was discovered. However, on 1 December 1882, in *La Nouvelle Rive
Gauche*, under the pseudonym of Karl Mohr, with all the assurance
of youth (he was twenty-two), Charles Morice had answered 'Art
poétique' in an article 'Boileau-Verlaine'.

> Verlaine wrote to me at once [Morice remembered]. He thanked
> me with ironic courtesy for gracing him with a handsome periwig, and
> he invited me to call on him. I called next day. I never thought as I
> walked up the rue de la Roquette, where Verlaine was then living with
> his mother, that a decisive period was opening for me and for an
> entire generation . . . Through me, Verlaine met all the young poets
> and was known by them; he became their leader, sharing that honour
> with Mallarmé and Villiers de l'Isle-Adam.[1]

'Verlaine would not have been less great without Morice,' wrote
Morice's biographer, 'but his glory would have come more
slowly. Morice imposed him on those around him with un-
wearying constancy.'[2]

Now, in 1888, with the shrewdness born of affection, Morice
indicated the cardinal points in Verlaine's character, his life and
work. He emphasised the significance of his appearance: 'The
forehead of a pensive monk, a forehead fashioned for ample

theologies, – and the jaws of a barbarian, made to assuage the most voracious hungers. – This antagonism of the spirit and the flesh . . . is the explanation of all his humanity.' This astonishing, haunting face was, to Morice, the outward sign of 'the sort of *double unity* of Verlaine – for he is wholly in his reason, as he is in his instinct.' Verlaine did not merely possess this double unity: he was fundamentally naïve. 'The soul of an immortal child: this is indeed the very soul of Verlaine, with all the benefits and all the dangers which it involves.' As Morice wrote, this unique man led an extraordinary life: 'an endless series of strange chances, of changes of direction in pursuit of different kinds of happiness: the dream of glory, the dream of love, and the dream, too – a Christian dream – of salvation. I really think that the dream of wealth is the only dream which has left Verlaine unmoved.' Verlaine wrote 'out of vital activity, as he loved, as he struggled, to add another realm to his own, or to prolong the echo of embraces and struggles'. But he was a man first and a poet afterwards. 'It is only by an excess of activity,' Morice concluded, 'by intensity of humanity, that he is a poet.'[3]

In November 1888, the month in which Morice published his study, Verlaine returned, once again, to Broussais; and there he stayed for three months. His financial situation was, as usual, far from happy, but he did not lack practical and generous admirers, and early in the New Year Cazals was in correspondence with the Association of Parisian Journalists, asking that Verlaine should be given a grant from the Boucicault legacy.[4] Maurice Barrès, the novelist and politician, also took an active interest in his affairs. On 7 February, he wrote to postpone the *déjeuner de délivrance* which had been planned for the day Verlaine left hospital. 'The previous evening,' he explained, 'I shall be busy getting you a lodging. I shall ask your approval before I conclude matters.'[5]

On 21 February, Verlaine left Broussais; under the auspices of Barrès, he was comfortably installed at the Hôtel de Lisbonne, 4, rue de Vaugirard. There he resumed his Wednesday receptions. These had begun when he was living in the rue Royer-Collard, but it was now that they reached their high-water mark. He himself left a sketch of his guests. Among them one can recognise Cazals, Rachilde, Moréas, Villiers de l'Isle-Adam, Tailhade, Tellier, and Paterne Berrichon.[6]

The journalists who chronicled social life did not forget to mention the weekly receptions of Mallarmé and Verlaine. In the late 1880s, from the small apartment at the top of the rue de Rome, to which all roads led, Mallarmé exercised his literary pontificate, and from hospital, from his café or his current furnished room, Verlaine reigned over modern poetry.[7]

45

During the first months of 1889, Verlaine had been in constant correspondence with Léon Vanier. 'Good morning, and a happy New Year!' went his letter on 1 January. 'Are you thinking about *Les Amis?*' . . . I'm working on the little book. It will be ready at the end of the month, at the latest.' 'I'm going on with *Les Amis,*' he continued on 3 April. 'May we draw up a contract AT ONCE for this little book, three-quarters of which is in your hands?'[1] *Les Amis,* which was later to be called *Dédicaces,* duly appeared in 1890; but it did not appear under Vanier's imprint. In the summer of 1889, Verlaine had broken with him.

Vanier was financially strict with Verlaine, but he was not unkind. Since February 1889 he had given him several sums of money as part of the advance for a reprint of *Sagesse*; the previous year he had drawn up a contract for *Amour* and *Parallèlement.* It was not meanness, but a knowledge of Verlaine's extravagance, which made him arrange to pay in instalments. But if Verlaine accepted Vanier's financial arrangements, he refused to accept his literary interference. On 12 June, confirming his urgent need for money, he wrote: 'I am against having CHASTETÉ, which doesn't belong to you, in PARALLÈLEMENT.'[2]

Verlaine's poem on '*la sainte Chasteté*' clearly had no place in *Parallèlement,* which had just been announced in the press. *Parallèlement* was the most erotic collection of poems which he had yet published under his name. However, this was not the only consideration. Verlaine was more concerned with money than he was with principles. He had given Vanier the exclusive right to publish his works in book form; but he was now dissatisfied with him. On 15 September 1888, in spite of his commitment to Vanier, he had signed a contract with Albert Savine for three still unfinished works. One of these was his collection of poems, *Bonheur*, and 'Chasteté' was intended for this book.

The first copies of *Parallèlement* were on sale on 20 June 1889; in some of them the poem appeared with a note by Vanier: 'We felt it would be of interest to give the reader of *Parallèlement* the first sight of the latest poem by *Paul Verlaine*, received from him for his next book, *Bonheur*.'

It is clear that Verlaine himself had given the manuscript of 'Chasteté' to Vanier, but on 22 June he wrote to him stiffly:

Monsieur,

Several people have told me about the inclusion of the poem from *Bonheur* called 'Chasteté': a poem which you have tipped into the book. You are not unaware that I had already opposed the proposals which you made to me on this subject, and you were sufficiently informed on this point to be careful not to tip in the poem which does not belong to you in the copies which you sent to me.

As for these copies, I cannot be satisfied with so few. I expected 15 copies of *Parallèlement* instead of the 5 which you have sent me, and I am therefore waiting for another 10. How many copies of *Sagesse* are you keeping at my disposal?

Accept my civilities, Monsieur.

P. VERLAINE.[3]

My dear Verlaine [answered Vanier, meekly],
Here are:

5 copies of *Parallèlement*

5 copies of *Sagesse* (2nd instalment) . . .

Yours,

VANIER.

If you formally refuse the innocent insertion of 'Chasteté', which seemed to me amusing and perhaps *useful*, I will readily give it up in future, as I don't want to offend you in any way.[4]

'Chasteté' was not included in future copies of *Parallèlement*;

but Verlaine chose to remain offended. It was to be many months before Vanier's imprint appeared again on his books.

Parallèlement, it has been said, was born in the early summer of 1885, when Verlaine was almost lost to sight. He had come out of prison at Vouziers in the middle of May, and for some weeks he had led a vagabond life. 'Poème saturnien', in *Parallèlement*, recalls his wanderings.

> Dans des troquets comme en ces bourgades,
> J'avais rôdé, suçant peu de glace.
> Trois galopins aux yeux de tribades
> Dévisageaient sans fin ma grimace . . .[5]

This outrageous vagabondage was a happy memory for Verlaine; it recalled his rejection of convention and hypocrisy, it recalled his freedom. In July 1885, when he had just moved to the Cour Saint-François, he published four poems in *Lutèce* which were a moral and aesthetic apology for homosexuality, with an aggressive repudiation of normal love. In the last of these poems, 'Lombes', which was possibly based on experience, he seemed to boast of his impotence with women as a sign that, henceforward, he belonged exclusively to men.

It was probably on his wanderings in the early summer of 1885, and on his return to Paris, that Verlaine conceived the idea of a book in which he could express his eroticism and his liberation, and disown his previous work. He would publish the poems for which there had been no room in *Jadis et Naguère*; he would re-publish *Les Amies*, the youthful Lesbian poems which Poulet-Malassis had printed in Belgium, under a pseudonym, in 1867. He would relieve himself of libidinous memories and dreams, present himself in all honesty; in a sense, he would make his confession. '*Parallèlement*,' he told Morice, 'is the waste-pipe, the night-soil deposit for all the "bad" feelings which I can express';[6] and, again, explaining the book to Félicien Rops: 'You will find in it, I think, what I wanted to put in it, a man who is sometimes myself – completely frank and honest in his vice, if you like. It is very sincere, and almost good by virtue of its sincerity.'[7] This sincerity probably included an element of exhibitionism, but it also showed a need to confess; and Verlaine made the point in his poem 'À propos de PARALLÈLEMENT':

> Ces vers durent être faits,
> Cet aveu fut nécessaire . . .
>
> Est-ce fini? Tu l'assures,
> Sorte de pressentiment
> D'un final apaisement . . .
>
> Ô mon Dieu, voyez mes vœux . . .
>
> Alors seront effacées
> À vos yeux inoffensés,
> Avec mes torts confessés,
> Ces lignes si peu pensées.[8]

'I believe, and I am a good Christian at one moment,' Verlaine wrote in *Les Poètes maudits*. 'I believe, and I am a bad Christian the moment after.'[9] *Parallèlement* was the book in which he was 'a bad Christian', or frankly un-Christian, and that makes it a much more honest book than the falsely innocent *Amour*.

Parallèlement, as Verlaine emphasised in his preface, was parallel to *Sagesse* and *Amour*, and to *Bonheur*, which was yet to come. It was the expression of carnal love after that of the love of God and the love – at least outwardly pure – of his friends. Verlaine had never felt such a need to explain a book; but he had to answer 'the objections which might be roused by the particular tone of the present work – a fragment of a whole work which is still in progress.' He himself considered *Parallèlement* to be a work of significance. On 17 August, from Broussais, he wrote to a literary colleague, enquiring if he had received the reprint of *Sagesse* 'and especially *Parallèlement* which, to my mind, has a considerable place in the kind of elegy which will be composed of *Sagesse, Amour* and *Bonheur* (which is still to appear).'[10]

Parallèlement expressed a trait in his nature which existed concurrently with religious and platonic love. It also included poems written during his imprisonment in Belgium, and poems inspired by his licence after his release from Vouziers. It contained brutal parodies of *Fêtes galantes* and *Poèmes saturniens*, and it adopted a new style in which he deliberately used slang and vulgarity. Verlaine renounces his past in the themes, and, again, in the technique of his verse; he renounces his 'Art poétique' and approaches banality. He has no time for subtleties, now; he shows a preference for octosyllabic verse, the rhythm of the songs composed by his young friends, the *poètes de café*. The poet is contriving a system for his decline.

So is the man. The author of *La Bonne Chanson* and *Sagesse* now shows his bitterness of spirit. In 'Dédicace', the first poem in the book, he attacks Mathilde, 'cocodette un peu mûre', who has recently remarried. He reminds her of her age (the *cocodettes* were Second Empire beauties), he taunts her ruthlessly:

> O grasse en des jerseys de poult-de-soie . . .

He reprints a sonnet, 'Allégorie', which had first appeared in 1867, largely for its reference to 'une naïade âgée'. In 'Le Sonnet de l'homme au sable' he attacks Mathilde obliquely, as he recalls the Hoffmann tale of the student enamoured of an automaton. In 'Guitare' he resumes the theme of Pierre Duchâtelet and the wife who abandoned him:

> 'Il paraît qu'elle couche depuis peu
> Avec un individu qui tient lieu
> D'époux à cette femme de querelle.
> Faut-il la tuer ou prier pour elle?'
>
> Et le pauvre sait très bien qu'il priera,
> Mais le diable parierait qu'il tuera.[11]

The sadism which had led Verlaine, more than once, to attack Mathilde, remained with him, frustrated but intense.

There is much cruelty in *Parallèlement*. There is the cruelty which leads Verlaine to include a poem to Mathilde among six poems inspired by prostitutes. There is the 'Ballade de la vie en rouge', which reflects the changes in a single heart: the heart of Verlaine. 'Mais moi je vois la vie en rouge': the refrain emphasises the murderous drunkenness which is with him still. And this poem is followed, immediately, by one of the most powerful poems in the collection. 'Mains' has been compared with Gautier's 'Études de mains' and with Rimbaud's 'Les Mains de Jeanne-Marie'. It comes nearest to Gautier's second 'Étude', inspired by the severed hand of the murderer Lacenaire. But Verlaine's poem transcends the work of both the other poets because he is writing about his own hands. This is not merely an essay in imaginative description, it is self-analysis, made with remembrance of the past and with fear of the future. It is a psychological document which frightens by its power of suggestion.

> Ce soir elles ont, ces mains sèches,
> Sous leurs rares poils hérissés,
> Des airs spécialement rêches,
> Comme en proie à d'âpres pensers.
>
> Le noir souci qui les agace,
> Leur quasi-songe aigre les font
> Faire une sinistre grimace
> À leur façon, mains qu'elles sont.
>
> J'ai peur à les voir sur la table
> Préméditer là, sous mes yeux,
> Quelque chose de redoutable,
> D'inflexible et de furieux.
>
> La main droite est bien à ma droite,
> L'autre à ma gauche, je suis seul.
> Les linges dans la chambre étroite
> Prennent des aspects de linceul,
>
> Dehors le vent hurle sans trêve,
> Le soir descend insidieux . . .
> Ah! si ce sont des mains de rêve,
> Tant mieux, – ou tant pis, – ou tant mieux![12]

There is little gentleness in this book to balance such cruelty and violence. The only gentleness is, perhaps, in the reprinted Lesbian poems, 'Amies', which were now more than twenty years old. 'Amies' lack the urgency, the conviction, of some of the poems in 'Filles': of 'Séguidille', or of the poem 'À la Princesse Roukhine' (written for Marie Gambier). They are far from showing the violent physical appetites of *Femmes*. But the most obvious parallel, in this book of parallels, remains the parallel between the *'prudents hyménées'* of man and woman and the passion and nobility of *'le Rite'* between woman and woman or man and man. Verlaine insisted that the poem 'Autre Explication' should be dedicated to Mathilde and Rimbaud. It was a defence of homosexual love, which he now defended as an act of courage and of beauty. 'L'Impénitent' is a vulgar catalogue of the charms of young men; but in 'Ces Passions' Verlaine praises homosexual love – *'le haut Rite'* – as a love beyond the love of women.

There follows a poem which had first appeared in *La Cravache* in September 1888: a poem which had been inspired by the rumour of Rimbaud's death. It was then fourteen years since Verlaine had last seen Rimbaud at Stuttgart; but his love for Lucien Létinois and for Cazals, his casual affairs with men and women had not lessened the intensity of his memories or his regrets. Rimbaud was in fact still alive when this poem was written; but the thought of his death had brought back more clearly, more delectably than ever, the recollection of a lost paradise. The title 'Læti et Errabundi' is modelled on Baudelaire's 'Mœsta et Errabunda'. But Baudelaire had dreamed of an innocent paradise of childhood, and dreamed of it with gentle melancholy. Verlaine recalled a paradise where mind and heart and body were exalted and completely satisfied. Now, as he knowingly faced his decline, he looked back on his years with Rimbaud as the supreme experience of his past. Rimbaud had been the paramount intellectual influence in his life; he remained the man he transcendently loved.

> Je n'y veux rien croire. Mort, vous,
> Toi, dieu parmi les demi-dieux!
> Ceux qui le disent sont des fous.
> Mort, mon grand péché radieux,

Tout ce passé brûlant encore
Dans mes veines et ma cervelle
Et qui rayonne et qui fulgore
Sur ma ferveur toujours nouvelle!

Mort tout ce triomphe inouï
Retentissant sans frein ni fin
Sur l'air jamais évanoui
Que bat mon cœur qui fut divin!

Quoi, le miraculeux poème
Et la toute-philosophie,
Et ma patrie et ma bohème
Morts? Allons donc! tu vis, ma vie![13]

46

On 8 July 1889, a little over a fortnight after the publication of *Parallèlement*, Verlaine returned to the hôpital Broussais.

He was to be uncommonly fortunate in his doctors; with one notable exception (to be recorded in *Invectives*), they showed him remarkable deference, understanding and affection. Verlaine could be the most difficult patient, undoing days of medical care by an afternoon of abandon on the Left Bank. More than once, he asked permission to visit an editor or a publisher, and he returned, blind drunk, to hospital. But the doctors who attended him tolerated his weaknesses, as they would have borne those of a child; they indulged his whims, and they recognised his distinction.

They had a heavy professional burden. In 1930, in his 'Essai de clinique littéraire: Paul Verlaine', Dr Benassis gave a sombre diagnosis of his condition.[1] The abuse of alcohol had, he wrote, affected Verlaine's digestive system; it had also – as usual with alcoholics – reduced his powers of resistance. If Verlaine finally died ot pneumonia, it was largely due to this general weakness. Verlaine also suffered from venereal disease; and Dr Benassis considered that his persistent 'rheumatism' might be partly due to gonorrhoea.

Indeed, Verlaine showed all the symptoms of gonorrhoea: not only intractable 'rheumatism' in the knee, but the abscesses which sometimes mark the acute stage of the disease. The heart condition which he mentioned may well have been endocarditis: the inflammation of the heart-valves, which also occurs occasionally during the acute stage of gonorrhoea. In 1935 the treatment of the disease was revolutionised by the introduction of sulphonamides, but in Verlaine's day there was little that could be done. Verlaine also suffered from the much more serious syphilis. In addition, he had diabetes. Little was known about this condition during his lifetime. When he died, he had cirrhosis of the liver; the doctor who certified his death said that his body was worn out: he had ten illnesses, rather than one. However, Verlaine did not go into hospital purely for medical reasons. M. de Massary, who attended him as a surgeon's assistant in 1889, recalled that he had 'anchylosis of the knee, but he did not come to Broussais because of the anchylosis: he came because of exhaustion, slight bronchitis, and, usually, because his purse was empty.'[2]

One of the most devoted of Verlaine's doctors was Dr Louis Jullien, a specialist in syphilis. Dr Jullien was already treating him for water on the knee in December 1885. It was Dr Jullien to whom he sent an urgent appeal when his leg grew worse the following summer; and no doubt it was Dr Jullien who got Verlaine into hospital, soon afterwards, and kept him there for more than six weeks. Dr Jullien became a friend and counsellor as well as Verlaine's medical adviser. Verlaine spoke to him about Mathilde's behaviour, about his financial troubles, about his writing; he asked the doctor to help him find a lodging when he left hospital. He asked him to lend him money. Dr Jullien paid the initial expenses, years later, to get him into the Hôpital Saint-Louis; and, at the end of Verlaine's life, he was one of the admirers who combined to assure him a monthly allowance.[3]

Now, in August 1889, after six weeks at Broussais, Verlaine was to leave for Aix-les-Bains. On Dr Jullien's advice, he was to take the waters in an attempt to cure his 'rheumatism', and, perhaps, to alleviate some of his other ills.

Dr Jullien could hardly have shown him more devotion.

My dear friend [he wrote on 15 August],

Alas! I cannot invite you on Sunday, because I'm leaving on Saturday for Lyons. But this is what I've thought of.

Before I go, I'll leave an envelope at home, containing the letters of recommendation and the money which – with great pleasure, believe me – I can put at your disposal. Fifty francs, I think. My servant knows you and he will be instructed to hand it over only to you in person . . .

The essential thing for you would be to go into hospital down there. You can do so through my friend Dr. Guilland.

Your most devoted
JULLIEN.[4]

Two days later, Jullien added:

My dear friend,

Dr. Guilland . . . has been told about your arrival. When you get out of the train go and see him, and he will probably give you a bed.

You should also announce your arrival to Dr. Monard, who did so much to help last year.

Finally our friend M. Cazalis will put his medical knowledge and his good literary brotherhood at your service. In this letter you will find the 50 francs which I am happy to put at your disposal.

Off you go, *mon cher*. Take heart, and come back to us cured . . .

DR. JULLIEN.

Hurry up and send your news.[5]

Dr Jullien was not alone in subsidising Verlaine. Dr Guilland, Dr Monard and Dr Cazalis opened a subscription at Aix-les-Bains to pay Verlaine's expenses and the cost of his treatment. Verlaine accepted such help without embarrassment.[6]

On 19 August, he left for Aix-les-Bains. The spa had every advantage. The surrounding country, said the guide, 'included every kind of beauty: the wild, sheer slopes of the Alps, a few hours from the town, and, near at hand, the brightest and most melancholy landscapes in Switzerland. Lake Le Bourget, immortalised by the pen of M. de Lamartine, and the music of M. de Niedermayer, lent a charm of its own to most of these views.'[7] 'One should come to Savoy in September,' suggested a second guide. 'The climate is delightful; the days are not too hot, and the evenings are warm. The countryside, covered with clover and buckwheat in flower, is as fresh as it is in springtime, and greener than the valleys of Scotland.' This idyllic corner of the department of the Savoy was not disturbed by untoward behaviour. As the guide reassured potential visitors: 'Brawls are virtually unknown in the valley of Aix, and in spite of the many taverns assiduously frequented by the lower orders, quarrels are very rarely found there.'[8]

The peace was broken by Verlaine. He had spent all his travel money on the journey; he arrived penniless, and completely drunk.

He was later to blame his condition on the railway company, which sent its trains through Burgundy, and allowed them to stop at Vougeot and Beaune. Mallarmé recorded in his usual kindly way: 'I'm told by some friends that Verlaine . . . . arrived drunk . . . at Aix-les-Bains, collared by the police, and followed by the populace. In a flash of lucidity, he remembered a letter of introduction to Cazalis, and Cazalis smoothed everything over; but I wager that he bears me a grudge for this damage to his reputation.'[9]

Henri Cazalis (or Jean Lahor, to give him his *nom de plume*) was the perfect doctor for men of letters. He was not only a doctor but a poet – indeed, his *Poésies complètes* had been published the previous year. As Maurice Fleury wrote, he had 'a perfect double intellect . . . He can sing superb rhymes for the five months of the winter (unlike the cricket), and look after his patients with care . . . in the watering-place where he practises for the seven months of the summer.' As medical consultant at Aix-les-Bains, Cazalis showed 'a rare professional honesty, a thorough knowledge of hydrology, and a proper understanding of therapeutic methods.'[10]

In 1889 Cazalis found himself in charge of Verlaine. Years later, he recalled the facts with terror.

In the first place [recorded Stuart Merrill], Verlaine refused to see Cazalis except in a café, and Cazalis – a society doctor – was obliged to frequent the lowest bistros in the small – excessively small – town. Then once or twice Verlaine was taken to the police station, where the respectable Cazalis had to go and claim him. And finally, as a prank, Verlaine showed an excessive, public and scandalous admiration for a certain marble Ganymede which adorns the public gardens at Aix-les-Bains. I don't want to look like a beastly bourgeois, but I still think one may sympathise with that excellent man Jean Lahor.[11]

On 21 August, apparently from the doctor's house, Verlaine reported to Cazals in a happy frame of mind. The punishing effects of the intoxication had gone, he was revelling in his surroundings, and he looked hopefully towards the future.

I've made a conquest!! The commissioner of police. He saw at once that I wasn't a brigand, as my dress might suggest. Have seen Cazalis, who's divine. Seen the hospital - more nursing Sisters. Haven't seen the town, which is terribly hilly. Will send you drawings. It's very fine.

Berets, carts drawn by cows. Italian patois. People very nice or seem to be, which is three-quarters of being it. (What do you think of that? And isn't that a more sensible observation than it seems?)

What's new in your life? I myself have become surprisingly serious all of a sudden. I'm going to pray for us, effectively, I think. I'm also going to work. Have done four lines of the second sonnet to Tellier. Have forgotten it. That'll come back to me.

Exhausted! Stupefied! But, as I say, I am spiritually better. Is it going to last? Well, YES!

I think that in your friendship, your serious and most deserving filial and brotherly affection, you will be glad of this news: my intellectual resurrection, my true Birth after this lamentable 'miscarriage'!

I am the sheep which was lost and is found again. Kill the fatted calf! And love me even more and write to me *bontément*, as the Ardennais say.

I have two addresses, and one of them – the proper one – is lost. Cazalis is going to give it to me again. He doesn't want me to go to the hospital and he has put me up. Write *poste restante* for the time being. I'll send you the proper address very soon . . .[12]

That day he settled in the Pension Héritier, and sent two further notes to Cazals. He desperately needed money, he had some literary errands to give him; but he needed to talk to him, by letter, to give himself the illusion of his company. During his stay at Aix-les-Bains, which lasted just under a month, he wrote to him twenty-seven times: sometimes briefly, but usually at length; and his letters, gay, spontaneous, affectionate, gossiping, serious, reveal Verlaine very much as he was in conversation with a close friend.

A wonderful welcome here from Drs. Guilland, Monard and Cazalis [he wrote on 23 August]. Have just seen the hospital almoner who has put himself at my disposal. In fact there's no one - including the commissioner of police, as I've already told you – who isn't very nice to me . . .
But, *mon ami*, how lonely I was the moment I got into the train . . . The loneliness! The loneliness![13]

For all his efforts to sublimate his love for Cazals, Verlaine was still immensely drawn to him. He sent him an unidentified flower and hoped that he would not be accused of sentimentality; but on his mantelpiece, with a picture of his son and a photograph of Lucien Létinois, he kept three likenesses of Cazals, including 'Cazals éphèbe' by Paterne Berrichon. 'Thank you for the charming *tone* of your letter,' he wrote on 26 August, 'although it is still a trifle too discreet.'[14] And, in a second letter that day, thinking of Villiers de l'Isle-Adam, who had just died, Verlaine compared their lives and considered his own nature. He made an illuminating assessment of his morals, his physical and emotional needs.

His life [he wrote of Villiers] was certainly more *dignified* than mine, but it was not really worthier. I have made more efforts than he did, and I was – alas, *I was*! – a more logical Christian. How can I explain my falls from grace? Shall I blame my blood, my education? But I was good and chaste . . . Oh, drink! The drink which so developed the acarus, the bacillus, the microbe of Lust in my flesh, though that flesh was made for normality and order! It is true that misfortune (I think an unparalleled misfortune) tempered me – for a time, and then weakened me because I didn't behave judiciously. For all my good sense, I lack judgment. I hardly like the moral, it looks as if it stinks of physiology: I'm feminine, – which would explain a good many things![15]

Verlaine's emotional life had not been entirely dictated by drink. Drink had only intensified the instincts he possessed, and released him from any frail inhibitions. But, as he recognised, he was 'feminine': feminine in his need for love, in his need to be dominated, in his possessiveness and his jealousy, and, above all, in his need for the love of men.

Now, compelled to sublimate his love for Cazals, he showed his profound affection and trust. He asked him to undertake a delicate task: to get news of Georges, to see him and talk to him. 'Nice of you to think it would give me pleasure to have news of my son,' he added, later that day. 'Yes, it gives me pleasure, but that doesn't stop what's written from being written.'[16] Some months earlier, in June, he had made Cazals his heir. 'And this novel of ours?' continued Verlaine on 28 August. 'For of course we shall collaborate closely. I shall announce it in my next book.'[17] It was a glittering prospect for the young man in Paris, but Verlaine was trying to bind Cazals by every bond of friendship. If, in a letter, he dwelt too long on the statue of Ganymede which adorned the public gardens at Aix, that was, perhaps, a means of expressing his love of 'Cazals éphèbe' without offending Cazals himself.

Verlaine was writing poetry – if not with inspiration, at least with fluency; and – since his sexual appetites were all-embracing – among the poems was the erotic 'À Celle que l'on dit froide'. He decorated his letters with drawings of himself: posting a letter, wearing his Sunday best, going to his douche. He added a sketch of Lamartine coming out of his douche in 1825. 'As soon as I have some sous I'll go to Lake Le Bourget,' he wrote on 1 September. '. . . This is Lamartine's famous lake, he lived for a long time in Aix itself, in a house a few yards from here . . .'[18]

'I believe you have gone to patch up your temporal shell at Aix-les-Bains,' wrote Huysmans on 15 September. '. . . Write to me, so that at least I know how you are, and whether one can bless the Pension Héritier where you are staying.'[19] Verlaine returned to Paris that day, and spent four days at the Hôtel de Lisbonne before he went back, inevitably, to Broussais. He sent a bulletin to Huysmans. 'My dear friend,' answered Huysmans, 'I'm glad to see that your leg is getting stronger. The relics of St Ganymede, the ancient one, may be omnipotent.'[20]

It was at Broussais, on 4 October, that Verlaine wrote a poem, 'Goûts royaux'. Like the poem 'À Celle que l'on dit froide', it was burning with desire for a woman, and it appeared in *Femmes*, which was privately published the following year.[1]

It was also at Broussais, in October, that a young Belgian came to see him. Henry Carton de Wiart had arrived from Brussels to finish his legal training in Paris. Léon Bloy took him to visit Verlaine.

He was in bed [remembered Carton de Wiart]; his black skull cap was pushed back on his knobbly skull, and, flat-faced, he looked at us with oblique and sparkling eyes. He seemed to me, that day, with his faun-like face, very much as Anatole France would enjoy describing him in *Gestas* and *Le Lys rouge* . . .

The memory I have kept of the man has hardly touched the admiration inspired in me by immortal masterpieces like *La Bonne Chanson* and *Sagesse*. For, in private, he did not feel obliged to put on a front, between a glass of absinthe and a pipe, in front of a few open-mouthed admirers, whom (old braggart of vice) he was trying to scandalise or to mystify; and then his fundamental nature . . . revealed its charming features.[2]

It was at Broussais, a few months later, that Pierre Louÿs and the young André Gide came to visit him.

His visage was extremely Socratic [so Louÿs recalled]. He had . . . an untrimmed beard, bushy towards the eyes but very sparse about the chin. Those were the characteristics that struck me first. Then I looked at his surroundings. What wretchedness! There, on a little iron bedstead with coarse and not overclean linen, propped up by a tiny pillow, was the poet. He was reading *L'Intransigeant*. He was wearing a cotton night cap, and a nightshirt marked 'HÔPITAL BROUSSAIS', in black capital letters.[3]

On 15 December *La Plume* announced that 'the greatest living poet lay dying . . . in hospital. Paul Verlaine, the heavenly dreamer of the *Fêtes galantes*, is too noble to complain, and it is for us to give him consolations . . .' The heavenly dreamer answered the editor in a down-to-earth style:

My dear Deschamps,

No, I'm not dying. I have never been dying, for that matter . . .
I am as well as I can be here, admirably looked after . . . So print this
note and reassure any readers who may take an interest in my health.

I'm sure that the sense of dignity with which you rightly invest me
will not be offended in the least by the things you say you are preparing
for me . . .

The letter appeared in *La Plume* with the editor's reply:

No, *mon cher Maître*, your dignity will not be offended; we all love
you, here, as much as we admire you. Your manuscript *Dédicaces* has
been unanimously chosen to open the new series of books which is
announced above. And in a few days . . . I hope to bring you some solid
consolations.

> Most affectionately yours, *mon cher Maître*,
> LÉON DESCHAMPS.[4]

Deschamps had known that Verlaine was not dying. He had
only been concerned to get publicity, and Verlaine had probably
been his accomplice. For Verlaine had told him about his financial
troubles and his difficulties with Vanier; and, touched by these
accounts, Deschamps had determined to publish *Dédicaces* by
subscription.

The project was so successful that he reported to René Ghil:
'*Dédicaces* is a triumph for our Review . . . He's having a terrible
celebration, the author of *Sagesse*. I've given him 600 francs in a
week, and he's spent it all. I'm going to turn the screw.'[5]

The first edition of *Dédicaces*, which appeared in March 1890,
consisted of forty-one poems. It included tributes to one or two
poets, and civilities to colleagues, and it showed, again, that
Verlaine had lost the secret of poetry. The seventy-two poems
which were added in 1894 merely emphasise this spiritual death.
Verlaine again escapes into entertainment, parody or mockery.
Whether he has become poetically impotent, or whether – which
is unlikely – he has disowned his past, he is now writing from
habit or from financial need; and he is clearly aware of his
degeneration:

'An innocent satyr . . .'

L'auteur de ces vers-ci, débris d'orage,
Ruine, épave, au vague et lent dessein . . .

The memory of Rimbaud still stirs some latent fire; and in
'À un Passant' the memories of Rimbaud and Létinois are
curiously fused with one another, and the poet is again touched by
the past. But the poems to his mistresses lack conviction and
quality; the poems to his friends and acquaintances impress only
by their mediocrity. When one recalls the exquisite accomplishment of *Fêtes galantes*, the impressionist, sometimes surrealist
brilliance of *Romances sans paroles*, one can measure the depth of
his decline.

Dédicaces was published with a drawing of its author by Cazals;
but relations between the two of them were strained. Verlaine
had hoped that their relationship would set him finally on the
path of rectitude, 'and help to suppress 2 demons in me, the
Drunkard, and the other one, which is worse!'[6] He hoped that
Cazals would make him suppress his homosexual instincts, and
give him the incentive to turn away from alcohol. The certainty
of his affection would give Verlaine a reason for living properly –
and, indeed, for living at all.

Alas, the dream of collaboration, of literary success and personal
happiness, of permanent reform, was not to be realised. On
20 September, five days after his return from Aix-les-Bains,
Verlaine was already reproaching Cazals for his lack of
punctuality; on 24 September he reproached him for failing to
visit him.

Verlaine – as he himself has said – had a feminine nature; he
would have accepted any sacrifice, provided that Cazals was
happy and that he continued to love him. But the relationship
grew tense. Verlaine remained in hospital for five months:
isolated enough to brood over Cazals' behaviour. When, on
19 February 1890, he finally left Broussais, his good intentions
were forgotten, and, after his long, enforced abstention, he
abandoned himself to homosexuality (his practices were to
inspire *Hombres*, which was published after his death).

In March 1890, after a serious quarrel, Verlaine told Cazals: 'Either you write or come as soon as possible, in a friendly way, or else you send me back *all* my things (including a certain paper) at once . . . Let us bend or break.'[7] Perhaps Cazals did return the will which Verlaine had made in his favour – for Georges Verlaine became his father's heir. In any case, Verlaine's correspondence reveals his jealousy, his misery and his possessiveness. Among Cazals' papers is a pencilled note from Fernand L'Anglois: undated, but probably written this March:

[My dear Cazals,]
I don't know what happened after I left yesterday evening. P.V. came to me in a fury at 2 o'clock, and we have been together ever since. Now come and explain things to him calmly. These perpetual quarrels are so futile! Come on, be reasonable.

Ever,
Fernand L'Anglois.

We are waiting for you downstairs. Turn over . . . P.V. is resting for a few hours on my divan. Or better still come to TARLE'S hurry up!

A second note, which follows this in the correspondence, is dated 24 March 1890, and appears to be the sequel.

Monday.

My dear Cazals,
As Verlaine is unable to hold a pen, he asks me to tell you how sorry he is for his anger yesterday. Only he'd like you to show a little goodwill, – and he sends you his best affection. When will you come?
I shake you warmly by the hand.
Fernand L'Anglois.[8]

Such appeals did not change the situation. Cazals was sometimes brusque and negligent and ungrateful. He did not want a closer relationship with Verlaine. The dream of collaboration vanished. In June, when Cazals had once again shown himself unpunctual, and Verlaine had made some sharp observations, there was a break between them.

On 19 June, Verlaine went into the Hôpital Cochin. On 22 July he left Cochin for Vincennes. He was to stay there until about 11 September, when he returned to the all-too-familiar Broussais.

PART TEN

Au temps du Quartier

(1890s)

THE Latin Quarter, between 1890 and 1896, was the Quarter of Bibi-la-Purée and Verlaine.

Bibi-la-Purée – or André Salis, to give him his real name – seemed like some grotesque survival from the Middle Ages: a figure from a Bacchanal by Breughel. He was in fact the son of a wine and spirit dealer in Angoulême; but he had long ago cut himself off from his relations, and the only remnant of his social status was an annuity of 300 francs, which he used to draw four times a year. To supplement these private means, Bibi used to do services for the lodgers at a hotel in the rue Broca: 'run errands for them, black their boots, and provide them at the lowest rates, consistent with a good article, with the umbrellas he used to steal in the various cafés of the Latin Quarter.' Bibi-la-Purée had no home, he had no means of existence, and he had no property except the ragged finery he stood up in. 'He was in perpetual masquerade. He usually wore a high hat, and never went abroad without a huge bouquet in his ragged frock coat . . . In the tails of his frock-coat he carried a pair of blacking-brushes; but his skill in the art of polishing boots was exercised rather for the benefit of his friends than for personal gain.' Bibi-la-Pureé was to die in the Hôtel-Dieu; he died of tuberculosis, and also of exposure, want and privation. He was known as Verlaine's 'secretary', and he is said to have exercised his talents as a thief on his behalf.[1] There was something touching in this association between the poet and the pariah.

Louis Roseyre recorded, in *Au temps du quartier*, how he had seen Verlaine attend the opening of a café in the rue Soufflot.

Bibi-la-Purée came first, clearing a way through the crowd, so that the reeling poet ... could find a seat. Verlaine followed, painfully, dragging his leg, and leaning on a stout stick ... He collapsed on to a chair ... Suddenly my heart, the heart of a boy of eighteen, bled with grief and fear at the sight of this old man, whining and infirm, demanding another absinthe. I knew the legend; but really Verlaine, this man who was trembling all over, this man with a dirty beard, his face half hidden by a filthy muffler, ... Verlaine collapsing on Bibi-la-Purée, with that horrible, grinning face, and a mouth slit to the ears, Bibi smelling of rat, old rotting rat! ... I have never been able to forget that sinister and pitiful vision.[2]

If Bibi was the faithful vassal, Verlaine himself, in the 1890s, was the unchallenged sovereign of the Latin Quarter. Camille Mauclair remembered how

... the students and prostitutes used to point him out to one another, and the waiters and owners of wine-bars would indicate him to foreign visitors. He was accompanied by his faithful nondescript followers. Sometimes, on his way to the Senate, Leconte de Lisle, impassible and wearing his monocle, would pass the group and turn away ostentatiously, and Verlaine would laugh and blow puffs of smoke from his cheap cigar in the path of the Olympian figure. They loathed each other.[3]

But it was not Leconte de Lisle whom the sons of the Right Bank used to come to see. 'We used to cross the Seine,' recalled Henri Duvernois,

... purely and simply to see Verlaine, with his old dosshouse overcoat, his battered felt hat, his vagabond's cudgel, and his hirsute face ennobled by suffering and sadness. When some young bourgeois timidly approached him and assured him of his passionate admiration, he would retort: 'In that case, monsieur, you might oblige me with a five-franc piece!' He didn't ask for more, because, with a sort of wisdom, he had reduced his needs to the level of his resources.[4]

This was not entirely true. Pierre-Eugène Vibert, the artist, once saw Verlaine alone in a café; he paid for his drink from a well-stocked purse which he took from his trouser pocket. Later that evening, when a few disciples had gathered around him, he took another purse from his waistcoat pocket, and emptied the contents on to the table, to show that it only contained a few sous.[5]

But these were the understandable wiles of a man who had forgotten the meaning of financial security; and his admirers were eager to help him. Some time in the 1890s, Charles Darantière wrote to him:

My dear poet,

... On Tuesday evening, with a few friends, I ventured as far as Sarrazin's: le Divan Japonais, at Montmartre ... Paterne Berrichon recited the magnificent sonnet which you addressed to him ... and Sarrazin told the audience that you were at Broussais, and made a collection for you. I just want to ask you, dear great Verlaine, if you actually received all the money – the collection seemed quite fruitful to me ...[6]

Verlaine frequented many bars and cafés on the Left Bank. Sometimes he would go to the Côte d'Or, a wine-bar opposite the Odéon, to meet Moréas. Iannis Pappadiamantopoulos had been born in Athens, of Greek parents, in 1856; but he had lived in Paris since 1870. Wholly French by culture and by tastes, he adopted the name Jean Moréas, and in the 1890s he was an ardent Symbolist, writing poetry and contributing to the little reviews. 'For some years, Jean Moréas passed for a great man in various artistic cellars,' noted Laurent Tailhade with aversion. 'He was small and skinny and sickly, with black skin, black nails, and black hair, and he dressed like a music-hall swell ...'[7] It was this ungainly creature who, in 1881, had made Verlaine's acquaintance; he became his ardent disciple. In the mid-1880s, the Quartier des Écoles echoed as Moréas declaimed his work.

Now Verlaine met Moréas at the Côte d'Or. As Stuart Merrill, the American expatriate, remembered:

Verlaine sometimes came there to share beef collops with onions and a demi-setier with us. When I say 'us', I mean Moréas, Raymond de la Tailhède, the great lyric writer who has too long been silent, Ernest Raynaud, Maurice du Plessys, with his nervous tics, sarcastic and dry-humoured, and Gauguin, who had arrived from the Antilles and was getting ready to leave for Tahiti . . . There was Édouard Dubus, a delightful soul who was to lose himself in every artificial paradise, Adolphe Retté, who was then hardly thinking of religion, Louis Le Cardonnel, who never ceased to think about it; and there were countless others, some of them have committed suicide, and others have met with terrible deaths . . .[8]

Café society on the Left Bank attracted all too many misfits; Verlaine outsoared them by his genius, but he was only one of hundreds who sought escape in drink. 'I get drunk to keep up my reputation,' he assured the novelist and diarist Jules Renard. 'I am the slave of my reputation.'[9] There was a fraction of truth in the statement; Verlaine was conscious of his image. But, reputation apart, he could not have abandoned his drinking habits. Verlaine was not only an alcoholic, he was unhappy with the fierce intensity of a child. Physically he depended on drink; emotionally he needed it as a curtain between himself and the past, the present and the future.

> Ah! si je bois c'est pour me saouler non pour boire.
> Être saoul vous ne savez pas quelle victoire
> C'est qu'on remporte sur la vie et quel don c'est!
> On oublie, on revoit, on ignore et l'on sait;
> C'est des mystères pleins d'aperçus, c'est du rêve
> Qui n'a jamais eu de naissance et ne s'achève
> Pas et ne se meut pas dans l'essence d'ici;
> C'est une espèce d'autre vie en raccourci.[10]

Some of those who drank with Verlaine grew more insignificant when they drank; but Gide recorded that when Verlaine was drunk he was formidable.[11] Perhaps, then, when reality became less real to him, when he moved in the world of his dreams, he became fully conscious of his powers.

Absinthe offered the quickest way to detach himself from the world; and absinthe was a taste which he shared with all too many of his contemporaries. As Fosca pointed out, in his book on Parisian cafés:

Après l'incision.

à Mon. jeun Ernest de Massary

h^t Broussais, 27 juillet 1893

P. Verlaine

'Messieurs, this is a great invalid – and the greatest Catholic poet of the century.' Verlaine at the Hôpital Broussais, 27 January 1893. This drawing by Cazals was presented to Ernest de Massary, one of the surgeons.

The would-be Academician, 1893 (photograph by Otto). Verlaine is no doubt wearing the top-hat and overcoat given to him by the staff at the Hôpital Broussais.

Verlaine lecturing in London, 21 November 1893. From a drawing by Charles Wellington Furse, ARA.

The absinthe habit had been brought back by soldiers from Algeria, and it developed considerably in the last ten years of the Second Empire ... There were many who had to suffer for their weakness for the 'green fairy': Villiers de l'Isle-Adam, Charles Cros, Glatigny, the artist André Gill, and the Communard Eugène Vermersch, whom it led to a padded cell. There were the musicians Chabrier, Cabaner and Charles de Sivry; and finally there was Verlaine, who abused it to the end of his days.

'Who can tell what damage was done by absinthe to this rash, unstable generation?' asked Michaud, in his *Message poétique du Symbolisme*.[12] Alphonse Daudet blamed absinthe for the alarming spread of alcoholism in France. Often, in his conversations with Robert Sherard, Wilde's biographer, Daudet insisted: 'Before those [Algerian] wars we were a very sober people.' Sherard noted that absinthe contained ninety per cent pure alcohol, three times as much as ordinary brandy. 'It is, moreover, an insidious drink,' Sherard continued,

... and the habit of consuming it grows upon its victim, who sooner or later has to abdicate all willpower in the control of his passion ... As a matter of fact, one has observed the usual effects of absinthism, the hoarse, guttural absinthe voice, the wandering, glazed absinthe eye, the cold and clammy hand, ... in people who have never drunk a glass of absinthe in their lives. Various *amers*, or bitters, even the supposed harmless *vermouth*, will, in due course, if taken in excess, conduct their man to epilepsy, paralysis and death. Absinthe gets in its work more speedily.

Since the absinthe drinker was often ashamed to be seen lingering over his glass, he acquired the habit of moving from one café to another. 'He takes his first drink at one café,' Sherard explained, 'his second somewhere else and his tenth or twelfth at some tenth or twelfth other café. I know a very distinguished musician who used to start off at the Café Napolitain and finish up at the Gare du Nord ...'[13]

Verlaine was only one of many who succumbed to absinthe. Tailhade said that his drunkenness was exaggerated by malicious journalists. Cazals declared that the literary circles he frequented hardly set an example of sobriety. 'It must also be observed,' said

Cazals, 'that, unlike many poets of that generation, Verlaine never took to hashish, opium, ether or morphine, which were then in fashion. He professed a genuine horror for these poisons of the mind.'[14] With rare exceptions, he drank nothing but absinthe, beer, and rum-and-water. When a journalist criticised him as an incorrigible drinker, Verlaine wrote indignantly to Vanier: 'I am – and I'll repeat it *ad nauseam* – basically a very worthy man, reduced to misery by excessive delicacy, a man with weaknesses and too much geniality but in every sense a *gentleman* and *hidalgo*. You must find someone to write that.'[15] In the last months of his life, he had almost given up his visits to cafés, and absinthe itself no longer tempted him.[16]

Yet many of his contemporaries recorded his addiction to drink with irony and disdain. Years after he had died, his alcoholic legend still persisted; and, in a novel, *Toute la Vie*, in 1913, M.-C. Poinsot introduced 'Jarlaine: an epic and Verlainian drunkard'.[17]

The Symbolists who gathered round Verlaine and Moréas held their sessions in cafés. Indeed, the café played an important part in the Symbolist movement, as it had always done in the history of French literature. Coppée made the fortune of the Café des Vosges, which later became, in his honour, the Café des Vosges et de François Coppée. Verlaine made the fortune of the François Ier, in the boulevard Saint-Michel. It was there, remembered Yvanhoe Rambosson,

... that, between his rustications in hospital, Paul Verlaine long found himself at home. Sitting in front of 'the humble ephemeral absinthe,' a scarf the colour of dregs worn anyhow over a shirt that was probably flannel, a short pipe held in a gloriously threatening or insistent fist, a jeer in his damp, limp moustache, good-humour in his faun's eyes, he used to talk, sometimes with gentleness, sometimes with trembling and rebellion, in a voice that was slightly husky and dull.

His preoccupations – in these hours of daily conversation – were not particularly orientated towards literature ... You should have heard him talk about 'Badinguet' or Boulanger. 'Le brav' général' had all his sympathies, and, faithful to the fallen god, Verlaine kept his sympathy for him to the end. As a good Lorrain from Metz, who had opted for French nationality, he displayed a chauvinism which seemed to us to be very out of season. But on this point he would never be contradicted. He abominated 'the Prussian' and Bismarck.[18]

It was at the François Ier that the Belgian artist Henry de Groux saw Verlaine in 1893. 'He had his huge and perpetual sly smile . . . He was still sober, but installed in front of a splendid *verte*. He was there, always on the edge of the seat, near the counter: stiff, imperious, upright, . . . his thick eyebrows raised, his forehead jutting out over the rest of his face, his eyes in which a silver jewel seemed to tremble: he was there in all his masculine and intellectual ugliness.'[19] The photographer who portrayed Verlaine at the François Ier in the series *Nos contemporains chez eux* had come sadly near the truth. Stuart Merrill kept the photograph on his desk, but he rarely went to the café, for it distressed him to see the 'hangers-on' drinking at Verlaine's expense when he was in pocket. 'His last years were spent in a kind of vulgar drinking-bout,' wrote Rémy de Gourmont. 'In this he was encouraged, to his misfortune and to their shame, by young men . . . whose only glory will have been that they drank with Verlaine.'[20]

But the François Ier – 'the café of splendours,' he called it – was Verlaine's headquarters. Some said that the first room was his throne-room; and Léo d'Orfer recalled that the café 'had a great vogue for several years. There the Symbolists met in full force almost every evening . . . There it was that Verlaine consolidated his reputation and displayed his mastery of the poetic art.'[21]

It was in this décor, in the spring of 1893, that Saint-Georges de Bouhélier first met him.

Georges de Bouhélier-Lepelletier had been born in 1876. He was the son of Edmond Lepelletier, the writer and politician who was Verlaine's lifelong friend. Saint-Georges de Bouhélier, as he came to call himself, soon gave proof of his literary tastes: he published a periodical at the age of seventeen. His parents later sent him to Switzerland, ostensibly to perfect his German, but really to cure him of his wilder literary dreams. When he returned to Paris, he earned a living as a clerk, and at night he devoted himself to literature. In 1896, in *L'Hiver en Méditation*, he was to lay the foundations of the Naturist doctrine.[22]

It would have been understandable if Bouhélier had first met Verlaine at his parents' house; but, as he wrote:

In the years which passed between his leaving prison at Mons, and the beginnings of his glory as a poet (1894–6), Verlaine was always badly dressed and living nobody knew how, lodging only in furnished rooms and covered with debts; he did not give a very favourable impression. My mother had a great appreciation of his talent, but when I was a child she always talked about him with marked disgust. In order not to expose her to affronts, my father met him only in cafés or in newspaper offices. Because of this proscription, imposed on him by his very way of life, Verlaine remained unknown to me for quite a long time, and I had to meet him independently. I was seventeen; in my eyes . . . his art had, as it were, freed him from all this filth, and I saw him, simply, as a kind of saint.[23]

One evening, with his friend Chapeyroux, a literary young man, Bouhélier went to the François Ier. It was, he remembered,

. . . a white-and-gold café, in the old French style, and at that time it was much frequented. We had not been there for five minutes, when someone, with his hat and shoulders streaming with rain, opened the door as if he had been hurled in by the storm. The bristling, reddish beard, like a tramp's, half hidden by thick woollen stuffs, would have been enough for anyone to recognise him at once: it was Paul Verlaine. At the sight of him, several customers had taken off their hats, and the manager rushed up to relieve him of his soaking wet coat. But Verlaine muttered, and brushed aside all assistance. He collapsed on a leather seat at the back of the café, and, with a rather sullen look, and a woeful voice, he asked the waiter for a grog. I was frightened by this cruel and unexpected vision . . .

'I'm going to take you to Verlaine,' said my friend a moment later. 'He will be delighted to see you.'

And . . . going over to the old man, who bore within himself all the poetry of a world of misery, Chapeyroux introduced me.

'Sit down there,' said Verlaine, indicating a seat beside him; and my friend vanished, as he had to go back to his paper . . .

It was appallingly hot in the François Ier. There was a stove which was constantly being fed with lumps of coal, and it was roaring away.

Nearly all the customers were puffing at long clay pipes, and what with the smell of the smoke and the gas, I was stifling.

Verlaine ordered a second grog, then a third . . . His clothes were so filthy they made me sick. I got up, feeling rather ill.

'I'm going, too,' cried Verlaine, in his husky, childlike voice . . . He called the waiter and paid the bill. He insisted on paying for everything . . .

Three minutes later, we were sitting side by side in a cab, and the vehicle had set off along the slippery streets. The rain was beating against the windows in a furious patter. It hadn't rained so hard for a long time. Verlaine had wrapped his old muffler round his neck again. . .

'My son is your age,' he said suddenly. 'I haven't had news of him for twenty years. I only know what outsiders tell me. He's doing his military service at the moment. I've written to him, but he hasn't answered. His mother is a bitch.'

And he began to vent a mass of complaints, . . . blaming all the world for his misfortune. What a life he had had! People had been determined to slander him. It was his wife's fault, she'd been jealous of Rimbaud – and there had been no reason at all for that . . .

I had had no experience of life. This great man, moaning beside me, made me ill. He clasped me against his breast, and sobbed . . . When he had calmed down again, he asked me to forgive him. All I wanted was to leave him. The omnibus was a very convenient excuse. I jumped out of the cab, and vanished into the darkness.

A few days later, I told my mother about this painful meeting.

'Poor Verlaine!' she cried. 'He hasn't changed.'[24]

Alas, Verlaine did not change in his affection for café life. He enjoyed it as a Parisian, as a man of letters, and as a bohemian who had no home.

Sometimes he was found in the Café Tabourey, in the rue de Vaugirard, opposite the Jardin du Luxembourg. The Tabourey had been patronised by Baudelaire, Leconte de Lisle and Banville, and one of the most pathetic habitués, until his death in 1889, had been Barbey d'Aurevilly, the novelist and critic, who, in his old age, with the help of corsets and cosmetics, had continued to play the youthful dandy. Verlaine also 'condescended to sit in state in the Café Vachette'. Years later, recalling the prostitutes at the Vachette, Antoine Albalat said that Verlaine had helped to give them respect for literature. One of them had discovered a 'very nice' book: *Discours de la méthode*, by Descartes.[25]

As for the Café Voltaire, in the place de l'Odéon, it was virtually an annexe of the Sorbonne and the Institut; it was also – as Paul Fort made clear – a centre for modern poetry. Fort and his young companions timidly ventured there to discover the mysteries of literature, and to admire the beauty of Rachilde, the imperial moustaches of Moréas, and the Socratic skull of Verlaine.[26]

In the Café Procope, in the rue de l'Ancienne Comédie, the mirrors had been replaced by portraits of the famous men who, since the eighteenth century, had gathered there. Voltaire and d'Alembert, Rousseau and Mirabeau had once gazed down from the walls on Anatole France, and on the young Gambetta. The Procope was now run by Théo, an original character, who determined that his café should earn renown. He ran a monthly paper, *Le Procope parlé* (Verlaine and Huysmans were contributors). In 1893, with the singer Xavier Privas, he founded the *soirées Procope*; and it was, remembered Privas, 'for a fête which was organised on behalf of Verlaine that Laurent Tailhade composed his admirable "Mystic Ballade to Paul Verlaine on the Sweetness of Poverty".'[27]

It was in the Café Procope, one evening in the nineties, that Bouhélier heard Verlaine recite his poetry. He recalled the occasion with affection, with transparent admiration, and with the inevitable sorrow which the sight of Verlaine inspired.

I had sat down at Signoret's table when . . . Verlaine appeared, with some or other escort, and a rather surly, ludicrous air. He did not acknowledge the numerous 'good evenings,' and, as if he was tired of these vanities, he went and settled down under a dim gas-lamp at the back of the room. And then, withdrawing into a hostile silence, he ordered a *stiff* pernod – 'un pernod *bien tassé*' – it was the current phrase. The regular customers were used to his moods, and began to drink and chat again. I was dismayed. Verlaine had clearly drunk more than he should. Signoret persisted in seeing only the *invisible god* in this fallen man . . . I remember that he rose, went to his table, and said a word to him. What passed between the two men I have no idea. But a moment later Signoret announced that the Master had agreed to recite some poetry . . . One could feel the veneration and the suspense. Verlaine had risen, awkwardly, to his feet. There was utter silence. And, in a gentle and almost inaudible voice, he announced that he would recite *Gaspard Hauser* . . .

While Verlaine was speaking, all these creatures who, a moment earlier, had merely been discussing their mistresses, or their petty quarrels, seemed to come out of the depths in which we are usually bogged down by everyday life. At the words of this vagabond, quite unconsciously, they had rediscovered their souls.[28]

49

It was in 1889 that Léon Deschamps had founded *La Plume*. The review gave generous hospitality to poets from the new schools, and Verlaine was one of Deschamps' first and dearest contributors. Late that summer, after the birth of *La Plume*, Deschamps had decided to organise a weekly gathering of artists and poets. The *soirées de la Plume* were held in the cellar of the café du Soleil d'Or, in the place Saint-Michel. They were to be a feature of literary Paris in the last decade of the century.

They took place at nine o'clock every Saturday night. Students, poets and artists, in their corduroy suits and musketeer hats, flocked down from Montmartre and Montparnasse for the occasion. 'It was a curious spectacle,' Ernest Raynaud remembered. 'Some two hundred people gathered there in a long stone passage, in clouds of tobacco smoke and a stifling atmosphere. Two bewildered and exhausted waiters wormed their way through a wilderness of chairs and tables . . . At about ten o'clock "the Master", Paul Verlaine, would come in.'[1] 'We used to induce him to come by means of a friendly little stratagem,' so remembered Léo d'Orfer. 'Knowing his failing and the emptiness of his purse, we got up a small subscription among ourselves and told the waiter to refuse payment when Verlaine offered it. When Verlaine had "yelled" a little, as he used to say, he would accept the situation and come again.'[2]

Deschamps was equally concerned about the Master's welfare. One evening, when Gabriel de Lautrec had accompanied Verlaine, Deschamps took the young man aside.

He handed me an envelope [remembered Lautrec], and said: 'Here's a little money which I ought to give Verlaine. It would be very kind of you if you'd see him to his door, and only give him the envelope once he's in.'
Which is what I did. When we reached the door, I wished him good-night, and handed him the precious envelope. I went off, calmly, down the street, taking care not to look round. I knew all too well that Verlaine was behind the door, waiting for me to disappear so that he could creep out and squander the 'gold'.[3]

We were all worshippers of Verlaine [remembered an American, Vance Thompson]. We had read *Sagesse*. We had lent the poet five-franc pieces, had bought him absinthe, had helped him up the hospital steps when his diseases were too many for him . . .
He sat among us there, this old man, with the dirty neckerchief and the ribald and unclean speech. And is it thus that I remember him? No. I remember him best when, with his glowing eyes half-closed, he recited some new sonnet or unforeseen verses – splendid as golden coins . . .
His art was at once subtle, refined, difficult, and inveterately young. His was the subtle simplicity of the Middle Ages . . . His individuality was dominant and insistent as of some great soul of the fifteenth century.[4]

There was another American admirer in the cellar of le Soleil d'Or. Stuart Merrill, poet, translator and critic, had been born in Long Island in 1863, but he had been educated in Paris. The spell of Paris had been so strong that in 1893, at the age of thirty, Merrill installed himself at 53, quai Bourbon. He gladly lost himself in the life of the Latin Quarter, and for Verlaine he felt profound affection.[5]
Some people felt only sorrow at the sight of him. Robert Sherard, who first saw him at le Soleil d'Or, remembered that 'Verlaine was drunk that night, and, as usual, he was dressed in rags. He had a false nose on his face (for it was carnival time), and he was piping on a little tin whistle. The spectacle had the terrible

comedy touch of Aristophanes.' 'He looked like a drunken god,' wrote Jules Renard, in 1892. 'There's nothing left of him except our cult. Above the wreck of a suit – a yellow cravat, an overcoat which must be sticking to his flesh in more places than one – is a head like a freestone being demolished.'[6] In 1893, at another *soirée de la Plume*, Jean Carrère, the man of letters, observed the drunken deity. The guests were about to sit down to dinner when Verlaine and Gabriel Vicaire staggered in, abominably drunk, and began to make their way to the top table.

'Come on, come on,' Vicaire was saying. 'Be brave, only two more steps!'
This funny, innocent remark from a kind-hearted drunkard roused general hilarity. And I . . . couldn't prevent myself from laughing, too. And then I happened to look towards the top table . . . Behind the official dignitaries who were sneering at this scene of humiliation, a man, a great poet, a being whose life was always one of admirable beauty, had turned away to hide his tears: it was Stéphane Mallarmé . . .
For the rest of my life I shall remember that eloquent lesson in human dignity.[7]

Mallarmé did not weep only at the sight of Verlaine's degradation. No doubt he also wept at the thought of Verlaine's grief. More than one observer in the 1890s had occasion to witness his misery. One evening, Merrill lingered late with friends at le Soleil d'Or. When they came out, the boulevard Saint-Michel was deserted.

We were walking on, more or less in silence [Merrill remembered], when we heard the weary, heavy tap of a stick on the asphalt. In front of us was a man in an Inverness cape, limping painfully. It was Verlaine. We hurried up to him, eagerly, and asked him to have supper with us . . . We had some trouble in making him accept the invitation. He remained silent throughout the meal. Finally one of us asked him, rather clumsily, to recite something. He did so, as if to pay his share, and recited *la Chanson de Gaspard Hauser* . . .
The lines themselves were infinitely moving . . . But all the moral and physical misery of the man wept, complained and growled in that voice.[8]

Adolphe Retté recorded an even sadder occasion.

One night, at about one in the morning, Stuart Merrill and I and two
English friends were crossing the Pont au Change. We had come from
a soirée de la Plume ...

When we had nearly reached the end of the bridge, I suddenly
noticed a silhouette and, despite the mist which was rising from the
river, I felt it was familiar. I went up to it, and recognised Verlaine.

He was leaning on the parapet, gazing down at the waters ...

I asked him what he was doing there so late and so alone. In a voice
which was broken by emotion, he answered: 'Oh, I'm weary, I'm
weary ... I was wondering if I should throw myself in the Seine.'

We couldn't leave him in such despair. And so we suggested that he
might do us the honour of supping with us ...

[At the restaurant], Verlaine remained silent, he only toyed with
his food and he left his glass untouched.

At last, when we came to dessert, I determined, whatever happened,
to make him relax, and I suddenly began to recite his *Colloque sentimental*. At the first line he shuddered, and even attempted a gesture of
protest. But, as I went on, ... he recovered his serenity. A gleam of
happiness crossed his great brow, his eyes shone with bright tears, and,
when I'd finished, he cried: 'Go on, go on!' ... And then I recited the
famous sonnet *Langueur*:

Je suis l'Empire à la fin de la décadence ...

Verlaine was radiant. And then he asked me to recite the last poem of
Sagesse: 'C'est la fête du blé, c'est la fête du pain ...'

... When the last line had been said, Verlaine turned to my friends
and, opening his hands in a droll gesture, he said to them: 'Voilà!'
What a world lay in that *voilà*!

It was at one of the *soirées de la Plume* that Xavier Privas, 'le
Prince des Chansonniers', met Verlaine. 'By a lucky chance,' he
remembered, 'one of the first songs I sang, "Le Luthier", pleased
Verlaine so much that he asked me to sing it again – this was the
happiest possible omen for me ... Ah, Verlaine! I lived for five
years in a little lodging at 133, Boulevard Saint-Michel, and I
shall never forget the honour I had of receiving him there.'
Xavier Privas became a regular performer at the *soirées de la
Plume*. 'And there,' he recalled, 'I met the poet-chansonnier Pierre

Trimouillat, who invited me to le Chat Noir and introduced me to Montmartre.'[10]

Le Chat Noir was the cabaret founded by Rodolphe Salis in the boulevard Rochechouart in 1881; it had moved to the rue Laval four years later. Its habitués were café cartoonists and chansonniers, but for a decade, until the mid-1890s, it was patronised by society and by famous artists and men of letters. The cabaret made an original contribution to the arts: the coloured shadow-plays, the *ombres chinoises*. This impressionistic anticipation of the cinema was the work of Henri Rivière, the painter, poet and inventor. He was assisted by a reciter, and by a pianist – often Charles de Sivry. Salis himself, funereal, jeering and grandiloquent, ruined by alcohol, disturbed the philistine and the conventional with his dramatic monologues. One gala evening in the 1890s, when the cabaret was full of elegant visitors, 'a man slipped in, timid, almost ashamed – a poor man, with fraying trousers and a dirty hat. People drew away from him; they expressed astonishment and began to ask what he was doing. "That man," answered Salis, "is Verlaine." The whole assembly rose to their feet, with one accord, in homage.'[11]

Verlaine paid a few visits to le Chat Noir; but, wrote Albert Lantoine in *Paul Verlaine et Quelques-uns*, he was 'stubbornly Left Bank both in his tastes and in his habits, and he felt rather out of his element among these young artists whom he hardly knew.'[12]

He remained a disturbing Left Bank figure, a man of dual nature. Maurice Spronck – like all the literary world – was acutely aware of the brute and the genius within him. One day in the 1890s, a number of Spronck's friends gave a dinner for Verlaine, and they invited Spronck to join them.

They had ordered the dinner in a private room of the restaurant concerned, which was an indispensable precaution. The poet arrived, wearing a sordid ulster with yellow checks, and a dirty felt hat; he was carrying an enormous cudgel. The cashier who sat enthroned at the counter gave us a glance full of meaning . . .

I remember that evening very clearly, and it might be divided into three parts.

In the first place, Verlaine sober. Insignificant, except perhaps for a certain preoccupation with extreme politeness. However odd it seemed from him, he was clearly anxious to show that he was 'accustomed to society'.

Then, Verlaine in a half-drunk state: and there he was infinitely strange, and – in his way – quite wonderful.

And, finally, Verlaine dead drunk; and then I have rarely witnessed such a lamentable spectacle ... He was sad and wicked and stupidly obscene ...

As soon as we sat down at table, he showed a childlike pleasure in the occasion; and when he had gulped down his soup, two slices of fish and three large glasses of wine, he became communicative. He ate legs of chicken without recourse to a knife or fork, holding the bone with both hands and biting into the meat without more ado. While he was busy eating, he laughed heartily at the slightest remark and the feeblest joke; at a certain point, I can't recall why, he told a series of barrack-room jokes about the Virgin ... Someone interrupted him:

'But, Maître, you are a believer?'

His satyr's face suddenly changed and assumed an expression of gravity, almost of sweetness:

'Believe in God!' he said. 'One must ... If it were not for His everlasting mercy ... Oh, I have sinned so much, so much! But I know that before God I am so humble, so humble! ... I go into His churches, and weep and pray ... Some people say that I've been refused confession. That's an utter lie ... They've lied, I tell you, they've lied ...'

The conversation continued more or less on the subject of theology. One of the guests suggested that perhaps Judas had not been damned. Verlaine started up: 'Who says that? He is damned, the scoundrel! He is damned for eternity! ... No, don't try to maintain otherwise. He is damned, and I know it. I am sure of it. Who dares to deny it?'

'No one, Maître. We're not making any objection. But you must agree that, however great his crime, an eternity of suffering still seems a very hard punishment.'

The poet's face was once again completely transformed. His unpleasant air of defiance disappeared; and he continued with the sudden splendour of a prophet on his mis-shapen face:

'I say that Judas is damned; but not because he betrayed Jesus Christ. No, not because of that. He is damned because he hanged himself in despair, because he had questioned the infinite mercy of God.'

I don't know if the words came from Verlaine himself, or if they were merely a reminiscence. But the idea seems to me so noble and so touching, and so in conformity with the particular genius of the man who pronounced them in my presence, that I should be inclined to consider him as the real author. The rest of his conversation, before the period of profound drunkenness, continued in the same tone, sometimes infamous, sometimes incomprehensibly obscure, sometimes with flashes which were almost sublime. Sometimes he cut his colleagues and friends to pieces in filthy terms which seemed to be borrowed from the slang of the hulks; then, suddenly, he would express his admiration for one of them and find a luminous and delicate formula which one was astonished to see springing from his lips . . . He proclaimed his vices with repugnant cynicism, and he spoke of his remorse with a mystic melancholy which revealed not the slightest exhibitionism. If I have tried to describe that evening, it is because, from beginning to end, the man was absolutely exactly, in his ugliness and his beauty, in the image of his work.[13]

50

In January 1891, after a break which had lasted for six months, Verlaine and Cazals were reconciled; but Cazals was no longer 'the Unique'. Verlaine felt deep affection for him, but the ardour of the past had finally gone. Henceforward there were no more quarrels, because there was no more passion, possessiveness or jealousy.

Cazals was now living with Marie Crance, a pretty young woman of humble origins, whom he eventually married. Verlaine was very fond of her, and she returned his affection. Sometimes, when he was ill and alone, she would dress his bad leg, and invite him to *déjeuner*. 'Verlaine had an excellent appetite,' remembered Cazals, 'and he was not a difficult guest. He adored simple country dishes, cabbage soup, mutton stew with potatoes, herrings, and *moules marinières* which were a favourite with him . . . One of his treats was a very rare rump steak surrounded, in English fashion, with potatoes in their jackets. He knew about good wine but, alas, he was often obliged to content himself with the most inferior "plonk".'[1]

While Marie Crance attended to Verlaine's gastronomic needs, Cazals became his secretary, counsellor and guide. Sometimes, however, in his fervour, Cazals went too far. He tried to save Verlaine from drunkenness by drinking his absinthe for him. One evening, he tossed down four in succession. Verlaine observed him, and each time he had the glass replaced. 'When Cazals got home, he stood besotted in front of his door, and speechless in front of his wife . . . She hauled him up as best she could to the third floor of the hôtel de Lisbonne, under the sly glance of Verlaine.'[2]

Cazals also showed his lasting affection for Verlaine in his drawings 'of *le bon saint Verlaine* of every day, in his infinite variety . . . I can never look at these drawings without emotion,' wrote Raynaud, '. . . for they recall the very tone of his voice. They bring back a whole atmosphere of ideals and misery.'[3] Cazals was not merely a caricaturist: he could give a certain grandeur to his style. As Émile Strauss observed: 'He has caught Verlaine in his simplicity; he has also fixed him in his legend.'[4]

Verlaine approved the drawings; for

. . . Verlaine had time for a joke and joked about himself. There is nothing more significant in this regard [wrote Raynaud] than the sketches which he tossed off in the margins of his letters. If he came to metamorphose himself, it was not into a god, or a laurelled leader of the Muses, but into a man of the world . . . an Academician, even a plain and simple well-to-do bourgeois, in other words all that he would have liked to be . . .

Cazals' sketches, which are quite as suggestive, are more assured in their art, for people have mentioned Forain in the same breath.[5]

Verlaine was to lapse at times into homosexuality (even Bibi-la-Purée claimed to have had relations with him); but, after he and Cazals were reconciled in January 1891, Verlaine was taken up with his *chères amies*.

During his last years, he enjoyed the favours of several women. One of them was a German in her thirties: Caroline Teisen. She was to go insane on the news of Verlaine's death, and she died in an asylum.[6] But this liaison lasted only a few days; and there were many prostitutes whose favours were still more ephemeral. Two women played a more substantial part in his life.

Philomène Boudin – generally known as Esther – was ten years younger than Verlaine. Lepelletier described her as 'an uncouth peasant, a massive, heavy-faced Ardennaise, hacked out of a block of wood'.[7] But 'Monsieur Verlein', as she called him, liked to hear her talk with his native accent. Esther had been a country girl, free with her favours, who had long ago found a man whom she loved. Delahaye said that she would have been a good farmer's wife, but her lover had abandoned her, and she had become a registered prostitute in Paris. She was now incapable of undivided love, incapable of happiness, perpetually suffering from regret.[8]

> Tu gardes le vertige et le goût du néant.
> Je le vois bien à ton regard souvent béant . . .

If she agreed to be Verlaine's mistress, it was, at first, as a means of earning a pittance. They were drawn together by their common need to forget their past, and by their present misery. Time and again, their quarrels revealed their underlying wretchedness; even Verlaine was torn by Esther's violence. Once, when she had reproached him for his interest in a passing woman, he left her, and – according to the *Élégies* – spent the next twenty nights with prostitutes. *Élégies* are a record of this degraded liaison: a plebeian liaison which still fulfilled a need, and created a primitive bond between the prostitute and the poet.

Verlaine himself would later recall the evening when he had first met her.

> Oui, c'était par un soir joyeux de cabaret,
> Un de ces soirs plutôt trop chauds où l'on dirait
> Que le gaz du plafond conspire à notre perte
> Avec le vin du zinc, saveur naïve et verte . . .[9]

The lines inevitably recall the lines in *La Bonne Chanson* in which, years earlier, he had greeted his approaching marriage: 'Donc, ce sera par un clair jour d'été . . .' Now the husband of Mathilde had become a middle-aged pariah, attracted by a woman of the streets. The date of the meeting is uncertain. Some say that it was as early as 1887; but one would be more inclined to place it early in 1891. On 6 February this year, when Verlaine left the hôpital Saint-Antoine, he took a room at the hôtel Montpellier, 18, rue Descartes. The manager was Paul Lacan, Esther's regular protector. This spring, while Verlaine was writing *Chansons pour Elle*, Esther was his constant companion.

She seems to have kept him happy at Lacan's instigation. Indeed, *'le souteneur aux belles moustaches'* used to boast in Left Bank cafés about the poet's passion for his 'woman', and he constantly proclaimed his respect for him. 'Monsieur Verlaine is a great writer,' he assured his boon companions. 'If anyone touched him, they'd have to deal with me. A good many times I've followed him home when he didn't know it, when he was going back late from the café to the *hôtel*. I didn't want anything nasty to happen to him.'[9] This solicitude was understandable. Verlaine was a useful source of money. The strange thing was that he found himself under the double protection of the underworld and the police. M. Lépine, the Prefect of Police, had given strict orders to his subordinates in the Latin Quarter that Verlaine must never be arrested, however eccentric his behaviour.[10]

It is said that the first time Verlaine earned a substantial sum of money, Esther seized it, and went off to join Lacan. The story is quite plausible. It was probably late in April or early in May 1891 that *Bonheur* appeared; and it was in May, in a wine-shop in the rue Saint-Jacques, that Verlaine met Eugénie Krantz, and abandoned himself to this new liaison. Delahaye observed that, by some piquant chance, the two women were neighbours in the religious calendar. The feast of St Philomène fell on the day before that of St Eugénie.

Eugénie was one degree higher than Esther in the social scale. Like the French Republic, she had been beautiful during the Empire. At the end of the Second Empire, she had been a star at the Bal Bullier, and no doubt one might find her portrait in some old number of *La Vie parisienne*. Ninie Mouton – as she was called because of her curly hair – had been an established cocotte in those distant days. She had known Gambetta, Jules Vallès, and all the writers and politicians who had frequented the Café Procope. After the war, she had been the *maîtresse en titre* of

Marius Constans, the politician. He had become the Minister of the Interior, and then Ambassador to Constantinople. For the rest of her life she kept his photograph, with a gallant inscription, on her mantelpiece. Verlaine was vexed that the photograph was so piously preserved, but no doubt Eugénie kept it from vanity rather than love. Once, when her former lover was a minister, she had written to him to ask for a tobacconist's shop, or some other sinecure; but he had seen fit to ignore her letter. 'Women!' said Constans to a young diplomat. 'They are a peril for a politician!' When Eugénie finally dropped out of the world of gallantry, she did sewing at home for La Belle Jardinière, and she was kept in work for the rest of her days.

Lepelletier said that she goaded Verlaine like an ox at the plough. He added that she was an alcoholic and that she died of drink not long after Verlaine's death. Cazals said that Eugénie was quarrelsome, indiscreet and rapacious. She thought that Verlaine would ensure her a peaceful old age. She took the presentation copies of books which were given him, and sold them by the basketful to the booksellers on the quais. She had seen how Vanier bought every scrap of manuscript from him, and she wanted to see him writing from morning till night. Verlaine was drawn to her by this bourgeois behaviour. He saw that she might save him from his own extravagance and assure him a regular life. Within a week of knowing her – so Cazals continued – he was disgusted by her avarice. He bundled up his shirts and papers, and left her.[11]

Cazals was hard on Eugénie; and Van Bever was unfair to dismiss her as 'a kind of virago'.[12] Eugénie understood the harshness of life, and she guarded against it while she could, showing a ruthless concern for money. But if she was practical and tough, and sometimes as uncontrolled as a fishwife, she also recognised that Verlaine, for all his penury and ill-health, for all his ugliness, for all his drunkenness and violence, for all his remaining homosexual instincts, was a man who deserved affection. She showed him a rough but always genuine love. In her simplicity, she matched him; as Barrès would observe, she had a grand simplicity about her.

Among Cazals' papers is a copy of a letter which she once sent to Verlaine. No translation can have the force of the original; misspelt as it is, it remains an illuminating comment on the relationship. It shows Verlaine's unending need for a mother-figure, his dependence on Eugénie; it reveals her own sense of purpose, her love of him and her belief in his powers.

My dear Paul and friend I want you to read this letter. Look why are you always *unkind and unfair* to me.

I think all the same I prove all my friendship and affection for you, by behaving like a Good little mistress Very faithful and good and better still like a Good little mother. I do love you very much That's why I'm often cross with you because I'd like you to be the divine poet that all the World admires and enjoys when they read you. Say what you like and especially when you spit out all the most horrible insults about me, you may curse yourself in the depths of your great soul, because you know I don't deserve them anyway god has put me on your path to help you so that your life does not seem so thorny and to stop you from committing sins, and as you sometimes call me your little mother, why scold me when I don't deserve it; little paul you hurt me, because you put me in the same class as your bad women. I'm giving you this little lecture because I have the right, you belong to me . . . for I have been your mistress for six years and I haven't gone with others, and if I'm jealous that proves that I *love you* without any shame.

Eugénie V. Krantz.

So come and kiss me Heartily.

Because I'm sure that you will reproach yourself for your cruelty to me you are Good paul and I don't like sharing when it means sharing you with other women.[13]

Eugénie, as Maurice Barrès wrote, was Verlaine's good angel; Esther was his bad angel. Marguerite Moreno said that Verlaine used to talk about 'the White Angel' and 'the Black Angel'.[14] Verlaine spent the last years of his life between these two fierce, exacting, plebeian women. Sometimes he was so exhausted by the unremitting struggle that he took refuge in hospital, or in some obscure *hôtel*, where, alas, he was soon discovered. 'I came out of hospital a week ago,' runs an undated letter, presumably sent to an editor. 'So if anyone comes on my behalf to talk to you of past, present or future interest, whether or not they are equipped with an authorisation from me, they will be attempting a swindle. Give them the reception they deserve.'[15] But Esther robbed him, with tranquil cynicism, on every possible occasion. On the back of Eugénie's letter is a copy of a letter from Esther, sent to Verlaine at the hôpital Broussais. It is hard not to see it as emotional blackmail.

Monday noon

My dear Paul,

I should like to come and see you very much but I am still so weak I can hardly drag myself from my bed to the window you see how ill I am try to have as much money as possible because I need a good deal of *looking after* I shall come tuesday whatever happens and stay as long as possible.

I embrace you because I love you *your devil*,

ESTHER.[16]

There was no love lost between the two women. Cazals recorded that when Mme Buffet, the singer, called on Verlaine, Eugénie mistook her for an envoy of Esther's, and attacked her literally tooth and nail. The concierge supported Eugénie, and threatened Mme Buffet and her companions with a revolver.

A terrible commotion followed. The crowd outside grew threatening, and called for their favourite singer; a window was smashed, and Eugénie Buffet (whose arm was quite badly hurt), went out into the street with bloodstained clothes. Verlaine had a bad leg and could not reach the battlefield in time; he was very upset by the altercation. That evening he told a reporter from the *Débats*: 'Poor Eugénie Buffet, she has no luck; she comes to see me, and she is bitten by a mad concierge!'[17]

PART ELEVEN

Enquête sur l'évolution littéraire

(1891)

51

ON 11 January 1891, Verlaine had gone back to hospital, this time to Saint-Antoine. He stayed there until 6 February. Four days before he left, a banquet was held to mark the publication of Moréas' new book of poems: *Le Pèlerin passionné*. It was not in fact simply Moréas who was consecrated by the occasion. The banquet made Symbolism the order of the day. Immediately afterwards, 'a courteous gentleman' from *Le Figaro* visited Verlaine in hospital, and asked him to define Symbolism. Verlaine contented himself with the observation that 'there are as many Symbolists as there are symbols ... The symbol is the metaphor, it is poetry itself.'[1]

Though the acclamation which greeted *Le Pèlerin passionné* was not exclusive acclaim for its author, Verlaine was vexed by Moréas' publicity (perhaps he knew that, in conversation, Moréas dismissed him as 'a good little poet').[2] Stuart Merrill remembered how Moréas went to the rue de Rome to present his book to Mallarmé.

Verlaine, the cunning old faun, was already lying in wait there. He and Moréas were then contending for the sceptre of the Latin Quarter ... Mallarmé received Moréas and his friends with his customary courtesy. As for Verlaine, he was bristling, and he never stopped riddling Moréas with poisoned barbs ... [He] really abused his old Parisian gift of the gab ...

When the time came to take leave of Mallarmé, I was immediately in front of Verlaine, and I heard the lovable old urchin ask him: 'Well, Stéphane, did I talk all right this evening? Did I astound the young ones properly?'[3]

Within a month of the banquet for *Le Pèlerin passionné*, Jules Huret took advantage of the current interest in Symbolism. Huret was later to be the first to interview Captain Dreyfus; now, at the age of twenty-seven, he established himself as the king of interviewers with his 'Enquête sur l'évolution littéraire'. He conducted a series of conversations with representative authors, he corresponded with those whom he did not meet; and his findings, published in *L'Écho de Paris*, and then as a book, gave a rich and authentic account of the decline of Naturalism and the future of the Symbolist movement. They also revealed the bickering and grandeur, the pettiness and vision, the jealousy and promise of men of letters. They offered an illuminating assessment of Verlaine's reputation.

The most critical of those who discussed him was, predictably, Moréas. His own fame has not survived as his contemporaries might have expected; but at the time of the enquiry he was a poet of standing and importance. His first collection of poems, published in 1884, had shown the spiritual and technical influence of Verlaine; his second collection, which appeared in 1886, had reflected the Symbolist love of the medieval and archaic. Now, after his third collection, *Le Pèlerin passionné*, Moréas was reverting to a more classical inspiration; and, in his letter to Huret, he revealed his abandonment of his old gods and a certain jealousy of Verlaine.

A good seven years ago [he said], I was singing the praises of Verlaine. In those days he was quite forgotten and a little despised. My opinion hasn't changed ... But I owe it to myself and to the poetic ideal which urges me on to say that Verlaine's immediate effect on the hoped-for poetic revival should be withstood ... It is true that, on certain points, he has been the precursor of the modern movement. But all that is over and done with; and the repercussions of his work would now be disastrous.[4]

It was significant that Huret had begun his survey by interviewing 'the two chief precursors of the Symbolo-decadent movement: MM. Stéphane Mallarmé and Paul Verlaine'. Mallarmé's comments are notably generous. He stands above the tumult, seeing literature in perspective, and ready to give honest, considered praise.

We are [he told Huret] witnessing a really extraordinary spectacle, and one which is unique in the whole history of poetry. Every poet is retiring into his corner to play a flute of his own, and to play the tunes he likes ... When the great Hugo died, I am sure he thought he had buried poetry for a century; and yet Paul Verlaine had already written *Sagesse* ...

I asked M. Mallarmé [continued Huret] where Verlaine stood in the history of poetry.
'He was the first to react against the impeccability and impassibility of the Parnassians ... The father, the real father of all young poets is Verlaine, the magnificent Verlaine, and I find his attitude as a man really quite as fine as his attitude as a writer. It is the only possible attitude in an age when the poet is outside the law – it makes us accept all suffering with pride and magnificent courage.'[5]

Huret's survey offered a series of character sketches, many of them implicit and unconscious; but the interview with Verlaine himself was remarkable for its vividness. His conversation rang with authenticity.

The figure of the author of *Sagesse* [began Huret] is more than familiar to the literary world and the different circles in the Latin Quarter. He has the head of an ageing fallen angel ...
I met him at his usual café, the François Ier ... During the day he had made expeditions *pour récupérer des ors*, as he puts it; and under his ample Inverness cape with its black and grey checks, there shone a superb golden yellow silk cravat, carefully tied round a stiff white collar ...
When I asked him for a definition of Symbolism, he answered:
'... Symbolism? ... Don't understand ... Must be a German word, eh? What can it mean? I don't care a damn, anyway. When I suffer or rejoice or weep, I know quite well that that isn't a symbol. Look, all those distinctions are Germanism. What does it matter to a

poet what Kant, Schopenhauer, Hegel and other Boches think about human feelings? I'm French, myself, do you understand? A chauvinistic Frenchman, first and foremost. Nothing in my instincts obliges me to seek the reason for the reason for my tears. When I'm unhappy, I write sad poems, that's all . . .'

His face clouded over . . .

'All the same,' he went on, 'that doesn't mean that you don't see the . . . *gulf stream* of my existence under my poems. There are currents of icy water and currents of boiling water, and débris – yes, sand, of course, and flowers, it may be . . .'

At every moment in Verlaine's conversation, one is surprised and delighted by these unexpected antitheses of brutality and grace, of gay irony and fierce indignation. But, I repeat, it is impossible to keep to the course of a conversation with him. That day, he was constantly straying from the subject, and as I was trying . . . to bring him back to Symbolism, he brought his fist down so heavily on the marble top of the table that his absinthe and my vermouth trembled.

'They drive me quite mad, the *cymbalistes* [he cried], they and their ridiculous manifestations! When you really want to cause a revolution in art, do you go on like that? . . . Every nonentity nowadays has his banner with the word ADVERTISEMENT! on it. And they've had their advertisement . . . Banquets . . . Just think of that . . .'

He shrugged his shoulders, and seemed to calm down, as if he had made a great effort. There was a moment's silence. Then he said:

'It's ridiculous, when you think of it! But ridicule has its limits, like everything else . . .'

He went on, in fits and snatches. His pipe was always going out and being relit.

'The Renaissance! To go back to the Renaissance! And ignore the seventeenth and eighteenth centuries! It's mad! So Racine and Corneille aren't French poets? And La Fontaine, the author of the *vers libre*, and Chénier! They don't count either. But it's crazy, crazy! And where are they, the *novelties*? Didn't Arthur Rimbaud . . . do all that before they did? And I've amused myself, too, with a bit of nonsense, in my time. But I don't have the pretention to impose it as Holy Scripture. Certainly I don't regret my fourteen-syllable lines; I've widened the discipline of the line, and that's a good thing; but I haven't suppressed it. If there's going to be a line of poetry, there must be rhythm. Nowadays, they write milliped lines. That isn't poetry any more, it's prose, and sometimes it's just gibberish . . .'

'The Symbolists are reproached for their obscurity,' I said ... 'Do you think they're obscure?'

'Oh, I don't understand everything, far from it!' ...

It seemed to me that the serious part of our conversation was ending, ... and I asked Verlaine:

'It is true you're jealous of Moréas?'

He threw back his torso, improvised a long gesture of the right hand, wetted his fingers, rhythmically twirled his moustache, and said, with emphasis:

'Yup!'[6]

52

Symbolism had become the intellectual topic of the year. As Joseph Capperon observed in *Notes d'art et de littérature*: 'the attention of men of letters has finally been drawn to Symbolism; from the little reviews where it took its first steps, it has come into the strong light of the stage and of publicity. The year 1891 marks one of those *moments*, one of those *nodes*, as Saint-Beuve would have said, in the history of poetry.'[1]

Symbolism was the essence of poetry – as the Symbolists believed; it was therefore as old as poetry itself. And so, in a sense, the Symbolist movement was elevating into a doctrine the principles which, consciously or unconsciously, poets had been using for centuries. 'Symbolism', so Adrien Remacle had told Huret, 'is the search for the unknown through the known, for the non-human through the human.' '*Suggestion*,' added Mallarmé. 'That is the dream. It is the perfect use of this mystery which constitutes the symbol.'[2] Such definitions were valid and lucid, but they said nothing new.

Yet if Symbolism re-presented truths as old as literature, it still remained, like Romanticism in the 1830s, an essential innovating force. French novelists had reacted against the excesses of Romanticism, and they had turned to Realism: a movement which had reached its height between 1850 and 1865. Realism had reflected the general distaste for the vague enthusiasm of the Romantics, and the interest of an increasingly positivist and scientific age in material facts. The intransigent realists had tried to give an accurate reproduction of life; and, in the hands of the extremist, the realistic novel was either an unselective catalogue of events, or a diligent account of vice and squalor. After 1865 the documentary and scientific aspects of the novel were still more heavily emphasised, and Realism developed into Naturalism. The difference between the two movements lay in the pseudo-scientific character given to Naturalism by its chief exponent, Émile Zola. Naturalism came to imply that the novel demanded scientific methods.

There was a clear reaction against the *roman naturaliste* before 1890, but in 1891 Huret's questionnaire showed that the movement was moribund. On 1 April that year, before Huret had finished his enquiry, Ferdinand Brunetière discussed *Le Symbolisme contemporain*. Brunetière was professor of French language and literature at the École normale supérieure; and he was, it has been said, the person outside Symbolism who understood it best. 'What we like, first of all, about modern Symbolism,' Brunetière explained, 'is its useful reaction against Naturalism.'[3] Verlaine, added Maurice Barrès, represented the poetic protest against Naturalism. It was this idea, as well as his gifts, which awoke the enthusiasm of a whole generation.[4]

Verlaine's poetry – and, indeed, Symbolism itself – was not only a protest against the prosaic and squalid in literature. It was also a protest against a deadening influence in poetry. The Parnassian school had carried poetry from the realm of personal inspiration into the ordered confines of the library. They had emphasised the supreme importance of technical perfection. Leconte de Lisle had taken Nordic and Oriental themes, and presented them in vivid, careful colour; Heredia had dwelt on the romantic world of the conquistadors. But the décors of their poems had been artificial, and the atmosphere had been rarefied. They had shown more concern for style than for humanity. Parnassian poetry had been impersonal; it had reflected the poets' impassibility. It had been, perhaps, a necessary intellectual discipline, and, in the hands of its masters, it was impressive. But its influence – like its inspiration – could only be limited, for it had lacked life. Verlaine and the Symbolists brought the human element into poetry: the dynamic and the eternally significant.

Verlaine himself had ridiculed the *cymbalistes* in his conversation with Huret. He did not consider himself to be a Symbolist; he sensibly refused to be classified. And if the Symbolists were ready to make use of his name, he had – said Brunetière – very little in common with them. Yet here, I think, Brunetière was wrong. Verlaine had no time for doctrine; but if Symbolism meant a return to the sources of poetry, 'a perfect use of the mystery', then he had been a Symbolist since the days of *Poèmes saturniens*. If Symbolist poetry embraced 'the *self* in the widest sense of the term, the universal *self*, translated into forms sufficiently universal to suit all mankind',[5] then – by the definition of Vigié-Lecocq – Verlaine had always been a Symbolist poet. 'Poetry,' said Brunetière, 'first developed what was rational in it, and then what was plastic; why should it not also develop what is musical? Why should poetry not attempt, like music, to dissolve the unity of the self in diverse and successive states of soul? Why should it not – again like music – restore this unity of soul to its original indeterminate state, and give it back the vagabond delight of the dream?'[6] This was not only an apology for Symbolist poetry; it was a definition of Verlaine's achievement.

If Symbolism was the search for essential poetry, and for the universal self, it was also the technical liberation of verse. Just as Wagner had set music free, so Verlaine liberated poetic rhythm.

Contemporary poetry received its decisive impulse from Verlaine [wrote Vigié-Lecocq] ... Verlaine freed French verse, which the Classical and Romantic poets had made more supple but not more free. While he respected the rules of prosody, he gave them a wider comprehension; from the technical point of view, his work is the transition from the Parnassian to the Symbolist form, from the classic verse submitted to laws which were fixed in the days of Ronsard and Malherbe to the *vers libre* of to-day.[7]

In the year of Verlaine's death, Verhaeren was to go further.

I maintain that . . . Paul Verlaine modified and revolutionised the prosody of his time, and that he did so profoundly. I maintain that he destroyed the prestige of rhyme, and deprived it of its position as queen of poetry – which is of capital importance. I maintain that he anticipated the modern evolution of verbal music in art, especially by rhythmic experiment, which is the essence of the poetry of the new generation . . . He was the man who made the modern school of poetry possible.[8]

It is, as Ernest Raynaud wrote, a recognised truth that every change of direction in French literature is the result of an outside influence. Romanticism, which had followed the defeat of Napoleon, had owed much to English and German literature. Symbolism followed the surrender of Napoleon III; it was again influenced by traditions and developments from the far side of the Channel and the Rhine.

The religion of beauty [concluded Raynaud]. All the refinements of Symbolism were implied in that formula: the hatred of the vulgar and common, the search for rare sensations, the taste for the precious, for archaisms, for neologisms, for unexpected, coruscating words. In this order of ideas, the English aesthetes had foreseen everything. In architecture, they chose the Queen Anne style; in painting, the primitives, chief among them Botticelli; in music, Liszt, Rubinstein and Wagner. They took as their watch-words constancy, purity and beauty, and they adopted their three emblems: the sunflower, the lily and the peacock feather. Finally, they wanted to transform everyday surroundings, and they took it into their heads to stylise even nature. Symbolism added nothing to the *aestheticism* from across the Channel.[9]

The Aesthetic School in England dated from 1848; and among those who helped to introduce it into France was Verlaine's friend Émile Blémont, with his articles in *La Renaissance*. Whistler, who had studied art in Paris, also helped to make the Pre-Raphaelites known in France; and in his own Symphonies, Harmonies and Nocturnes he showed 'how musical colour is when it is freed from entangling associations'. This comment, made by one of the artist's biographers, suggests that Whistler and Verlaine had the same liberating purpose. Verlaine's landscapes, exquisitely melting, came close to those of Whistler. And there was another link between Symbolism and the aesthetic movement across the Channel. 'Gustave Moreau had a great influence,' wrote Michaud, in his *Message poétique du Symbolisme*. 'In the chain which joins our Symbolism to English idealism, and to the Pre-Raphaelites, that is an indispensable link.'[10] In the Paris Exhibition of 1878 a panel by Moreau had opened the door on to a world of legend. And Raynaud made some other points:

Apart from the fact that its law was essentially musical, and that it had learned from the English Æstheticists, by way of the Parnassians, to moderate its effusions, Symbolism is no different from Romanticism. It offers its particular characteristics: unease, pride, mystic sensuality, the disdain of science, disgust with ordinary life. It has, above all, the same misanthropy and pessimism. It has no delight which is not sombre and tormented. It reveals a deep, incurable sadness, come from across the Channel and the Rhine, that is to say from the Biblical countries, intensified, on its way, by a Slav element: nihilist madness ... Symbolism, cosmopolitan, individualist, enamoured of dreams, did not, therefore, correspond at all, in France, to the sensible and generous aspirations of the race, or to its spiritual habits, and, which is even more serious, it went against the traditions of French art, the heir of the Greek genius, by trying to replace the gods of light by the idols of the mists. It was the thing of a small élite, subtle, but troubled and unhealthy, and of an ardent young generation which had gone astray ...[11]

Symbolism had not been inspired only by the English Æsthetic movement. It coincided with the rebirth of an interest in music in France. Essentially musical, it was also much affected by the 'music of the future', by the passion for Wagner. As Adolphe Boschot pointed out:

The generation of Symbolists and *vers-libristes* became aware of itself, and began to manifest itself in literature, during the ten years or so in which the Wagnerian crisis was at its height; these were roughly the ten years which followed the death of Hugo ...

One must also remember some political events which revealed the general state of mind: one was the meteoric popularity of General Boulanger; there was a fever of nationalism, stimulated by the songs of the café-concert ... and by the popular Press ...

The young generation of French artists reacted against this nationalist fever, and went beyond the opposite extreme. For them, *nationalist* meant vulgar, banal, old-fashioned ... The new art, whether it was labelled Symbolist, Decadent, *vers-libriste*, Instrumentalist, Impressionist, or anything else, was conceived as a reaction against everything that was generally considered French.[12]

Just before 1890 [wrote another critic], the influence of Wagner – or, rather, that of *Wagnerism*, ... was at least as active as that of Shakespeare before the great battles of Romanticism ...

Wagner, musician and musical philosopher, profoundly German, took up the formulas of the school of Kant once again, and talked about the *en-soi* of things, of the *essence* as opposed to appearances ... [He insisted] that the purpose of art, and especially of music, was to express the depths of the *purely human*, a mystery which we glimpsed *beyond* what our senses and ideas perceived ...

The Symbolists were attracted by this *en-soi*. Most of them, without knowing it, were impregnated by such ideas, which were then in the air around them ...

The Symbolist and *vers-libriste* movement reached its twilight from 1900. The Wagnerian fever had subsided.[13]

Raynaud, one of the wisest historians of Symbolism, also emphasised the importance of its background: intellectual, social and political; and he set Verlaine, very properly, in his disturbing perspective.

The generation of Paul Verlaine lived in the disarray of a stage of transition. It suffered its unease. It reflected its versatile and changing character. Brought up to the sound of the tol-de-rols of Offenbach and Hervé, it reached its apogee with the effervescence of Boulangism and with anarchists' bombs ... Tossed from dictatorship to anarchy, it greeted Ravachol and General Boulanger with the same ephemeral hope. It was a searching, artistic, refined but unstable generation; and, drawn by diverse influences, it struggled desperately, in the general débâcle, in search of some or other certainty; it limped on, disabled, from Darwin to Hegel, from Taine to Nietszche, from Ruskin to Tolstoy, and from Renan to Karl Marx, without finally being satisfied.

Verlaine is the voice of this generation 'of carnal spirit and unhappy flesh'. He reflects its vain agitation, its incoherence and its ungovernable impotence.[14]

À bas le symbolisme, mythe
Et termite, et encore à bas
Ce décadisme parasite
Dont tels rimeurs ne voudraient pas!
À bas tous faiseurs d'embarras!
Amis, partons en caravane,
Combattons de taille et d'estoc,
Que le sang coule comm' d'un broc
Pour la sainte école romane![2]

'La Ballade de l'École Romane' was not to be published until after Verlaine's death. But by 1891 he had already tried to dissociate himself from his early poetry; and, for a moment, he accepted the new creed that poets should return to traditional forms, and not attempt to make poetry a personal adventure. In the poem 'J'ai dit à l'esprit vain . . .,' which he had written in 1890, Verlaine recorded his new 'Art poétique'.

L'art, mes enfants, c'est d'être absolument soi-même.
Et qui m'aime me suive, et qui me suit qu'il m'aime,
Et si personne n'aime ou ne suit, allons seul
Mais traditionnel et soyons notre aïeul!
Obéissons au sang qui coule dans nos veines
Et qui ne peut broncher en conjectures vaines,
Flux de verve gauloise et flot d'aplomb romain
Avec, puisqu'un peu Franc, de bon limon germain.
Moyennant cette allure et par cette assurance
Il pourra bien germer des artistes en France.
Mais, plus de vos fioritures, bons petits,
Ni de ce pessimisme et ni du cliquetis
De ce ricanement comme d'armes faussées,
Et ni de ce scepticisme en sottes fusées;
Autrement c'est la mort et je vous le prédis
De ma voix de bonhomme, encore un peu, Jadis.[3]

This movement back to the classical and the traditional was a natural reaction against the excesses of the Decadents and Symbolists; it suited Verlaine in his mood of renunciation, a Verlaine who was no longer interested in experiment, perhaps no longer capable of invention. Most of the poems in *Bonheur*

are monotonous in form, some of them are tortuous in expression.
Verlaine himself is aware that he lacks lucidity:

> Mais hélas! je ratiocine
> Sur mes fautes et mes douleurs,
> Espèce de mauvais Racine
> Analysant jusqu'à mes pleurs.
> Dans ma raison mal assagie
> Je fais de la psychologie
> Au lieu d'être un cœur pénitent
> Tout simple . . .[4]

These lines indicate both Verlaine's intellectual weakening, and
his lack of spiritual fervour. *Sagesse* had been inspired by real, if
transient, piety. *Bonheur* was published seventeen years after
Verlaine's conversion, and his ardour had long since grown cool.
Bonheur is a religious book written without conviction: a series
of poems which seem more like literary exercises than a record
of belief, or of the need to believe. In *Bonheur,* Verlaine is denying
his poetic self; he has disowned his old inspiration, and found no
inspiration to replace it.

Yet, once or twice, his honest feeling comes to the surface.
His poem to Cazals ('Mon ami, ma plus belle amitié, ma meilleure
. . .') is spoiled by an attempt to invest the friendship with religious
significance; but the first verses are vivified by emotion. In the
poem 'Un projet de mon âge mûr . . .', Verlaine attacks his
former wife with a vehemence which is all too convincing. In his
poem 'À propos de *Parallèlement*', he explains his need to confess
his sins of the flesh:

> Ces vers durent être faits . . . ,

and here, as he recalls his past, his hope that he has purged himself
in poetry, Verlaine is briefly speaking. 'In *Bonheur,*' he would
explain, 'I finished the confession I had to make. Now I feel free
to act as I choose.'[5]

Only one poem in *Bonheur* recalls the essential Verlaine; and
this is a poem in which he follows his natural inclinations. It is a
poem religious in inspiration, but eminently personal in tone. It is

written with that dream-like suggestive power, that delicate symbolism which marks Verlaine at his best.

> La cathédrale est majestueuse
> Que j'imagine en pleine campagne
> Sur quelque affluent de quelque Meuse
> Non loin de l'Océan qu'il regagne,
>
> L'Océan pas vu que je devine
> Par l'air chargé de sels et d'arômes.
> La croix est d'or dans la nuit divine
> D'entre l'envol des tours et des dômes.
>
> Des angélus font aux campaniles
> Une couronne d'argent qui chante.
> De blancs hiboux, aux longs cris graciles,
> Tournent sans fin de sorte charmante.
>
> Des processions jeunes et claires
> Vont et viennent de porches sans nombre,
> Soie et perles de vivants rosaires,
> Rogations pour de chers fruits d'ombre.
>
> Ce n'est pas un rêve ni la vie,
> C est ma belle et ma chaste pensée,
> Si vous voulez, ma philosophie,
> Ma mort bien mienne ainsi déguisée.[6]

PART TWELVE

Gestas
(1891–2)

54

WHEN Verlaine left the hôpital Saint-Antoine for the rue Descartes in February 1891, he was once again in financial straits. On 24 April, he signed the order for press for the half-title of his *Choix de Poésies*. It was to be published by Charpentier and Fasquelle. Verlaine, who was desperate for money, simply saw the project as a question of author's rights; he had therefore made an agreement with Fasquelle, without consulting Vanier. Vanier naturally protested. However, the book appeared on 20 June, adorned – at Verlaine's suggestion – with a reproduction of his portrait by Eugène Carrière.

This had been painted the previous year. Charles Morice recalled: 'Throughout the sitting, which lasted several hours, Verlaine was pacing up and down the studio, talking with that effervescent verve which was all his own . . . I sometimes answered him, so as to . . . get him to glance towards the easel. Not for a moment did Carrière stop working. I really believe that Verlaine left without having noticed him.'[1] But the portrait had somehow been finished, and Morice had been moved to poetry by the sight. His poem 'Paul Verlaine', dedicated to Carrière, was published in February in the newly-founded *Mercure de France*. 'Carrière did not measure the poet's head with a square rule and compass,' he wrote, later. 'He saw, and he caught for all time, the grief . . . of this man who was crucified.'[2]

Verlaine's poverty was part of his growing legend, and he himself was not unaware of the nobility of poverty. He once told Ernest Raynaud of an idea for a short story.

Two great ladies are coming out of Mass, laden with jewels. A crowd of distinguished men are paying court to them. Their pride in this adulation is shining from their eyes. Suddenly they stop, and bow their heads, overcome by shame, at the sight of a saintly man, a beggar who is passing by, barefoot. They kneel and, in all humility and piety, they kiss the hem of his garment, as if to do him homage and to show contrition for their opulence.[3]

If Verlaine identified himself with the saintly beggar, others found the identification difficult.

Even then, in the 1890s [wrote Camille Mauclair], I could not accept the legend created round him, the legend of symbolic poverty, the figure of the great social pariah, of the sacred poet reduced to the infirmary to the exemplary shame of France.

His Bacchic and anarchist legend should be destroyed: yes, even the anarchists have claimed Verlaine as a social outcast, a victim of bourgeois society! The truth is different: discreet and devoted assistance was not wanting, but he liked irregularity, and he was aboulic, obsessed by saintliness and then by the gutter, and finally he became extremely attached to his role of accursed poet, of the poor man burdened with the sins of the world.[4]

Verlaine's contemporaries took opposing views about his poverty. Adolphe Brisson wrote, in *La Comédie littéraire*, that it was 'a fortunate poverty, a civilised poverty. It is sweetened by the very fact that everyone knows about it and sympathises.'[5] Henri de Régnier did not sympathise. He was horrified by Verlaine's degradation. He recalled going to see him in some Latin Quarter *hôtel*. The room was beyond description, and Verlaine was sprawling, fully dressed, on the bed, in drunken sleep. Another writer remembered him arriving at a café. 'He had come on foot because he hadn't got the 30 sous for a cab, and he was wearing a coat green with age, fiercely buttoned over a bare torso.'[6] Marcel Schwob, the essayist and critic, saw the grandeur which lay beyond the squalor. He had once visited Verlaine in the hideous Cour Saint-François:

> I pushed open the door . . . Verlaine was in bed. One could see locks of hair and beard, and a little of his face, like dirty yellow wax, decayed.
> 'Are you ill, maître?'
> 'Hou, hou!'
> 'Did you come back late, maître?'
> 'Hou, hou!'
> He turned round. I saw the whole ball of wax. Part of it, covered in mud - the lower jaw – looked as if it might fall away.
> Verlaine stretched out a fingertip to me. He was completely dressed. His dirty shoes were sticking out of the sheets. He turned round to face the wall, with his Hou! Hou! On the bedside table was a book. It was a Racine.[7]

Marguerite Moreno, the young *pensionnaire* at the Comédie-Française, was one day to become the wife of Schwob. She, too, was fascinated by Verlaine's legend – though at times she felt that he loved poverty, and that he loved sin and the fear of hell. She hoped – against hope, so it seemed – that she might meet him.

> The phrases that I used to hear:
> 'When Verlaine came out of prison . . .'
> 'When I saw Verlaine in hospital . . .'
> 'The duchess wrote to Verlaine yesterday . . .'
> All excited my curiosity. It was finally satisfied – and disappointed.
> I saw him at the Café Procope, le Pauvre Lélian, he was then holding his sessions there, surrounded by disciples burning incense, sitting like a Mexican god in the acrid smoke from their pipes . . . Wearing a slipper on his bad foot, a grubby muffler round his neck, he was gazing silently at his rowdy court and at the faded gilding on the walls. He was certainly far away. In an enchanted garden or an exquisite hell? I do not know, but he was far from the place where I watched him, far from everyone, far away from himself . . .[8]

Marguerite Moreno recalled how, in the ardour of youth, Paul Fort had founded the Théâtre d'Art. 'A theatre for poets, and poets only! It was too fine, and it did not last. But at least this dramatic Utopia was the reason why Verlaine's play, *Les Uns et les*

Autres, came out of the book where it was drying like some rare flower.'⁹

If any literary movement was, by its very principles, incapable of dramatic presentation, that movement was Symbolism; and yet it laid its claim to the stage. One evening in the café Voltaire, carried away by his fervour, Alfred Vallette, the editor of the *Mercure de France*,

. . . the organ of the purest Symbolism, . . . let fall the following words: 'What our school needs is a theatre.' The words fell on my youthful ears [remembered Paul Fort] . . . I, a boy of seventeen, determined to create this theatre and to be its director . . .

It is very difficult for me to boast about the work of the youth I used to be . . .¹⁰

His achievement was remarkable. In 1891 he duly created the Théâtre d'Art. He was the first to think of presenting the modern theatre alongside old dramas, and of showing the foreign and the French, Shelley and Verlaine.

It was soon decided that the Théâtre d'Art should honour art as well as literature: that there should be two joint benefit performances for Gauguin and Verlaine. These matinées would be given on 20 and 21 May at the Théâtre du Vaudeville, and one of the plays to be performed would be *Les Uns et les Autres*, in which Verlaine treated a theme from the *Fêtes galantes*. The part of Rosalinde was given to Marguerite Moreno.

On 20 May the curtain duly rose. 'Not an empty seat!' cried Mlle Moreno. 'Not a bracket-seat to spare! . . . It was a triumph, an apotheosis.'¹¹ Others were less enthusiastic. The pontifical critic Francisque Sarcey decided that the acting was poor and the costumes were shabby. He also decided, rightly, that the play was *une pièce de collégien*.¹²

Gauguin had hoped to come home from Tahiti with the money raised for him, and he recorded his disappointment. 'As for my return, you know that my half-benefit performance produced nothing. I was counting on some fifteen hundred francs from it. And I shall miss them terribly . . .'¹³ Four days after the second performance, Verlaine wrote to Carrière:

Since my 'Benefit' has brought me very little except vexation, I am approaching you with a proposition, and I beg your forgiveness for doing so.

That very fine portrait you did of me – would you buy it from me? And how much for?

As rapidly and expensively as possible?

Forgive me a thousand times, and let me shake you very warmly by the hand.

Through the intervention of Carrière, Jean Dolent bought the portrait for 300 francs, and on his death it was acquired by the Musée du Luxembourg.[14]

Soon afterwards, Verlaine signed a document which revealed the depths of his poverty. For ten years, since the publication of *Sagesse*, he had carried round the manuscript of *Voyage en France par un Français*: an intensely critical pamphlet about modern France. 'Alas, it all seems to be over, now, and really over, for France! The eloquent defeats of 1870–1 appear to have passed unheeded.' Impiety, violent republicanism, duplicity, intrigue, materialism, the decline of family bonds: Verlaine found much to criticise; and he contrasted the degeneration of France with the religious inspiration, the incontestable dignity, and the constant prosperity of England.

No French publisher would accept the pamphlet. Now, in July 1891, Verlaine had reached the end of his resources, and he owed two hundred francs to Lacan, his landlord in the rue Descartes. By some happy chance, he persuaded him to accept his manuscript in payment. Lacan tried, in vain, to sell it to a publisher. At last M. Delzant, a friend of Verlaine's, bought it back from him. *Voyage en France par un Français* was finally published by Delzant's son-in-law, Louis Loviot, eleven years after Verlaine had died.[15]

Meanwhile, in 1891, Verlaine remained bitter about the behaviour of literary critics: about the long conspiracy of silence, about the sudden and intense publicity, and about the poverty which beset him, even in his glory.

Ah, si l'on pouvait m'étouffer
Sous cette pile de journaux
Où mon nom qu'on feint de trouver
Comme on rencontre des cerneaux
Se gonfle à le faire crever !

C'est ce qu'on appelle la Gloire
– Avec le droit à la famine,
À la grande Misère noire
Et presque jusqu'à la vermine –
C'est ce qu'on appelle la Gloire![16]

'Déception' appeared in *La Revue blanche* in November.

Vanier had not neglected his most celebrated author. After the performances at the Vaudeville, he republished *Les Uns et les Autres*. He published new editions of *Jadis et Naguère* and *La Bonne Chanson*. On 1 November, in an interview in *Le Figaro*, he announced Verlaine's forthcoming prose work, *Mes Hôpitaux*, and his new book of poetry.

When *Mes Hôpitaux* appeared that month, Verlaine had returned to Broussais. 'I've come back to my winter residence,' he told Gabriel Vicaire. '. . . *Rerhumatismes*, palpitations, the beginnings of diabetes and the end of syphilis. Nice programme, isn't it? And it will take TIME.'[17]

His book reflected his prolonged ill-health. *Mes Hôpitaux* was a lamentable work. But 'what a title and what a book!' exclaimed Philippe Gille, in *La Bataille littéraire*. 'A shudder of fear runs through you as the author paints the surroundings in which he has been cast by the cruel and terrifying chances of life. He does so with a philosophy which is born of custom. Verlaine . . . sets the title down without hatred or rancour, and with a certain affection born of habit.'[18]

If Verlaine had come to look on hospital life with affection, journalists had come to recognise it as part of the Verlaine legend. It was a recurrent theme for the Press. The literary world did not congregate, now, only in cafés and in salons. It was found at Vincennes, Saint-Louis, Saint-Antoine, Tenon, Bichat, and, above all, at Broussais.

When hospital lights were turned out at night, Verlaine was
allowed to combat his insomnia, to keep his lamp lit, and to write
his poetry. The concierge and the commissionaire at the admis-
sions desk agreed that all his friends should be admitted, and that
visiting hours should be ignored. Doctors and nurses overlooked
the small bottles of absinthe pushed under his pillow by thoughtful
friends; they noticed the orchids sent to him by American
admirers, the inscribed books presented by their authors, the visits
of young and promising writers like Pierre Louÿs and André
Gide (and Francis Poictevin, who knelt to kiss the hands of the
Master). Established writers came to see him: Anatole France,
Huysmans and Mallarmé. Foreign critics were followed by pub-
lishers and editors. There were artists of every degree, working
on sketches or 'official' portraits. Aesthetes and society women sat
beside the poet's bed; humble friends arrived from the Latin
Quarter (and some of them, said Rodenbach, were so poor that
they came to share his hospital meals). Bulletins on Verlaine's
health were published in the papers. In summer, under the plane
trees in the courtyard or the garden, draped in his Public Assistance
dressing-gown, wearing his hospital cap, Verlaine presided over
Socratic conversations which became part of the literary scene.
A visit to Verlaine in hospital became a form of snobbery, a cult
among the intelligentsia. Dr Chauffart did not only take his
patient out to dinner; when he reached his bed on his morning
round, he would inform his students: 'Messieurs, this is a great
invalid – and the greatest Catholic poet of the century.' And,
before he went on to the next bed, Dr Chauffart would pronounce
a lengthy dissertation on *Sagesse*.

In the last years of Verlaine's life, the hospitals of Paris would
have fought for the honour of having him.

55

On 10 November 1891, after years in Abyssinia, Rimbaud died of
cancer at Marseilles. Charles Maurras wrote: 'His legend had its
interest as long as no-one knew whether he was dead or alive.

I don't think it will last.'[1] In January, in *L'Ermitage*, Adolphe Retté reviewed *Les Illuminations* and *Une Saison en Enfer*, which Vanier had carefully republished. Under the signature Fra Diabolico, he also addressed a letter to the editor. 'Do you not agree,' he asked, 'that the legend which haloes Rimbaud's memory is admirable as it is, and that we must be careful not to destroy it?'[2]

Soon afterwards, Retté went to see Verlaine at Broussais. He found him lost in dejection. 'What weighs upon me are my dreams,' Verlaine confessed. 'Since Rimbaud died, I see him again, every night . . .'

Retté encouraged him to talk; and Verlaine recalled the scene in the hotel in Brussels, the brainstorm which had led him to shoot at Rimbaud. He talked as if he was suppressing violent emotion.

'Once you were in prison,' I said, 'when you heard that Rimbaud's wound was slight, were you relieved?'

'No,' Verlaine replied at once. 'I was so furious at losing him that I'd have liked to know that he was dead . . . It was later, in my cell at Mons, and then when I was freed, that I thought about him with some gentleness . . . And yet, no, it wasn't gentleness. The boy had diabolical powers of seduction. The memory of the days we had spent wandering on the roads, wild and intoxicated with art, came back to me like a swelling tide laden with perfumes of dreadful delight . . .

'I have known happiness twice in my life. First with my wife – the only woman I have deeply loved – and if I had been the master of my senses, that happiness would have made me a different man. And then, with Rimbaud, I tasted pleasures which were painful, they were so intense . . . I have never consoled myself for losing both of them.'

For a few seconds he was silent; then he said: 'You wrote, the other day, that Rimbaud was a legend. No doubt, from the point of view of literature, you were right. But for me Rimbaud is an ever-living reality, a sun aflame within me, a sun that will not suffer eclipse.'[3]

Since Rimbaud's death, Verlaine had published another book of poetry. *Chansons pour Elle* would one day be illustrated by Maillol. Some of the poems had been inspired by Esther, but most of them by Eugénie.

The tone is more sincere than that of *Bonheur*. Verlaine's attempt to recall his religious inspiration had been unconvincing; but there is no doubt, now, of his physical passion. The banality of the language and of certain rhythms, the facility or vulgarity of many of the themes bring the poems close to the songs of the café-concert. But there is still something in this poetically poor book besides sensuality or a willing decline and fall. The eroticism of *Parallèlement* had shown a strong element of perversity; it had seemed like a last, unsuccessful attempt to stifle the soul beneath the body. The eroticism of *Chansons pour Elle* shows a determination to be '*pareil aux purs animaux*', a desire to give new innocence to the flesh. The simple physical love between man and woman has briefly become a sort of morality. But it has little to do with religion. Verlaine's days of mysticism are over.

> Quant à nos âmes, dis, Madame,
> Tu sais, mon âme et puis ton âme,
> Nous en moquons-nous? Que non pas!
> Seulement nous sommes au monde.
> Ici-bas, sur la terre ronde,
> Et non au ciel, mais ici-bas.[4]

Verlaine, as usual, is moved by remorse; but he tries to take refuge in the satisfaction of primitive needs:

> Jouir et dormir ce sera, veux-tu?
> Notre fonction première et dernière,
> Notre seule et notre double vertu,
> Conscience unique, unique lumière.[5]

But he cannot remain at this level. *Chansons pour Elle*, inspired by two inferior women, remains an inferior work in thought and manner. 'Doggerel by a poet of genius,' said *Le Mercure de France* in December. That month, in *La Revue blanche*, Lucien Muhlfeld reached the same conclusion. 'The *Chansons* of to-day are a long way from the *Fêtes galantes*. These are *fêtes paillardes*, or lewd revels . . . This is not tipsiness any more, it's dead-drunkenness . . . But it is still the drunkenness and lewdness of Verlaine . . . Verlaine is the man whom nothing can diminish.'[6]

He could not be diminished by drunkenness or lewdness, or by his need of Public Assistance. 'It is in hospital that he writes his poems,' said Anatole France in *Le Temps*. 'He hardly works any more except in hospital. His poetic and bizarre imagination casts a spell for him over the big, cold, sparsely furnished ward . . .'[7] And once again, with his familiar sympathy and irony, Anatole France paid tribute to Verlaine:

There is a poet in hospital to-day, as there was in 1780. But to-day (and one did not find that at the Hôtel-Dieu in the days of Gilbert) the bed has white curtains and its occupant is a real poet. He is called Paul Verlaine. He isn't a pale and melancholy young man, he's an old vagabond, tired from having wandered on every road for the past thirty years . . .

[He is] the most singular poet, the most monstrous and the most mystic, the most complicated and the simplest, the most disturbed, the maddest, but certainly the most inspired and the most real of modern poets . . .

But beware, for this poor madman has created a new art, and there is some chance that people will say of him, one day, what they say today of François Villon, with whom he must be compared: 'He was the best poet of his time!'[8]

56

On 20 January 1892, Verlaine left Broussais, and went to live with Eugénie Krantz at 272, rue Saint-Jacques. She gave him a rough kind of domesticity, and, as Gabriel de Lautrec was to recognise, Verlaine had bourgeois ambitions or, rather, bourgeois regrets.

Gabriel de Lautrec had come from the South of France to begin his student life in Paris; he had settled in humble fourth-floor lodgings in the impasse Nicole, near the boulevard du Port-Royal. It was here that he entertained Verlaine with touching devotion.

He used to come, more and more often, to spend the evening with me. I used to go and fetch him, of course, for an apéritif. It was strictly understood that he should have only one. And then we used to go and dine at Touzery's, in the rue de la Huchette . . . For 25 sous, or 30 sous on our days of orgy, we had a sumptuous meal . . .

And then we used to walk slowly up the boulevard Saint-Michel, smoking our pipes, to get our dinner down. And Verlaine would struggle up my four flights of stairs ... Once we'd got up there, I would settle him on my divan, with a carafe of cold coffee on the table beside him. He used to study the carafe with the resigned expression of a medieval victim about to suffer the water torture. But he used to talk simply and nicely ...

However, when the evening was over, and the friends had said good-bye, and Verlaine, heroically, had drunk half his carafe, I thought this heroism deserved its reward. We went downstairs ... and, after many peregrinations, we reached the place Maubert ... There was a bar where they sold absinthe at 4 sous a glass. I never dared to ask what these absinthes were made of ... But Verlaine was content ...

On these nocturnal escapades he sometimes slipped away, furtively. And then God knows where he went. But no doubt it was on these days that he was suddenly seized by remorse for the criminal life which he thought he led, and went at about four o'clock in the morning to batter the door of Saint-Jacques du Haut-Pas with his thick stick, shouting: 'In God's name, I want to confess!' ...[1]

For all his weaknesses, he remained the convert of *Sagesse*; he still sought religious comfort. *Liturgies intimes*, his new book of poems, appeared in March 1892. It was published by subscription, by the Bibliothèque du Saint-Graal; and it was a continuation of *Bonheur*. 'This little work,' wrote Verlaine in his preface, 'is again an exposition of the Doctrine and of its reflection in a soul.' He added seven poems to the second edition of the book, which was published by Vanier the following April.

Among them was the sonnet *À Charles Baudelaire*, which he set at the beginning of the collection. It has been suggested, with good reason, that he had meant to include it in *Dédicaces*; certainly it seems out of place in *Liturgies intimes*, for it is a sceptical comment on Baudelaire's Catholicism. Verlaine is also at pains to disown his poetic debt to Baudelaire:

> Je ne t'ai pas connu, je ne t'ai pas aimé,
> Je ne te connais point et je t'aime encor moins ...

It is an extraordinary sonnet to find in this collection of pious poems, and it can only be interpreted as part of Verlaine's attempt to disown the past. Just as he had ridiculed his earlier styles and inspirations, so he now tries to diminish Baudelaire: the poet who, after Rimbaud, had had the deepest and the most natural influence on his work.[2]

'It would be useless to analyse the poems in *Liturgies* at length,' wrote Adolphe Retté in *L'Ermitage*. 'Their absoluteness hardly admits discussion: either you feel them or you do not – for they are, above all, poems of feeling. One must simply proclaim that they are as beautiful as the most perfect poems of M. Verlaine's, and that he remains the *greatest* poet of the late nineteenth century, the Master against whom no school, even the École romane, will prevail.'[3] But the inspiration of *Liturgies intimes* is in fact sadly wanting. Verlaine attempts to construct a convincing religious metaphysic, a creed which is both reassuring and orthodox. Apology is nearly always stronger than vision. Verlaine's inspiration sounds authentic only when he is expressing nostalgia or remorse.

> Pénitence, du fond de mes crimes affreux,
> Luxure, orgueil, colère, et toute la filière,
> J'invoque ton secours, vertu particulière,
> Seule agréable à Dieu qui voit mon cœur affreux.[4]

Many men of letters accepted this self-portrait of Verlaine. Goncourt, in the privacy of his journal, called him a homosexual murderer. Rémy de Gourmont, time and again, would mutter to Léautaud: 'Verlaine! The gentle Verlaine! *Mon cher*, he was a bandit – a bandit!'[5]

The bandit was complacently aware of his legend. 'I have,' he said, 'long been considered an absolute monster, something like a murderer crossed with what respectable people call an "immoral" man. I don't know anyone of mark who hasn't got his halo – in reverse.'[6]

Years later, Léautaud asked Alfred Vallette if Verlaine's contemporaries recognised his worth. 'I'm sure they did,' replied Vallette. 'Absolutely sure. People knew quite well that he was a

great poet. People like Barrès, for example ... And Montesquiou ... Only, people preferred not to see him. When one saw
him, he was generally rather drunk, surrounded by bohemians
like himself. There was nothing attractive about it.'[7]

57

Maurice Barrès had made his literary début in 1884, when he
founded an ephemeral periodical, *Les Taches d'Encre*. He had
immediately published his allegiance to Verlaine, and he would
proclaim it all his life.

Comte Robert de Montesquiou-Fezensac was well known in the
literary and fashionable worlds. He was a poet, an aesthete, and a
man of letters. His mannerisms and his luxurious habits had
inspired Huysmans with the character of Des Esseintes in *À
Rebours*. The novel was often quoted as the supreme expression of
l'esprit décadent. Montesquiou was later to inspire Proust with the
character of Charlus in *À la recherche du temps perdu*, and it has been
said that his association with Proust is his most lasting claim to be
remembered. Perhaps he may also be recalled as the friend and
patron of Verlaine.

The letters from Verlaine, which Montesquiou was piously
to bind in morocco, were the notes of a beggar rather than a
master. They were written on rough hospital paper, on the pink
and lilac cards which were favoured by cocottes, and on wine-
merchants' bills, and they smelt of tobacco. Montesquiou showed
Verlaine much patience and kindness. In the last months of the
poet's life, through the offices of *Le Figaro*, he and Barrès, with a
number of other admirers, assured him a monthly allowance.
'You know,' he wrote, 'you can always count on me to look after
your interests ...'[1]

Verlaine recognised Montesquiou as a useful source of money.
He sold manuscripts to him, he wrote to him from hospital,
asking for a hundred francs for clothes, and for lodging money.
'Find letters after absence,' goes a telegram from Montesquiou,
sent to Broussais in 1892. 'Will manage it act quickly for the best

stop repeat affection.'[2] In 1893 Verlaine sent his benefactor some poems, 'copied out in a poor hand, the hand of a feverish invalid and a skeleton. The people who give me money are slow, very slow ... God! What a bloody nuisance it all is!' Montesquiou despatched Yturri, his secretary and companion, with help. Verlaine shared in the festivities which Montesquiou organised to raise funds for a statue to Mme Desbordes-Valmore. The memorial committee was to dine at Foyot's, the elegant restaurant in the rue Tournon. Verlaine asked for shoes for the occasion.[3]

If Montesquiou was drawn to the poet, Verlaine must have been enthralled by this aristocrat who epitomised all the refinements and excesses of the fin de siècle. In the 1890s Montesquiou lived in the rue Franklin; and, following the current fashion for *japonaiseries*, he engaged a Japanese gardener. When he had dinner parties, a Japanese valet set out strings of lanterns in the rock garden. 'I could, if you let me know, send my carriage and my secretary at two o'clock to bring you here in complete comfort.'[4] So goes a note from Montesquiou in 1892. Whether or not he came by carriage, Verlaine called at the small apartment; and, in his memoirs, *Les Pas effacés*, Montesquiou recalled him: a man who was still in his forties, but who already seemed old.

A poor old man of letters [wrote Montesquiou], as poignant as the wreck of a gondola, was the guest of the rue Franklin: I mean Verlaine. He had heard of my predilection for his work, and no doubt he was ill informed about the kind which was most likely to please me; he had me sounded to see how interested I was in acquiring a manuscript (which, I hope, remained unpublished, because it contained things which did not do him honour) ... I once invited him, with Stevens, to Foyot's, where he behaved amiably; I also went to see him in various lodgings, notably at the hôpital Broussais ... I pride myself that I was the first to give the great composer [Fauré] the slim volume which contained the starting-point of their collaboration.[5]

Whoever put the poems of Verlaine into his hands, it was in 1887 that Fauré had set 'Clair de Lune' to music; in 1889 he had set 'Spleen'. In 1892 he composed the music for *La Bonne Chanson*. Léautaud recorded that Verlaine asked Fauré: 'What possessed you to add music to my music?' But the comment seems improbable. In 1922, in his article 'Gabriel Fauré et les Poètes', Réne Chalupt wrote that

... Verlaine occupies a preponderant place in the work of M. Fauré; he comes nearly at the top of this prize-list with seventeen poems. This is not the effect of chance but of a fundamental relationship ...

Nearly every composer in the last thirty years has taken up the challenge to add music to this music. Two, and only two, have succeeded in matching the genius of Lélian: Claude Debussy and M. Gabriel Fauré ...

By familiarising itself with the poetry of the Symbolists, [Fauré's music] grows lighter, more diaphanous, more docile to the suggestions of the words, it lends itself to more flexible flourishes and arabesques. The connection with Verlaine takes it to its point of perfection.[6]

In 1916, in *La Musique française d'aujourd'hui*, G. Jean-Aubry set the relationship between Verlaine and Fauré in perspective.

Even if we consider only its musical aspect, the history of the *lied* in France must include the name and work of Paul Verlaine. Of course this poet did not, alone, determine the remarkable movement which, in about 1867, transformed the romantic melody into the *lied*, as we understand the form to-day; but the publication of *Fêtes galantes, La Bonne Chanson*, and *Romances sans paroles*, offered musicians poems which were excellently, and indeed uniquely suited to this melodic form ... Gabriel Fauré was among the first to feel how much these poems of Verlaine's could give to music, ... and Verlaine's sensibility has no more faithful translator.[7]

As Chalupt said, there were two composers who interpreted Verlaine with a tact and genius which approached his own. One was Fauré; the other was Debussy, whose relationship with Verlaine was even closer. By some strange chance, Debussy's father had come to know Charles de Sivry during the Commune; he had told him of his promising son, and Sivry had recommended the boy to his mother, Mme Mauté. In 1871 young Debussy had begun to learn the piano with her.

As Edward Lockspeiser points out, in his study of the composer, Debussy could have spent only a few months as her pupil. There were only seventeen months between the overthrow of the

Commune on 28 May 1871, and his admission to the Conservatoire on 22 October the following year. But, so Lockspeiser maintains: 'I do not think there can be any doubt that the child was in some way made aware during these months of the agonising strife between Verlaine, Rimbaud and Mathilde. The fact that, despite exhaustive research, no mention can be traced of a meeting in later years between Debussy and Verlaine is a mystery, but it may also be significant.'[8] It is hard to know the truth. In *Claude Debussy et son temps*, Léon Vallas states categorically that, in about 1890, Debussy met Verlaine at Mallarmé's.[9]

Debussy did not only belong to the musical movement of his time; as a student, he had lived among young writers whose masters were Mallarmé and Verlaine. His friend Dukas remembered: 'Verlaine, Mallarmé and Laforgue brought us new tones and new sonorities ... Above all, they conceived verse or prose like musicians, they combined images and their echoing correspondences. The strong influence on Debussy was not that of musicians, but that of men of letters.' It was a fruitful time, when music, painting and literature gave strength to one another.[10]

In 1880, at the age of eighteen, Debussy set Verlaine's poem, 'Mandoline', to music. He remained drawn to *Fêtes galantes*: in 1882, he composed the first version of 'Clair de Lune'. In 1887, a student at the Villa Médicis in Rome, he was sending to Paris for works by Verlaine. In 1888 he published six songs on poems by Verlaine, and in 1891 he wrote *Trois Mélodies* on Verlainian poems inspired by English scenes. As Vallas wrote: 'Debussy was then completely absorbed by the art of Paul Verlaine. "That is all I like, now," he said one day to the publisher Hamelle ... And he gave Hamelle a volume of poems by Verlaine, and asked him to choose the pieces to set to music. Was there negligence on both sides? The book remained with the publisher, who did not make the choice as was suggested.'[11]

In 1900 *L'Écho de Paris* called Debussy 'the Verlaine of music'. Almost until his death in 1918, he was drawn, consistently, to Verlaine; and, as Jean-Aubry pointed out:

The admirable alliance in Debussy's music between the sense of reality and the sense of mystery, its character at once legendary and true, material and immaterial, profoundly intellectual and yet profoundly sensual, could not be applied more exactly than it was to this poet.

For there is no question here of decorative music pure and simple; with Verlaine, as with Debussy, the landscapes cannot be separated from the spirit which considers and animates them.[12]

Jean-Aubry regretted that César Franck had not set Verlaine's poetry to music; but with every day, he wrote, the interpretation of Verlaine increased.

Music, in all its forms, is the soul of Verlainian poetry, and that is why musicians have loved it and will love it with passion. Fauré, Chausson, Lenormand, Debussy, Charpentier, Bordes, Sylvio Lazzari, Ravel, Sévérac, and others, too, have mingled their voices with that of the vagabond singer.

If so many musicians have been tempted by his poems, if such cohesion is found between their notes and his words, Verlaine must indeed have been one of them, for the genius of the composer would not alone have been enough.[13]

58

They say that there is a wicked man called Gestas, who sings the sweetest songs in the world. It was written on his snub-nosed face that he would sin the sins of the flesh and, towards the evening, wicked pleasures shine in his green eyes. He is no longer young. The bumps on his skull have acquired the glow of copper; and down his neck hangs his long discoloured hair. And yet he is innocent and he has kept the simple faith of his childhood. When he is not in hospital, he lodges in some little hotel room between the Panthéon and the Jardin des Plantes. There, in the old poor quarter, all the stones know him, and the sombre alleyways are indulgent to him, and one of these alleyways is after his own heart, for it is lined with low taverns and drinking dens and, at the corner of a house, there is a Holy Virgin in her blue niche behind her grille . . .[1]

Gestas made his appearance in French literature in 1892; he inspired a short story in *L'Étui de Nacre*, by Anatole France. The portrait of Gestas was an unmistakable portrait of Verlaine. Gestas, like Verlaine, had kept a curious innocence; he had had the same longing for purity, he had felt the same periodic self-disgust. Just as Verlaine thundered on the doors of Saint-Jacques du Haut-Pas, so Gestas, in despair, sought a priest who would hear his confession. Gestas was thrown out of church by the halberdier, but this earthly rejection was not final. If he had sinned, he did at least remain aware of his sin, honest in his need to be forgiven. Like the author of *Sagesse*, he was near the Kingdom of Heaven.

It was Anatole France, this same year, who contributed a preface to *Un Hollandais à Paris en 1891*. The book was the work of W. G. C. Byvanck, one day to be director of the Royal Library at The Hague. By a stroke of good fortune, a friend of Byvanck's had interviewed Verlaine for *Le Figaro*, and he had allowed Byvanck to come and meet him.

They had found Verlaine-Gestas at the François Ier, staring into space. 'His face was worn and weary. His long box-coat gave him the appearance of a poor old street singer, long exposed to wind and rain . . .' The reporter from *Le Figaro* showed the brashness of the journalist. He asked Verlaine what had happened to his wife. Then, uncouth but determined, he asked about Verlaine's conviction in Brussels. 'Verlaine was gently drumming his fingers on the marble top of the little table. At this request, he suddenly looked up. His eyes flashed – but just for a moment. Almost at once his face resumed its impassibility, and one felt that, behind that vague expression, he had a wounded soul that was still unhealed.'

It was not the first time that he had recalled his imprisonment with gratitude; but now he looked back on the years in prison, the years of conversion, the tranquil life in England, the months at Rethel, with regret and affection. He alluded, rapidly, to the death of his mother and the death of Lucien, as if he was hurrying over dangerous ice. It seemed to Byvanck as if he felt not only regrets for the past, but apprehension about the future. 'I'm going to begin a new work. What will it be? Theatre? That's not impossible. Oh, if I could only count on a few years of good health! But I'm ill, and then I have my passions, which don't leave me.' He went off, dragging his leg, as if he was broken by life. 'And yet,' wrote Byvanck, 'I felt, confusedly, that beneath the humiliation of the man lay something very great which passed the bounds of my understanding.'[2]

Despite his undeniable squalor, Verlaine gave a strange impression of grandeur: or, rather, from his worn features, his sometimes incoherent words, there emanated a sense of genius. Byvanck remained aware of it when, one evening in 1891, he met him in the deserted boulevard. His eyes were half-closed, and he was groping with his stick, as if he was blind.

Suddenly he stopped. With one hand he made his usual gesture, and caught hold of his clothes; with the other hand, holding his stick, he sketched out a vague semi-circle on the pavement. He opened his eyes; he uttered a few inarticulate words, as if he was preparing a speech for some unseen audience.

'Cher maître, would you dine with us? We're going to some quiet place with Marcel Schwob and Cazals . . .'

'Very good; but I'm rather unwell to-day', answered Verlaine, emerging from his dream. 'I had some trouble this morning . . . Oh, these quarrels! . . . I've been trying to find relief . . . You know I've been haunted, recently, by a terrible picture. I can't stop thinking about the people in Huysmans' novel, *Là-Bas*. The black mass, the contamination of the host, and then Canon Docre, who says the Satanic mass for the Devil's faithful! What a man, Canon Docre!'

Verlaine went on repeating the name; obviously he was drawn by its strange sonority. 'Canon Docre!' He paused to enjoy, at leisure, all the pictures which this combination of sounds evoked . . .

Suddenly his expression changed.

'Mass! Just think that for centuries the ceremony has been the same, always invariable, and that it will remain unchanged until the end of the world . . .'

We had nearly reached the Panthéon . . .

Verlaine continued in another tone, picking up the thread of his early ideas.

'The black mass! But the real Satanic mass is the mass said by a priest who has no belief in it . . .'

And the subtle play of the poet's imagination led him to change places with the servant of Satan.

'There is no sin that I have not committed,' he said, proudly, raising his head. 'I have committed all the deadly sins, in thought and in deed! I am damned indeed.'

His thoughts, that evening, continued to run on religion and literature; and, during dinner, stimulated by drink and by the gullible foreign visitor, he happily enlarged on his themes. He spoke of his need of God; he declared that Racine was the first poet in the world, and that Shakespeare was a pedant and a Jansenist. And then, having tried to shock Byvanck, Verlaine made a comment that rang poignantly true:

'When you lead a dog's life, like I do, you must have friends every-where, and you must have some very strange friends, if only to cover your tracks.' And this remark, with its infinite vista of misery, was only the transition to his last words: 'If I had enough money to live on, I shouldn't get out of my chair, I should just dream away all the time, with my legs stretched out by the fire. I hate working, I hate talking to people ... But I'm poor, you see!'[3]

He was also ill. On 11 August 1892, 'rheumaticky, with heart trouble and vague diabetes', he entered Broussais yet again, this time for two months.

PART THIRTEEN

Apotheosis

(1892–3)

59

No doubt Byvanck was partly responsible for inviting Verlaine to Holland; and, on 2 November, Verlaine set out from the Gare du Nord for a lecture tour.

At The Hague, some twenty people had gathered to greet him, and he was borne off to a banquet. 'How simple he was!' remembered a Dutch admirer. 'He ate as if he was eating with his best friends. He paid no attention to all the eyes which were fixed on him. He found it natural that we should all be sketching him . . . When he arrived, he'd put on a top hat; but it wasn't long before he took a felt hat and a silk scarf out of his case, and said: "That's more like me".' And with the modesty of greatness, he added: 'What I do is . . . nothing to boast about. It's not my fault if I am what I am. These things depend on chance, so I mustn't consider myself superior. Art is a trade, and I am a working man.'[1]

After the banquet Philippe Zilcken, the artist, took him off to his house just outside The Hague, and presented him to his wife and child. 'My little daughter was then only two,' wrote Zilcken, after Verlaine's death. 'They were friends at once. The great Bohemian played with her for hours, and, long afterwards, he always remembered her in his letters, called her 'my literary god-daughter', and sent her kisses from the "mossieu".'[2]

On the day after his arrival, Verlaine lectured in The Hague on contemporary poetry. 'My dear Vanier [this on 4 November], complete success yesterday. New lecture here this evening. Monday to Leyden, then to Amsterdam. . . . If Mlle Krantz needs some money, I recommend the good lady to you.'[3] The recommendation was probably wise. 'My compliments to Eugénigre or to Estègre,' wrote Delahaye next day. 'Oh, fickle sultan, which beauty is in favour?'[4]

On 11 November Verlaine gave his fifth, and last, lecture in Holland; among the papers of Cazals is the draft of his conclusion: formal and polite, as became the occasion, but personal and unexpectedly touching, 'Ladies and Gentlemen, I have had the honour of speaking to an élite and I hope that I have not proved too unworthy . . . I will take back to France . . . the happiest and most comforting memory for the life of struggle which awaits me.'[5]

Verlaine left Holland on 14 November. On 19 December, suffering, this time, from diabetes, he returned to the Hôpital Broussais.

On 1 January, inspired by his recollection of Holland, he wrote to Octave Maus, the secretary of the Cercle des XX, and suggested that he might lecture in Belgium.

The Vingtistes were a group of avant-garde artists who had made themselves independent, and held their own exhibitions (a sort of annual *Salon des Refusés*). The first Vingtistes had set down the basis of their association in 1883, and the following year they had appointed Maus, a lawyer at the Brussels Court of Appeal, to be secretary of the Cercle des XX. The Vingtistes had later widened their interests, and organised lectures and concerts, and in 1892 the concerts had included settings of poems by Verlaine. The Cercle des XX was to be dissolved in the summer of 1893, and immediately afterwards Maus would lay the basis of La Libre Esthétique. This was the natural extension of the Vingtiste movement; but while the Cercle des XX was a federation of artists, La Libre Esthétique was an association of amateurs, bound together only by the desire to encourage modern art.[6]

The Cercle des XX was the most appreciative audience to which Verlaine could have lectured in Belgium; and Maus greeted his suggestion with enthusiasm. 'Your project pleases me immensely,' he wrote on 4 January, 'and I shall be happy to welcome you in February at the Salon des XX . . . But if your idea is to be usefully realised, you will need the support of provincial societies . . .'[7]

Even before Maus had answered, Verlaine was dreaming of a triumphal progress through Belgium. It would, he told Montesquiou, last about a month. In more practical mood, he added: 'My wardrobe is more than incomplete, especially for travelling at this time of year and for keeping up my dignity abroad.'[8]

Yet now that his plans seemed about to be realised, Verlaine also felt apprehensive. It was almost exactly eighteen years since his release from Mons. On 16 January 1875, two gendarmes had escorted him to the Belgian frontier. If he went back to Belgium now, what would his reception be? On 5 January – on receipt of the letter from Maus – Verlaine wrote to Edmond Picard, the Brussels lawyer and man of letters, and asked if it would be safe for him to return. Picard made enquiries at the Ministry of Justice.

Dear friend [he explained to Maus],
Verlaine was not expelled by royal decree, he was just escorted to the frontier as a non-resident. Strictly speaking, his return does not, therefore, expose him to anything.

All the same, to avoid any unpleasantness which might be caused by ignorance or by excessive zeal in a subordinate, let him send the Minister a request to stay in Belgium; it will be granted.

Picard also sent an encouraging answer to Verlaine; and, at Verlaine's request, he drafted a suitable letter to the Belgian Minister of Justice. It was a draft for Verlaine to copy.[9]

These formalities were soon settled, for on 18 January Maus wrote again to Verlaine:

The President of Conference of the Junior Bar at Brussels . . . told me that he would be glad to offer you the platform, if you cared to give a talk to them. But, according to our traditions, the lecture would have to have a little bearing on the Law. It occurred to us that it might be interesting to hear the account of your judicial dealings in Belgium . . .
My Prisons by Paul Verlaine – what an alluring title for a lecture![10]

On 17 January Verlaine had left Broussais, and gone to live with Eugénie at 9, rue des Fossés-Saint-Jacques. Ten days later he drafted a letter to an unnamed dignitary, asking for financial assistance.[11] His poverty was crippling. Octave Maus arranged that he should come to Charleroi on 25 February, and lecture there the following afternoon. 'Cher Monsieur,' replied Verlaine, 'I shall leave for Charleroi on the 25th . . . But since I am abominably poor, I should definitely need some money to dress decently and to catch the train.'[12] Jules Destrée asked Verlaine to stay at his house in Charleroi; Verlaine not only accepted, but asked him for 150 francs if he was to leave Paris at all. At the request of Maus, Léon Vanier gave Verlaine an advance of fifty francs. Destrée had also answered his appeal, but the fifty francs he sent reached Vanier after Verlaine's departure. Verlaine had been obliged to set out in his vagabond's clothes.[13]

On 25 February, he arrived at Charleroi. Next day a large audience in the Eden Theatre heard him talk on modern poetry. 'I'm not an orator at all,' he had warned them. 'At best I am a reader with a cold.' But he was heard with deference, and applauded when he read from *Sagesse*.[14]

The following day, Carton de Wiart met him at the Gare du Midi in Brussels.

When I saw him get out of the train [he recalled], with a scarf wound round his neck, and no tie, I felt I could advise him to equip himself with a collar . . . He had a very thick neck and we went to several shops in the rue Neuve before we found a collar that fitted him. He was delighted to see himself so handsome . . .

When I introduced him to my mother, he greeted her in the grand manner, and when she asked what sort of food he would like, he bowed and said: 'I must admit, Madame, that I am a little diabetic.'

Alas, his old-fashioned courtesy was rapidly forgotten. As his host remembered:

We were wrong to give him the key of the house . . . He came in at the most unearthly hours. We worked together on the lecture which he was to give to the Cercle Artistique – he hadn't bothered much about it before he left Paris. Then, as the old guard of La Jeune Belgique had invited him to dinner, he made his appearance at about seven o'clock in the evening at a hotel in the rue de la Fourche. He was soon drunk with homage, and also with a variety of drinks to which he did too much honour. When I managed to tear him away from this cordial reception, the time for the lecture had long passed, and at the Cercle Artistique we found an audience whose impatience was growing rather nasty.

Verlaine hurried, tripped on one of the steps of the platform, and fell down flat. His papers . . . were scattered far and wide. He had to pick them up and sort them out again as best he could, and they did not always find their proper place. After this unfortunate beginning, things grew even worse. A good many listeners were disappointed by the poet's thin voice – indeed, it could hardly be heard. They were also disappointed by the increasing incoherence of an ill-paginated lecture, and they left before the end. They hardly disguised their expressions and gestures of disapproval. It was a fiasco.[15]

On 2 March, Verlaine lectured to the Cercle des XX. Émile Verhaeren remembered: 'He went up to the platform, awkwardly, leaning on a stick, and indifferent to conventional dress: a poet – one would have said a passer-by. In a neutral voice, as if he was only reading for himself, he talked about art and poetry.' His lectures were in fact readings from his own poems, with anecdotes about their composition, and a few aesthetic observations. Now he confessed his faults, and, as he remembered them, the tears filled his eyes. 'He comes from the Middle Ages,' wrote Verhaeren. 'He has their faith and their licence. Such is the power of this disposition of soul in Verlaine that, even in public, in the middle of a lecture, he could not fail to show himself as he was, insisting on his errors, criticising himself, accusing some of his poems of lacking virtue.' In this morality, this humility, lay the difference between Verlaine and the poets who had preceded him. 'He towers above us all,' Verhaeren concluded, 'from the height of his simplicity.'[16]

At Verlaine's request, Maus had organised a lecture tour in the Belgian provinces; but there had been difficulties to overcome. The president of one provincial club had hesitated 'to exhibit the strange animal' which 'could not perhaps be shown out of a cage'.[17] However, Verlaine had been to Antwerp and, on 4 March, he lectured happily in Liége. 'Verlaine adored Belgium,' wrote Gustave Kahn, 'all he was afraid of now were its streets. The stones were generally round, and laid out in an astonishing variety of traps and ruts, especially near the churches, all of which he persisted in seeing. These stones accompanied his spiritual pleasures with mortifications of the flesh which he did not suffer without a few profane oaths.'[18]

On Monday, 6 March, he lectured on *Mes Prisons* to the Junior Bar of Brussels.

The lecture [remembered Kahn] took place in a room at the Palais de Justice . . . Verlaine had once found himself in a similar room, condemned to suffer the rigours of Belgian law . . . He described this affair of long ago . . . He joked about the Verlaine of those days, the tall, thin, violent, gawky creature, so different from *le pauvre Lélian* who was present now, happy but unwell, in slippers because of his arthritis, and wearing a magnificent gold silk scarf round his neck . . .

Chance – or, rather, the change of circumstances, the victory of his art, gave him a breath of youth: it brought him a welcome triumph in the very place where he had known one of his worst griefs.

He was moved to tears, and almost fainted with emotion.[19]

Next day he set off for Ghent. Maurice Maeterlinck left a vivid impression of the visit.

One fine morning, we waited for our guest at the railway station (my friends the poets Grégoire Le Roy and Charles van Leberghe, and I). We were accompanied by a certain Jean Casier, the son of an ultra-Catholic senator . . . Casier was a fervent admirer of Verlaine, because he had read *Sagesse*, and believed him to be a saint . . . The Brussels train came to a halt in the almost deserted station. A window in a third-class carriage opened with a great clatter and framed the faun-like face of the old poet. 'I take sugar with it!' he cried. This was apparently his usual greeting when he was on his travels: a sort of war-cry or password, which meant that he took sugar with his absinthe. We greeted one another effusively; we helped him to carry his bundle of clothes and his worn old tapestry workbag, . . . and off we went to the Taverne Saint-Jean, the best restaurant in the city . . .

Verlaine looked delighted, and smiled like a shaggy angel. He was offered port, but he preferred gin. Just as we were sitting down at the flower-decorated table, he asked with Franciscan simplicity: 'Where can I pee?' The seraphic Jean Casier gripped the arms of his chair so as not to faint. Verlaine came back more smiling than ever and confided to us that everything had gone well. The meal began, and continued in familiar fashion . . .

I knew that our good Verlaine readily forgot himself in the presence of strong liquor, and I discreetly restrained the zealous maître-d'hôtel; I had to remember that our guest was to talk that evening to a strait-laced and rather susceptible audience.

The collar which Carton de Wiart had bought Verlaine in Brussels had already been discarded, and Verlaine was now wearing a pinkish-grey flannel shirt, which was more grey than pink. It was held together, at the neck, by a cord with tassels on it. The question of dress became urgent once more. Maeterlinck observed to Verlaine that a white shirt with a stiff collar was essential,

. . . and I suggested [he went on] taking him to my shirtmaker. He benevolently agreed. The manager of the shop showed him some remarkable masterpieces . . . He pushed them on one side disdainfully. What he wanted was a simple triangular dickey like the head-waiters in wine-bars. It was more practical, less expensive and very satisfactory.

And so he was rigged out; and we had to wait through the afternoon without letting him out of our sight. Since he had discovered the as yet unsuspected powers of a gin called 'Hasselt vieux système', he had a dangerous tendency to prefer the humblest dives to the most distinguished bars, and to the ancient sights of the city.

At last, the evening came . . .

Grégoire Le Roy, Georges Minne the artist and I, all three of us good boxers, undertook to police the session, which might have been stormy. The hall was nearly full. Verlaine was introduced by the president of the Cercle artistique et littéraire. He came up and bowed with dignity. There were a few ominous tremors in the audience, and we clenched our fists. He sat down at the official table and, with an occasional stammer, read a few dozen lines. But soon he mixed up the pages, and lost the thread of his ideas . . . A billiard-player from the next-door room opened the door, and listened for a moment, cue in hand; then he went off, noisily, muttering: 'The man's drunk.'

We were trembling, ready to spring, but, faced with the imperturbable calm of our old master, everything settled down and finally turned out all right. When we came out, the president of le Cercle Artistique gave the lecturer a carefully sealed envelope . . .

At the first street light we came to, Verlaine opened the envelope in a fever:

'Three hundred francs!' he cried, pale with emotion. 'Where is the nearest bank?'

'They're all shut, now,' I said.

'But what shall I do? I can't spend all night guarding a sum like this!'

We soothed him down as best we could by assuring him that, if he lost it, Jean Casier and I would be completely responsible. It was nearly eleven o'clock. I was dropping with fatigue, and I entrusted our ruffianly hero to Grégoire Le Roy, an inveterate noctambulist. Next day he told me that he had struggled until two o'clock in the morning to stop the good Lélian from getting drunk and from standing drinks to everyone he met. In the morning he escorted him to the station.[20]

Maeterlinck omitted one of the stranger episodes of the visit. At Ghent, Verlaine had been the guest of the innocent Casier. 'Alas! Jean Casier . . . had put his family carriage at Verlaine's disposal. The carriage had panels charged with great painted coats-of-arms, and it was known throughout the city . . . Verlaine was delighted to be the momentary master of such a turn-out, . . . and the passers-by had a good laugh one evening, when this patrician carriage stood waiting, until the small hours, outside some house in a quarter of ill repute.'[21]

Verlaine kept a happy memory of his Belgian tour, and so did his Belgian admirers. In October, when he was in Broussais, he received a heartwarming telegram: 'The assembly of the Junior Bar of Brussels drinks to your health.'[22]

Soon after his return to Paris, Adolphe Retté found him in joyful mood:

He had grown fatter; his leg was not so stiff; and as he had brought back some money which assured him his daily pittance, he was making plans – not, alas, to be realised – for a life of work and regularity.

'I'm going to furnish an apartment!' he repeated, delightedly, clicking his fingers like castanets.

And then he told me about his travels. Like a mischievous child, he gave an imitation of the mild, solemn Dutch, and he joked – without malice – about the *snobbery* of his Belgian audiences. 'What surprised me most,' he added, 'was Maurice Maeterlinck . . . A phenomenon, Maeterlinck! A revelation! . . . After his drama and poetry, I expected to find a thin, pale, corpse-green individual, muffled up in flannel and sipping constant cups of tea. Well, he wasn't like that at all . . . He made me drink some excellent brown *gueuze*; and then he said to me – and you can imagine his Flemish accent: "And now, cher Maître, we're going to eat a good steak . . ."

'And we ate the steak, and a good many other succulent things as well. That Maeterlinck is a good trencherman. So am I, by the way. And afterwards he puffed at his pipe, and talked about his bees . . . I like that kind of mystic!'[23]

60

On 5 May 1893, a few weeks after Verlaine's return from Belgium, Vanier published *Élégies*.

It was late the previous August, at Broussais, that Verlaine had begun 'this complement to the *Chansons* and the *Odes*'.[1] By the end of October, he had finished it; and it bears evidence of its hasty composition. It is one of the works of the Esther cycle; but it shows no erotic verve, let alone transcendent passion. Apart from some rare Verlainian phrase, it is a prosaic record of a turbulent and common liaison.

On 6 May, the day after the appearance of *Élégies*, Vanier published *Odes en son honneur*. The book had been conceived in the summer of 1891. Between its conception and its birth, Verlaine had constantly been torn between Eugénie and Esther, not to mention more ephemeral loves; but nearly all the poems are addressed to Esther or inspired by her.

Verlaine took them seriously, and he worked on them carefully, but they remain pedestrian: a repetitive catalogue of his mistress's charms, a description of everyday incidents in their life. The poems have no depth, no general significance; they remain his tribute to one particular middle-aged prostitute in the Paris of the

1890s. As celebrations of physical love, they are less passionate than *Femmes*, less alluring than Verlaine's Lesbian poems. They lack abandon and mystery, and they also lack the attraction of forbidden love. There is a pitiful difference between 'Colloque sentimental', the poem which had ended *Fêtes galantes*, and the dream dialogue in *Odes en son honneur*. Verlaine had long ago lost his touch.

Yet, biographically, the poems have their interest. They proclaim Verlaine's conversion to heterosexual love. They show his pleasure in his humble ménage, his gratitude for sharing Esther's favours, his strange but characteristic pleasure in being dominated – and, now, his pleasure even in being deceived. There is a certain masochism in his devotion:

> S'il arrive que tu me battes,
> Soufflettes, égratignes, tu
> Es le maître dans nos pénates,
> Et moi le cocu, le battu,
>
> Suis content et vois tout en rose.[2]

Such lines rouse our contempt and our pity.

It has been said that Verlaine shows little charity to the woman who inspired these poems. The comment is strange; repeatedly he shows his compassionate understanding of her past.

> Pense à Phaon pour l'oublier dans mon étreinte
> Plus douce et plus fidèle, amant d'après-midi,
> D'extrême après-midi, mais non pas attiédi,
> Que me voici, tout plein d'extases et de crainte.
>
> Va, je t'aime . . . mieux que l'autre: il faut l'oublier.
> Toi: souris-moi entre deux confidences,
> Amazone blessée ès belles imprudences
> Qui se réveille au sein d'un vieux brave écuyer.[3]

Such lines are not fine poetry, but they give a touching likeness of a rejected man, a rejected woman, both of them wounded and disappointed, finding a latter-day consolation in one another.

In May 1893, when Verlaine's two collections of poems appeared, his health grew considerably worse. He was now suffering from erysipelas on his left leg. On 14 June he returned to Broussais, where Dr Chauffart once again took charge of him. Verlaine was delirious. His abscesses were lanced, but he could not be given an anaesthetic because of his heart condition. Eugénie had chosen this moment to desert him.

But if Eugénie had departed, Esther had returned. Affectionate and diligent, she came to visit him. Between July and November, during his periods in hospital, he wrote five poems which appeared in *La Revue parisienne* on 25 November. They were published as *Le Livre posthume – Fragments*; they were probably inspired by Esther. Gone are the religious faith and the belief in poetic immortality; gone, too, is the physical desire. Verlaine has reached the point where temporal and spiritual comforts have alike vanished. He hopes only that he will live in her memory, that his final absence will be remembered, and that her benediction will absolve him from his sins. And in these poems, for a brief moment, his poetic gift returns.

> Dis, sérieusement, lorsque je serai mort,
> Plein de toi, sens, esprit, âme, et dans la prunelle
> Ton image à jamais pour la nuit éternelle;
> Au cœur tout ce passé tendre et farouche, sort
>
> Divin, l'incomparable entre les jouissances
> Immenses de ma vie excessive, ô toi, dis,
> Pense parfois à moi qui ne pensais jadis
> Qu'à t'aimer, t'adorer de toutes les puissances
>
> D'un être fait exprès pour toi seule t'aimer,
> Toi seule te servir et vivre pour toi seule
> Et mourir en toi seule. Et puis quand belle aïeule
> Tu penseras à moi, garde-toi d'exhumer
>
> Mes jours de jalousie et mes nuits d'humeur noire:
> Plutôt évoque l'abandon entre tes mains
> De tout moi, tout au bon présent, aux chers demains,
> Et qu'une bénédiction de la mémoire
>
> M'absolve et soit mon guide en les sombres chemins.[4]

Verlaine was far from inactive at Broussais in this summer of 1893. In July he wrote the preface to *Dans les limbes* (which would appear the following year); he also copied out *Quinze Jours en Hollande*, his account of his Dutch tour. He did so in spite of continued ill-health. Dr Chauffart's house-surgeon, Ernest de Massary, was to remember: 'He had lymphangitis of a leg, the result of an abrasion on his foot. This lymphangitis was followed by inflammation of the glands: I believe I lanced his leg twenty-four times in a fortnight.'[5] 'The scalpel is very busy,' Verlaine told Cazals on 11 August.[6]

Despite his physical condition, and despite the tone of *Le Livre posthume*, he had many plans for the future. He had been so pleased with his Belgian tour that he wanted to make another. On 1 July he told Carton de Wiart: 'As soon as "science" has let me go – in a month at the latest, so I hope – I'm thinking of lecturing in Bruges through Casier and Maeterlinck. Why shouldn't I go on afterwards, by way of Louvain, to Verviers (where I was invited) and to Mons, where I might have a certain success?'[7] The idea persisted. On 19 September, he wrote again:

> I'm getting better every day. I really hope that I'll be able to travel in December. I mean to lecture in Bruges, Louvain, Verviers, and perhaps Mons. Maybe in Brussels, too, if you think this would be useful. I shall have a whole new stock of unpublished and appropriate poems, prepared well in advance. So let me know what you think. I also expect to go to London, Cambridge, Oxford, and I have my stakes there already. Switzerland awaits me. Lyons and Nancy *are fighting over me*.[8]

Verlaine knew, now, that he had become an international poet; and he did not intend to restrict his ambitions. On 24 July *Le Figaro* announced:

> Paul Verlaine ... is now in hospital; he is presenting himself for M. Taine's Chair at the Académie-Française.
>
> He tells us that he will send his letter to M. Camille Doucet [the permanent secretary] as soon as he is better.

'Why shouldn't I join the Assembly of the Forty? Haven't I got as good a right to the Chair as anyone? I've published 12 volumes of poetry, 5 prose works, a play, and hundreds of articles in different papers. It seems to me that many Immortals can't boast of such a body of work. I am quite determined to stand for the Académie. I may not be elected, but rest assured that I shall have a certain number of votes . . .'[9]

The reaction was immediate. Two days later, Henri Fouquier, the journalist and politician, published his comments on 'Verlaine Candidat à l'Académie'. Fouquier's article, in *Paris*, was not really malicious: he maintained that Verlaine had been ill-advised by his friends. On the same day, in *L'Écho de Paris*, there appeared an article which was less forgivable.

From the decorative and physical point of view [wrote Edmond Lepelletier], Verlaine would be a quite adequate Immortal. Although he is still young, he is very seedy . . . What with his stubbly beard, his mutilated nostrils, his sharp grey eyes, and a skull which is almost obscene in its baldness, he looks like a vicious monk. He would be very suitable for this gallery of wretched old men. All he needs is a green eye-shade . . .

[But] through all his wanderings and follies, Verlaine has kept the sound reason and the clear judgment of the Northerner. How can he fail to understand that his candidature, especially at this period in his life, seems like a wager and a practical joke? . . .

Poor Lélian, the national Bohemian . . . has made himself a dazzling reputation out of the purple of vice. He is the nomad guest of quick-service bars and nocturnal rookeries where you sleep it off by the night, he is the wandering tourist of drab furnished lodgings and white hospital wards. Verlaine has proudly worn the shame of being poor, insulted and rejected. How can he aspire to come down from his Olympus of scum and filth and gold to be red-taped again among forty bourgeois of literature?[10]

Verlaine took the article with surprising tolerance. '*Zut à Lepelletier!*' he observed to Cazals.[11] On 4 August he wrote to Doucet, and announced himself as a candidate.

It was now – so the story goes – that the medical staff at Broussais subscribed to buy him a top hat and a coat with fur collar and cuffs. If Verlaine was to canvass votes, to make the statutory visits to the Academicians, he must be suitably dressed. Verlaine was so charmed by this unaccustomed sartorial splendour that he had his photograph taken. Next day, short of money, he sold the hat and coat without compunction.[12]

On 15 February 1894, he wrote once more to Doucet, and confirmed that he would be standing; but, since he was ill, he asked to be excused from making the regulation Academic visits.

Verlaine had no illusions about his chances of election. He knew that he was not *Académisable*. He and Zola, a rival candidate for the Chair, received no votes; Albert Sorel, the historian, was chosen. But the gesture was significant, and Verlaine himself explained it to a visitor at Broussais. 'I want to shake some of the vermin who don't take me seriously; I want to affirm my dignity.' The vagrant poet of the Left Bank remained at heart a bourgeois, and he was not averse to official recognition. The Académie-Française, he had written in 1885, 'is the object of a good deal of derision, and occasionally this is deserved. But, whatever they say, it is the Académie, the Académie-Française, the great foundation of a great man, a respectable institution, and one that is fundamentally respected, even by those who sneer at it.'[13] There is a touching story that, during a *déjeuner* in Liége, someone had asked him if, one day, he hoped to be elected to the Académie. 'Verlaine rose, tried to clear his throat, and, almost without hesitation, delivered the whole of the speech he had prepared for his reception.'[14]

For all his Academic activity, he remained very ill. In October he seemed at the point of death. One evening Yvanhoe Rambosson was told of Verlaine's critical condition. 'The following morning,' remembered Rambosson, 'I was at Broussais . . . I was afraid there might be bad news, but as soon as I entered I saw the poet, propped up on his elbow on the pillow, surrounded by books and papers. The previous evening he had been at his lowest ebb; the force of his extraordinary temperament had again overcome death.'[15]

On 3 November, a revived Verlaine left Broussais for a lecture-tour in Lorraine. On 8 November he lectured at Nancy, and next day he spoke at Lunéville.

Ten days later he left France to lecture in the country which he had 'so greatly loved and admired' since the days of *Romances sans paroles*.[16]

61

If, in his years of misfortune, Verlaine had often thought of England, England had also thought of Verlaine; but it was William Rothenstein who suggested that Verlaine should come back to England and make a lecture-tour. Rothenstein – now an eager youth of twenty-one – had studied art for four years in Paris. Late in 1893, he had drawn three noble portraits of Verlaine, and he had wanted, discreetly, to come to his aid. On 18 September, from Broussais, Verlaine had written, in English, to an unspecified correspondent – probably John Lane or Herbert Horne.

Dear Sir,

Mr Rothenstein sent to you, yesterday, four poems of mine which may be intitled *Apaisement*.

My intention would be to have them printed in the 'Hobby Horse' at the price of two guineas each. If it agrees to you, please advise me by an early letter in which you should be very good to give me some details about the intended books.

I beg you to believe me

Yours truly,
PAUL VERLAINE.[1]

But Rothenstein wanted to give Verlaine more ambitious help. Verlaine had already lectured in Holland and Belgium, he was then about to lecture in Lorraine. In London all the literary world would want to see him; and in Oxford the academic world would welcome him. Early in October, Verlaine agreed to come over soon, lecture on contemporary French poetry, and read from his own work. Arthur Symons (who was to write the most sympathetic study of Symbolism) was enlisted to arrange Verlaine's visit to London. York Powell, of Christ Church, was invited to make arrangements in Oxford.

Stuart Merrill recalled some details of Verlaine's English

odyssey. Robert Sherard was, he said, given the responsible task of seeing him on to the night train from Paris. Symons had undertaken to meet him at Charing Cross. On 19 November, Sherard duly took Verlaine out to dinner, ensured that he did not drink too much, and put him on to the train, entrusting him to the guard as if he had been a child. Then he sent Symons a telegram to announce Verlaine's departure, and went home to bed with an easy conscience. Unfortunately, continued Merrill, there was such a storm over the Channel that the mail boat could not leave, and Verlaine spent the night in the buffet at Calais.[2]

Merrill's account should be read with caution. It was quite probably Sherard who had seen Verlaine on to the train; but in 'My Visit to London' Verlaine recorded that he had travelled from Dieppe to Newhaven.

> I reached London at two in the morning [so he continued], and had a quarter of an hour's drive to the Temple, in the fine moonlight ... London so impressive as one passes its superb buildings from the formidable T[h]ames towards Westminster, the rich, elegant London between Victoria Station and the Strand, seemed to me that night exquisite, delicate, almost dainty, luminous.
>
> At the Temple awaited me the poet Arthur Symons ... He had been to look for me three or four times in vain at Victoria Station ... My host led me up into his charming little flat, from which, next day, I was to have one of the most ravishing and peaceful views ... Blithe birds, blackbirds even, on the infinitely twisted branches of those beautiful immense English trees; to the left, the fountain, which gives its name to the place (Fountain Court), with its babbling jet of water. But for the moment I was hungry, fagged out by those hours of vehement sea; and Symons, following my example, ate – while we talked for two good hours, about everything under the sun, Paris, poetry, money too (Poets think of nothing else ... and with reason!), my future lectures – an entire box, one of those long, tall, tin boxes, of tea-biscuits, 'muffins' in English, washed down with plenty of gin and soda and perfumed with vague cigarettes. And it was, I assure you, one of the best and gayest meals I ever had in my life![3]

At eleven o'clock in the morning, when Verlaine and his host had enjoyed some rest, Edmund Gosse, 'the very sympathetic journalist', arrived to take them out to lunch. Verlaine returned to Fountain Court to put the final touches to his lecture, and, it seems, to receive a stream of visitors, including William Heinemann, the publisher, and Herbert Horne, the editor of *The Hobby Horse*, who was a considerable influence among the poets and artists of the nineties. Rothenstein came, and John Lane, who had recently set up The Bodley Head in Vigo Street. Merrill recorded a less satisfactory aspect of the visit. Symons asked Verlaine if he had brought a suit. It was the familiar story.

A suit! Poor Lelian just had the barest necessities. So Symons rushed from place to place, borrowing a suit there and a shirt here, and pumps from somewhere else; and when, that evening, Verlaine made his appearance on the platform, he looked like a respectable clergyman. It was not what the public had expected. The Press had whetted their appetite by announcing a lecture by Paul Verlaine, 'the convict poet'.[4]

Ernest Dowson went to hear him that evening; and Charles Furse sketched him as he lectured in Barnard's Inn, in Holborn: sober, steadfast, and unusually demure. 'Ladies and Gentlemen. I should be unworthy of the title of poet . . . if I were to forget that I speak here in the country which is par excellence that of poetry . . .'[5] 'Verlaine's lecture last night was a great success,' wrote John Lane next day to Rothenstein, who had gone to await the poet at Oxford.[6]

On the morning of 23 November, Verlaine was deposited on the Oxford train at Paddington, and Symons sent a telegram to Rothenstein, announcing that the poet was on his way. Verlaine arrived at Oxford station wearing a long greatcoat, a muffler, and a cloth shoe on his bad foot. He was met by Rothenstein, York Powell, and by Dr Charles Bonnier, a French schoolmaster who was an old friend of Mallarmé's.

At the age of forty-three, a Student of Christ Church, York Powell was already a legend of omniscience. He not only possessed 'a good set of Verlaine', he was an Icelandic scholar, an authority on Roman law, on boxing, on Provençal and Middle High Dutch. He knew Hebrew and Old Irish. He was also the chief influence on the teaching of history in Oxford long before he became Regius Professor of Modern History in 1894.[7]

Large, dark-haired, with a spade beard, he looked like a sea captain: an impression which was strengthened by his bluff, impulsive manner.

A sudden laugh or a grave expression, a feeling of strength and kindness: so it is [wrote Bonnier] that he appeared to us in that décor he had devised for himself ... And the impression was immediate: the impression of the large room ... with the vast foliage of the Broad Walk swaying outside the windows: the illumination of an English setting of field and avenue: of trees seen through the fallen piles of books.

It was there that he received his friends and the foreign visitors who felt drawn towards him.

It was there, in his rooms in the Meadow Building, at Christ Church, that York Powell gave a lunch for Verlaine. Max Beerbohm, then an undergraduate at Merton, was a guest; and so was a young don from New College, H. A. L. Fisher.

Bonnier recalled the scene:

The vague, bewildered undergraduates, who had come to admire a poet in the flesh, with the feeling of a slightly risky pleasure jaunt; Powell striding up and down, smoking and laughing; and Verlaine! But not the Verlaine of ... some or other Latin Quarter café. What a transformation! He had been told, no doubt, to behave well in front of the Oxford public, to be 'good,' and so he did and so he was, with an effort that was comic. Across his face, the face of a genial good Silenus, ran creases of laughter and cunning: it evidently amused him to play a part and to wear evening dress [*sic*] once in a while. He talked all the time, but with many half-tints, as grey as those in his portrait by Carrière; he recalled his memories as a French and drawing master in English schools, and as a Press censor during the Commune; he talked about his drama on Louis XVII ...

The faces of those few undergraduates are lost in the unchangeable background of Oxford; all that stand out, illuminated, are Verlaine, talking and reminiscing, and Powell showing his appreciation with his hearty laughter.[8]

Powell had reserved a guest-room in college for Verlaine, and there Verlaine asked for time to prepare his lecture. It was in fact his usual lecture, but he did not know any poems by heart.

While Powell and Rothenstein collected books for him, he wrote a letter to Esther; he missed her desperately, he said, but would she forgive him if he stayed longer? 'Another three or four hundred francs would not be useless.' He asked her to send her answer, by telegram, to London. In the meanwhile, he sent her fifty francs.[9]

The letter was written, the lecture prepared; and then, recalled Verlaine, 'with the aid of hansoms, we were able to see some of the town, . . . unique in its medieval majesty.'

> Oxford est une ville qui me consola,
> Moi rêvant toujours de ce Moyen Âge-là . . .

He wrote a poem on this 'exquisite city', which so outshone *'la vieille Sorbonne'*.

> Ô toi, cité charmante et mémorable, Oxford![10]

Verlaine, with his lifelong love of the Middle Ages, his particular affection for England, was captivated by this medieval city – this city that was English to the point of symbolism.

Last Thursday [reported *The Oxford Magazine*, a few days later], a small number of enthusiasts met in the room behind Mr Blackwell's shop to hear M. Verlaine lecture on 'Contemporary French Poetry.' Fortunately M. Verlaine was persuaded to deal more largely with his own work than with that of poets with whom Oxford men are but little acquainted. He practically gave an autobiography, illustrating the varied phases of his life, by reciting his own poems, intensely dramatic and pathetic alternately. 'Le poète doit vivre beaucoup, vivre dans tous les sens.' This was his text, his justification; and upon it he founded a lecture of great interest and originality. His audience was small – too small, but it thoroughly appreciated seeing and hearing the eminent French poet.[11]

Rothenstein was to remember: 'There was only a sprinkling of persons present; . . . but Verlaine was tickled with the idea of having lectured before what he believed was an audience of doctors and scholars of the ancient University of Oxford.'[12]

Next morning, Powell escorted him round Christ Church and its gardens. Verlaine was now so enamoured of Oxford that the problem was to make him go. He later said that his visit had lasted twenty-four hours; York Powell referred to two days. Rothenstein spoke of two or three days, and added that Verlaine 'needed a good deal of gentle persuasion' before he departed. Many years later, in conversation, Rothenstein explained that Verlaine's lecture fee had been withheld until he was safely on the London train.[13]

There were other complications; Verlaine was trying to pacify both his fierce, demanding and possessive mistresses in Paris. Numerous letters were despatched to his *chère femme* (Esther) and his *chère amie* (Eugénie). Esther agreed that he should stay longer and lecture in Manchester. In the meanwhile, as Symons was away, Verlaine's admirers found him another room in London: at 63, York Terrace, Regent's Park. He led, he reported, 'a pasha's life', and 'all this did but increase my long and profoundly felt sympathy for a city which I have praised so often for its force, its splendour, its infinite charm, too, in fine weather and foul, and which I am forced, in all good faith, to praise now for its charm of the moment, and a limitless hospitality.'[14]

The hospitality did seem limitless. He spent a few days 'dawdling through a London of theatres (a very fairy-tale), Music-halls (a very paradise!)';[15] and on 29 November, Ernest Dowson told Victor Plarr: 'Verlaine is after all still in London. I am dining with Horne & Horne Père at the Constitutional to-night to meet him. So that if I have the courage I will even suggest to the Master that he should honour his disciples with a visit to the Cheese . . .'[26] There is no record that Verlaine went to the Cheshire Cheese, but he did go to that latter-day Mermaid Tavern, the Crown in Charing Cross Road.

On 1 December, still in a state of euphoria, he took a train from 'the admirable station of St Pancras', and set off to lecture in Manchester. Symons had already sent a description of him to his host. Verlaine, he wrote, was 'an old gentleman [he was in fact forty-nine], who is very lame in his left leg; he has a face all eyes, a black felt hat, a big overcoat made venerable by age and use and a faded multicoloured scarf.'

The portrait had been sent to Theodore Craig London.[17] A schoolfriend of Richard Le Gallienne, 'Theo' was now the Pastor of the New Windsor Congregational Church at Windsor Bridge in Salford. But he was much more than a preacher; he organised incredible lecture programmes and, still more astonishing, carried them out. In the years of his ministry at the Congregational Church, 'some of the greatest figures of the age were ushered through that ugly façade with its graceless round-headed windows, its yellowing plaster and its cage of iron railings, and there, amidst the pitch-pine and linoleum, they played and sang and lectured to the folk of this obscure corner of Lancashire . . .' This winter his congregation heard Herkomer, the artist, Jerome K. Jerome, and Stanley the explorer. On 1 December, in the New Windsor Schools, near the Congregational Church, Verlaine repeated the lecture which he had given in London and Oxford; it was followed by a reception in the presbytery.[18]

Verlaine returned to London and to a whirl of activity. He gave a long interview to *The Sketch*; he wrote a poem inspired by his Channel crossing, and a poem on Oxford. He also wrote numerous letters dictated by financial and amorous affairs. The lectures in London and Oxford had produced a thousand francs, he was asking 375 francs for his lecture in Manchester. He had been invited to contribute to English periodicals. It seemed, at last, as if a new and prosperous era had begun, and Verlaine indulged in a pasha's dreams. He hoped to give Esther a bracelet which she had long coveted. Even marriage seemed possible. 'As for the marriage,' he wrote to her, 'you would give me *the greatest pleasure in my life* and we'll go and see M. le Maire whenever you like. Anyway, it's the most effective way of assuring you something regular after my death . . . You are the only one I love – and how I love you!'[19]

And yet, for all these protestations, Verlaine was acting a little in his letters. He was not sure of Esther's fidelity. Cazals, who disliked her, was sending reports on her, and Eugénie was doing her best to discredit her rival. On 1 December, after his long journey to Manchester, Verlaine wrote to Esther: 'Oh no, don't be unfaithful to me! Don't be unkind any more. I can tell you I'm almost out of my mind . . . You know it's you I'm working for, I'm doing everything, and I *shall* do everything for you.' If she was faithful to him, he still wanted to marry her.[20] Eugénie, determined to disparage her, told Verlaine of Esther's infidelities and of her theft of 3,000 francs. On 5 December, from the French Hospital in London, where his leg was being dressed, Verlaine wrote to Cazals: 'The question is the eternal Esther (*a bad name*. I prefer Philomène). I am jealous in this land of Othello. So jealous I could die, if I had decided to break with her – *cette trop aimée, bizarre et savoureuse middle-aged woman*! Is it true that she is unfaithful to me? . . . You can find out and let me know.'[21]

Verlaine was not entirely honest. He had already decided to break with her. That day he wrote to Eugénie, telling her to come next day, Wednesday, at seven o'clock in the evening, to meet him at the Gare du Nord. He was, he said, parting from Esther-Philomène 'with profound grief. I love that woman, and I'll always love her. But she is dangerous for me . . .' He added – and Eugénie had to forgive him for the comparison: 'I love you, too. You have always been good to me, and I only work well when I'm with you . . . Have a nicer nature, and all will be well.'[22] He also sent a farewell note to Esther-Philomène, and indulged in a little mystification. 'If you want to see me, I'll be at the Gare du Nord on *Thursday*, the day after tomorrow, by the train which gets in from Calais at 7 in the evening.'[23]

He returned to Paris with 'deep affection and boundless esteem' for his London friends. He also returned with a handsome sum of money. His home was now a fifth-floor room at 187, rue Saint-Jacques, where he went to live with Eugénie.

PART FOURTEEN

Prince of Poets

(1893–6)

62

HE remained in a state of euphoria. The day after his return, he wrote to Carton de Wiart. 'I should like to lecture in Belgium again. Do you think there's some chance of earning a little money in Brussels?'[1]

Alas, the question was decided for him. Soon afterwards, he was ill yet again. 'I've got a recurrence of my trouble,' he explained to Rothenstein. 'I'm looking after it carefully, but it's made me incapable of writing much . . . Thanks to this recurrence, I haven't been able to go to Belgium, let alone to Switzerland. I have moved house and divorced. Write to me at 187, rue Saint-Jacques . . . *Above all don't send anything to the rue Broca.*' This was no doubt Esther's address. Verlaine announced that he had got rid of '*cette harlot*'. He added: 'The household is in ecstasy. We're going to have some little – canaries! And we've acquired an aquarium with two goldfish.'[2]

In 'L'Hôpital chez soi', Verlaine described the attic, so dark that he had to keep a lamp lit until noon. Through the curtainless window he could see a forest of chimneys, and, in the attic opposite, a woman making immortelles for tombs. The window had unexpected uses. One day, two admirers were loyally sharing a plate of leeks and a litre of cheap wine with the Master, when the postman arrived with five pounds from an English editor. Verlaine emptied the plate of leeks out of the window. '*Et maintenant, mes enfants, nous allons déjeuner comme des tigres!*' They were soon enjoying pâté and vintage wine.³

Achille Segard had a less attractive recollection of the rue Saint-Jacques.

'The 'proper apartment' consisted simply of a long, narrow room, all cluttered up by the huge bed, a wardrobe which had lost its mirror, the cooking-stove, the chest-of-drawers, and the kitchen utensils. When I went in, I had not even caught sight of Verlaine, who was stretched out on the bed, before I bumped into the caretaker of the basement at le Soleil d'or, and into Bibi-la-Purée, who was decked out that day in a tail-coat with one tail missing, and into Eugénie, who might have been hovering somewhere between forty and fifty, and had certainly never been pretty or distinguished.

Verlaine enjoyed my discomfiture and my astonishment; he looked at me with amusement out of his small mischievous eyes, and when, as was proper, I had sent for a little vermouth and absinthe, we should have been good friends at once, if Eugénie had not – despite my presence – overwhelmed Verlaine with bitter reproaches for his infidelity.

That day, no doubt to do me honour, he bore her outbursts with untiring patience. But we know from the *Chansons pour elle* that he was far from being so benign all the time. The attic often echoed with arguments and blows ... These plebeian scenes did not displease Verlaine; he liked simple things, humble women and sordid clothes. When he went down the boulevard Saint-Michel, wearing an old threadbare coat and the broad-brimmed felt hat which he used to call *le chapeau d'Infortunatus*, a red muffler round his neck, and a big stick in his hand, which he brandished at passers-by, he was really a very curious figure ...⁴

It was in this curious dress that Verlaine had called on the artist Aman-Jean at the quai Bourbon.

He had been drinking, as his gait suggested, and he was all the more unsteady because he could hardly bend his left knee. He came along, limping, feeling the pavement with his iron-tipped stick, like a street singer. The concierge appeared at her attic window, and shouted: 'You, there! No singers here!' Verlaine went quietly towards her. 'I sing, Madame, but a different sort of song.' Aman-Jean, who had watched the scene, opened his window. 'Come up, Monsieur Verlaine.'

And, to the concierge: 'Madame Beugnat, you have just been talking to the greatest poet in France.'[5]

Some might have given the palm to Mallarmé, but there was no doubt that Verlaine was now haloed by extraordinary prestige.

It was not the prestige of his recent poetry, or of his prose. When, in April 1893, Léon Bloy received *Mes Prisons*, he reported in his journal: 'Drunkard's literature. Poor great Verlaine!' Poor great Verlaine! For this account of his prison life and his conversion, published at the height of his renown, Vanier gave him ninety-five francs.[6]

But if Verlaine had long since ceased to write significant poetry, if he contented himself with scribbling undistinguished verse and pedestrian prose, with writing out of a desperate need for money, it was still clear, from a sight of him, from a sudden flash of his conversation, that he was the poet of *Fêtes Galantes*, of *Romances sans paroles* and *Sagesse*. Verlaine, wrote Carrère,

. . . was born for a great purpose. He bore all the marks of it. Physically, he was robust and lofty like an oak in his native Ardennes. Even in his lamentable decline, when, worn by vice, by misery, and by self-neglect, he wandered, limping, through the Latin Quarter, one saw in his square shoulders, in the proud way he bore his torso, in his muscular neck, in the bearing of his head, which was still superb, the mighty relic of a man made to command those about him . . . Some-times, in the middle of the imbecile conversations with which his companions enlivened the long and smoky sessions round café tables, one saw the old poet suddenly shake the torpor from his veiled eyes. He would raise his proud head, and look scornfully, fiercely round the band of aesthetes . . . Eyes aglow, and lips disdainful, he would sweep aside the whole mass of nonsense and silliness with one or two decisive syllables . . . And really at such moments he flashed like an awakening lion.[7]

His destiny had ended after the apotheosis of 1891, at the Vaudeville, recorded Rémy de Gourmont. 'It ended in a kind of tremulous calm, among friends who were excessively familiar and admirers who were too inquisitive. People came to sense in his present the odour of his past.'[8] 'The future,' wrote Lucien

Muhlfeld, 'will certainly be more just to him than his contemporaries. Young people admired him, some of them even compromised him, for during those last years every puerile scribbler wanted to monopolise him . . . But his older companions were mediocre, or worse.'⁹

Sometimes he felt inclined to exploit the admiration which was professed for him. One day, in the Boul' Mich', he found himself face to face with a student whom he met every evening, gazing at him, in ecstasy, in a café.

'Young man,' he said to him, and stopped. 'Listen to me.'

'Maître,' stammered the student, mad with pride and delight. 'Maître . . .'

'Listen, young man, what I want to say is this: Have you got 50 centimes to lend me?'¹⁰

Verlaine sometimes thought that he was cursed. 'Do you know what it is to be a poet?' he asked Georges Beaujon. 'Well, it's a curse, it's a malediction . . . You understand? . . . a ma-le-dic-tion!'¹¹ He had become a sort of incarnation of the protests of the individual against society. And yet he was a curious mixture of bitterness and pride, of humility and self-respect. 'What I do is nothing to boast about,' he had said in Holland. 'These things depend on chance.'¹² But towards the end of his life, remembered Delahaye, a student stopped him in the street, and declared his admiration. Verlaine replied coldly: 'Monsieur, my name is Paul Verlaine and my address is 16, rue Saint-Victor.' Delahaye was impressed by such insistence on formality. Verlaine was conscious of his status; he refused to have admiration offered to him like alms.¹³ 'Verlaine, the real Verlaine,' confirmed Gabriel de Lautrec, 'knew his proper value. I won't say that he was perpetually stupefied to be himself. But . . . this impenitent street Arab had the greatest respect for the poet whom he bore within himself. He knew his worth.'¹⁴

It was no stupid vanity, but a proper sense of proportion, a considered literary judgment. And if, in the presence of the profane, Verlaine proclaimed enormous pride, the pride did not come from his heart. Gheusi had set him near Baudelaire; and

one day he asked him if he accepted the comparison. 'Baudelaire!'
cried Verlaine. 'He is my god. I think his lines are a little "well-
groomed": that was the period. But I won't let people compare
me with him. I should be crushed by his shadow. He completely
dominates us. We have no genius beside his own.'[15]

Verlaine himself had the humility of genius. It was easy to
approach him, remembered Merrill. No great man ever showed
less haughtiness. 'He talked at once to the first comer,' confirmed
Delahaye, 'with the same spontaneity, trust, and expansiveness
that one might show to friends one had known since childhood.'
Delayaye also mentioned 'his delicacy, his education as a man of
the world, which prevented familiarity from turning into rude-
ness'.[16] Certainly he was recognised as a man apart.

Everyone knew him in the Latin Quarter [remembered Saint-
Georges de Bouhélier]. Especially the waiters in the cafés, who showed
him a certain consideration, not that he was particularly generous to
them – he couldn't have been, even if he had wanted – but because of
his renown. Mankind have such a deep sense of the divine and the
eternal, that, even in the wreck of a body, under the appearance of
triviality, they only ask to acknowledge and adore it. When Verlaine
went down the boulevard Saint-Michel, with muddy feet and vague
curses, he was greeted on every side . . . Bibi-la-Purée went so far as to
brush his suits, in the middle of the street, and to clean his shoes. It was
his way of honouring the poet.[17]

Time and again Verlaine's contemporaries paid tribute to him.
Émile Gallé, the glass-maker and cabinet-maker in Nancy, and
one of the pioneers of Art Nouveau, inscribed a vase with a line
from Verlaine:

Je récolte en secret des fleurs mystérieuses.

Early in the 1890s he made a number of *meubles parlants*: pieces
of furniture engraved with quotations from his poems. By 1895
there was a rue Paul Verlaine in Nancy. Reynaldo Hahn played
three or four of his settings of Verlaine at a dinner given by Daudet
for Princess Mathilde. The *Mercure de France* recorded some 'very
remarkable transpositions' of part of *Sagesse* into German; it also
published an article, 'Le Symbolisme jugé par une Russe', in which

a Mlle Wenguerow concluded 'that Verlaine touches the drama in the very heart of modern man'.[18]

The interest in Verlaine now spread throughout Europe and beyond. The first English version of his poems had appeared in 1881. The first studies of his poetry and reprints of his work had appeared in Italy, Germany and Spain in 1890; the first in Russia and Sweden had been published in 1892 (*Romances sans paroles* was translated into Russian two years later). In Norway and Denmark, the interest began in 1893. In 1894 a book of translations, *Poems of the Symbolists*, including versions of Verlaine, made its appearance in Chicago; in 1895 there were articles about him in Poland, Bohemia and Hungary. In 1896 his fame had spread to Greece, and in 1903 it reached Rumania.[19]

He was constantly portrayed; for, as Arthur Symons said, his face was 'a face devoured by dreams . . . : it had earthly passions, intellectual pride, spiritual humility.'[20] In 1893 De Gaspari's plaster bust of Verlaine was shown at the Artistes Français exhibition. Robert Vallin painted his portrait at Broussais (as Aman-Jean had done before him). And when, that October, Le Barc de Boutteville held an exhibition, 'Portraits du prochain siècle', Niederhausen's bust of Verlaine was 'rightly and properly placed in the centre, like a patriarch in the middle of his family'. The exhibition led an enterprising publisher to announce a book with the same title, 'in which one will see not only the silhouettes of the artists and men of letters whose portraits actually figured in the show . . . but all the young personalities of the moment.'[21]

Portraits du prochain siècle was published in 1894. In the first section of the book, 'Les Précurseurs', Charles Morice paid tribute to Verlaine. 'By his honest and intense humanity, his perpetual communion with the eternal essences of things, his prodigiously subtle simplicity, Verlaine procures, for those who know how to love him, that austere and flattering spiritual delight which proclaims that a *new beauty* is revealed.' *Portraits du prochain siècle* was also notable for another portrait of a 'precursor': for Verlaine's appreciation of Rimbaud. It was now nineteen years since he had seen Rimbaud, and three years since Rimbaud's death, but Verlaine's love remained, his admiration was as strong and confident as ever. 'In the sadness of the premature death of this unique poet, I "rejoice",' he wrote, 'that, in a sense, I inaugurated his glory.'[22]

In March 1894, Rothenstein paid a visit to the rue Saint-Jacques. It was just before Verlaine's fiftieth birthday, but his leg was too bad for him to go out. Rothenstein arranged to have a party in Verlaine's room. Eugénie was to buy the food from a nearby restaurant. On 30 March Rothenstein and a friend arrived with a bottle of vintage wine; they had hidden it in a large bunch of flowers.[23] The present moved Verlaine to write 'Anniversaire': a poem of poignant gratitude and poignant regret.[24]

The following month his leg became considerably worse; and on 1 May his old friend Dr Jullien sent him to the Hôpital Saint-Louis. He was there when he began to write his memoirs for the periodical *La Fin de Siècle*. He was paid ten sous a line.

He was still at Saint-Louis when, on 26 May, Vanier published his new collection of poems. *Dans les limbes* had been conceived at Broussais in October 1892. 'Les Limbes,' Verlaine explained, '*c'est l'hôpital avec une visiteuse.*' The visitor had been Esther; and the poems reflect the humiliated, jealous, but undoubtedly real love which Verlaine felt for her. The poetic element which fires *Le Livre posthume* is almost entirely lacking from *Dans les limbes*. But, once again, Verlaine illuminates himself. He records his need for this impulsive, passionate woman, who sometimes loses her grief in brittle gaiety.

> Quelle chaude gaîté quand ton chagrin s'oublie,
> Ce chagrin qui pudiquement rêve en sa tente . . .

The latter-day Verlaine is here, blessing the vigorous mistress who has saved him from decline, and rescued him from nothingness. Esther is the dominant woman he has always sought:

> Ah! courbe-le, mon caractère,
> Piétine-le donc sous le tien . . .[25]

Esther is jealous of his friends, possessive, invigorating, foul-mouthed, tender and unfaithful. But Verlaine only asks to be the servant of her whims.

It was not the first time that his love poems were out of date when they appeared. There is no record that Esther came to fetch him on 10 July 1894, when he left Saint-Louis. And Eugénie, with whom he had been living in the spring, now refused to have him back at the rue Saint-Jacques. Verlaine returned to an old address: to the hôtel de Lisbonne, 4, rue de Vaugirard.

63

Within the week, on 17 July, at the age of seventy-six, Leconte de Lisle died. Since the distant Saturdays in the Boulevard des Invalides, master and pupil had changed. For years they had detested one another. Leconte de Lisle, rigid and high-principled, had learned about Verlaine's broken marriage and his flight with Rimbaud. Louis Gaillard heard a young disciple ask: 'Mon cher Maître, what is Mallarmé?' 'A Symbolist poet.' 'And Moréas?' 'A Decadent poet.' 'And Paul Verlaine?' Leconte de Lisle looked scornfully over his monocle. 'He's a queer.'[1]

Leconte de Lisle had also come to believe that Verlaine was a Communard. However despicable Verlaine's war record had been, he had not in fact been an active Communard, and he had taken no part in the bloodshed. But Leconte de Lisle had not changed his opinion; and, after the Commune, he had ostracised him. In the 1880s and 1890s, if by chance they met, their mutual detestation was evident. Leconte de Lisle used to patronise a tobacconist's in the rue Gay-Lussac, and here, from time to time, he would find himself in the presence of Verlaine. Leconte de Lisle would light his cigar with a lordly air. Verlaine would re-light his pipe. And, standing before the lighting apparatus, the two poets would bow to one another in silence. Sometimes Verlaine would follow Leconte de Lisle into the shop; 'and when his enemy had bought a one-sou cigar, he himself would make his lordly purchase: "Madame," he would say, "a demi-londrès!" And, telling the story, Verlaine would add: "You should have seen the poor man's humiliation"!' Once, when Leconte de Lisle had left, Verlaine confided to the tobacconist: 'That was the old actor, Mélingue.'[2]

Such was Verlaine's revenge for the personal remarks which had duly been repeated to him. 'Verlaine is terrible, quite terrible!' Leconte de Lisle would say. 'He looks like a fat skeleton.' And when a disciple was walking with him in the Jardin du Luxembourg, he snapped: 'If they put up my bust here, I don't want it near Verlaine's ... because of the smell!'

Now, in July 1894, the old Parnassian died; and Verlaine set down his recollections. They were remarkably generous to the man who had called him 'the dishonour of French youth'.[3] Two years later, when Verlaine himself had died, there appeared his final word:

> Fleur de cuistrerie et de méchanceté
> Au parfum de lucre et de servilité,
> Et poussée en plein terrain d'hypocrisie,
>
> Cet individu fait de la poésie ...

'Portrait Académique' appeared among Verlaine's *Invectives*.[4] It was a savage revenge for the Master's behaviour.

Since Verlaine had come out of hospital in July 1894, Eugénie had returned to him. But he was as poor as ever; and Rothenstein, on a visit to Paris, had a note from him: 'I count on you for Wednesday ... Would you and could you contribute *a little* to our frugal orgies?' Verlaine was not well enough to dine out, and Rothenstein, who often went to dinner with him and Eugénie, 'usually procured some addition to their larder'.[5]

On 24 August, as Paul Léautaud was passing the Café Mayeux, on the corner of the rue Soufflot, he saw Verlaine on the terrace 'with that woman who is always with him. I bought a small bunch of violets from the florist,' Léautaud recorded, 'and I had it sent by a commissionaire. I took up my position ... to watch the effect from a distance. He raised the violets to his nose, to smell them, and looked all round to see where they could have come from. I went on my way again, delighted with my gesture.'[6]

Soon after this idyllic scene there came the inevitable quarrel. De Langle recorded how,

... one evening when ... Mlle Eugénie had created a commotion at the Café Procope, she left, and then came back again – and threw some letters, two or three dirty shirts, and Verlaine's manuscripts, right in the middle of the café, pell mell, in a very sorry state. Théo [the proprietor] piously gathered them up and put them in the café library where they stayed for two months. Verlaine took them back in a series of little parcels. He received the last at the hôpital Bichat.[7]

Among Cazals' papers is a 'warrant', addressed to Marie Crance, dated by Cazals 1894. 'I authorise Mme Crance to remove my belongings from my rooms, 48, rue du Cardinal Lemoine, where I have lodged Mlle Krantz. Wednesday, 19 September. Paul Verlaine.'[8]

In September, Verlaine was not only looking back on his broken liaison; he was still looking back on his childhood, and writing his memoirs. He began to publish them in *La Fin de Siècle* on 30 September (and he enlarged them into a book in 1895, under the title of *Confessions*). He had little, now, except regrets; and no-one recognised this more clearly than Carrère, when, on an autumn morning this year, he saw him for the last time.

Carrère had just come back to Paris from the South of France. He had the good fortune to spend a few days with Mistral, the Provençal poet, at Maillane, and,

... full of youthful intoxication [he wrote], I was telling all comers about the splendour of my sunlit journey. I met Verlaine at the corner of the rue Monge and the rue des Écoles. And, as it happened, the author of *Mireille* had spoken to me with the greatest warmth about the author of *La Bonne Chanson* ...

'Dear Verlaine,' he had said to me, 'how I should like to see him!'

So I repeated the compliments which I brought from Maillane, and Verlaine felt great joy and delight.

'Dear Mistral! What a poet! What a man! I'm so pleased about what you say!'

At that moment, despite its premature signs of age, Verlaine's face took on an air of childlike innocence; it seemed as if recollections of verdant childhood welled up from the depths of his memory. His eyes shone with tears. He made me recall, again and again, all the impressions which I had brought back from my pilgrimage in the

South. And after every phrase he interrupted: 'Isn't that fine? Isn't that the true life?'

Then, little by little, he grew roused ...

'And what about us? What are we? What are we doing here? Oh, cursed city! How squalid to live in all this!'

And I saw him gradually working himself into a rage ... And suddenly, sombre, frowning, without farewell or explanation, he left me and went off, muttering: 'Pig! Pig!'

And his heavy stick struck the pavement, his free arm gesticulated in the air, his head was bent and no longer proudly held. He went off alone, swearing, threatening invisible enemies; then I saw him disappear at the corner of a street, fierce, formidable, sinister, walking on straight ahead, oblivious of carriages and pedestrians ...

What was happening then in his poor, helpless, wounded soul? What regret of youth, and of wasted life, so stirred all the memories of his mis-spent hours? ... Some time later, in *L'Éclair*, I read a touching letter which the ailing poet, already near his end, wrote to Mistral, and I remembered that autumn morning when I saw in the gestures of Verlaine all the lucid awareness, all the devastating remorse that was in him.[9]

His private life was misery; his financial situation remained as precarious as ever. In August, Barrès had persuaded Montesquiou that a committee of fifteen subscribers should be formed, each of whom, through *Le Figaro*, would send Verlaine ten francs a month. On 9 August, in answer to Verlaine's appeal, the Minister of Public Instruction had made him a grant of five hundred francs. Deschamps, the editor of *La Plume*, and many other friends, had supported his application, and on 25 August Verlaine had thanked Zola for his help. He and Zola stood at opposite poles of literature, but they kept an affectionate respect for one another. In 1892, Zola had sent Verlaine an inscribed copy of *La Débâcle*: the last but one of the Rougon-Macquart novels, a study of the Franco-Prussian War. '*Monsieur et cher éminent confrère,*' answered Verlaine. 'This book is your masterpiece ... It has made me shudder and tremble with grief and with absolute admiration.' Now, in the summer of 1894, Verlaine acknowledged Zola's support. He took the occasion to express his admiration for Zola's latest book: *Lourdes*, the first of his trilogy *Les Trois Villes*. 'I find it supremely interesting,' Verlaine assured him, 'both as a Catholic and as your admirer.'[10]

Verlaine's own fame was now to be more solidly established. The death of Leconte de Lisle had left vacant not only his Chair at the Académie, but the controversial title of Prince of Poets. Stuart Merrill urged that Verlaine should be given the title as compensation for an unjust destiny.[11] Two hundred men of letters, aged from eighteen to twenty-five, took part in the ballot that October. The election was made at the Café Procope. Verlaine came at the top of the list with 77 votes, Heredia had 38, Mallarmé 36, and Coppée received only 12. Verlaine was given the result in his room at the Hôtel de Lisbonne. The new Prince of Poets gazed out of the window at the Jardin du Luxembourg. 'I have no palace,' was his comment, 'but there is my royal park.'[12] Immediately after the ballot, wrote Adolphe Brisson, 'M. Paul Verlaine retired to the Hôpital Broussais, to take up his winter quarters.'[13]

It was in fact the Hôpital Bichat to which he was admitted on 1 December. A fortnight later, *Épigrammes* was published, through the good offices of *La Plume*. In his preface, Verlaine explained that it was the work of an invalid, who wanted to amuse himself and not to bore his contemporaries excessively. Posterity, he added, should see the book as a jest.

It was, indeed, a lighthearted return to old inspirations and old methods: a collection of pastiches and reconstructed forms. There was no invention or creation, merely a playing with themes and techniques.

> J'admire l'ambition du Vers Libre
> – Et moi-même, que fais-je en ce moment
> Que d'essayer d'émouvoir l'équilibre
> D'un nombre ayant deux rhythmes seulement? . . .[14]

In the fifth epigram, Verlaine returns to the mood of *Fêtes galantes*: to an eighteenth-century, theatrical world, its elegance and gaiety. In the seventh epigram, he vaguely recalls the 'Paysages tristes' of his *Poèmes saturniens*. In the twenty-ninth, asking for grace from God, he echoes the inspiration of *Sagesse*. But *Épigrammes* remains superficial, a medley of poems with no consistent theme, and no fire.

The Prince of Poets had not lost his will to work. 'Despite so many mortifications,' he had written in October, 'he is still alive ... And, if God should grant him the cure which, perhaps, he deserves after eight years of ill-health, he does not despair of filling French literature with impersonal works, critical and historical.'[15]

It was a strange and unlikely programme for a man whose work was supremely personal: a man who admitted that he was not a critic. But among his historical works was his play about Louis XVII. More than once he had talked to his friends about writing a *Louis XVII*, and he used to sketch out the plot or indicate a few episodes. Verlaine was sceptical about Naundorff, the watchmaker who had claimed to be Louis XVII in the days of the Bourbon Restoration. But he was convinced that the Dauphin had not died in the Temple.[16]

He was, perhaps, preparing to write his *Louis XVII* when Rémy de Gourmont saw him for the first time.

It was in the Bibliothèque nationale ... Even if the ticket with his name on it had not signalled him out for my attention, his face would have struck me. It was the face I imagined for a Swabian or a Hun, one of those formidable barbarians who so terrified Sidonius Apollinaris that he trembled as he described them. The impression was not so bad. Had he not just laid waste the art of poetry as they had laid waste the majesty of Rome? I did not see him again except in the cafés and on the pavements of the boulevard Saint-Michel. He no longer left the Latin Quarter, except for the distant and friendly refuge of the hospitals, into which he was cast by his hazardous health.[17]

Some time in December 1894, Saint-Georges de Bouhélier went, with Chapeyroux, to visit him in hospital. He took him a bag of sweets. He had slipped a small gold coin among them; for the poor, he wrote,

... are grateful for the smallest thing, and I felt as if Verlaine was a relation ...

We found the poet in bed, with a brownish woollen cover over him . . .

He had gone into Bichat, because his usual trouble had recurred, and he was coughing fit to burst. I didn't know whether to pity him, or to be silent in the presence of such misery.

'Here are some sweets for you,' said Chapeyroux.

'That's nice of you,' said Verlaine.

I took the little bag from my pocket, and he began – rather clumsily – to take off the gold cord; . . . and then, at last, he opened the bag, and took out a handful of sweets . . .

'Very good, these!' he said, and licked his chops with great delight. A party seemed to have started inside him. His eyes were shining.

'What are you working on?' asked Chapeyroux.

A book of poems, which he planned to call *Esther*, was in preparation . . .

'What would you say to another title: *Le Livre posthume*?, Verlaine asked suddenly.

The title was not a new inspiration. Since May 1893 several poems had appeared 'from *Le Livre posthume*, a book to be published by Léon Vanier'. But Chapeyroux had not seen them. Now, when Verlaine mentioned the title,

Chapeyroux could not restrain himself. 'Oh, Verlaine! What an idea!'

'You haven't read Fouquier's column in *Le Figaro* today?' continued the old genius in profound depression.

I caught sight of a paper on the bed [continued Bouhélier] . . . Fouquier had . . . lashed out at the new poets . . . He attacked those whom he considered to be their guides, and, in particular, poor Verlaine, whose influence he called exceedingly corrosive . . .

Verlaine's face was clouded by infinite melancholy. He had been eating away at his chocolates with a sort of fury, all the time . . . It was a mechanical gesture and he did not notice the flavour . . .

'Why say that something isn't poetry?' asked Verlaine, suddenly . . . 'The diamond is in the coal, there are gold nuggets in the mud of the rivers of California. It's a question of having good eyes . . .'[18]

There are experiences which one has to be poor and fallen to understand: there are the smiles of beggars, the dreams of prisoners, the repentance of sinners and the sleep of vagabonds. Verlaine had found this poetic gold in the mud of the rivers. Maurice Barrès called his work 'the poetry of the good thief'.[19]

The year which brought Verlaine's election as the Prince of Poets brought him a less orthodox tribute. It is a sign of fame to inspire not only the writers of fact but the writers of fiction; and Anatole France, who had drawn him in *Gestas*, now presented him again in *Le Lys rouge*. From this novel of contemporary manners, there rose the figure of Choulette, the poet. It was hard not to recognise him as the poet of *Sagesse*. 'Choulette,' wrote Anatole France, 'is not very different from the saints whose extraordinary lives we read. He is sincere, as they are, with an exquisite delicacy of feeling and a terrible violence of spirit. If he shocks us by many of his actions, that is because he is weaker, less enduring, or perhaps just more closely observed. And then there are bad saints, just as there are bad angels: Choulette is a bad saint, that's all!'

There is the spiritual profile of Verlaine, drawn with a touch of humour, and with understanding; and, physically, Anatole France presented him to perfection, with his Socratic features, his Inverness cape and red muffler, and his reputation for drunkenness. 'He was limping along the quai, his hat pushed back on his bumpy head, his beard unkempt, lugging an old carpet bag. He was almost terrible, and, although he was fifty, he seemed young. His blue eyes were so bright and shining, his worn and yellowed face had kept such innocent audacity. From this old ruin of a man there emanated the eternal youth of the poet.'[20]

If Verlaine found his artists in Cazals and Rothenstein, he found his verbal portrait-painter in Anatole France.

64

On 21 January 1895, Verlaine left Bichat. It had been his last stay in a Paris hospital. He had spent nearly four of the last nine years in a hospital bed.

This time Esther had come to fetch him, but they seem to have quarrelled at once, and she abandoned him. At last the break was final. Verlaine could no longer bear her rapacity and her infidelity. Among the papers of Cazals are two undated notes, clearly written under the influence of drink. The first, which is scrawled at all angles, is addressed to 'Mme Esther', at 18, rue Descartes.

> I demand, by postcard, the portrait of my mother and all my other things, too, in spite of what your favourite lover or filthy pimp requires.
>
> Merde!
>
> P.V.

The second card is addressed to the proprietor of the Hôtel de Rennes, 277, rue Saint-Jacques.

> Please return all the things of mine which are with YOU. As for Miss Esther and her 'bloke', they have ceased to please me, and I should be obliged to complain in high places or to see that justice is done myself.
>
> PAUL VERLAINE.[1]

Verlaine had been physically drawn to Esther, but he had recognised her inferiority; and, talking one day to Gheusi about Baudelaire's former mistress, Jeanne Duval, he said: 'I know her, she's still alive and she isn't even old – the negress he immortalised in his poems. She is as superior to my Esther as his pages are to mine.'[2] Now, said Cazals, when Esther repented, and tried to win him over with her smiles, 'Verlaine did not answer, but turned away, and raised his stick in a gesture of malediction and horror.'[3] De Langle went further, and said that Verlaine 'nearly murdered Esther one fine evening, at the corner of the rue Soufflot.'[4] Eventually she retired to live with a new protector in the country. In February 1895, after a few days of wandering from one furnished room to another, Verlaine went to live in an attic near the École polytechnique, with Eugénie.

Dear Sir [he announced to the manager of the Procope, on 8 March],
I am now living at 16 rue St Victor where I shall be very happy to see you when you come and visit a bedridden man – myself, once

again. I have an abscess under my foot, it was lanced yesterday and it's dressed every day. Impossible to put my foot on the ground.

Don't give the rest of my old papers to Esther or anyone else. I'd rather you brought them to me when you come and see me – anyway, keep them carefully.

Yours ever,

P. VERLAINE.[5]

On 19 February he had been given a second grant of five hundred francs by the Minister of Public Instruction. He would receive a third on 30 September. His health grew worse, and he was forced to keep to his bed, but he continued to write, and to keep a watchful eye on his editors. 'What news of you?' This to Gustave Kahn on 18 April. '... And what news of the poems I sent you from Bichat? Have they appeared, will they appear, and what's happening about them?' On 9 June, in a letter to an unnamed correspondent, he asked for some books he needed to write an article.[6]

On 27 June, Edmond de Goncourt dined with Rodenbach at Voisin's. Rodenbach told him that he had been present when Verlaine and Vanier agreed on a contract.

The publisher wanted to give only 25 francs for a few poems he had just written, and Verlaine was determined to have 30 francs. And it ended with Verlaine holding his receipt in one hand, and staying there until he received a napoleon and two hundred-sou pieces in the other ... And, when Rodenbach congratulated him on his victory: 'No, no, I shouldn't have given in ... I'd have had a scene!' said Verlaine, alluding to the authority of a low woman he was living with.[7]

It was easy to denigrate Eugénie, but she deserved some gratitude. In September, she and Verlaine finally settled in two rooms at 39, rue Descartes. The street was in a working-class quarter, perpetually buzzing with housewives' gossip and with children's chatter. The house itself had been recently built, but already it seemed shabby, and the paint was flaking on the staircase. The concierge, remembered Gaston Stiegler, was 'a tiny little phantom of an old woman'. On the third floor above the *entresol* he knocked on a narrow door. It was opened by Eugénie: a simple woman, with a worn face, wearing a jacket and skirt.

She was not perhaps the 'charming companion' praised by the sculptor Rodo Niederhausern, but there was no doubt of her devotion. And, thanks to her, for the few remaining months of his life, Verlaine was to enjoy what seemed to him an almost bourgeois home. It was 'a small and very decent apartment', recorded Gabriel de Lautrec, 'and there I found him, one day, delighted because he was having strawberries for pudding.'[8]

Eugénie really looked after him with great devotion [wrote de Langle], though her devotion was punctuated by a few bursts of temper – excusable, after all – the kind of temper one shows to an excessively naughty child. He used to lay the table, while she went shopping; and, alluding to his love and to the rudimentary education of Mlle Eugénie, his compatriot, he would say: 'What do you expect? When I love her, I seem to hear the bells of my native countryside.'[9]

Verlaine now talked calmly about his former wife. At moments, when they recalled the past, Eugénie would take sides with Mathilde; and (recorded Delahaye), after a little rum she would sparkle and describe her distant triumphs at the Théâtre du Châtelet.

'I haven't always been a humble sempstress, you know, Monsieur!... Once upon a time they threw flowers on stage for me!... Yes, they did!... Listen, when I sang ...'
And then she would take up a mincing attitude, raise her arms above her old head, and, with an affected lisp of indescribable comedy, she would recite some or other quatrain from a revue which had delighted the *petits crevés* in the reign of Napoleon III.

She was too emotional, now, to be a good nurse, but at least she saw that Verlaine's shirts and bedclothes were always clean. One day she bought him some peroxide to dye his greying beard. Verlaine used the dye with abandon, and appalled his friends.[10]
It was possibly now that Rothenstein went to see him again.

He was obviously far from well, and he looked terribly yellow. He was still living with Eugénie Krantz in a single room [*sic*] ... One day

I arrived to find he had gilded all the chairs with cheap bronze paint, and was childishly delighted with the effect. 'That is how a poet should live,' he said, 'with golden furniture,' and he laughed, half childlike and half cynical. No-one ever seemed to visit him; at least I never met any of his old associates there. Only Cazals was faithful still.[11]

Cazals, who often climbed the steep stairs, recorded Verlaine's last apartment. On the right, as you entered, was the dining-room: poorly furnished, and looking over the courtyard. Facing you was the kitchen. On the left was the bedroom, with two windows looking over the street. These windows were adorned with the canary cage and the pots of flowers dear to Murger's heroines. One side of the room was taken up by a faded red plush sofa. In the middle of the room was Verlaine's work table, covered with neat piles of papers. Beside them stood an oil lamp: its base in the shape of an owl. On the mantelpiece, among the photographs, he had set out a row of oranges: it was an old Ardennais custom, and he liked the bright colour. It was Eugénie, said Cazals, who had bought him the gold paint to gild the canary cage; and he had gilded everything within reach. These childish pleasures, and his work, and reading, and the visits of the few friends who came to see him, filled his days until, at last, illness overcame him.[12]

It was probably in the autumn of 1895 that Verlaine met Pierre Dauze, the editor of *La Revue biblio-iconographique*. Dauze arranged to publish twenty-four 'Biblio-Sonnets' by Verlaine in his review, and then as a book.

On 12 October, Verlaine wrote 'Bibliophilie'. It appeared a fortnight later, and it recalls Renard's comment that he was no longer writing poetry, he was playing knucklebones with words. But Verlaine wrote on. 'I'm going to settle down to work,' he told Dauze on 31 October. 'It's true that, in this cold weather, one's mind is clearer.' On 12 November he complained of 'a terrible cold. I'm afraid it's complicated by gastralgia, and it has literally brutalised me.'

Dauze went to see him; he found the apartment 'clean and well-kept, bright and rather gay.' He thought Eugénie 'a good woman, pretty common, with thick features, but she seemed to me to have a good character, and I think that she was really attached to him.'[13]

Despite his ill-health, Verlaine had finished the first part of a large-scale work (apparently his *Louis XVII*). He also tried to sell Dauze a new article on Rimbaud;[14] and when, this year, Vanier published Rimbaud's *Poésies complètes*, they appeared with a preface by Verlaine. In October, in *La Plume*, he recalled the evening, twenty-four years earlier, when Rimbaud had arrived at the rue Nicolet: an adolescent, with his voice still breaking. He had shaped Verlaine's destiny; now, largely through Verlaine, his poems were 'virtual classics'.[15]

65

In about mid October another figure emerged from the past. For many years, now, Verlaine had had no direct news of his son. He had heard that Georges had lived in England, and in Algeria with the Delportes. Now Georges himself wrote from Soignies, in Belgium; he wanted to meet his father, 'if the question could be solved by a railway ticket or, if possible, some money in advance'. He wrote more than once; and Verlaine sent affectionate answers. He did not have the money for his fare. Silence followed, and Verlaine made enquiries of the Burgomaster of Soignies. Georges, it appeared, had left Soignies three or four weeks earlier; he had been ill, and, after a brief visit to hospital, he had returned to his mother in Brussels. Her address was given as 451, avenue Louise. On 28 November, Verlaine wrote urgently to Carton de Wiart: 'It would be infinitely kind of you if you would make enquiries about the young man, and find out if he is content with his lot. If you can get him alone, you might talk to him, discreetly, about me, and see what he thinks . . . And, in brackets: if you do see my son, tell him not to say anything to his mother, because I think he's rather naïve.'

Carton de Wiart tried in vain to find Georges Verlaine. There was no-one by the name of Delporte at the address in the avenue Louise. 'I am very sad,' replied Verlaine, 'about what you say of the avenue Louise and its nominal occupants. But it hardly surprises me . . . I see it as a maternal manoeuvre.'[1]

In fact the Delportes lived at 454, avenue Louise. It was the ultimate irony of Verlaine's life that he himself had given Carton de Wiart the wrong address.

Georges did not come to the rue Descartes, but two other eager visitors arrived. Le Blond, the young writer, was a friend of Saint-Georges de Bouhélier. For a long time he had begged him to introduce him to Verlaine. At last, one day late in 1895, a meeting was arranged.

That November afternoon [Bouhélier recalled] was all diapered with pale sunlight. We reached the floor where he lived, and we were about to pull the bell-rope when a commotion burst out from behind the door . . .

[Eugénie Krantz] was calling him a dirty old man and a filthy pimp, and he was answering in the same tone . . .

[Le Blond rang the bell] and then all was silent . . . We heard someone coming.

'Who is that?' enquired a voice in sudden honeyed tones.

The door was opened at once.

'Ah! It's you!' said Eugénie Krantz, who was now displaying an unconvincing if appropriate sweetness. 'You should have said so!'

And she shouted:

'A visitor for you!'

The poet appeared, and stretched out his hand in a gesture at once embarrassed and relieved . . .

Verlaine took visible delight in showing me his little lodgings. Some have declared that he loved squalor, but I should say myself that he only endured it with bitterness . . .[2]

The visit was interrupted by a call from Yturri, Montesquiou's companion and secretary. The Count had sent him to enquire after Verlaine's health.

There was a certain controversy about Montesquiou's patronage of Verlaine, and some considered that he played the Maecenas with unjustified ostentation. Cazals and Delahaye, wrote a critic, were more concerned about Verlaine than Montesquiou ever was; and if the Count gave him a sumptuous dinner at Foyot's, he was content to send his secretary to represent him. This dinner, on 7 December, was possibly the dinner which Barrès mentioned in his *Cahiers*. 'Verlaine's last outing was to dine with the president of some South American republic. He was ready, like a child, at four o'clock! He was dancing with delight when Yturri came to fetch him. After the highly spiced *écrevisses*, he leant over and said slyly: "I feel young this evening." And, later: "Did I behave all right?" '³

In his article 'Derniers moments de Verlaine', Georges Berthou gave a different account of the occasion.

For the past year Verlaine's sufferings had increased, he hardly went out any more ... The last time, it was a general from a [South] American republic who had come to invite him to dinner at Foyot's. The poet went there by cab. But his state of health no longer allowed him to enjoy the good food and wine, and it was with a certain bitterness that he came home and told his mistress: 'My dear, there were *timbales d'écrevisses* and I couldn't eat them.'

At the very end of his life, his only food was milk and Vichy water.⁴

'If you only knew, monsieur, how nice he'd become,' Eugénie was to tell a journalist. 'No, he didn't drink any more. I had managed *to curb him*. No more absinthe, or anything.'⁵ She herself thought that Verlaine died of cancer of the stomach. In fact he was suffering from more than one disease which could have killed him. He had cirrhosis of the liver and diabetes, he had a heart condition, and he had syphilis. He had once had a fine physique, and he might have reached old age if he had chosen another way of life. Finally he was to die of pneumonia. Years of alcoholism had weakened his resistance. His body was worn out.

It was, apparently, in December that Ernest Dowson saw 'our dear and incomparable Verlaine', and thought him 'at about the end of his tether'.⁶ That month, Verlaine also dined with Bouhélier in a restaurant in the rue Racine; and during the evening he took him, touchingly, into his confidence, and talked to him about Eugénie. Perhaps he hoped to make him forget the humiliating scene he had witnessed.

'Do you know that she was a dancer when she was young?' he said to me [reported Bouhélier]. 'I have a picture of her as a dancer. I'll show it to you.'

From one of the pockets of his jacket, which was all threadbare and covered with stains, he pulled out an old leather wallet. The photo he took out of it must have been twenty or twenty-five years old. The face it represented bore only a very distant likeness to the Eugénie Krantz, with the thick waist and the hard, stubborn expression, whom I knew. The photo showed a woman whom Manet might have painted, with very beautiful hair, a wreath of flowers in her hat, and a dress with a train.

'She was pretty,' said Verlaine, whose eyes seemed to caress this evocation.

The years which had since passed over this graceful head really did not seem to count for him ...

> Là! je l'ai, ta photographie
> Quand t'étais galopine,
> Avec, jà, tes yeux de défi,
>
> Tes petits yeux en trous de vrille,
> Avec alors de fiers tétins
> Promus en fiers seins aujourd'hui.
>
> Sous la longue robe si bien
> Qu'on portait vers soixante-seize
> Et sous la traîne et tout son train,
>
> On devine bien ton manège ...[7]

Now, for some minutes, recalled Bouhélier, Verlaine talked about Eugénie, 'and congratulated himself on living with her ... I could not bring myself to respond to his enthusiasm. I could not forget the terrible words she had used to him. If some presiding spirit had warned me that, in twenty or thirty days at most, Verlaine would be dead, I should have agreed with him in all he said.'[8]

Verlaine himself was now aware that he had not long to live. As Christmas approached, he made a final attempt to trace his son. On 23 December he wrote to Carton de Wiart:

Cher Monsieur,

I am going to bother you yet again – for the last time – about this son of mine. He was living with his employer, a watchmaker at Soignies, then he was ill for a day or two at Braine-le-Comte, which he left to live with his mother in a non-existent house in Brussels.

I should be so very grateful if you would have another look at this phantasmagoria, and let me know what you find out, even if there are 'horrors' to tell me . . .

My health isn't very good. I now have not only my old foe (increasingly painful lameness), but bronchitis, which has come to be chronic, a cough, fits of nausea, etc., and the beginnings of gastralgia. I'm taking great care of myself this time, but is it really too late? Anyway, what does it matter? . . .[9]

On 2 January he sent some corrected proofs to Dauze, with a covering note: 'Excuse my scrawl. I am writing in bed and in a fever, with a very severe kind of gastritis.'[10] That day he also wrote to Montesquiou, acknowledging a further hundred francs.

During the next few days, he grew worse. He spoke of death with serenity, even with macabre irony. To Gustave Lenglet, the editor of *La Revue rouge*, he said: 'What an irony of fate! . . . I shall die holding a bottle of Saint-Galmier [mineral water] . . . Do you see me cast in bronze like that?' And when Lenglet protested that Verlaine was not dying, Verlaine shook his head: 'No, I feel death coming . . . Death does not surprise the sage.'

On 5 January, he was delirious for a time; but he recovered by the afternoon. Lenglet returned with a colleague and brought the proof of a poem which Verlaine had written a few days earlier. Thirty-eight years ago, he had sent Victor Hugo his earliest known poem, 'La Mort'. Now, with visible emotion, he re-read the last poem he would write. It, too, was called 'Mort'; but he was aware that death was upon him.[11]

> Les Armes ont tu leurs ordres en attendant
> De vibrer à nouveau dans des mains admirables
> Ou scélérates, et, tristes, le bras pendant,
> Nous allons, mal rêveurs, dans le vague des Fables.

Les Armes ont tu leurs ordres qu'on attendait
Même chez les rêveurs mensongers que nous sommes,
Honteux de notre bras qui pendait et tardait,
Et nous allons, désappointés, parmi les hommes.

Armes, vibrez! mains admirables, prenez-les,
Mains scélérates à défaut des admirables!
Prenez-les donc et faites signe aux En-allés
Dans les fables plus incertaines que les sables.

Tirez du rêve notre exode, voulez-vous?
Nous mourons d'être ainsi languides, presqu'infâmes!
Armes, parlez! Vos ordres vont être pour nous
La vie enfin fleurie au bout, s'il faut des lames.

La mort que nous aimons, que nous eûmes toujours
Pour but de ce chemin où prospèrent la ronce
Et l'ortie, ô la mort sans plus ces émois lourds,
Délicieuse et dont la victoire est l'annonce![12]

On 7 January, Verlaine felt slightly better; and, at about ten
o'clock, when he had read the papers in bed, Eugénie and Zélie,
an old charwoman, helped him to get up. Cazals recorded: 'Dr.
Parisot had put him on a strict diet: no alcohol at all, and milk
diluted with Vichy water. Was he perhaps beginning to hope?...
But as Verlaine felt a need to see his friends, and Albert Cornuty
[a would-be poet and fervent disciple] had just arrived to get
news of the Master, Verlaine sent him to find Gustave Le Rouge
and his mistress for a friendly *déjeuner*. Verlaine, incidentally, only
drank a few sips of white wine mixed with Vichy water. The
meal was quite gay.'[13] Verlaine told them how, the previous week,
an admirer in San Francisco had sent him a lapis-lazuli paper-
knife as big as a sabre, and a huge bottle of rum. Alas, he had not
been able to drink rum for a long time, and the paper-knife had
arrived smashed to pieces. The pudding was served on old plates
with pictures on them. Verlaine took a childish pleasure in finding
likenesses between the people on the plates and some of his friends.
One plate showed a watchmaker in his shop. 'That's my son,

Georges,' he said. 'I'll probably never see him again.' He added: 'All the same, I'll leave him a name as good as any other.' At the end of the meal, he felt very tired, and went back to bed.[14]

That night, wrote Cazals, he wanted to get up, 'but his strength failed him, and he collapsed on the rug beside the bed, to the great anxiety of Eugénie. She tried in vain to lift him up. She did not dare to wake her neighbours across the landing, and she left him sprawling on the floor.' Eugénie would not have been too timid to ask for help; she was probably drunk. She and Zélie, said Delahaye, used to drink themselves into a stupor with punch. However, she covered Verlaine with blankets, and there he lay till morning, when she and Zélie lifted him on to his bed.

Dr Chauffart arrived from Broussais, and he prescribed mustard poultice in an attempt to revive the prostrate body, but he saw that all prescriptions were useless. Verlaine tried to tear away the poulticer, which was scorching him.[15] Montesquiou apparently misunderstood the gesture. He said that Verlaine attempted to move imaginary funeral wreaths from his bed.[16] Then, at about five o'clock, Verlaine asked for a priest. A young priest from Saint-Étienne-du-Mont, the future abbé Schoenhentz, received his confession, and gave him the last sacraments.[17]

Verlaine died at seven o'clock that evening, 8 January 1896. He had been deeply in love with life; he had always spoken of death 'with a shuddering revolt for the thought of ever going away into the cold'.[18]

66

Maurice Barrès came that evening; he was the first to pay homage. He was followed by Mendès, who recalled that Verlaine's face was the colour of snow, and by Montesquiou, accompanied by his secretary. Yturri took an orange from the mantelpiece, and peeled it; he ate it, and threw the peel under the deathbed. Huysmans came, and Albert Mérat, who had known Verlaine in the days of the Hôtel de Ville, and Léon Dierx, who would succeed Verlaine as Prince of Poets. Cazals sat by the embers of the fire in Verlaine's room, drawing him for the last time.[1]

Next morning, in *L'Écho de Paris*, Saint-Georges de Bouhélier read the news of Verlaine's death. He was in the rue de Rome, and, by some strange coincidence, he was standing under Mallarmé's windows. 'And if, by chance, that old magician had paused at one of them, he might have seen me, weeping, with a paper in my hand, standing there as if I was petrified.'[2]

Three-quarters of an hour later, Bouhélier was in the rue Descartes. The news of Verlaine's death was already spreading, and neighbours were standing, gossiping, on doorsteps. They blamed everything on Eugénie's negligence.

My throat was constricted [wrote Bouhélier]. When I reached the dead man's rooms, and met friends I knew, I burst into tears. Even if I had lost a relation, I shouldn't have felt more grief.

The room itself had been hung with black, but the little canary in its gilded cage was singing desperately. In the dining-room I found Eugénie ... When I appeared, she went hysterical, wept bitterly, and insisted that what had happened hadn't been her fault. I hadn't yet accused her of anything, but she forestalled me. And then she told me how the poor man had died.

'A moment ago,' she continued, without transition, 'an Englishman arrived. He wanted a memento of Paul at any price. I let him take a pen-holder. Do you know how much he paid me? A louis. What do you think of that?'

Obviously she was astounded. She was now looking through the drawers to rummage out things to sell. I learned afterwards that she had had to go to a local stationer's to buy pencils and pen-holders. She did not want to be taken unawares.

'Do you want to see him?' she asked.

I left her to her researches and slipped into the death chamber ... My heart was pounding. I had never until then found myself in the presence of death. Verlaine had been laid out on his bed. He was wearing a white shirt, and an evening-dress cravat ... His face gave the impression of deep peace ... He looked as if he lay in Paradise. I only stayed for a moment. I was overcome by emotion. Some fine pink candles had been set out round the bed: they were party candles, probably the only ones they had found.[3]

Verlaine, remembered Merrill, looked 'unimaginably fine.

There was still a smile of beatitude on his lips. His head was tilted slightly to the left, as if he had been peacefully asleep. The poor old faun was dead indeed: only the soul of the saint shone forth from his body. I had forgotten, long ago, how one ought to pray. But I bent over the dead Verlaine, and I kissed his brow.'[4]

Achille Segard would recall how 'young men were disputing the honour of keeping a final vigil ... The little room, hung with a cheap, faded wallpaper, was completely filled with flowers, and in the restricted space groups of friends stood silent, in such grief that it seemed as if each of them had lost his dearest friend.'[5]

Verlaine's former wife, in Brussels, learned of his death from the papers; and she was moved to unexpected tears. 'Certainly, if I had known he was so near his end, I should have done all I could to send Georges to him. Only a few months earlier, Georges had written to his father, and his father had replied. But now he was doing his military service at Lille, and he was in the army hospital.'[6] Cazals had sent him the news by telegram.

At about noon a doctor came to establish the cause of death. He said that Verlaine's body was worn out; there were ten illnesses rather than one.[7] Meoni came to make a death-mask;[8] Mallarmé, overcome with grief, slipped into the death-chamber, and, among the palms and wreaths, he left a bunch of violets.[9]

When Gabriel de Lautrec arrived that evening, he found Cazals ... alone with three devoted women. They were all distraught after nights of vigil, and they counted on me [he wrote] to let them rest a little on the night before the funeral.

Paul Verlaine seemed to be sleeping peacefully. I settled down in an armchair by the window, and I found myself alone with him. It was January, and it was as cold as that winter month can be. I huddled up in my overcoat. They hadn't been able to light a fire *pour des raisons*, as the dead man would have said. Luckily I had some tobacco, so I filled my pipe, and lit it. I don't know how many pipes I smoked, on that funeral night ... but I certainly know that I've never been so cold in my life. I tried in vain to comfort myself with the thought that I was burning a kind of incense at the deathbed of a man of genius. That only gave me moral warmth. And he himself, I am sure, would rather have been stretched out on my little divan in the impasse Nicole, even to drink cold coffee.

And so the night passed, endless, in that silent tête-à-tête. And, when dawn appeared, ... I thought that the undertaker would be arriving soon. There was a pair of scissors on the mantelpiece. I took them, ... and cut off a lock of the poet's greying hair, ... and put it in my wallet. A few moments later, the door opened, and there was Léon Vanier, the publisher and friend of Paul Verlaine. He was really overcome by grief.

Then came a photographer from *Le Monde illustré*. He had no doubt kindly taken it on himself to represent, single-handed, the illustrated papers of France. Then came the gentlemen in black who are the last servants of the dead.[10]

On Friday, 10 January, the day of the funeral, the humble *quartier* was stupefied by the distinction of the mourners. On the threshold of the squalid house in the rue Descartes, the most famous poets and men of letters in France waited to accompany the body of Verlaine.

As the undertakers were about to bear away the coffin, Eugénie said: 'Someone's taken Verlaine's religious book. If they don't give it back at once, I'll create a commotion at the grave.' Someone had taken it as a memento, but it was returned. There was no doubt that Eugénie had loved Verlaine, but her love was primitive and possessive. Before they left for the church, she said: 'If Esther comes, I'll create a scene.' It was no doubt Montesquiou who reminded her: 'You have had Verlaine all to yourself. You have been wonderful. Now you must make sacrifices. You can't insist that Esther doesn't enter the church. The church is for everyone.' Eugénie accepted.[11] It is said that Verlaine's admirers had seriously considered whether or not she should attend the funeral. Finally, wearing a widow's weeds, she drove to the church with Rachilde. She had been allowed to attend largely on the insistence of Maurice Barrès.[12]

At ten o'clock that morning, a congregation of several hundred assembled at Saint-Étienne-du-Mont. There, behind the high altar, rested the earthly remains of Pascal and Racine; and there, now, the funeral service was held for Verlaine.

The organist was Fauré, who had set Verlaine's poetry to music. In the congregation stood Heredia and Sully-Prudhomme, the representative of the Parnassians, and Moréas, who had been Verlaine's disciple. There was Jean Lahor, Dr Henri Cazalis, who had attempted to safeguard Verlaine's health, and Camille Mauclair, who would put Verlaine's funeral into his novel, *Le Soleil des morts*. There was Vanier, who had published Verlaine, and was now among the principal mourners.[13]

Among Verlaine's young admirers were some of the Naturists; they included Le Blond and Bouhélier. 'However different we were in our everyday behaviour and in our conception of poetry, we united,' wrote Bouhélier, 'in our common admiration for Verlaine.' Among the more celebrated mourners they could see Jean Richepin and the tall, distinctive figure of Barrès. Barrès himself was watching Eugénie, who was looking fiercely for Esther. 'From my place,' he remembered, 'I could see that terrible *frog's* face, a flat, broad face convulsed by grief, turning round, keeping watch on the door. Beside her were two other prostitutes, utter rabble! Oh, they were three unforgettable mourners!'[14]

Edmond Lepelletier stood near the coffin. The chief mourner was Charles de Sivry, whom some of the congregation recognised as the pianist from le Chat Noir. He was only the half-brother of the former Mme Verlaine, but Georges Verlaine had been unable to come, and Sivry had been asked to represent the poet's family. As Bouhélier said, he symbolised its dispersal and its ruin.

At about eleven o'clock the procession formed for the hour-long journey to the Cimetière des Batignolles. Robert de Montesquiou complained because Bibi-la-Purée was given the place of honour behind the hearse. Crowds lined the streets of the Latin Quarter. Coppée and Barrès, Mendès and Lepelletier were the pallbearers. When they reached the quais, Coppée was exhausted, and had to continue the journey in a carriage. Mallarmé took his place beside the coffin. Lepelletier struggled with his emotion. Mendès lit a cigar and smoked it. Suddenly, aware of his gross impropriety, he threw it into the gutter. But Cazals said that, when they reached the avenue de Clichy, Mendès bought a paper, and read it as he walked beside the coffin.[15]

Paul Fort had overstrained himself with his work for the Théâtre d'Art, but he had risen from his sick-bed to join the procession; and nearly half a century later he recalled that army of poets,

... on a morning of swirling snow, coming down the Boulevard Saint-Michel, that white army whose tears were frozen by the cold ...

More than two thousand poets, songwriters and men of letters followed the procession to the end – and, among them, side by side, were the ragged Bibi-la-Purée, and the 'illustrious' count and poet Robert de Montesquiou, elegantly dressed, and as glossy as a good cigar ...

The descent down the Boulevard Saint-Michel ... of the whole of French – or at least Parisian – literature ... was a vision not to be effaced from any memory.[16]

The sun shone like a benediction. Never in January, so it seemed, had a more brilliant azure sky sparkled over Paris. When the procession began to make its way along the quais, the air appeared diamanté. The mourners kept the slow pace of the horses which, with their funeral plumage nodding, drew the hearse. The driver of the hearse looked like a messenger from the world of ghosts. The procession moved on; and then, suddenly, remembered Lautrec,

... the street grew wider, and the décor changed. In the distance, against the intense blue sky, stood the Opéra. In front of us, the coachman's black three-cornered hat appeared in dramatic silhouette against the golden blue from above. A cold wind blew across the procession, and made the flowers shiver. The hearse was bearing the poet to the last Opéra ball. Chance brings such encounters. We passed the shops where they sold lace and fans. The sun was inimitable. It was the décor of the *fêtes galantes*, witnessing the funeral of Watteau.[17]

At the cemetery, Lepelletier was finally overcome. Barrès delivered an oration in a voice as resonant as a mausoleum. 'Before he spoke,' wrote Renard, 'he had handed his hat to Montesquiou. For a moment I wanted to applaud, to thump my cane on the tomb, but suppose the dead had awakened?'[18] Barrès was still watching Eugénie. 'At the cemetery, she leant over the grave:

"Verlaine! All your friends are here!" A magnificent cry. And that was why he loved her.'[19]

Then Mendès, so Renard recalled,

... spoke of climbing a staircase of aereal marble, with rose-laurels on either side, and candles shining at the top. It was very pretty, and it could have been applied to any one.

Coppée was applauded at first. People turned cold when he reserved himself a place near Verlaine, in Paradise ...

Mallarmé. One will have to read his speech again. Lepelletier made a materialistic profession of faith, although he had no constituents. The great virtue of Barrès is his tact ...

At the restaurant, we were joking: we reserved a table and ordered a meal for Coppée's funeral.[20]

The literary world had lost none of its harshness or its malice.

> Hommes durs! Vie atroce et laide d'ici-bas!
> Ah! que du moins, loin des baisers et des combats,
> Quelque chose demeure un peu sur la montagne,
>
> Quelque chose du cœur enfantin et subtil,
> Bonté, respect! Car qu'est-ce qui nous accompagne,
> Et vraiment, quand la mort viendra, que reste-t-il?[21]

67

Today, three-quarters of a century later, there remains the legend of the vagabond, the prisoner and the supreme bohemian. Verlaine, the husband of Mathilde, slips from the memory. Verlaine's odyssey with Rimbaud holds the imagination. Never has there been a comparable liaison between two poets of recognised genius. After these brilliant months of freedom, Verlaine becomes the prisoner; the renegade becomes a Catholic convert. And, finally, the social pariah, living in the Cour Saint-François, in fifth-floor attics and in Left Bank cafés, lingering in hospitals on public assistance, dependent on the charity of admirers, torn between two middle-aged women of dubious virtue, becomes the poet of international fame. Alcoholic, worn by years of illness and disease, sometimes destitute, sometimes tempted to seek release in death, unable, any more, to write his poetry, Verlaine is elected Prince of Poets.

Verlaine published his first book at a moment when French poetry was dominated by the Parnassians: by a belief in technical perfection and by the creed of impassibility. Verlaine was a technician of consummate skill, he understood the value of discipline; but he could not be impassible. He was, by his nature, from the first, the most responsive and personal of poets.

To be a poet [he maintained, at the end of his life], I think one must live intensely, in every way – and remember it . . .

As I see it, then, the poet must be absolutely sincere, but completely conscientious as a writer. He must hide nothing of himself; but, in his honesty, he must show all the dignity which can be expected of him. He must show his concern for this dignity, as far as he can, if not in the perfection of form, at least in the imperceptible but effective effort towards this high and demanding ideal: I was going to say this virtue.

A poet – myself – has attempted this task. Perhaps he has failed, but he has certainly done all he can to come out of it with honour.[1]

Verlaine, in his best work, had practised this creed. He had lived intensely, and no poet had recorded his life more consistently. At times, it is true, he had hinted rather than recorded, he had suppressed when he might have told, he had spoken when he might have been silent. He had been ambiguous and exhibitionist, he had occasionally played a part. But his life and his poetry cannot be separated, and he reflects his changing moods, his inconsistencies, his spiritual progress, as much as his permanent qualities and his weaknesses; and this he does in a way that no French poet had done before him. Beside the poems of Verlaine, the more personal poems of Hugo sound like theatrical rhetoric, the melancholy and piety of Lamartine sound dated, academic and unconvincing. Musset had lived intensely, as a poet should; but Musset, as Verlaine emphasised, had not given himself completely in his work, and Musset had not been a perfect artist, for he had not laboured to achieve perfect form.

Of all his predecessors in French poetry, it was Baudelaire who was Verlaine's spiritual ancestor. There was a manliness, an intellectual depth, a spiritual power in Baudelaire with which Verlaine was simply not endowed. Verlaine could not rise to the majesty of the poems which Baudelaire addressed to Mme Sabatier; and he did not approach the fierce, exotic passion of the poems to Jeanne Duval. Baudelaire's despair and grief, his anguish of soul, were more bitter and more profound. But there remains a remarkable affinity between their poems of mood. Verlaine was instinctively in sympathy with him. *Poèmes saturniens* was a tribute to this poetic kinship. Verlaine, like Baudelaire, recognised the correspondences between the arts, and between the senses; Verlaine, like Baudelaire, recorded the inescapable *mal du siècle*.

The profound originality of Charles Baudelaire is, to my mind [Verlaine had written], his powerful presentation of the essential modern man: ... the physical man of to-day, as he has been made by the refinements of an excessive civilisation: modern man, with his sharpened, vibrant senses, his painfully subtle mind, his intellect steeped in tobacco, his blood burned up by alcohol ... It is, I repeat, Charles Baudelaire who presents the sensitive man, and he presents him as a type, or, if you like, as a *hero* ... The future historian of our age should study *Les Fleurs du mal* with pious attention. It is the quintessence, the extreme concentration of a whole element of this century.[2]

This was not only an acute assessment of Baudelaire; it proved to be an unconscious self-portrait. Where Baudelaire had recorded the Parisian of the 1840s and 1850s, Verlaine recorded the man of the following generation: the man who lived through the Franco-Prussian War, the Siege of Paris, the Commune and the Republic, the outbursts of anarchy, the moods of defeat, disgust and despair, the aimlessness, the excessive chauvinism. A hundred different and often conflicting influences were felt. It was an increasingly philistine and materialistic age which judged success, American fashion, by money. It was the age of 'carnal spirit and unhappy flesh', which welcomed Naturalism and the novels of Zola. It was also the age of aesthetes like Robert de Montesquiou and Huysmans' Des Esseintes. There were influences from abroad: the influence of English aestheticism, of German music, of Russian nihilism. There were disturbing signs of technical progress. The generation of Verlaine lived in the disarray of a stage of transition; as Raynaud observed: 'It was a searching, artistic, refined, but unstable generation; and, drawn by diverse influences, it struggled desperately, in the general débâcle, in search of some or other certainty ... Verlaine is the voice of this generation ... He reflects its vain agitation, its incoherence and its ungovernable impotence.'[3]

He did so in a manner that was entirely his own. If Baudelaire had inspired him at the start of his career, Rimbaud had reminded him that poetry must be distilled till it became a new language and expressed the hitherto unknown. Rimbaud – like Baudelaire – had entered Verlaine's life with marvellous precision. He was not only supreme in Verlaine's emotional existence, he was also his poetic kin.

Baudelaire and Rimbaud were Verlaine's literary mentors. Verlaine's own life, brief though it was, embraced a world of experience. He lived feverishly, and, as he told Vance Thompson, he wrote *en fièvre*. As Arthur Symons recognised:

Few men ever got so much out of their lives, or lived so fully, so intensely, with such a genius for living. That, indeed, is why he was a great poet. Verlaine was a man who gave its full value to every moment, who got out of every moment all that that moment had to give him. It was not always, not often, perhaps, pleasure. But it was energy, the vital force of a nature which was always receiving and giving out, never at rest, never passive, or indifferent, or hesitating ... He sinned, and it was with all his humanity; he repented, and it was with all his soul. And to every occurrence of the day, to every mood of the mind, to every impulse of the creative instinct, he brought the same unparalleled sharpness of sensation.[4]

As a literary critic, Verlaine had introduced Mallarmé, Rimbaud and Corbière to the French public; and *Les Poètes maudits*, with his eager, repeated appreciations of Rimbaud, and his early assessment of Baudelaire, were his most significant contributions to criticism. The twenty-seven biographies of poets and men of letters which he wrote for the series *Les Hommes d'aujourd'hui* were often generous, but they were not profound. Verlaine, as he said himself, was not a critic, he was a man of feeling.

As a writer of prose, he is little more than an unreliable source for the biographer or the literary historian. Charles Le Goffic wrote: 'His prose works, rough and strange, with a syntax dictated only by the impression of the moment, will always surprise those who have not heard him talk. They will delight the others: they were exactly like his conversation, unpredictable, with all its brackets and parentheses. In a few minutes it went through every shade of mischievousness and passion.'[5]

As a poet, he had done service to modern literature. He had restored the free use of metre: given back to poets the unfettered use of their instrument of work. He had deliberately broken every rule of prosody, used every metre from five to thirteen syllables; he had used combinations of metres which had not been used since the sixteenth century. He had done as he pleased with cesuras and *enjambements*, with masculine and feminine rhymes. He had introduced foreign words, and vulgarisms. He had refined the French language until it became a new instrument in his hands. '*Suggestion*,' said Mallarmé. 'That is the dream. It is the perfect use of this mystery which constitutes the symbol.' Verlaine used his marvellous technical powers, as well as his instincts, to record suggestion. Only his two literary mentors, and, perhaps, Gérard de Nerval, or Mallarmé, understood the art of mystery and suggestion like Verlaine. He understood it in his first book, in 'Mon rêve familier'; he understood it, perfectly, in 'Kaléidoscope' in *Jadis et Naguère*, where a broken mosaic of memories crowds upon him, some apparently trivial, some serious, all of them invested with an undefined, disturbing significance.

> Ce sera comme quand on rêve et qu'on s'éveille !
> Et que l'on se rendort et que l'on rêve encor
> De la même féerie et du même décor,
> L'été, dans l'herbe, au bruit moiré d'un vol d'abeille . . .[6]

No-one else catches, like Verlaine, this infinitely fragile state between dreaming and waking, between imagination and reality. He expresses a thought before it is formulated, an instinct before it is recognised, an emotion which has yet to be acknowledged. 'In many short poems which are like the tremors of a soul, caught as they pass, it is hardly Verlaine who is talking any more, it is some or other human soul, impersonal, intemporal, it is almost the soul of things gaining awareness of itself in the soul of a man.'[7]

The best of Verlaine's landscapes are, again, the landscapes of the soul, the 'Paysages tristes' of *Poèmes saturniens*, some of the 'Ariettes oubliées' in *Romances sans paroles*, and certain poems in *Sagesse*: 'Le son du cor s'afflige vers les bois . . . ,' or 'L'échelonnement des haies'. 'Bournemouth', in *Amour*, is both a landscape and an impression of serenity. Symons wrote wisely that, to Verlaine, 'physical sight and spiritual vision, by some strange alchemical operation, were one'.[8] *Fêtes galantes*, which was one of the most accomplished of his books, contains a series of tiny pictures of an eighteenth-century world; and yet these are not mere transpositions of art. They give a brilliant suggestion of theatre, of elegant and artificial revelry, of fugitive pleasures watched by a hard and brooding destiny. They are charming, in the style of Watteau, delicately licentious, in the manner of Fragonard; and yet they are undoubtedly disturbing. They create an atmosphere as much as a scene.

> Votre âme est un paysage choisi
> Que vont charmant masques et bergamasques . . .

There is a poem written by Verlaine on the threshold of manhood: a poem which he alone could have written. It is at once the landscape of a soul, and a microcosm of the world which Watteau and his contemporaries painted. It is the first poem in *Fêtes galantes*. The last poem, 'Colloque sentimental', concentrates within itself a world of anguish: an anguish half explained, yet completely told. It is a marvel of suggestive power.

No French poet has recorded certain moods with the exquisite touch of Verlaine: the vague melancholy of *Chanson d'automne* and 'Il pleure dans mon cœur . . .'; the vast peace of 'La lune blanche . . .', written for Mathilde: a poem which was music long before Fauré discovered it. In such poems as these, and in

'C'est l'extase langoureuse . . .', which he wrote for Rimbaud, and in the poem of infinite regret which he wrote, in prison: 'Le ciel est, par-dessus le toit . . . ,' Verlaine is unequalled in French literature. Simple in word and form, he seems to write almost without effort. In their own inherent melody, in their emotive power, his lyrics come as close as any poems have ever come to music.

As a poet of love, Verlaine is uneven. The Lesbian poems of the early years are written with gentle tact, under the influence of Baudelaire. The poems he addressed to Mathilde generally suggest a suitor who is trying to conform. The poems to his mistresses, in his later years, were set down when his mind was dulled, his inspiration gone. They are sometimes trivial, sometimes crude; only rarely (one recalls a fragment in *Le Livre posthume*) does Verlaine remind us that he was a great poet. Verlaine wrote no poem to a woman which, in intensity of feeling, approached the poem that he wrote on the rumour of Rimbaud's death. 'Læti et Errabundi' was not simply a record of physical passion, it was a tribute to the only complete relationship in his life.

In 1923 Georg Brandes, the Danish critic, wrote: 'The historian . . . will probably point out the ground swell which seems to be bearing modern French literature towards Rome and Catholicism. It seems to me at the moment to be almost entirely ultra-Catholic; it had already been so since the conversion of Verlaine . . . To-day Paul Claudel is setting the tone for French literature, and it is the same tone.'[9] It was ironic that Claudel should be mentioned. At the thought of Verlaine and Rimbaud, he reached instinctively for his chaplet; and he found hypocrisy in *Sagesse*. Perhaps, as a religious poet, Verlaine has been overestimated. His religious poems lack the conviction of some of his love poems, the original-ity of his landscapes and his poems of mood. Some critics maintain that his dialogue with God in *Sagesse* is the height of his poetic achievement; yet, honest though his conversion was, there remains a certain convention about the work. It was remarkable that *Sagesse* appeared when Naturalism was at its height; it was remark-able that he should write a book religious in inspiration. And yet the poems in *Sagesse* which one now recalls are not the more theological pieces: they are, yet again, the poems of mood and suggestion, the recollection of forbidden pleasures.

'*L'art, mes enfants, c'est d'être absolument soi-même.*' So Verlaine had explained in *Bonheur*. No poet had been more himself than Verlaine. He recorded all his life, all his raptures and regrets, all his bitterness, licentiousness and melancholy, all his humour, violence, weakness, and simplicity. Verlaine's was at times a subtle simplicity. It was that of a child; it was also that of a consummate poet.

For his genius is not in doubt. French poetry was changed by Verlaine. As Verhaeren said: 'He fused himself so profoundly with beauty, that he left upon it an imprint which was new and henceforth eternal.'[10]

NOTES

Bib. Nat.＝Bibliothèque Nationale
Corr.＝Correspondance
Œs cs.＝Œuvres complètes
Œs posths.＝Œuvres posthumes

For Verlaine's prose works and correspondence, I have generally used
the Messein edition. For his poetry I have generally used the Garnier
edition by Jacques Robichez and the Pléiade edition by Jacques Borel;
these are referred to, in the notes, as Robichez and Borel.

I

1　For an appreciation of Metz, see *Confessions*: *Œs cs.*, v, 7 sqq.,
　　and *Metz. Fragment*: *Œs posths.*, II, 129–30
2　Verlaine: 'Paysages', Robichez, 394
3　'Conférence faite à Anvers', *Œs posths.*, III, 216
4　The best account of Verlaine's Belgian connections is given by
　　Gustave Vanwelkenhuyzen: *Verlaine en Belgique*
5　*Ibid.*
6　*Confessions*: *Œs cs.*, v, 8

2

1　*Confessions*: *Œs cs.*, v, 18
2　*Ibid.*, 21–2
3　*Ibid.*, 23
4　*Ibid.*, 26–7
5　Ad. van Bever: *La Vie douloureuse de Verlaine*, 9

3

1　*Confessions*, 55
2　*Ibid.*, 69–70, note. This testimonial was later in the Barthou
　　Collection (*Bibliothèque de M. Louis Barthou*, II, 204)

3 Quoted from the catalogue of the sale of the Collection J.D. at the Palais Galliéra, 6 and 7 December 1961
4 Edmond Lepelletier: *Paul Verlaine*, 55
5 *Confessions*, 80

4

1 Lepelletier: *op. cit.*, 65–6
2 Mme Alphonse Daudet: *Souvenirs autour d'un groupe littéraire*, 37–41. A letter from Heredia among the Cazals papers illumines his relationship with Verlaine (Bib. Nat. N. A. Fr. 13150 ff 79–80). It is postmarked 13 December 1891; it was presumably sent to Verlaine when he was writing his essay on Heredia for the series *Les Hommes d'Aujourd'hui*.

> Excusez-moi, mon cher Verlaine, d'avoir tant tardé à répondre à votre aimable lettre. Elle a couru après moi par toute la Bretagne. Elle n'en est pas moins la bien revenue. Je suis très fier de l'honneur qu'un poète tel que vous me veut faire et je me tiens à la disposition de votre dessinateur. Il est venu le lendemain de mon arrivée. J'étais souffrant et je regrette qu'on l'ait renvoyé sans me prévenir. Veuillez m'excuser auprès de lui et croire à toute ma vieille et cordiale admiration.
>
> J. M. De Heredia
> 11 *bis* rue Balzac

The essay on Heredia (reprinted in Verlaine: *Œs cs.*, v, 459 et sqq.) appeared with a drawing of Heredia by Cazals. One suspects that it was this portrait which Cazals later tried to sell to the author of *Les Trophées*. Heredia replied (Bib. Nat. N.A. Fr. 13152 f 170):

> Mon cher artiste,
> Merci de votre gracieuseté. Mais je ne veux pas accepter ce portrait dont je vous autorise à tirer profit. Je ne suis malheureusement pas assez riche pour vous en offrir le prix qu'il vaut. Excusez-moi et faites mes amitiés à Verlaine.
>
> J. M. De Heredia
> Ce 15 Xbre 94

3 Lepelletier: *op. cit.*, 67, 76, 90; Claude Cuénot: *L'État présent des études verlainiennes*, 49–50

5

1   Laurent Tailhade: *Quelques fantômes de jadis*, 182. See also Armand
    Lods: *Les Premières éditions de Verlaine. Mercure de France*, 15
    October 1924, 402–24
2   Quoted in Georges Servières: *Emmanuel Chabrier, 1841–1894*
3   Joseph Desaymard: *Emmanuel Chabrier d'après ses Lettres*, 53.
    Francis Poulenc: *Emmanuel Chabrier*, 28 sqq., 37
4   Servières: *op. cit., passim*; Poulenc: *op. cit.*, 185–7
5   Fernand Clerget: *Émile Blémont*, 27–8, 30
6   A. de Bersaucourt: *Au Temps des Parnassiens. Nina de Villard et ses
    amis*, 7–8, 12–14 and *passim*.
7   George Moore: *Memoirs of my dead life*, 66–7, 69
8   For Charles Cros, see Jean-Émile Bayard: *The Latin Quarter past
    and present*, 83–4; A. de Bersaucourt: *Au temps des Parnassiens;*
    Jacques Brenner: *Charles Cros*
9   Catulle Mendès: *La Légende du Parnasse contemporain*, 224–6
10 François Coppée: *Mon Franc parler*, 3e série, 62 sqq.
11 14 September 1867. Bib. Nat. N.A. Fr. 24803, ff 371–2
12 Fernand Calmettes: *Leconte de Lisle et ses amis*, 279

6

1   *Confessions*, 81
2   *Çavitri*. Robichez, 45
3   *Épilogue*. Robichez, 62
4   'Conférence faite à Anvers', *Œs posths.*, III, 218
5   *L'Éclair*. Undated cutting in the Doucet Collection
6   *Charles Baudelaire*. Verlaine: *Œs posths.*, II, 8–9
7   Verlaine: *Critique et Conférences. Œs posths.*, II, 248
8   Jules Lemaître: *Les Contemporains*, 4e série, 88
9   *Chanson d'automne*. Robichez, 39
10 22 November 1866. Henri Mondor: *L'Amitié de Verlaine et de
    Mallarmé*, 18
11 Undated letter, probably written late in 1866. *Ibid.*, 21–2
12 Charles de Martrin-Donos: *Verlaine intime*, 33
13 Lepelletier: *op. cit.*, 145–6

7

1 *Le Temps*. Undated cutting in the Doucet Collection
2 Vœu. Robichez, 28
3 Lepelletier; *op. cit.*, 183–4
4 *Ibid.*, 142–3
5 Borel, xix
6 For Verlaine's *Louis XVII*, see pp. 318, 335
7 Coppée was not entirely loyal to Verlaine, and he was not averse to making sharp personal criticisms, as the *Goncourt Journal* bears witness (xviii, 190; xx, 227–8)

8

1 Robichez, 68
2 Robichez, 67–71
3 It seems unlikely that Verlaine missed the Exposition du boulevard des Italiens, which embraced the work of Pater, Lancret, Boucher, Chardin, Fragonard and Greuze – and that of other French artists. Gautier devoted seven articles to the exhibition in *Le Moniteur universel* between 30 August and 15 December 1860. For Gautier's art criticism, see: Joanna Richardson: *Théophile Gautier: His Life and Times*, 130 et sqq.
4 Robichez: *op. cit.*, 69
5 *Ibid.*, 86
6 *Ibid.*, 83–4
7 *Ibid.*, 91
8 George Moore: *Confessions of a Young Man*, 51
9 Colloque sentimental. Robichez, 96–7

9

1 François Porché: *Verlaine tel qu'il fut*, 71–3
2 For this account of Mathilde Mauté and her family, I am largely indebted to her own *Mémoires de ma vie*, and to François Porché's introduction to them

3 Ex-Mme Paul Verlaine: *Mémoires de ma vie*, 61. In *La Passion de Claude Debussy*, 22, Marcel Dietschy records that in 1852 Mme Sivry married Théodore-Jean Mauté, 'propriétaire, fils d'épicier (10 à 15.000 fr. de rente, précise un rapport de police)'

4 Porché: Introduction to *Mémoires de ma vie*, 18–19. Dietschy confirms that Mme Mauté was a music teacher (*op. cit.*, 23). He describes her as '*unsurpatrice du titre d'ancienne élève de Chopin, fausse marquise, . . . excellente pianiste*' (*ibid.*, 24)

5 Ex-Mme Paul Verlaine: *op. cit.*, 58. Dietschy (*op. cit.*, 22) says that the records of Saint-Germain-en-Laye state that the 'Marquis de Sivry' was the son of the hatmaker Michel Sivry

6 Porché: Introduction to Ex-Mme Paul Verlaine: *op. cit.*, 10

7 For some appreciations of Charles de Sivry, who died in 1900, see ex-Mme Paul Verlaine, *op. cit.*, 269–72.

8 Ex-Mme Paul Verlaine, *op. cit.*, 42

9 *Ibid.*, 82

10 *Ibid.*, 86–7. Mathilde is often an unreliable witness. She had in fact met Verlaine before *Fêtes galantes* had appeared. Perhaps she had read 'Colloque sentimental' in *L'Artiste* on 1 July 1868, but she could not have read 'Le Parc': Verlaine wrote no poem with that title. Possibly she was thinking again of 'Dans le vieux parc solitaire et glacé . . .' Incidentally, Mathilde was sixteen, not fourteen, when *Fêtes galantes* appeared.

10

1 Ex-Mme Paul Verlaine: *op. cit.*, 89

2 *Ibid.*, 91–2

3 Robichez, 102, note

4 *Ibid.*

5 Porché, *op, cit.*, 89

6 Robichez, 102–3, note

7 *Ibid.*, 103, note

8 *Ibid.*

9 Ex-Mme Paul Verlaine: *op. cit.*, 93

10 *Ibid.*, 79

11 *Ibid.*, 93–4

12 Doucet MS 7203–58

13 Robichez, 103–4

II

1 Ex-Mme Paul Verlaine: *op. cit.*, 98–100
2 Robichez, 118–19
3 *Ibid.*, 119
4 Ex-Mme Paul Verlaine: *op. cit.*, 101
5 Robichez, 120
6 *Ibid.*, 120–1
7 *Ibid.*, 122
8 *Ibid.*, 124–5
9 Ex-Mme Paul Verlaine: *op. cit.*, 105–6
10 *Ibid.*, 107–8
11 *Ibid.*, 108
12 *Ibid.*, 108–9
13 *Ibid.*, 109
14 *Ibid.*, 109–10; and see Jean Rousselot: *De quoi vivait Verlaine?*, 18

12

1 Fernand Gregh: *La Fenêtre ouverte*, 20
2 Ex-Mme Paul Verlaine: *op. cit.*, 112–14
3 Robichez, 126
4 Ex-Mme Paul Verlaine: *op. cit.*, 114–16
5 *Ibid.*, 118–19
6 Doucet MS 7203–415
7 Ex-Mme Paul Verlaine: *op. cit.*, 124
8 *Ibid.*, 97

13

1 Ex-Mme Paul Verlaine: *op. cit.*, 97
2 *Ibid.*, 125–6
3 Quoted by Jules Claretie in *Le Temps*, 16 January 1896; reprinted in Claretie: *La Vie à Paris, 1896*, 17–18
4 Ex-Mme Paul Verlaine: *op. cit.*, 126; Doucet MS 7203–92
5 Paul Verlaine: *Edmund de Goncourt. Les Hommes d'Aujourd'hui*, Œs cs., v, 317 sqq.

6 Ex-Mme Paul Verlaine: *op. cit.*, 160–2
7 *Mémoires d'un Veuf, Œs cs.*, IV, 215
8 Ex-Mme Paul Verlaine: *op. cit.*, 162–70
9 28 May 1871; Goncourt *Journal*, X, 13
10 Clerget: *op. cit.*, 47
11 Lepelletier: *op. cit.*, 248
12 Clerget: *op. cit.*, 212–13
13 Ex-Mme Paul Verlaine: *op. cit.*, 172–5
14 For my account of Rimbaud, I am very much indebted to Enid Starkie's *Arthur Rimbaud* (London, 1961)

14

1 Years later, Verlaine's friend Cazals was concerned with the disagreements between Georges Izambard and Rimbaud's brother-in-law, Paterne Berrichon. These had been aired in the *Mercure de France* in December 1910, and in the following January and February. On 23 October 1913, Izambard wrote to Cazals from Neuilly (N. A. Fr. 13152 ff 177–8):

> Voici les dates que vous me demandez (celles de mes articles) ... Après quoi je ne lui ai plus répondu, le laissant *contester* les dates dont j'avais les *preuves*. Quand il est revenu à la charge, parlant d'une rupture violente entre Rimbaud et moi (Rimbaud 'à la suite d'une dénonciation de moi', m'aurait écrit une lettre grossièrement insolente) j'ai relevé cette *infamie* comme il convenait, me réservant de lui cracher mon mépris sans périphrase quand le moment sera venu; c'est à dire dans mon livre ... Mon article dans *Vers et Prose* est dans le No de Jan.–Fév.–Mars 1911 (tome XXIV).

The same folio of letters contains a note from J. Anquetil, post-marked 15 January 1939 (f 124). Anquetil mentions the letters from Verlaine and Rimbaud which he has possessed. 'Mais la plus belle qui soit passée dans mon coffre est une lettre de Rimbaud à Izambard, critiquant les Poèmes Saturniens, lettre de 4 pages, qui, aujourd'hui vaudrait cher.'

2 Porché: *op. cit.*, 118–19
3 Georges Rodenbach: 'La Poésie nouvelle'. *Revue politique et littéraire. Revue bleue*, 4 April 1891, 422–30. This is an interesting account of the literary impact of Rimbaud.

15

1   *Nouvelles Notes sur Rimbaud, Œs. posths.*, II, 277
2   Porché: *op. cit.*, 121
3   *Écho de Paris*, 25 July 1900. Bib. Nat. N. A. Fr. 13156 ff 96 (1 and 2); see also Lepelletier in *Écho de Paris*, September 1897. N. A. Fr. 13156 f 94
4   Ex-Mme Paul Verlaine: *op. cit.*, 181
5   Starkie: *op. cit.*, 147
6   *Ibid.*, 148, 150. In Jean-Émile Bayard: *The Latin Quarter past and present*, Jean Richepin wrote (p. 255): 'Arthur Rimbaud was one of my intimate friends. He was my guest on his arrival in Paris and I have a mass of interesting letters written by him from England and Belgium.'
7   Ex-Mme Paul Verlaine: *op. cit.*, 183–4
8   *Ibid.*, 184–5
9   Saint-Georges de Bouhélier: *Le Printemps d'Une Génération*, 22
10   Ex-Mme Paul Verlaine: *op. cit.*, 186
11   Adolphe Jullien: *Fantin-Latour. Sa Vie et ses amitiés*, 45; Goncourt *Journal*, 18 March 1872 (x, 80); Lepelletier: *op. cit.*, 258. In *La Pêche aux souvenirs*, 123, Jacques-Émile Blanche records that Edmond Maître, musician, art-lover and amateur of literature, had introduced Verlaine and Rimbaud to Fantin-Latour. Mr Michael Pakenham has brought to my notice a letter from Verlaine to Albert Mérat, described in *Livres et autographes*, 25 February 1965. The letter is dated simply '16 février', but it may be ascribed to 1872.

> Verlaine accuse Mérat de colporter de '*prétendus propos de lui*' qui peuvent être mal interprétés; il le prie '*de cesser toute blague de ce genre,*' et de lui affirmer '*qu'il n'a absolument voulu* que rire.' '*Un ami averti en vaut deux, c'est pourquoi je vous préviens.*'

This letter sheds some light on the personal relationships of the sitters in *Coin de table*.

12   Ex-Mme Paul Verlaine: *op. cit.*, 200–2
13   Undated letter, quoted by Léandre Vaillat: *En écoutant Forain*, 101
14   *Ariettes oubliées*. I. Borel, 191

16

1 Starkie: *op. cit.*, 178, 182
2 Charles Maurras: *Arthur Rimbaud. La Revue encyclopédique*, 1 January 1892, 10
3 Léon Valade to Émile Blémont, 2 October 1871. Note to Maurice Dullaert: *L'Affaire Verlaine* (pages unnumbered)
4 *Écho de Paris*, September 1897. Bib. Nat. N. A. Fr. 13156 f 94
5 18 April 1886. Goncourt *Journal*, XIV, 116–17
6 Robichez, 318
7 *Ibid.*, 479–82
8 Ex-Mme Paul Verlaine: *op. cit.*, 210-11
9 *Ibid.*, 211-12
10 *Ibid.*, 212–14
11 *Ibid.*, 216
12 *Ibid.*, 217
13 *Ibid.*, 217–18

17

1 Robichez, 159
2 *Ibid.*, 161
3 For Rimbaud's influence on Verlaine, see: Georges Rodenbach: *L'Élite*, 75-6, Guy Michaud: *Message poétique du Symbolisme*, I, 124; Henri Strentz: *Paul Verlaine. Son Œuvre*, 27; Henri Clouard: *La Poésie française moderne*, 80

18

1 Ex-Mme Paul Verlaine: *op. cit.*, 219
2 *Ibid.*, 219–22
3 Starkie: *op. cit.*, 247–8
4 Félix Régamey: *Verlaine dessinateur*, 225
5 Paul Valéry to J.-M. Carré, 25 February 1923; quoted in Carré, *op. cit.*, VI–VII
6 *Corr.*, I, 41
7 *Ibid.*, 41-2
8 Robichez, 163

9 Lepelletier: *op. cit.*, 39–40
10 24 September 1872; *Corr.*, I, 44–6
11 *Ibid.*, 46, note; and 319–20

19

1 For Rimbaud's literary development, see especially Starkie: *op. cit.*, 83 et sqq.
2 Robichez, 148
3 *Ibid.*
4 *Ibid.*, 149
5 *Ibid.*, 159
6 *La Vie parisienne*, 26 September 1891, 537

20

1 *Corr.*, I, 47, 50
2 [October 1872]; *Corr.*, I, 53
3 *Corr.*, I, 67–70
4 Ex-Mme Paul Verlaine: *op. cit.*, 267–9
5 *Corr.*, I, 55
6 *Corr.*, I, 63
7 *Corr.*, I, 71–3, 78
8 *Corr.*, I, 82–3
9 26 December 1872; *Corr.*, I, 80
10 *Corr.*, I, 302–3
11 Letter to Lepelletier [January 1873]; *Corr.*, I, 86
12 [February 1873]; *Corr.*, I, 89
13 Robichez, *op. cit.*, 166

21

1 Starkie: *op. cit.*, 265
2 15 April 1873; *Corr.*, I, 92–3
3 Lepelletier: *op. cit.*, 319
4 *Ibid.*, 318–19
5 22 April 1873; *Corr.*, I, 307–9

6 16 May 1873; *Corr.*, I, 95–7
7 *Corr.*, I, 98–9
8 Letter to Francis Poictevin, 4 March 1888; *Corr.*, III, 277
9 'Art poétique'. Robichez, 261–2
10 *Corr.*, I, 100
11 19 May 1873; *Corr.*, I, 101–2

22

1 23 May [1873]; *Corr.*, I, 106
2 *Corr.*, I, 312
3 *Ibid.*
4 21 June [1873]; *Corr.*, I, 313
5 25 June [1873]; *Corr.*, I, 315–18
6 [June 1873]; *Corr.*, I, 108
7 Lepelletier: *op. cit.*, 331
8 Starkie: *op. cit.*, 269
9 Ex-Mme Paul Verlaine: *op. cit.*, 223
10 See Starkie: *op. cit.*, 278
11 *Ibid.*, 279–80
12 *Ibid.*, 280–2
13 Lepelletier: *op. cit.*, 334–5
14 *Ibid.*, 344–5
15 Dullaert: *op. cit.*, note (pages unnumbered)
16 Adolphe Retté: *Le Symbolisme. Anecdotes et Souvenirs*, 102–10
17 Lepelletier: *op. cit.*, 345
18 *Ibid.*
19 *Ibid.*, 346

23

1 Starkie: *op. cit.*, 286–7
2 Lepelletier: *op. cit.*, 347–8
3 According to ex-Mme-Paul Verlaine; but see pp. 157-158 of this book.
4 *Ibid.*, 226
5 Porché: *op. cit.*, 324–5
6 Verlaine: *Mes Prisons, Œs cs.*, IV, 393–4
7 *Ibid.*, 397–8; Robichez, 226

8 W. G. C. Byvanck: *Un Hollandais à Paris*, 114 et sqq.
9 Robichez, 456
10 *Ibid.*, 225; Barthou, *op. cit.*, II, 308
11 18 June 1929. Gide: *Journal*, III, 193
12 Robichez, 323–4; Barthou, II, 311
13 Jean-Arthur Rimbaud: *Œuvres complètes*, 201
14 Robichez, 319; Barthou, II, 308
15 Robichez, 266; *Corr.*, I, 126–30; Barthou, II, 310
16 28 September [1873]; *Corr.*, I, 109–11
17 Robichez, 256–7; Barthou, II, 310
18 'Écrit en 1875', *Amour*. Robichez, 363
19 *Mes Prisons. Œs cs.*, IV, 412
20 22 November [1873]; *Corr.*, I, 111–13
21 Lepelletier: *op. cit.*, 362–3
22 24–28 November [1873]; *Corr.*, I, 117–18
23 Ex-Mme Paul Verlaine: *op. cit.*, 227–8
24 *Ibid.*, 228

24

1 Letter of 8 January 1881; published by Claretie in *La Vie à Paris, 1880*, 505–6
2 W. G. C. Byvanck: *op. cit.*, 133–4
3 In *Conversations in Ebury Street*, 161–6, Moore added that Verlaine's 'attachment to religion was stinted to stained-glass windows and the Pope's indulgences'.
4 Byvanck: *op. cit.*, 132–3
5 *Ibid.*, 119–20
6 Edmond Pilon in *L'Ermitage*, February 1896, 59–60
7 Lepelletier: *op. cit.*, 386–7
8 *Ibid.*, 393
9 *Corr.*, I, 146–7
10 Robichez, 216–17
11 Lepelletier: *op. cit.*, 396
12 Robichez, 318; and note, 650–1
13 Rémy de Gourmont: *Promenades littéraires*, IV, 30–2
14 Ex-Mme Paul Verlaine: *op. cit.*, 236
15 Rémy de Gourmont: *op. cit.*, IV, 28. See also Maurice Barrès: *Mes Cahiers*, I, 55 sqq.

25

1 Robichez, 186
2 *Corr.*, I, 164
3 Porché: *op. cit.*, 209
4 *Ibid.*, 211
5 Letter to Lepelletier, 27 March 1874; *Corr.*, I, 136
6 Robichez, 230–1
7 *Notes on England, Œs posths.*, III, 231–4
8 F. S. de Carteret-Bisson. *Our Schools and Colleges*, I, 866. Miss J. M. Bunker wrote to the present author (11 December 1968): 'My connections are with the village of Stickney, where my grandfather William Andrews was headmaster in the 1870s and '80s. I never met him as he died in his middle forties when my mother, the youngest of his seven children, was seven years old. I am told he was a cultured man who had previously been a tutor at Burgh Theological College ... I feel great pride to see the brass tablet in the church in memory of my grandfather.'
9 *Notes on England, loc. cit.*
10 *Ibid.*, 241–4
11 *Ibid.*, 249–50
12 *Corr.*, I, 165–6
13 For the most complete account of Verlaine in Lincolnshire, see: V. P. Underwood: *Verlaine et l'Angleterre*, 185 sqq.
14 Robichez, 193
15 29 April 1875; *Corr.*, III, 105
16 *Ibid.*, 107; Delahaye; *op. cit.*, 22–3; *Corr.*, III, 101. Delahaye: Letters to Verlaine, from the Doucet Collection. Quoted by Carré: *Autour de Verlaine et de Rimbaud*, 13, 15. Mallarmé: *Divagations*, 89–90
17 29 April 1875; *Corr.* III, 105
18 For the vicissitudes of this work, see p. 285

26

1 V. P. Underwood: *op. cit.*, 217 sqq.
2 See also: Ernest Delahaye. *Verlaine*, 222
3 Alfred, Lord Tennyson: *Works*, 45

4 Robichez, 36
5 Tennyson: *op. cit.*, 13
6 Robichez, 37

27

1 6 September [1875]; *Corr.*, II, 3
2 7 July 1875; Maggs catalogue, 1937, 35
3 Anatole France was later to make amends for his behaviour. See p. 290.
4 Robichez, 364
5 27 November [1875]; *Corr.*, III, 113–14
6 Quoted by Underwood: *op. cit.*, 284
7 Verlaine: *Notes on England, Œs posths.*, 257–8
8 Underwood: *op. cit.*, 290

28

1 Anon: *A Descriptive Guide to Bournemouth*, 1 sqq.
2 *Ibid.*, 5
3 'Bournemouth', *Amour*, Borel, 413
4 F. S. de Carteret-Bisson: *op. cit.*, I, 927, lxxi
5 Tennyson: *op. cit.*, 250
6 Robichez, 375
7 In an undated note in the Doucet Collection (7203–184), Delahaye writes to Verlaine:

> Ne manque pas d'écrire vite et long, et surtout envoie les vers recopiés. Je n'ai pas les deux pièces dont tu parles: Écoutez la chanson bien douce, ni: Les chères mains qui furent miennes. Inutile de dire que je compte dessus.

A drawing by Delahaye in the same collection (7203–186) illustrates Verlaine's attempts to be reconciled with his wife and son. Verlaine is shown as a soldier, carrying his son under his arm. He is standing triumphantly on a cannon labelled '*papa beau-père*'. The sun – with the caption '*Soleil d'Austerlitz*' – is shining on his victory.

8 Catalogue de la bibliothèque J. Claretie, 1re partie, 1918, no 1208
9 Ex-Mme Paul Verlaine: *op. cit.*, 237
10 Letter in Doucet Collection; quoted by Underwood, 318
11 For Mr Remington's testimonial see Underwood, 321
12 Letter of [1877]. Doucet: 7203–196

29

1 Charles Leleux: *Quand nous étions jeunes.* (*Souvenirs du Collège Notre-Dame de Rethel*), 97–9
2 *Ibid.*, 64–5
3 Eugène Prévost; quoted by Charles Leleux in *Mémorial du Collège Notre-Dame de Rethel, 1854–1910*, 72
4 Henri Regnault; quoted in *ibid.*, 72–4
5 Ex-Mme Paul Verlaine: *op. cit.*, 237–8
6 Robichez, 202
7 Ex-Mme Verlaine: *op. cit.*, 240
8 *Ibid.*, 243–4; Underwood, 319; Ernest Delahaye: *Verlaine*, 284
9 Leleux: *op. cit.*, 79, note. Bib. Nat. N. A. Fr. 13154, f 313; N. A. Fr. 13155, f 171. In the Doucet Collection (7203–238) is a letter from Delahaye to Verlaine, dated in pencil 1881. It sheds a little light on Verlaine's stay at Rethel.

> . . . Je te disais bien que Rethel est un endroit charmant, et si tu n'étais pas un anglomane hideux (oui, hideux!) ne connaissant que ton London et autres Sohos, tu aurais, depuis longtemps, partagé avec exetase Ma façon de pancer . . .
> Vrai que tu n'as jamais su comprendre Rethompe, ça c'est connu. Et si tu y resté [*sic*] six mois de plus que bibi, c'était vitement poussé par des intérêts bassement commerciaux.

10 Leleux: *op. cit.*, 72–4
11 Henri Mondor: *L'Amitié de Verlaine et de Mallarmé*, 49
12 *Ibid.*, 50
13 *Ibid.*, 51
14 *Ibid.*, 51–2. Anatole Mallarmé died on 6 October 1879, at the age of eight.
15 Saint-Georges de Bouhélier: *loc. cit.*

30

1 Bib. Nat. N. A. Fr. 13155 f 171; Robichez, p. 1. Note in Doucet Collection, quoted by Underwood, *op. cit.*, 326
2 Quoted by François Porché: *Verlaine tel qu'il fut*, 231
3 Underwood (p. 332) mentions a photograph of Verlaine dated 29 August; but this does not seem to be the date of the visit to

Boston. On 1 and 11 September, Verlaine wrote to Mallarmé from Arras.

4 The most complete account of Verlaine in Lymington is given by Underwood, *op. cit.*

5 *Amour*, XXII. Robichez, 414

6 Doucet Collection: MS 7203–215

7 *Amour*, XXII; Robichez, 414

8 *Amour*, VII. Robichez, 401–2

9 *Ibid.*, I, 307; and Porché, *op. cit.*, 237

31

1 Lepelletier: *op. cit.*, 401; and Alfred Poizat: *Le Symbolisme – de Baudelaire à Claudel*, 110–11

2 *Amour*, XIII. Robichez, 406

3 *Ibid.*, VI, 400

4 *Voyage en France par un Français, Œs posths.*, II, 87–8.

32

1 Ernest Delahaye: *Souvenirs familiers à propos de Rimbaud, Verlaine, Germain Nouveau*, 173–4

2 Jules Claretie in *Le Temps*, 28 December 1880. Reprinted in Claretie: *La Vie à Paris, 1880*, 505–6

3 Published by Jules Claretie in *Le Temps*, 2 June 1911. Reprinted in Claretie: *La Vie à Paris, 1911–13*, 52–8

4 *Ibid.*

5 Émile Zola: *Documents littéraires*, 178–9, 194

6 H. Carton de Wiart: *Le Droit à la Joie*, 149

7 Maurice Barrès: *op. cit.*, I, 55 sqq.

8 Carton de Wiart: *op. cit.*, 156–7

9 Jules Lemaître: *Les Contemporains*, 4e série, 93, 95

10 See also Moore: *Conversations in Ebury Street*, 161–6; *Le Gaulois*, 9 January 1896

11 1 December 1905. Gide: *Journal*, I, 223

12 Robichez, 226

13 *Ibid.*, 193

14 *Ibid.*, 179

33

1 Lepelletier: *op. cit.*, 424
2 *Ibid.*, 424–5
3 *Notes on England, Œs posths.*, III, 269; *Œs posths.*, II, 131–4
4 Porché: *op. cit.*, 246
5 Verlaine's request is reproduced by Lepelletier: *op. cit.*, 124–5
6 *Ibid.*, 124 sqq.
7 A. E. Carter: *Verlaine: a Study in Parallels*, 186–7
8 Lepelletier: *op. cit.*, 128
9 Quoted by François Porché: *Verlaine tel qu'il fut*, 248
10 *Amour. Lucien Létinois.* XV. Robichez, 407–8

34

1 Mondor: *op. cit.*
2 Ernest Raynaud: *En Marge de la Mêlée symboliste*, 63–6
3 22 August 1883; Mondor: *op. cit.*, 60–1
4 *Ibid.*, 65–6
5 Ernest Raynaud: *Considérations*, 41–2
6 Lods: *op. cit.*, 409–10; Carteret: *Le Trésor du Bibliophile* . . . , II, 422
7 Ad. van Bever: *La Vie douloureuse de Verlaine*, 38
8 Albert Lantoine: *Paul Verlaine et Quelques-uns*, 24–6; Maurice Barrès: *op. cit.*, I, 55 sqq.
9 Mondor: *op. cit.*, 78–9
10 P.-V. Stock: *Mémorandum d'un Éditeur*, I, 265
11 J.-K. Huysmans: *À Rebours*, 245 sqq.
12 Robert Baldick: *The Life of J.-K. Huysmans*, 109
13 André Germain: *Verlaine et Huysmans. La Revue Européenne*, 1 May 1923, 23–5. For another version of this story, see Paul Léautaud: *Journal littéraire, 1893–1956*, I, 188. See also Rousselot: *op. cit.*, 84–5

35

1 Robichez, 314
2 M.-L. Henry: *La Contribution d'un Américain au Symbolisme*

français. Stuart Merrill, 29. H. d'Alméras: *Avant la Gloire. Leurs Débuts*. 1re série, 81

3   Raynaud: *La Mêlée Symboliste* (*1870–1890*), 63–5

36

1   Lepelletier: *op. cit.*, 475–6
2   *Ibid.*, 483; and Verlaine: *Invectives*, XVIII. Borel, 916–17
3   Lepelletier: *op. cit.*, 484
4   Gustave Vanwelkenhuyzen: *Verlaine en Belgique*, 100–3
6   'La Goutte'. *Œs posths.*, I, 249
7   Robichez, *loc. cit.*
8   'La Goutte', *loc. cit.*

37

1   Ernest Raynaud: *La Mêlée symboliste*, II, 18 sqq. In the Dauze library (Vol. II, No. 2284) was an undated letter from Charles Morice to Mme Verlaine, which may possibly belong to 1885. It asks her to forgive Verlaine his wrongs and to come back and live with him. 'He has told me his troubles,' wrote Morice, 'and I know that he has since religiously confessed them to a priest . . . I am convinced that solitude is very dangerous for him . . . No company could be so good for him as his mother's . . .'
2   Raynaud: *loc. cit.*
3   René Ghil: *Les Dates et les Œuvres*, 44–5
4   *Ibid.*, 46–7
5   *Ibid.*, 48–50
6   Mondor: *op. cit.*, 92–3
7   Ghil: *op. cit.*, 51–2
8   George Moore: *Conversations in Ebury Street*, 162–6
9   Robichez, 381
10   Léon Vallas: *Claude Debussy et son temps*, 97–8

38

1   4 April 1886. Goncourt *Journal*, XIV, 107
2   Ex-Mme Paul Verlaine: *op. cit.*, 250–3

3 Georges Barrelle: *Le Pèlerin lyrique*, 51–2
4 Ex-Mme Paul Verlaine: *loc cit.*
5 *Ibid.*, 255
6 Porché: Introduction, *op. cit.*, 30

39

1 Borel, XXXIV
2 *Bonheur*, XV; *Œs cs.*, II, 246
3 Bayard: *op. cit.*, 154
4 Georges Zayed (ed.): *Lettres inédites de Verlaine à Cazals*
5 *Ibid.*
6 I, 21 September 1888; Zayed: *op. cit.*, 93, 95
7 25 December 1888, 14 [January 1889]; *ibid.*, 103, 113
8 [12 January 1889]; *ibid.*, 111
9 [20 June 1889]; *ibid.*, 140
10 [26 June 1889]; *ibid.*, 144–5
11 *Œs posths.*, III, 109 sqq.
12 F.-A. Cazals and Gustave Le Rouge: *Les derniers jours de Paul Verlaine*, 69–72

40

1 Gustave Kahn: *Les Origines du Symbolisme*, 52–7. See also R. Darzens: *Enquêtes littéraires: Arthur Rimbaud. La Revue indépendante*, January–February 1889, 190 sqq.
2 See also Verlaine's introduction to *Les Poètes maudits; Œs cs.*, IV, 9
3 Kahn: *loc. cit.*
4 Laurent Tailhade: *Quelques fantômes de jadis*, 23; *Lettres à sa mère*, 93
5 Tailhade: *Quelques fantômes de jadis*, 23
6 Ex-Mme Paul Verlaine: *op. cit.*, 245
7 Mme Mauté had been paralysed by a stroke in 1882, and died two years later.
8 Ex-Mme Paul Verlaine: *op. cit.*, 256

41

1 For an account of Rachilde, see André David: *Rachilde. Homme de Lettres*. The friendship inspired a correspondence which she refused to publish, as it seemed to her 'absolutely *private*'.
2 12 November 1886. *Corr.*, III, 279–281
3 Mondor: *op. cit.*, 105–7
4 Letter of 22 December 1886; Charavay catalogue No. 699 (February 1958), No. 26, 907
5 Raynaud: *La Mêlée symboliste*, II, 18 sqq.
6 Barrelle: *loc. cit.*; Raymond Christoflour: *Louis Le Cardonnel*, 24
7 Letter of 26 April 1887. Bib. Nat. N. A. Fr. 13152 f 152
8 Mondor: *op. cit.*, 115–16
9 2 May 1887; *ibid.*, 116–17
10 Ex-Mme Paul Verlaine: *op. cit.*, 250–1; Lepelletier, *op. cit.*, 540–1
11 Martrin-Donos: *op. cit.*, 144–5
12 Doucet MS 5093
13 Doucet MS 5094
14 Ex-Mme Paul Verlaine: *op. cit.*, 256–7
15 Doucet MS 5095
16 Ex-Mme Paul Verlaine: *loc. cit.*
17 Lepelletier: *op. cit.*, 420
18 Lepelletier: *op. cit.*, *passim.* 9 February 1909: Jules Renard: *Journal intime, 1906–10*, p. 1490. Porché: introduction to Mme Verlaine's memoirs.
19 For an illuminating commentary on Mathilde, see Porché's introduction to her memoirs. He notes that her son Félix Delporte died on 16 April 1918, aged twenty-five; her daughter, Suzanne Delporte, died on 23 March 1923. On her second marriage certificate is a note: 'En vertu d'un jugement du tribunal d'Alger, en date du 12 mai 1905, transcrit le 1er août 1906, le mariage a été dissous par le divorce' (*op. cit.*, 30–2).

42

1 Undated note in Charavay catalogue No. 691, November 1954; No. 25,420
2 Raymond de la Tailhède: introduction to Jules Tellier: *Œuvres*,

1, xxiii–xxv. For Tellier's comments on Verlaine, see *Œuvres*, II, 27, 181 sqq.; and *Les Écrivains d'Aujourd'hui. Nos Poètes*, 211 sqq.

3 15 July 1887. Ad. van Bever: *Paul Verlaine. Lettres à Léon Vanier. Mercure de France*, 1 June 1923, 407

4 Jules Lemaître: *Les Contemporains*, 4e série, 63–78

5 Raymond de la Tailhède: *loc. cit.*

6 David: *op. cit.*, 28–9

7 Bib. Nat. N. A. Fr., 13150 f 41. Envelope postmarked 12 mars [18]88, and addressed to Verlaine at Broussais.

Paris, 11 rue de Sèvres

Merci et vraiment, mon cher ami, de votre affectueuse lettre – et aussi de la promesse que vous me faites de nous voir, vers la fin du mois, alors que vous serez sorti de Broussais.

Cela, il le faut! – ne serait-ce que pour soulager un peu nos biles sur les immondes bourgeois que nous connaissons – car nous sommes à peu près logés à la même enseigne, en tant que dols familiaux et affection de proches.

Puis, il me semble que dans ce colossal Empire du Panmuflisme où nous vivons, nous sommes quelques uns d'égarés, croyant à l'art, et que nous devrions nous serrer un peu les coudes, car sans cela, nous ne sommes faits pour vivre avec personne.

Quelle singulière époque tout de même!

J'attends Amour avec une sacrée impatience, je vous jure, et suis véritablement fier que vous ayez bien voulu me dédicacer une pièce. Écrivez moi donc un petit mot, dès que vous serez libre – nous dînerons ensemble et frotterons, à table, nos plaies.

votre bien dévoué
J. K. HUYSMANS

On 29 March, Huysmans wrote again (Bib. Nat. N. A. Fr. 13150 f 84); this letter-card was addressed to Verlaine at 14, rue Royer-Collard.

Mon cher ami, il demeure convenu que le lundi pascal, soit lundi prochain, 2, nous irons chez vous avec Bloy, entre 4 et 5 heures. Je vais lui faire apporter son œuvre sur vous et cela nous préparera pour le dîner voisin.

J'ai relu, hier soir, au lit, le Liétinois [*sic*] c'est plein de choses neuves et superbes, oh mais oui!

Je vais m'occuper demain de l'affaire avec la maison quentin dont je vous ai parlé.

à lundi donc, mon cher Verlaine, et jusque là, une vraie bonne poignée de main.

de votre
J. K. HUYSMANS

43

1 For a review of *Amour*, see Gustave Kahn in *La Revue indépendante*, May 1888
2 'In Memoriam', Tennyson: *op. cit.*, 247. *Amour*, I. Robichez, 397
3 *Ibid.*, v. Robichez, 400
4 *Ibid.*, vi. Robichez, 401
5 *Ibid.*, vii. Robichez, 401-2
6 *Ibid.*, ix. Robichez, 403

44

1 Charles Morice: quoted in Bayard: *op. cit.*, 216
2 Louis Lefebvre: *Charles Morice*, 23-4
3 Charles Morice: *Paul Verlaine*, 10 and *passim*.
4 Bib. Nat. N. A. Fr. 13152 ff 189–90, 192–3
5 Bib. Nat. N. A. Fr. 13150 f 6
6 Ernest Raynaud: *La Mêlée Symboliste*, ii, 14–16
7 *Ibid.*, 13–14; and Lefebvre: *op. cit.*, 12

45

1 *Corr.*, ii, 152-3, 153
2 *Ibid.*, 157
3 *Ibid.*, 158
4 Bib. Nat. N. A. Fr. 13150 f 171
5 'Poème saturnien', *Parallèlement*. Robichez. 468
6 Georges Zayed (éditeur): *Paul Verlaine. Lettres inédites à Charles Morice*, 89
7 Quoted by Robichez, 422
8 Borel, 694
9 *Œs cs.*, iv, 89
10 Preface to *Parallèlement*. Robichez, 433. Letter in Barthou, ii, 208-9
11 Borel, 515-16
12 'Mains', *Parallèlement*. Robichez, 475
13 'Læti et Errabundi', *Parallèlement*. Robichez, 481-2

46

1. 'Essai de clinique littéraire. Paul Verlaine', *Revue thérapeutique des Alcaloides*. March, April 1930. Magazine cuttings in Bib. Nat. N. A. Fr. 13157 ff 61 sqq.
2. *Ibid.*, f 87
3. For Dr Jullien and Verlaine, see Paul Marsan: 'Paul Verlaine et son médecin. Lettres inédites au Dr Jullien', *Mercure de France*, 1 July 1925, 60–91
4. Bib. Nat. N. A. Fr. 13154 f 227
5. *Ibid.*, f 228
6. Porché: *op. cit.*, 299–300
7. Anon.: *Nouveau Guide Pratique médical et pittoresque aux Eaux d'Aix en Savoie* (1864), 57–8
8. *Aix-les-Bains . . . Nouveau Guide* (1872), 8, 19, 37
9. Mondor: *op. cit.*, 132–3; for Verlaine's account of his journey, see *Mes Hôpitaux. Œs cs.*, IV, 347–54
10. Quoted by Joseph Uzanne: *Figures contemporaines tirées de l'album Mariani*, x. (Henry Floury, 1906). Uzanne adds: 'Licencié en droit (1861); interne en médecine; docteur en médecine (1875). Médecin consultant aux Bains d'Aix, M. le docteur Henri Cazalis est chevalier de la Légion d'honneur et chevalier ou officier de plusieurs ordres étrangers.' Cazalis was born in 1840 and died in 1909.
11. Stuart Merrill: *Prose et Vers*, 171–2
12. [21 August 1889]: Zayed: *op. cit.*, 154–5
13. [23 August 1889]: *ibid.*, 158
14. [26 August 1889]: *ibid.*, 171
15. [26 August 1889]: *ibid.*, 174
16. [26 August 1889]: *ibid.*, 176
17. [28 August 1889]: *ibid.*, 183
18. [1 September 1889]: *ibid.*, 198
19. Delahaye, *op. cit.*, 13–15
20. Bib. Nat. N. A. Fr. 13150 f 86

47

1. For *Femmes*, which was originally meant to appear as *Auculnes*,

see: *Collection de Mme C * * *.* Vente du 21 novembre 1936 (Blaizot. 1936), Nos. 198–204

2   H. Carton de Wiart: *Souvenirs littéraires*, 60–2

3   Louÿs, quoted by Bayard: *op. cit.*, 206–7. See also André Gide: *Journal*, II, 11

4   Bib. Nat. N. A. Fr. 13152 f 116

5   Armand Lods: 'Les Premières éditions de Verlaine', *Mercure de France*, 15 October 1924, 412–13; Deschamps' letter is undated here.

6   Letter to Cazals [12 September 1889]. Zayed *op. cit.*, 223

7   16 [March 1890]: *ibid.*, 225

8   Bib. Nat. N. A. Fr. 13152 ff 195, 197–8

48

1   Alphonse Séché: *Ah! Jeunesse! Petits souvenirs du Quartier Latin. Les Œuvres Libres*, July 1931, 202. R. H. Sherard: *Modern Paris*, 137–8 and *passim*

2   Quoted by Antoine Albalat: *Trente Ans de Quartier Latin*, 21–2

3   Camille Mauclair: *Servitude et Grandeur littéraires*, 23

4   Henri Duvernois: *Apprentissages*, 63–4

5   Élie Moroy: *La Guirlande de Verlaine*, 20

6   Bib. Nat. N. A. Fr. 13150 ff 61–2

7   Laurent Tailhade: *Quelques fantômes de jadis*, 87–8

8   Stuart Merrill: *op. cit.*, 168–9

9   29 March 1894. Jules Renard: *Journal inédit, 1887–95*, 250

10 Quoted by Cazals and Le Rouge: *op. cit.*, 139

11 20 March 1906; André Gide: *Journal*, I, 243

12 François Fosca: *Histoire des Cafés de Paris*, 176: Guy Michaud: *Message poétique du Symbolisme*, I, 215

13 R. H. Sherard: *My Friends the French*, 39–41, 112

14 Cazals and Le Rouge: *op. cit.*, 134

15 Martrin-Donos: *op. cit.*, 163

16 Cazals and Le Rouge: *op. cit.*, 1–2

17 M.-C. Poinsot: *Toute la Vie*, 14–15, 156–7

18 Yvanhoe Rambosson: 'In Memoriam', *L'Ermitage*, February 1896, 66–7

19 Émile Baumann: *La Vie terrible d'Henri de Groux*, 104

20 Rémy de Gourmont: *Promenades littéraires*, IV, 29

21 Léo d'Orfer; quoted in Jean-Émile Bayard: *The Latin Quarter past and present*, 226

22 See Paul Blanchart: *Saint-Georges de Bouhélier. Son Œuvre. Étude critique*

23 Saint-Georges de Bouhélier: *Le Printemps d'une génération*, 206–9

24 *Ibid.*

25 Léo d'Orfer, quoted in Bayard: *op. cit.*, 225. Albalat: *op. cit.*, 30–1

26 Paul Fort: *Mes Mémoires*, 9–10

27 Fosca: *op. cit.*, 174; Aressy: *op. cit.*, 155–6; Bayard: *op. cit.*, 240–1

28 Saint-Georges de Bouhélier: *op. cit.*, 144–5

49

1 Raynaud: *La Mêlée symboliste*, 137; and Bayard, *op. cit.*, 249–50

2 Léo d'Orfer; quoted in Bayard: *op. cit.*, 228

3 Gabriel de Lautrec: *Souvenirs des jours sans souci*, 14–18

4 Vance Thompson: *French Portraits*, 1–3

5 Henry: *op. cit.*, 87–8, 89

6 R. H. Sherard: *Twenty years in Paris*, 384; Renard: *op. cit.*, 144–5

7 Jean Carrère: *Les Mauvais Maîtres*, 175–6

8 Merrill: *op. cit.*, 175–6

9 Adolphe Retté: *Le Symbolisme. Anecdotes et Souvenirs*, 96–101

10 Xavier Privas; quoted in Bayard: *op. cit.*, 239–41

11 *Demain*, 19 January 1896. Newspaper cutting in Bib. Nat. N. A. Fr. 13157 f 10

12 Albert Lantoine: *Paul Verlaine et quelques-uns*, 103–4. For Verlaine at Le Chat Noir, see also Maurice Donnay: *Mes Débuts à Paris*, 193–4

13 Maurice Spronck: *Notes et Impressions. Revue politique et littéraire. Revue bleue*, 29 August 1896, 284–5

50

1 Cazals and Le Rouge: *op. cit.*

2 For an understanding account of Verlaine's drinking habits, see Cazals and Le Rouge, *op. cit.*, 127 sqq.

3 Ernest Raynaud: *En Marge de la Mêlée Symboliste*, 106–8

4 Émile Strauss in *La Critique*, 5 July 1897; quoted by Raynaud: *op. cit.*, 109

5   Raynaud: *op. cit.*, 106–8
6   Aressy: *op. cit.*, 168–9
7   Lepelletier: *op. cit.*, 535–6
8   Ernest Delahaye: *Verlaine*, 354–5
9   *Élégies*, II. Borel, 790
10 Cazals and Le Rouge: *op. cit.*, 87, note
11 There are a few sidelights on Constans in Octave Homberg: *Les Coulisses de l'histoire* (Fayard 1938) and in W. F. Lonergan: *Forty Years of Paris* (T. Fisher Unwin. 1907)
12 Van Bever: *op. cit.*, 39
13 Bib. Nat. N. A. Fr. 13154 f 227. Copy dated 1893 or '94
14 Maurice Barrès: *Mes Cahiers*, I, 55 sqq.; Marguerite Moreno: *Souvenirs de ma vie*, 26–7
15 Undated letter in Dauze library: catalogue, Vol. II, p. 326
16 Bib. Nat. N. A. Fr. 13154 f 227. Copy of letter dated 5 September 1892
17 Cazals and Le Rouge: *op. cit.*, 97–8

51

1   Guy Michaud: *Message poétique du Symbolisme*, II, 393–4
2   Camille Mauclair: *Servitude et Grandeur littéraires*, 22
3   Stuart Merrill: *Prose et Verse*, 169–70
4   Jules Huret: *Enquête sur l'évolution littéraire*, 80–1
5   *Ibid.*, 62
6   *Ibid.*, 65–71

52

1   Joseph Capperon: *Notes d'art et de littérature*, 35
2   Huret: *op. cit.*, 107; and Michaud: *op. cit.*, II, 409
3   Ferdinand Brunetière: 'Le Symbolisme contemporain'. Reprinted in *Essais sur la littérature contemporaine*, 133–56. See also Georges Rodenbach: 'La Poésie nouvelle', *Revue bleue*, 4 April 1891, 422–5
4   Barrès: *op. cit.*, I, 279
5   E. Vigié-Lecocq: *La Poésie contemporaine, 1884–1896*, 241
6   Brunetière: *loc. cit.*
7   E. Vigié-Lecocq: *loc. cit.*

8 Émile Verhaeren: *Impressions*, 3e série, 75
9 Ernest Raynaud: *La Mêlée Symboliste*, III, 167–8
10 Arthur James Eddy: *Recollections and Impressions of James McNeill Whistler*, 211; Michaud: *op. cit.*, I, 221
11 Raynaud: *op. cit.*, III, 154–5
12 Adolphe Boschot: *Chez nos poètes*, 81–2
13 Camille Mauclair: *L'Art indépendant français sous la Troisième République*, 83–4, 86, 109
14 Ernest Raynaud: *Considérations*, 38–42
15 Alfred Poizat: *Le Symbolisme – de Baudelaire à Claudel*, 130–2
16 Mauclair: *op. cit.*, 102–3

53

1 Byvanck: *op. cit.*, 134
2 Borel, 908
3 'J'ai dit à l'esprit vain . . .' *Bonheur*, XVIII. Borel, 682–5
4 'Seigneur, vous m'avez laissé vivre . . .' *Bonheur*, XVI. Borel, 681
5 Byvanck: *op. cit.*, 119–20
6 *Bonheur*, XXXII. Borel, 701–2

54

1 Charles Morice: *Eugène Carrière*, 193 sqq.
2 *Ibid.*
3 Ernest Raynaud: *La Mêlée Symboliste*, I, 144–5
4 Camille Mauclair: *Servitude et Grandeur littéraires*, 23–5
5 Adolphe Brisson: *La Comédie littéraire*, 105–19
6 Henri de Régnier: *Nos Rencontres*, 45–7; *Le Journal*, 18 January 1896 (Doucet Collection).
7 Pierre Champion: *Marcel Schwob et son temps*, 96–7
8 Marguerite Moreno: *op. cit.*, 23 sqq.
9 *Ibid.*
10 Paul Fort: *Mes Mémoires*, 10–13
11 Marguerite Moreno: *loc. cit.*
12 Jacques Robichez: *Le Symbolisme au théâtre*, 121
13 7 November 1891. *Lettres de Paul Gauguin à G.-D. de Monfreid*, 81–2

14 *La Connaissance*, November 1920, 911–12, and 912, note
15 Louis Loviot: Preface to *Voyage en France par un Français*, 7–9
16 Published under the title 'Littérature' in *Invectives*. Borel, 902
17 13 [November 1891]. Bib. Nat. N. A. Fr. 13151 f 23
18 Philippe Gille: *La Bataille littéraire (1891–1892)*, 145

55

1 Charles Maurras in *La Revue encyclopédique*, 1 January 1892, 7 sqq.
   Among the papers of Cazals are a series of letters from Paterne
   Berrichon, who had known Verlaine and had married Rimbaud's
   sister Isabelle. They include a letter begun on 4 July 1914 (Bib.
   Nat. N. A. Fr. 13152 f 97). This casts some light on Rimbaud's
   family. It seems that the poet's nephew – the son of his brother
   Frederick – had inherited the Rimbaud taste for travel.

8 juillet

Cette lettre a été interrompue par une angoisse terrible. Notre neveu,
Léon Rimbaud, retour [*sic*] du Sénégal depuis une quinzaine, a été subitement
atteint de broncho-pneumonie. Le médecin a ordonné son transport d'urgence
à l'hôpital. Il est maintenant à la maison Dubois, dans un état très inquiétant.

Je n'ai pas le cœur à t'expliquer ce que signifie le propos de Kahn sur
Verlaine et les Illuminations. Ce sera pour plus tard.

Léon Rimbaud died two days later, at the age of twenty-six.
Paterne Berrichon sent a *faire-part* to Cazals (f 99). Léon Rimbaud's
parents were presumably dead, since the announcement was
made by:

M et Mme Dufour-Rimbaud (Paterne Berrichon), ses oncle et tante; M et
Mme Teissier-Rimbaud, M et Mme Lecourt-Rimbaud, ses sœurs et beaux-
frères; MM Serge, Pierre et Léon Teissier, ses neveux; Mlle Hélène Lecourt,
sa nièce.

Léon Rimbaud was buried on 13 July at the Cimetière de la
Chapelle
2 Adolphe Retté in *L'Ermitage*, January 1892, 58
3 Adolphe Retté: *Le Symbolisme*, 102–10
4 *Chansons pour Elle*, VIII. Borel, 715
5 *Chansons pour Elle*, XVIII. Borel, 723
6 *Mercure de France*, December 1891, 361; *La Revue blanche*,
   December 1891, 215

7 Anatole France: *Le Temps*, 15 November 1891; quoted in F.-A. Cazals: *Paul Verlaine. Ses Portraits*.
8 Anatole France: *La Vie littéraire*, 3e série, 309 sqq.

56

1 Gabriel de Lautrec: *Souvenirs des jours sans souci*, 44–51
2 Verlaine was on the Committee for the Baudelaire Monument (*Mercure de France*, October 1892, 188–9)
3 *L'Ermitage*, 15 May 1892, 308–9
4 'Pénitence'. *Liturgies intimes*, XXII. Borel. 755
5 15 November 1910; Léautaud: *op. cit.*, III, 17
6 *À Propos de Desbordes-Valmore*, *Œs posths.*, III, 152–3
7 3 February 1933. Léautaud: *op. cit.*, X, 125

57

1 Undated note. Doucet MS 7203–11
2 Telegram of 30 December 1892. Bib. Nat. N. A. Fr. 13150 f 121
3 Philippe Jullian: *Robert de Montesquiou. Un prince 1900*, 169 sqq.
4 25 May 1892. Bib. Nat. N. A. Fr. 13150 ff 119–20
5 Robert de Montesquiou: *Les Pas Effacés. Mémoires*, II, 229–31
6 René Chalupt: 'Gabriel Fauré et les Poètes.' *La Revue musicale*, October 1922, 30–2
7 G. Jean-Aubry: *La Musique française d'aujourd'hui*, 239–44
8 Lockspeiser: *Debussy*, I, 22–3
9 Léon Vallas: *Claude Debussy et son temps*, 103
10 *Ibid.*, 97–8
11 *Ibid.*, 129–30, 189
12 Jean-Aubry: *loc. cit.*, 243–8
13 *Ibid.*, 251–2

58

1 Anatole France: 'Gestas'. *L'Étui de Nacre*, 145–57
2 Byvanck: *op. cit.*, 114 sqq.
3 *Ibid.*, 139

59

1 Quoted by G. Jean-Aubry: 'Verlaine en Hollande. Souvenirs et Documents', *Mercure de France*, 1 June 1923, 341

2 Philippe Zilcken: 'Un manuscrit de Verlaine', *Revue blanche*, 1 February 1896, 112, note

3 Bib. Nat. N. A. Fr. 13154 f 66; Verlaine's lecture programme in Holland is sketched out on ff 72 and 316

4 Bib. Nat. N. A. Fr. 13150 ff 64–5

5 Bib. Nat. N. A. Fr. 13154 f 4

6 For the history of the Vingtiste movement and La Libre Esthétique, see Madeleine Octave Maus: *Trente Années de lutte pour l'Art, 1884–1914*

7 Copy of letter. Bib. Nat. N. A. Fr. 13154 f 51

8 3 January 1893. Quoted by Gustave Vanwelkenhuyzen: *Verlaine en Belgique*, 141

9 7 January 1893; and draft note: Bib. Nat. N. A. Fr. 13154 f 53

10 Octave Maus to Verlaine, 18 January 1893. Bib. Nat. N. A. Fr. 13154 f 51

11 Bib. Nat. N. A. Fr. 13154 f 48. Draft letter found among Verlaine's papers.

Paris, 27 Janv. 93

Monsieur le Président,

Le soussigné, homme de lettres de quelque notoriété, pouvant se recommander d'un passé très agité mais resté hautement honorable a l'honneur de vous exposer que par suite de bien des circonstances, notamment un état de santé qui le force à vivre le trois-quarts du temps à l'hôpital, ainsi qu'en pourraient témoigner les docteurs Dujardin-Beaumetz de Cochin, Tapret de St Antoine, et Cochard [*sic*] de Broussais, et la perte toute récente de manuscrits des plus importants, il se trouve dans les circonstances les plus critiques.

Il ose en conséquence solliciter de votre bienveillance un secours immédiat qui le mit [*sic*] à même de reprendre ses travaux.

Il est avec le plus profond respect, Monsieur le Président,

votre très humble serviteur
PAUL VERLAINE

9 rue des fossés St Jacques.

12 Letter from Maus, 14 February 1893. Bib. Nat. N. A. Fr. 13154 f 52

13 Vanwelkenhuyzen: *op. cit.*, 152–4

14 *Ibid.*, 159–60

15 H. Carton de Wiart: *Souvenirs littéraires*, 147 sqq.
16 Quoted by Maus: *op. cit.*, 149–51
17 *Ibid.*
18 Gustave Kahn: *Silhouettes littéraires*, 49–51
19 *Ibid.*, and Verlaine: 'La Prison nulle part'. *Œs posths.*, 170
20 'Une Conférence de Paul Verlaine', Maurice Maeterlinck: *Bulles bleues*, 189–93
21 Carton de Wiart: *loc. cit.*
22 Telegram dated 14 October 1893. Bib. Nat. N. A. Fr. 13154 f 78
23 Retté: *op. cit.*, 101–2

60

1 Borel, 785
2 *Odes en son honneur.* IX. Borel, 770–1
3 *Odes en son honneur.* XVI. Borel, 779
4 *Fragments, I, Le Livre Posthume.* Borel, 817–18
5 Quoted by Benassis: *loc. cit.*
6 Bib. Nat. N. A. Fr. 13154 f 55
7 Letter quoted by Zayed: *op. cit.*, 275
8 *Ibid.*
9 *Ibid.*, 275, note
10 *Ibid.*, 275–6, note
11 10 August 1893
12 Porché: *op. cit.*, 290
13 Undated cutting from *L'Éclair* (Doucet Collection). Verlaine: 'Leconte de Lisle', *Les Hommes d'Aujourd'hui*, Vol. V, No. 241
14 Vanwelkenhuyzen: *op. cit.*, 187–8
15 Rambosson: *op. cit.*, 67
16 'My Visit to London', *Œs posths.*, III, 316

61

1 Bodleian Library. MS. Autogr. d. 11 f 312. (No poems with this title appear in the Pléiade edition of Verlaine.) William Rothenstein: *Men and Memories*, 148 sqq.
2 Stuart Merrill: *op. cit.*, 173–5
3 'My Visit to London', *Œs posths.*, III, 301–8

4   Merrill: *loc. cit.*

5   'My Visit to London': *loc. cit.*, 316

6   Rothenstein: *op. cit.*, 149. Underwood says (*op. cit.*, 408) that
    Verlaine stayed with Rothenstein at 19, Merton Street, Oxford;
    but Rothenstein says (*op. cit.*, p. 150): 'I took him at once to
    Christ Church, where Powell had a room for him.'

    In the Doucet Collection (7203–89) is a photocopy of the printed
    announcement:

    M. Paul Verlaine, the French poet, is coming to London for a short visit
    in the course of this month. At the request of some friends, he will give a
    lecture, in French, on 'Contemporary French Poetry' in the hall of Barnard's
    Inn, Holborn, on Tuesday, November 21, at 8.45 p.m. As there will only be
    accommodation for a limited number, immediate application for tickets,
    price 10s., should be made ...

    On the back of this notice, Rothenstein has written: 'M. Verlaine
    will deliver the same lecture at Oxford on Thursday afternoon the
    23 November, at 4.30 p.m., in Mr Blackwell's rooms in the Broad.
    The price of admission will be 5s.'

7   For an account of York Powell, see Oliver Elton: *Frederick York
    Powell. A Life and a Selection from his Letters and Occasional Writings.*
    See also Rothenstein: *op. cit., passim*

8   Elton: *op. cit.*, I, 153

9   [23 November 1893]; *Corr.*, II, 303

10 'My Visit to London: *loc. cit.*, 318; *Confessions. Œs cs.*, V, 67–8

11 *The Oxford Magazine*, Vol. XII, No. 7, 29 November 1893, 106

12 Rothenstein: *op. cit.*, 150; and Verlaine: 'My Visit to London': *loc.
    cit.*, 319–20

13 'Verlaine was delighted with Oxford. He showed no sign of
    wanting to leave; he was gay and talkative, and wished to be
    taken everywhere; but York Powell, admirer of Verlaine though
    he was, was in terror, lest the poet should get drunk while staying
    at Christ Church ... After two or three days, Powell suggested
    that I should give poor Verlaine a hint that guest-rooms were
    only to be occupied for a short period ... He needed a good deal
    of gentle persuasion before he was put into the train again for
    London.' Rothenstein: *op. cit.*, 150. Many years later, Rothenstein
    told Dr Enid Starkie that Verlaine had not been given his fee until
    he was safely on the London train.

    In the Doucet Collection (7203–74) is a postcard from York
    Powell to Verlaine, sent from Oxford on 2 January 1894:

Cher Monsieur,

Bien de bonheur pour l'année qui commence ! Je suis heureux de savoir que vous tenez en mémoire vox deux jours d'Oxford, et que la mémoire vous sourit. J'espère vous y voir encore un de ces jours.

Quant au livre, je m'en occupe instamment, et j'espère pouvoir vous envoyer bientôt [la] liste des poèmes que je crois choisir pour [le] petit volume, avec votre approbation toujours . . .

On 6 February, Powell adds (7203–75) :

Cher Monsieur,

J'ai presque prêt [*sic*] la choix des Poésies et je suis en correspondence [*sic*] active avec M. Lane là dessus. J'espère cette semaine ci d'envoyer la copie vous ayant d'abord envoyé liste des pièces choisies.

Je viens d'écrire à M. Rothenstein (26 Tite St. Chelsea) à propos du Budget [?]

Les mauvaises nouvelles que vous m'envoyez de votre santé m'ont attristé. J'espérais que vous auriez une convalescence plus rapide après vous avoir reposé des fatigues de voyage.

J'espère en recevoir de meilleures nouvelles et je suis à vous,

bien sincèrement
F. York Powell

Powell's selection from Verlaine was, alas, not published.

14 'My Visit to London': *loc. cit.*, 320–1
15 *Ibid.*, 323
16 Victor Plarr: *Ernest Dowson, 1888–1897*, 299
17 For Theodore Craig London, see: Richard Whittington-Egan and Geoffrey Smerdon: *The Quest of the Golden Boy. The Life and Letters of Richard Le Gallienne*
18 Verlaine noted that a Manchester art lover had bought *Coin de Table*, by Fantin-Latour
19 Desmond Flower and Henry Maas (ed.): *The Letters of Ernest Dowson*, 302, note
20 28 [November 1893]. *Corr.*, II, 309–10
21 5 December 1893; N. A. Fr. 13155 f 200. Cazals and Le Rouge: *op. cit.*, 95–6, note
22 5 December 1893; *Corr.*, II, 321–2
23 5 December 1893; *Corr.*, II, 323

62

1 7 December 1893. Quoted by Carton de Wiart in *Paul Verlaine*

en Belgique. Académie Royale de Langue et de Littérature Françaises. *Bulletin*, (x, 1, April 1931, p. 11.)

2 Rothenstein: *op. cit.*, 164

3 'L'Hopital chez soi'. *Œs posths.*, III, 156. sqq Cazals and Le Rouge, *op. cit.*, 120-3

4 Achille Segard: *Itineraire fantaisiste*, 15–19

5 François Aman-Jean: *L'Enfant oublié*, 49–50

6 Léon Bloy: *Le Mendiant ingrat. Journal, 1892–1895*, 149: L. Carteret: *Le Trésor du Bibliophile*, II, 432

7 Jean Carrère: *Les Mauvais Maîtres*, 169–70

8 Rémy de Gourmont: *Promenades littéraires*, IV, 20

9 Lucien Muhlfeld: *op. cit.*, 31–2

10 Marguerite Moreno: *op. cit.*, 23–6

11 Georges Beaujon: *L'École symboliste*

12 G. Jean-Aubry: 'Verlaine en Hollande', *loc. cit.*, 341

13 Delahaye: *op. cit.*, 180–2

14 Gabriel de Lautrec: *op. cit.*, 20–1

15 P.-B. Gheusi: *Cinquante Ans de Paris*, II, 382–6

16 Merrill: *op. cit.*, 167; Delahaye: *Souvenirs . . .* 161

17 Saint-Georges de Bouhélier: *op. cit.*

18 *Mercure de France*, February 1893, 186–7, 173–8. S. T. Madsen: *Sources of Art Nouveau*, 262, 263–4

19 For bibliographies of Verlaine, see G. Tournoux; *Bibliographie Verlainienne*, and A. van Bever and M. Monda: *Bibliographie et Iconographie de Paul Verlaine*

20 Arthur Symons: *The Symbolist Movement in Literature*, 79 sqq.

21 *Mercure de France*, October 1893, 172; November 1893, 288

22 *Portraits du prochain siècle*, XXV–XXVI, XXIV–XXV

23 Rothenstein: *op. cit.*, 264–5

24 Borel, 593

25 *Dans les limbes*, XII, Borel 838; *ibid.*, V, Borel, 833

63

1 Moreno; *op. cit.*, 26–7; Bayard; *op. cit.*, 89

2 *Écho de Paris*. Undated cutting in the Doucet Collection. Henri de Régnier, in *Nos Rencontres*, p. 48, tells the story of Mélingue. Verlaine doubtless knew that Mélingue had died in 1875 – at least ten years before the incident.

3 Among Cazals' papers are Verlaine's recollections of Leconte de Lisle, written on the inside of an envelope (Bib. Nat. N. A. Fr. 13151 f 18). There is a note with them: 'Le *Journal* du 20 juillet 94. Souvenirs sur L. de L.'

4 *Invectives*, VI. Borel, 905

5 Rothenstein: *op. cit.*, 163–4

6 Paul Léautaud: *Journal littéraire*, I, 10

7 De Langle: *op. cit.* A postscript to this incident may be found among Cazals' papers, in a copy of a note to the proprietor of the Procope (Bib. Nat. N. A. Fr. 13155 f 203):

Le 9 Xbre 94

Mon cher Théo, – Voudrez vous bien, dès ceci reçu, m'envoyer sous enveloppe les morceaux déchirés du manuscrit – en même temps prenez soin des quelques nippes miennes, n'est-ce pas?

Tout à vous
P. VERLAINE

hôpl. Bichat . . .

8 Bib. Nat. N. A. Fr. 13151 f 24

9 Jean Carrère: *op. cit.*, 176–9

10 These letters from Verlaine to Zola may be found among Zola's papers at the Bibliothèque Nationale (N. A. Fr. 24524 ff 529, 530)

Paris 4 Juillet 92

Monsieur et cher éminent confrère,

J'ai lu et je viens de relire *la Débâcle* que je vous remercie de m'avoir envoyé. Ce livre qui est votre chef d'œuvre entre tant d'autres m'a fait frémir et vibrer de douleur et d'absolue admiration.

Encore une fois merci et pour l'envoi grâcieux et pour le glorieux livre. Agréez mes très confraternelles et très cordiales poignées de main.

P. VERLAINE
15, rue Descartes

Le 25 Août 1894

Mon cher Monsieur Zola,

Je viens vous remercier bien cordialement de vous [*word illegible*] à la demande de pension dont Deschamps s'est fait le propagateur et qui a reçu un commencement d'exécution.

Je profite de cette occasion pour vous recommander la reproduction d'un portrait de moi à quatre ans que vient de faire mon ami et 'peintre ordinaire' que vous connaissez d'ailleurs, Cazals, à qui vous rendriez service si vous vouliez l'acheter et qui vous est porté par sa femme.

Je suis en train de lire 'Lourdes' qui m'intéresse au suprême degré, à titre de catholique et de votre admirateur.

P. VERLAINE
48 rue du Cardinal Lemoine

For an appreciation of Verlaine by Zola, see *Le Figaro*, 18 January 1896; the article was reprinted as *Le Solitaire* in *Nouvelle Campagne – 1896*, 35 sqq.

11 For a commentary on the election, see René Doumic: *La Vie et les Mœurs au jour le jour*, (Perrin – 1895), 61–3

12 Martrin-Donos: *op. cit.*, 244

13 Adolphe Brisson: *La Comédie littéraire*, 105–19

14 *Épigrammes*, II. Borel, 854

15 *Opinions sur la littérature. Œs posths.*, III, 350

16 Gustave Kahn: *op cit.*, 49

17 Rémy de Gourmont: *Promenades littéraires*, IV, 19–20

18 Saint-Georges de Bouhélier: *op. cit.*, 222–7

19 Fernand Gregh: *La Fenêtre ouverte*, 8; and Maurice Barrès: *Mes Cahiers*, X, 181

20 Anatole France: *Le Lys rouge*, 95–6, 112

64

1 Bib. Nat. N. A. Fr. 13151 ff 26–8, 29

2 P.-B. Gheusi: *op. cit.*, 386

3 Cazals and Le Rouge: *op. cit.*, 96

4 L. de Langle: *op. cit.*

5 Bib. Nat. N. A. Fr. 13155 f 203 (copy)

6 Charavay catalogue No. 685 (October 1961), No. 24, 388; catalogue No. 718 (June 1965), No. 30, 539

7 27 June 1895. Goncourt *Journal*, XXI, 75

8 Article by Gaston Stiegler in an unidentified newspaper (Doucet Collection); Gabriel de Lautrec: *loc. cit.*

9 De Langle: *loc. cit.*

10 Ernest Delahaye: *Verlaine*, 533–5

11 Rothenstein: *op. cit.*, 264–5

12 Cazals and Le Rouge: *op. cit.*, 2–4

13 Pierre Dauze (Paul Louis Dreyfus Bing): preface to Paul Verlaine: *Biblio-Sonnets*, I–III

14 *Ibid.*, 6, 7, 9; Dauze also publishes (p. 14) a note from Eugénie Krantz, dated 7 January 1896:

Monsieur,

Monsieur Verlaine, très malade et alité, serait bien aise de vous voir et de vous serrer la main.

Pour M. P. Verlaine
M. KRANTZ [*sic*]

15   'Nouvelles notes sur Rimbaud'. *Œs posths.*, II, 275–80

65

1   H. Carton de Wiart: *Verlaine en Belgique: loc. cit.*, 12–13. The inventory of Verlaine's effects, 25 March 1896 (Doucet: A IV 10: 7203–426) gives Mme Delporte's address as 454, avenue Louise, Brussels. For Georges Verlaine, see also: 'Le Fils de Verlaine'. *Demain*, 19 January 1896 (Bib. Nat. N.A.Fr. 13157 f 11): *Le Rappel*, 26 January 1896 (ibid, f 25). The most complete account is given by A. E. Carter in *Verlaine: A Study in Parallels*, 241 sqq.

2   Saint-Georges de Bouhélier: *op. cit.*, 244 sqq.

3   Maurice Barrès: *Mes Cahiers*, I, 55 sqq.

4   *Demain*, 19 January 1896. Bib. Nat. N. A. Fr. 13157, f 10; *Le Gaulois*, 9 January 1896, says that Verlaine had *déjenner* with M. Marsilia, ex-president of the Argentine Republic.

5   *Journal des Débats* [January 1896]. Doucet Collection.

6   Letter to Arthur Moore, about 12 January 1896. Flower and Maas: *op. cit.*, 339

7   Borel, 886–7

8   Saint-Georges de Bouhélier: *op. cit.*, 294–350

9   Carton de Wiart: *op. cit.*, 14–15

10   Gustave Kahn: *op. cit.*, 45–6

11   Undated cutting from *Le Journal des Débats*, January 1896, in the Doucet Collection

12   Borel, 1039–40

13   Notes by Cazals. Bib. Nat. N. A. Fr. 13155 ff 488 sqq.

14   Cazals and Le Rouge: *op. cit.*, 7–9

15   Notes by Cazals. Bib. Nat. N. A. Fr. 13155 ff 488 sqq.

16   Robert de Montesquiou: *Autels privilégiés*, 99

17   Porché: *op. cit.*, 342–3. Talking to Porché in 1931, the abbé Schoenhentz had recalled Verlaine's last confession, and he still remembered his piety. 'Monsieur, c'était un chrétien.'

18   Arthur Symons: *The Symbolist Movement in Literature*, 79 sqq.

66

1   Antoine Albalat (*op. cit.*, 181–2), records that Cazals remained the generous defender of Verlaine. Paul Léautaud maintained, in his *Journal littéraire*, 12 October 1931 (IX, 129–30) that Cazals was given the post of tax-collector by Jean-Louis Barthou, the politician and writer, in exchange for the Verlaine papers he possessed. Certainly Barthou's correspondence with Cazals shows his eager interest in his papers (Bib. Nat. N. A. Fr. 13152 ff 66 sqq.). According to a note among Cazals' papers (Bib. Nat. N. A. Fr. 13152 f 211), Y.-G. Le Dantec asked him, in March 1938, for help in preparing an edition of Verlaine's poems.

2   Saint-Georges de Bouhélier: *op. cit.*, 251–5

3   *Ibid.* According to the *Revue biblio-iconographique*, 7 March 1896, Verlaine's property consisted of five clay pipes, one cherry-wood pipe, a plaster cigarette-holder, two pairs of pince-nez, a pair of shoes and a cotton cap.

4   Merrill: *op. cit.*, 176

5   Segard: *loc. cit.*

6   Ex-Mme Paul Verlaine: *op. cit.*, 258

7   Harold Nicolson records in *Paul Verlaine*, 221: 'The doctor diagnosed diabetes, syphilis, heart disease and bronchitis, to say nothing of the acute arthritic affection of his knee.' *Le Journal des Débats* maintained on 10 January 1896 that Verlaine had suffered from advanced tuberculosis and physical exhaustion.

8   Among the papers of Cazals (Bib. Nat. N. A. Fr. 13152 f 249) is a receipt from A. Meoni, '*mouleur en tous genres à façon: prix modérés*'. It is dated 11 January 1896, and acknowledges the sum of 50 fr. from Cazals for the '*moulage de la tête du Poète Verlaine*'.

9   Mallarmé eagerly fostered Verlaine's posthumous reputation, as may be seen from his correspondence with Cazals (Bib. Nat. N. A. Fr. 13152 ff 231 sqq.). The bunch of violets which he left on Verlaine's deathbed are kept in the Doucet Collection in Paris; and there (A IV 10; 7203–426) is the inventory of Verlaine's effects, valued at 72 francs. This document, dated 25 March 1896, records that Vanier is still owed 329 francs for the funeral expenses; Eugénie Krantz claims for the expenses incurred on Verlaine's death (327 francs 90). Georges Verlaine, then convalescent with his mother in Brussels, is named as the sole heir.

10 Gabriel de Lautrec: *op. cit.*, 44–51
11 Maurice Barrès: *Mes Cahiers*, I, 55 sqq. Ernest Delahaye recorded in *Verlaine* (pp. 544–5), that he saw Eugénie wearing widow's weeds, and weeping bitterly, and Esther almost smiling with pride at being forgiven. Martrin-Donos notes (*Verlaine intime*, 254), that when the mourners had left the cemetery, Esther 'posa pieusement auprès des géantes couronnes étalées en regrets appointés une minuscule gerbe de mimosas et de violettes'.
12 Harold Nicolson: *op. cit.*, 222.
La Revue Biblio-iconographique, 7 March 1896, gives some account of Eugénie Krantz and the problems of Verlaine's inheritance. Lantoine (*op. cit.*, 21) says that Maurice Barrès had taken steps at La Samaritaine [*sic*] so that Eugénie could resume the work she had had there before she became Verlaine's mistress. Rothenstein records (*op. cit.*, 264–5) that Eugénie wrote to tell him of Verlaine's death:

> She added that he had kept a reproduction of one of my drawings hung over the bed on which he died. I wrote to enquire for further details, and received the following characteristic letter, the last, I think, I had from Eugénie.
> '. . . Je vous remercie de vous occuper de moi.
> Vous me demandez si l'on doit à Monsieur Paul Verlaine en Angleterre; oui monsieur on lui doit encore 250 francs que je serais bien heureuse d'avoir car je suis resté[é] sans un sou. Adieu Monsieur Will Rothenstein veuillez accepter l'assurance de ma cordialeté sympathic.
>
> EUGÉNIE KRANTZ.'

Eugénie remained in poverty. A few days before the anniversary mass for Verlaine in 1897, she appealed to Cazals and to Maurice du Plessys for help. Among Cazals' papers (Bib. Nat. N. A. Fr. 13154 f 266) is the counterfoil of the postal order for 5 francs which they sent her. On 8 January, from 13 rue Valette, she had also appealed for help to Sully-Prudhomme.

> Monsieur,
> Je vous emprie ne m'oublié pas. Je serai si malheureuse si je ne pouvai pas asister au Bou de lans de paul Verlaine. Je n'ai pas ma robes il sont toute engagé. Ce que vous ferais pour moi Vous sera comté pardonnez-moi monsieur de vous écrire comme cela.
> Veulier recevoire mes salutations respectueuses.
>
> Votre trai obligé
> E. KRANTZ

This letter is published in the Barthou catalogue, IV, p. 145. Sully-Prudhomme seems to have written about this letter to the Sec-

rétaire perpétuel de l'Académie-Française. It was the final chance
to show Eugénie some sort of gratitude. In April, Maurice Barrès
recorded (*op. cit.*, I, 145):

> J'ai vu Mme J. Rioli, une écrivain, elle m'a dit: Mme Krantz est morte;
> elle est morte en nous appelant *tous*; elle disait: 'Je veux qu'ils assistent à mon
> enterrement.
>
> 'J'ai enterré Verlaine dans de beaux draps de lit; des draps de Cambrai; ils
> avaient un ourlet large comme la main. Vous voyez que le maître a été bien
> enterré.'

Eugénie Krantz is said to have died at the Hôpital Cochin.

13 Léon Vanier did not long outlive Verlaine. He died in October.
Vanier, went an obituary, 'was above all the publisher and
friend of our poet Paul Verlaine. And this last claim to the gratitude
of literature and of men of letters is as good as any.'

14 Barrès: *loc. cit.*; see also 'Obsèques de Paul Verlaine', *La Revue
encyclopédique*, 25 January 1896, 54–5

15 Cazals and Le Rouge: *op. cit.*, 26, 27, notes

16 Paul Fort: *op. cit.*, 14–16

17 Gabriel de Lautrec: *op. cit.*, 51

18 Jules Renard: *Journal inédit, 1896–9*, 377–8

19 Barrès: *loc cit.*

20 Renard: *loc. cit.* Philippe Jullian (*op. cit.*, 171–2), writes that, on the
day of the funeral, the Minister sent 50 francs for wreaths. The
cost of the ceremony was shared between Montesquiou, Barrès
and Mendès. Reynoldo Hahn recorded next day that he had sent
Montesquiou some money towards the funeral expenses, but it had
not been needed, and Montesquiou – no doubt jealous of his
position as a patron – had returned it with a tactless note. Feelings
were running high: Hahn despatched a prompt and acid answer.

21 Borel, 247

67

1 *Critique et conferences*, *Œs posths.*, II, 387–8

2 'Charles Baudelaire', *Œs posths.*, II, 8–9

3 Raynaud: *Considérations*, *loc. cit.*

4 Symons: *loc. cit.*

5 Charles Le Goffic. *Revue bleue*, 25 January 1896, 112–13

6 'Kaléidoscope', *Jadis et Naguère*. Borel, 322

7 Fernand Gregh: *La Fenêtre ouverte*, 21–2
8 Symons: *op. cit.*, 79–84
9 24 November 1923. F. Lefèvre: *Une heure avec* . . . , 2e série, 89
10 Quoted by Symons: *op. cit.*, 93

SELECTED BIBLIOGRAPHY

The following are among the books consulted. English books are published in London, French books in Paris, unless otherwise stated.

ADAM, A.: *Verlaine* (Hatier, 1965)

ALBALAT, Antoine: *Souvenirs de la Vie littéraire* (Arthème Fayard, 1920)

——: *Trente Ans de Quartier Latin. Nouveaux Souvenirs de la Vie littéraire* (Société Française d'Éditions Littéraires et Techniques, 1930)

ALMÉRAS, Henri d': *Avant la Gloire. Leurs Débuts*. Ire série (Société Française d'Imprimerie et de Librairie, 1902)

AMAN-JEAN, François: *L'Enfant oublié. Chronique* (Buchet/Chastel, 1963)

ANON.: *A Descriptive Guide to Bournemouth* (Simpkin, Marshall, 1876)

——: *Nouveau Guide Pratique médical et pittoresque aux Eaux d'Aix en Savoie* (Chambéry, 1864)

——: *Aix-les-Bains, Marlioz et leurs Environs. Nouveau guide médical et pittoresque* (Asselin, 1872)

——: *Paul Verlaine et ses contemporains. Par un témoin impartial* (Bibliothèque de l'Association, 1897)

ANTHEAUME, A., et DROMARD, G.: *Poésie et Folie. Essai de psychologie et de critique* (Doin, 1908)

ARESSY, Lucien: *La Dernière Bohème. Verlaine et son Milieu. Fantaisie*, Préface de Rachilde. (Jouve, 1923)

BAJU, Anatole: *L'Anarchie littéraire* (Vanier, 1892)

BALDICK, Robert: *The Life of J.-K. Huysmans* (Oxford, The Clarendon Press, 1955)

BARRE, André: *Le Symbolisme. Essai historique sur le mouvement symboliste en France de 1885 à 1900, suivi d'une bibliographie de la poésie symboliste* (Jouve, 1911)

BARRELLE, Georges: *Le Pèlerin Lyrique. Entretiens avec Louis Le Cardonnel au Palais du Roure. Notes et Souvenirs* (Lethielleux, 1937)

BARRÈS, Maurice: *Mes Cahiers* (Plon, 1929–57)

[BARTHOU, Louis]: *Bibliothèque de M. Louis Barthou* (Blaizot & Fils, 1935–7)

BAUDELAIRE, Charles: *Les Fleurs du mal*. Edited by Enid Starkie (Oxford, Blackwell, 1943)

BAUMANN, Émile: *La Vie Terrible d'Henry de Groux* (Bernard Grasset, 1936)

BAYARD, Jean-Émile: *The Latin Quarter past and present*. Translated by Percy Mitchell (T. Fisher Unwin, 1926)

BEAUJON, Georges: *L'École symboliste* (Basle, 1900)

BERSAUCOURT, A. de: *Au Temps des Parnassiens. Nina de Villard et ses amis* (La Renaissance du livre, 1921)

BEVER, Ad. van: *La Vie douloureuse de Verlaine* (Monaco, Imprimerie de Monaco, 1926)

BEVER, Ad. van, et MONDA, Maurice: *Bibliographie et Iconographie de Paul Verlaine*. Publiées d'après des documents inédits (Messein, 1926)

BINET, Léon, et VALLERY-RADOT, Pierre: *Verlaine à Aix-les-Bains*. Préface de M. Daniel-Rops (L'Expansion scientifique française, 1958)

BLANCHART, Paul: *Saint-Georges de Bouhélier. Son Œuvre*. Étude critique (Édition du Carnet-Critique, 1920)

BLOY, Léon: *Le Mendiant ingrat. Journal, 1892–5* (Deman, 1898)

BORGEAUD, Henri (éd.): *Correspondence de Claude Debussy et Pierre Louÿs (1893–1904)*. Recueillie et annotée par Henri Borgeaud. Avec une introduction de G. Jean-Aubry (Corti, 1945)

BORNECQUE, Jacques-Henry: *Lumière sur les* Fêtes galantes *de Paul Verlaine* (Nizet, 1959)

——: *Verlaine par lui-même* (Éditions du Seuil, 1966)

BOSCHOT, Adolphe: *Chez nos poètes* (Plon, 1925)

BOURGET, Paul: *Études et Portraits* (Plon, Nourrit, 1900)

BRENNER, Jacques: *Charles Cros* (Seghers, 1955)

BRISSON, Adolphe: *La Comédie littéraire*. Notes et Impressions de littérature (Colin, 1895)

BRUNETIÈRE, Ferdinand: *Essais sur la littérature contemporaine* (Calmann Lévy, 1892)

——: *L'Évolution de la poésie lyrique en France au XIXᵉ siècle*. Leçons professées à la Sorbonne. Tome II (Hachette, 1894)

BURNAND, Robert: *La Vie Quotidienne en France de 1870 à 1900* (Hachette, 1947)

BYVANCK, W. G. C.: *Un Hollandais à Paris en 1891. Sensations de littérature et d'art.* Préface d'Anatole France (Perrin, 1892)

CALMETTES, Fernand: *Leconte de Lisle et ses amis* (Librairies-Imprimeries réunies, 1902)

CAPPERON, Joseph: *Notes d'art et de littérature.* Avec une notice bibliographique par Max Leclerc (Colin, 1897)

CARCO, Francis: *À la gloire de Verlaine* (Nouvelle Revue Critique, 1939)

——: *Verlaine, poète maudit* (Albin Michel, 1948)

CARRÉ, Jean-Marie: *Autour de Verlaine et de Rimbaud.* Dessins inédits de Paul Verlaine, de Germain Nouveau, et d'Ernest Delahaye. Classés et présentés par Jean-Marie Carré (Cahiers Jacques Doucet, Université de Paris, 1949)

CARRÈRE, Jean: *Les Mauvais Maîtres* (Plon, 1922)

CARTER, A. E.: *Verlaine. A Study in Parallels* (Toronto University Press; London, Oxford University Press, 1970)

CARTERET, L.: *Le Trésor du Bibliophile Romantique et moderne 1801–75.* Tome II (Carteret, 1925)

——: *Le Trésor du Bibliophile* (Carteret, 1946)

CARTERET-BISSON, F. S. de: *Our Schools and Colleges* (Simpkin, Marshall, 1879)

CARTON DE WIART, H.: *Le Droit à la Joie* (Perrin, 1922)

——: *Souvenirs Littéraires* (Lethielleux, 1938)

CAZALS, F.-A.: *Paul Verlaine. Ses Portraits* (Bibliothèque de l'Association, 1896)

——: *Le Jardin des Ronces. 1889–99* (Éditions de la Plume, 1902)

CAZALS, F.-A., & LE ROUGE, Gustave: *Les derniers Jours de Paul Verlaine.* Nombreux documents et dessins. Avec une préface de Maurice Barrès (Mercure de France, 1923)

CHAMPION, Pierre: *Marcel Schwob et son Temps* (Grasset, 1927)

CHRISTOFLOUR, Raymond: *Louis Le Cardonnel. Pèlerin de l'Invisible.* Préface de Georges Bernanos (Plon, 1938)

CLARETIE, Jules: *La Vie à Paris, 1880* (Havard, 1881)

——: *La Vie à Paris, 1896* (Charpentier/Fasquelle, 1897)

——: *La Vie à Paris, 1911–12–13* (Charpentier/Fasquelle, 1914)

CLAUDEL, Paul: *Verlaine* (Éditions de la Nouvelle Revue Française, 1922)

CLERGET, Fernand: *Émile Blémont* (Bibliothèque de l'Association, 1906)

COLLET, Georges-Paul: *George Moore et la France* (Minard, 1957)

COPPÉE, François: *Mon Franc parler*. 3ᵉ série; Juin 1894-Février 1895 (Lemerre, 1895)

CORDIER DELAPORTERIE, Dr: *Étude médico-psychologique sur Paul Verlaine (1844–96)*. Alcoolisme et Génie (Coulommiers, Imprimerie Paul Brodard, 1922)

COULON, Marcel: *Verlaine. Poète Saturnien*. Avec des Documents inédits (Grasset, 1929)

——: *Au cœur de Verlaine et de Rimbaud* ('Le Livre', 1925)

CUÉNOT, Claude: *État présent des études verlainiennes* (Société d'Édition 'Les Belles Lettres', 1938)

DABOT, Henri: *Souvenirs et impressions d'un bourgeois du Quartier Latin de mai 1854 à mai 1869* (Péronne, Imprimerie E. Quentin, 1899)

DAUDET, Mme Alphonse: *Souvenirs autour d'un groupe littéraire* (Charpentier, 1910)

[DAUZE, Pierre]: *Catalogue de la Bibliothèque de feu M. Pierre Dauze* (Leclerc/Blaizot, 1914)

DAVID, André: *Rachilde. Homme de Lettres* (Nouvelle Revue Critique, 1924)

DELAHAYE, Ernest: *Documents relatifs à Paul Verlaine*. Lettres, dessins, pages inédites recueillis et décrits par Ernest Delahaye (Maison du Livre, 1919)

——: *Verlaine* (Messein, 1919)

——: *Souvenirs familiers à propos de Rimbaud, Verlaine, Germain Nouveau* (Messein, 1925)

DELSEMME, Paul: *Un Théoricien du symbolisme. Charles Morice* (Nizet, 1958)

DESAYMARD, Joseph: *Emmanuel Chabrier d'après ses lettres. L'homme et l'œuvre* (Roches, 1934)

DESCHAMPS, Gaston: *La Vie et les Livres*. 3ᵉ série (Armand Colin, 1896)

DIETSCHY, Marcel: *La Passion de Claude Debussy* (Neuchatel, À la Baconnière, 1962)

DONNAY, Maurice: *Mes Débuts à Paris* (Librairie Arthème Fayard, 1937)

DOUMIC, René: *Hommes et idées du XIXᵉ siècle* (Perrin, 1903)

DUGAS, Marcel: *Verlaine. Essai* (Radot, 1928)

DULLAERT, Maurice: *Verlaine* (Ghent, Imprimerie A. Siffer, 1896)

——: *L'Affaire Verlaine* (Messein, 1930)

DUPUY, Ernest: *Poètes et Critiques* (Hachette, 1913)

DURAND, Jacques: *Quelques souvenirs d'un Éditeur de musique* (A. Durand et fils, 1924)

DURAND, Jacques (éd.): *Lettres de Claude Debussy à son éditeur.* Publiées par Jacques Durand (A. Durand & Fils, 1927)

DUVERNOIS, Henri: *Apprentissages. Souvenirs des années 1885–1900* (Hachette, 1930)

EAUBONNE, Francoise d': *Verlaine et Rimbaud, ou la fausse évasion* (Albin Michel, 1960)

ELTON, Oliver: *Frederick York Powell. A Life and a Selection from his Letters and Occasional Writings* (Oxford, Clarendon Press, 1906)

FARMER, Albert J.: *Le Mouvement esthétique et 'décadent' en Angleterre (1873–1900)* (Champion, 1931)

FLOWER, Desmond, and Maas, Henry (ed.): *The Letters of Ernest Dowson,* (Cassell, 1967)

FONTAINAS, André: *Verlaine-Rimbaud. Ce qu'on présume de leurs relations. Ce qu'on en sait* (Librairie de France, 1931)

FONTAINE, André: *Verlaine, homme de lettres* (Delagrave, 1937)

FORT, Paul: *Mes Mémoires. Toute la vie d'un Poète, 1872–1944* (Flammarion, 1944)

FOSCA, François: *Histoire des Cafés de Paris* (Firmin-Didot, 1934)

FRANCE, Anatole: *La Vie littéraire.* 3ᵉ série (Calmann Lévy, 1891)

——: *L'Étui de Nacre* (Calmann Lévy, 1892)

——: *Le Lys rouge.* 13ᵉ edition (Calmann Lévy, 1894)

GAUGUIN, Paul: *Lettres de Paul Gauguin à Georges-Daniel de Monfreid.* Précédées d'un hommage par Victor Segalen (Crès, 1919)

GHEUSI, P.-B.: *Cinquante Ans de Paris* (Plon, 1939–40)

GHIL, René: *Les Dates et les Œuvres. Symbolisme et Poésie scientifique* (Crès, 1923)

GIDE, André: *Journal, 1889–1939.* 4 tomes (Rio de Janeiro, Americ-Edit, 1943)

GILLE, Philippe: *La Bataille littéraire (1891–92)* (Victor-Havard, 1894)

GONCOURT, Edmond et Jules de: *Journal. Mémoires de la vie littéraire* (Monaco, Imprimerie Nationale, 1956)

GOSSE, Edmund: *French Profiles* (Heinemann, 1913)

GOURMONT, Rémy de: *Le Livre des Masques. Portraits symbolistes* (Société du Mercure de France, 1896)

——: *Promenades littéraires* (Mercure de France, 1904)

——: *Promenades littéraires. Quatrième série. Souvenirs du Symbolisme et autres études* (Mercure de France, 1912)

GREGH, Fernand: *L'Âge d'or. Souvenirs d'enfance et de jeunesse* (Grasset, 1947)

GREGH, Fernand: *La Fenêtre ouverte* (Charpentier-Fasquelle, 1901)

HENRY, Marjorie Louise: *La Contribution d'un Américain au Symbolisme français - Stuart Merrill* (Champion, 1927)

HURET, Jules: *Enquête sur l'évolution littéraire* (Charpentier, 1891)

HUYSMANS, J.-K.: *À Rebours* (Charpentier, 1891)

JACKSON, Holbrook: *The Eighteen Nineties. A Review of Art and Ideas at the Close of the Nineteenth Century* (Grant Richards, 1913)

JEAN-AUBRY, G.: *La Musique française d'aujourd'hui* (Perrin, 1916)

JEPSON, Edgar: *Memories of a Victorian.* Vol. I (Gollancz, 1933)

JULLIAN, Philippe: *Robert de Montesquiou. Un Prince 1900* (Librairie Académique Perrin, 1965)

JULLIEN, Adolphe: *Fantin-Latour. Sa Vie et ses amitiés* (Laveur, 1909)

KAHN, Gustave: *Silhouettes littéraires* (Éditions Montaigne, 1925)

——: *Les Origines du Symbolisme* (Messein, 1936)

LANTOINE, Albert: *Paul Verlaine et quelques-uns* (Direction du Livre mensuel, 1920)

LAURENT, Dr Émile: *La Poésie décadente devant la science psychiatrique* (Alexandre Maloine, 1897)

LAUTREC, Gabriel de: *Souvenirs des jours sans souci* (Éditions de la Tournelle, 1938)

LÉAUTAUD, Paul: *Journal littéraire, 1893-1956* (Mercure de France, 1954–66)

LEFEBVRE, Louis: *Charles Morice* (Perrin, 1926)

LEFÈVRE, F.: *Une heure avec . . .* (N.R.F., 1924)

LE GALLIENNE, Richard: *The Romantic '90s* (G. P. Putnam's Sons, 1925)

LELEUX, Charles: *Mémorial du Collège Notre-Dame de Rethel, 1854–1910* (No publisher given, 1933)

——: *Quand nous étions jeunes (Souvenirs du Collège Notre-Dame de Rethel)* (No publisher given; Printer: G. de Malherbe, 1930)

LEMAÎTRE, Jules: *Les Contemporains.* 4e série (Lecène & Oudin, 1889)

LEPELLETIER, Edmond: *Paul Verlaine. Sa Vie-Son Œuvre* (Société du Mercure de France, 1907)

LE ROUGE, Gustave: *Verlainiens et décadents* (Éditions Seheur, 1928)

LOCKSPEISER, Edward: *Debussy - his Life and Mind* (Cassell, 1962, 1965)

LOUŸS, Pierre: *Journal intime, 1882-91* (Éditions Montaigne, Fernand Aubier, 1929)

MADSEN, Stephan Tschudi: *Sources of Art Nouveau* (Oslo, H. Asche-houg, 1956)

MAETERLINCK, Maurice: *Bulles Bleues. Souvenirs heureux* (Monaco, Éditions du Rocher, 1948)

MALLARMÉ, Stéphane: *Divagations* (Charpentier-Fasquelle, 1897)

MARTINO, Pierre: *Verlaine* (Boivin, 1951)

MARTRIN-DONOS, Charles de: *Verlaine intime.* Rédigé d'après les documents recueillis sur le Roi des Poètes par son ami et éditeur Léon Vanier (Vanier, 1898)

MAUCLAIR, Camille: *L'Art Indépendant Français sous la troisième république (peinture, lettres, musique)* (La Renaissance du Livre, 1919)
——: *Servitude et Grandeur littéraires* (Ollendorff, 1922)

MAURRAS, Charles: *Poètes* (Le Divan, 1923)

MAUS, Madeleine Octave: *Trente Années de lutte pour l'Art, 1884–1914* (Brussels, Librairie l'oiseau bleu, 1926)

MAY, J. Lewis: *John Lane and the Nineties* (John Lane, The Bodley Head, 1936)

MENDÈS, Catulle: *La Légende du Parnasse contemporain* (Brussels, Auguste Brancart, 1884)

MERRILL, Stuart: *Prose et Vers. Œuvres Posthumes.* Préface d'André Fontainas (Messein, 1925)

MICHAUD, Guy: *Message poétique du Symbolisme* (Nizet, 1947)

MITHOUARD, Adrien: *Paul Verlaine ou le Scrupule de la Beauté* (Au 'Spectateur Catholique', 1897)

MONDOR, Henri: *L'Amitié de Verlaine et de Mallarmé* (Gallimard, 1939)

MONKIEWICZ, Bronislawa: *Verlaine, critique littéraire* (Messein, 1928)

MONTESQUIOU, Robert de: *Autels privilégiés* (Charpentier, 1898)
——: *Les Pas Effacés. Mémoires* (Émile-Paul, 1923)

MOORE, George: *Confessions of a Young Man* (Heinemann, 1937)
——: *Conversations in Ebury Street* (Heinemann, 1936)
——: *Memoirs of my dead life* (Heinemann, 1936)

MORÉAS, Jean: *Esquisses et Souvenirs* (Société du Mercure de France, 1908)

MORENO, Marguerite: *Souvenirs de la vie* (Éditions de Flore, 1948)

MORICE, Charles: *Eugène Carrière* (Société du Mercure de France, 1906)
——: *Paul Verlaine* (Vanier, 1888)

MORICE, Louis: *Verlaine. Le drame religieux* (Beauchesn eet ses fils, 1946)

MOROY, Élie: *La Guirlande de Verlaine* (Geneva, Éditions de la Semaine, 1926)

MUHLFELD, Lucien: *Le Monde où l'on imprime. Regards sur quelques lettrés et divers illettrés contemporains* (Perrin, 1897)

NADAL, Octave: *Paul Verlaine* (Mercure de France, 1961)

NICOLSON, Harold: *Paul Verlaine* (Constable, 1921)

PLARR, Victor: *Ernest Dowson, 1888–98. Reminiscences, unpublished letters and marginalia* (Elkin Mathews, 1914)

POINSOT, M.-C.: *Toute la vie* (Figuière, 1913)

POIZAT, Alfred: *Le Symbolisme – de Baudelaire à Claudel* (La Renaissance du Livre, 1919)

PORCHÉ, François: *Verlaine tel qu'il fut* (Flammarion, 1933)

POULENC, Francis: *Emmanuel Chabrier* (La Palatine, 1961)

RACHILDE: *Portraits d'Hommes* (Mercure de France, 1930)

——: *Quand j'étais jeune* (Mercure de France, 1948)

RAYNAUD, Ernest: *L'Assomption de Paul Verlaine.* Scène pastorale, représentée pour la première fois sur la scène de l'Odéon, le 28 mai 1911. Précédée de considérations sur Paul Verlaine (Mercure de France, 1912)

——: *La Bohème sous le second empire. Charles Cros et Nina* (L'Artisan du Livre, 1930)

——: *La Mêlée symboliste (1870–90). Portraits et Souvenirs* (La Renaissance du Livre, 1918)

——: *La Mêlée Symboliste (1890–1900). Portraits et Souvenirs* (La Renaissance du Livre, 1920)

——: *La Mêlée Symboliste (1900–1910). Portraits et Souvenirs* (La Renaissance du Livre, 1922)

——: *En Marge de la Mêlée Symboliste.* 2ᵉ édition (Mercure de France, 1936)

RÉGAMEY, Félix: *Verlaine Dessinateur* (Floury, 1896)

RÉGNIER, Henri de: *Figures et caractères.* 2ᵉ édition (Société du Mercure de France, 1901)

——: *Nos Rencontres* (Mercure de France, 1931)

RENARD, Jules: *Journal inédit, 1887–95* (Bernouard, 1925)

——: *Journal inédit, 1896–9* (Bernouard, 1926)

——: *Journal inédit, 1906–10* (Bernouard, 1927)

RETTÉ, Adolphe: *Le Symbolisme. Anecdotes et Souvenirs.* (Librairie Léon Vanier, Éditeur: A. Messein, Succr. 1903)

RICHARDSON, Joanna: *Théophile Gautier: His Life and Times* (Reinhardt, 1958)

RICHER, Jean: *Paul Verlaine* (Seghers, 1967)

RIMBAUD, Jean-Arthur: *Œuvres complètes* (Montreal, Valiquette, n.d.)

RODENBACH, Georges: *L'Élite. Écrivains. Orateurs sacrés. Peintres. Sculpteurs* (Charpentier, 1899)

ROINARD, P. N.: *Portraits du Prochain Siècle*. Tome 1ᵉʳ. Poètes et Prosateurs (Girard, 1894)

ROTHENSTEIN, John: *The Portrait Drawings of William Rothenstein (1889–1925)*. An iconography by John Rothenstein with a preface by Max Beerbohm and 101 collotype plates (Chapman and Hall, 1926)

ROTHENSTEIN, William: *Paul Verlaine*. Three Drawings on lithographic paper by Will Rothenstein done from the life. With a short prefatory note by Professor F. York Powell. (Hacon & Ricketts, 1898)

——: *Men and Memories. Recollections, 1872–1900* (Faber and Faber, 1931)

ROUSSELOT, Jean: *De quoi vivait Verlaine?* (Deux Rives, 1950)

RUCHON, François (éditeur): *Verlaine. Documents iconographiques* (Genève, Cailler, 1947)

SAINT-GEORGES DE BOUHÉLIER: *Le Printemps d'une Génération* (Éditions Nagel, 1946)

SÉCHÉ, Alphonse, et BERTAUT, Jules: *La Vie anecdotique et pittoresque des Grands Écrivains. Paul Verlaine* (Louis-Michaud, 1909)

SEGARD, Achille: *Itinéraire fantaisiste* (Ollendorff, 1899)

SERVIÈRES, Georges: *Emmanuel Chabrier, 1841–94* (Librairie Félix Alcan, 1912)

——: *Gabriel Fauré. Étude critique* (Laurens, 1930)

SHERARD, R. H.: *Twenty Years in Paris* (Hutchinson, 1905)

——: *My Friends the French* (T. Werner Laurie, 1909)

SIGNORET, Emmanuel: *Ode à Paul Verlaine* (Léon Vanier, 1892)

SPEAIGHT, Robert: *William Rothenstein. The Portrait of an artist in his time* (Eyre and Spottiswoode, 1962)

STARKIE, Enid: *Baudelaire* (Faber, 1957)

——: *Arthur Rimbaud* (Faber, 1961)

STOCK, P.-V.: *Mémorandum d'un Éditeur*. I (Stock, 1935)

STRENTZ, Henri: *Paul Verlaine. Son Œuvre* (La Nouvelle Revue Critique, 1925)

SYMONS, Arthur: *The Symbolist Movement in Literature* (Heinemann, 1899)

TAILHADE, Laurent: *Lettres à sa mère, 1874–91*. Introduction, notes et index par Pierre Dufay (Van Den Berg & Enlart, 1926)

——: *Quelques fantômes de jadis* (L'Édition française illustrée, 1920)

TELLIER, Jules: *Les Écrivains d'Aujourd'hui. Nos Poètes* (Dupret, 1888)

——: *Œuvres*. Publiées par Raymond de la Tailhède. I, II (Émile-Paul, 1923, 1925)

TENNYSON, Alfred, Lord: *Works* (Macmillan, 1909)

THOMPSON, Vance: *French Portraits* (Boston, Richard G. Badger & Co., 1900)

TOLSTOI, Comte Léon: *Qu'est-ce que l'Art?* Traduit du russe et précédée d'une Introduction par Teodor de Wyzewa (Perrin, 1898)

TOURNOUX, G. A.: *Bibliographie Verlainienne* (Leipzig, E. Rowohlt, 1912)

UNDERWOOD, V. P.: *Le Carnet personnel de Verlaine* (Lille, Revue des Sciences Humaines, 1955)

——: *Verlaine et l'Angleterre* (Nizet, 1956)

VAILAT, Léandre: *En écoutant Forain* (Flammarion, 1931)

VALÉRY, Paul: *Villon et Verlaine* (Maestricht, Éditions A.A.M. Stols, 1937)

VALLAS, Léon: *Claude Debussy et son temps* (Albin Michel, 1958)

VALLERY-RADOT, Pierre: *Un habitué de nos Hôpitaux. Verlaine à Broussais* (Guillemot et De Lamothe, 1956)

VANWELKENHUYZEN, Gustave: *Verlaine en Belgique* (Brussels, La Renaissance du Livre, 1945)

VERHAEREN, Émile: *Impressions*. 3ᵉ série (Mercure de France, 1928)

VERLAINE, ex-Madame Paul: *Mémoires de ma vie*. Précédés d'une introduction de M. François Porché (Flammarion, 1935)

VERLAINE, Paul: *Œuvres complètes* (5 tomes) (Messein, 1923–49)

——: *Œuvres poétiques*. Édition de Jacques Robichez (Garnier, 1969)

——: *Œuvres posthumes*. 3 tomes (Messein, 1922–9)

——: *Œuvres oubliées*. Recueillies par Maurice Monda (Tome I, Éditions Baudinière, 1926; Tome II, Messein, 1929)

——: *Œuvres poétiques complètes*. Texte établi et annoté par Y.-G. Le Dantec. Édition revue, complétée et présentée par Jacques Borel (Bibliothèque de la Pléiade, N.R.F., 1968)

——: *Poèmes saturniens*. Texte critique, étude et commentaire par J.-H. Bornecque (Nizet, 1967)

——: *Fêtes Galantes. La Bonne Chanson. Romances sans paroles*. Avec introduction et notes de V. P. Underwood. (Manchester, Éditions de l'Université de Manchester, 1963)

VERLAINE, Paul: *Sagesse*. Édition critique commentée par Louis Morice (Nizet, 1964)

——: *Biblio-Sonnets*. Poèmes inédits. Préface de Pierre Dauze (H. Floury, 1913)

——: *Correspondance*. Publiée sur les manuscrits originaux avec une préface et des notes par Ad. Van Bever. 3 tomes (Messein, 1922–9)

——: Paul Verlaine. Correspondance et documents inédits relatifs à son livre 'Quinze jours en Hollande'. Avec une lettre de Stéphane Mallarmé et un portrait de Verlaine écrivant d'après la pointe-sèche de Ph. Zilcken, sir un croquis de J. Toorop (Floury, 1897)

——: *Voyage en France par un Français*. Publié d'après le manuscrit inédit. Préface de Louis Loviot. 2ᵉ edition (Librairie Léon Vanier, Éditeur: A. Messein, Succr. 1907)

——: *Nos Ardennes*. Huit dessins de Paul Verlaine, Ernest Delahaye, Germain Nouveau. Introduction et notes par Jules Mouquet (Genève, Cailler, 1948)

VIGIÉ-LECOCQ, E.: *La Poésie contemporaine, 1884–96* (Mercure de France, 1896)

WHITTINGTON-EGAN, Richard, & SMERDON, Geoffrey: *The Quest of the Golden Boy. The Life and Letters of Richard Le Gallienne* (The Unicorn Press, 1960)

ZAYED, Georges (éditeur): *Lettres inédites de Verlaine à Cazals* (Genève, Droz, 1957)

——: *Paul Verlaine. Lettres inédites à Charles Morice* (Genève, Droz, 1964)

ZIMMERMANN, Éléonore M.: *Magies de Verlaine. Étude de l'évolution poétique de Paul Verlaine* (Corti, 1967)

ZOLA, Émile: *Documents Littéraires. Études et Portraits* (Charpentier, 1881)

——: *Nouvelle Campagne, 1896* (Charpentier, 1897)

The following are among the articles consulted:

AUBAULT DE LA HAULTE-CHAMBRE, G.: 'Lettres inédites de Verlaine et de Huysmans', *La Revue Européene*, 1 May 1923, pp. 19–22

BENASSIS, Dr: 'Essais de clinique littéraire. Paul Verlaine,' *Revue thérapeutique des Alcaloïdes*. March, April, 1930

BERRICHON, Paterne: 'Verlaine héroïque', *La Revue blanche*, 15 February 1896, pp. 177–81

——: 'Pour Verlaine', *La Revue blanche*, 15 September 1896, pp. 264–8

BEVER, Ad. van: 'Paul Verlaine. Lettres à Léon Vanier', *Mercure de France*, 1 June 1923, pp. 405 sqq.

CARTON DE WIART, H.: 'Paul Verlaine en Belgique. Souvenirs et documents inédits', *Bulletin de l'Académie Royale de Langue et de Littérature Françaises*, Tome X, No. 1, Brussels, April 1931, pp. 5 sqq.

CASTETS, Henri: 'Étude biographique. Paul Verlaine', *La Revue encyclopédique*, 25 January 1896, pp. 51–3

CHALUPT, René: 'Gabriel Fauré et les Poètes', *La Revue Musicale*, October, 1922

DELINES, Michel: 'Un Russe à la recherche de Verlaine', *La Revue hebdomadaire*, 25 September 1897, pp. 521–34

DUFAY, Pierre: 'Une lettre et quelques billets inédits de Paul Verlaine', *La Connaissance*, November 1920, pp. 897–912

GAULTIER, Jules de: 'Essai de physiologie poétique. À propos des poèmes de M. Paul Verlaine', *La Revue blanche*, May and June 1894, pp. 393–408 and 527–35

GERMAIN, André: 'Verlaine et Huysmans', *La Revue Européenne*, 1 May 1923, pp. 23–5

GOURMONT, Jean de: 'Revue de la Quinzaine. Littérature. Correspondance de Paul Verlaine', *Mercure de France*, 1 October 1923, pp. 189–90

JEAN-AUBREY, G.: 'Sainte-Beuve et Paul Verlaine', *Mercure de France*, November 1919, pp. 80 sqq.

——: 'Verlaine en Hollande. Souvenirs et Documents', *Mercure de France*, 1 June 1923, pp. 318 sqq.

KAHN, Gustave: 'Chronique de la littérature et de l'art ... Les Poètes Maudits', *La Revue indépendante*, October, 1888, pp. 119–28

——: 'La Vie Mentale', *La Revue blanche*, 1 February 1896, pp. 118–28

KAHN, Gustave: 'Doumic contre Verlaine', *La Revue blanche*, 15 February 1901, pp. 256–9

LARROUMET, Gustave: 'La Littérature et l'Art. Paul Verlaine', *La Vie contemporaine*, 1 February 1896, pp. 279–92

LE GOFFIC, Charles: 'Paul Verlaine', *Revue politique et littéraire, Revue bleue*, 25 January 1896, pp. 111–13

LEMAÎTRE, Jules: 'M. Paul Verlaine et les poètes "symbolistes" et "décadents", *Revue politique et littéraire. Revue bleue*, 7 January 1888, pp. 2–14

LODS, Armand: 'Les Premières éditions de Verlaine', *Mercure de France*, 15 October 1924, pp. 402–24

MALLARME, Stéphane: 'Propos sur la poésie' (Lettres inédites), *La Table ronde*, August 1952

MARSAN, Jules: 'Paul Verlaine et son médecin. Lettres inédites au Dr Jullien', *Mercure de France*, 1 July 1925, pp. 60–91

MAURRAS, Charles: 'Arthur Rimbaud', *Revue encyclopédique*, 1 January 1892, pp. 7–13

——: 'Paul Verlaine. Les époques de sa poésie', *La Revue encyclopédique*, 1 January 1895, pp. 1–8

——: 'La Mémoire de Verlaine', *La Revue encyclopédique*, 25 January 1896, p. 54

MORICE, Charles: 'Le Fauteuil de Leconte de Lisle', *Mercure de France*, October 1894, pp. 151 sqq.

MUHLFELD, Lucien: 'Mort de Paul Verlaine', *La Revue blanche*, 15 January 1896, pp. 49–51

RAYNAUD, Ernest: 'Les Soirées de la Plume', *La Plume*, 15 April 1903, pp. 425 sqq.

RODENBACH, Georges: 'La Poésie nouvelle. À propos des décadents et symbolistes', *Revue politique et littéraire, Revue bleue*, 4 April 1891, pp. 422–30

[ROPS, Félicien]: 'Lettres inédites à Félicien Rops', *Mercure de France*, January–February 1905, pp. 30–43

SAINT-POL-ROUX: 'Verlaine le Pâtre. Souvenirs de Belgique', *La Revue blanche*, 1 September 1900, pp. 26–35

SÉCHÉ, Alphonse: 'Ah! Jeunesse! Petits Souvenirs du Quartier Latin', *Les Œuvres Libres*, July 1931

SIMON, Gustave: 'Paul Verlaine et Victor Hugo', *La Revue de France*, 1 October 1924, pp. 500–11

SPRONCK, Maurice: 'Notes et Impressions', *Revue politique et littéraire. Revue bleue*, 29 August 1896, pp. 283–6

STARKIE, Enid: '*Coin de Table* by H. Fantin-Latour', *The French Mind*. Studies in honour of Gustave Rudler, Oxford, Clarendon Press, 1952, pp. 318–26

VERHAEREN, Émile: 'Paul Verlaine', *La Revue blanche*, 15 April 1897, pp. 409–12

VERLAINE, Paul: 'Croquis de Belgique', *La Revue encyclopédique*, 1 May 1895, pp. 157–61

[VERLAINE, Paul]: 'Lettres de Paul Verlaine' (Une Saison à Aix-les-Bains: Août-Septembre, 1889), *La Revue blanche*, 15 November 1896, pp. 433–52; 1 December 1896, pp. 505–15

VICAIRE, Gabriel: 'Paul Verlaine', *La Revue hebdomadaire*, 21 April 1894, pp. 433–51

ZILCKEN, Philippe: 'Un manuscrit de Verlaine', *La Revue blanche*, 1 February 1896, pp. 112–14

Index

Bracketed figures refer to pages of notes.

Index